HamRadioSchool.com

Technician License Course

*Complete Element 2 Exam Preparation
and more,
to help you really understand ham radio!*

by
**Stu Turner
WØSTU**

Third Edition: Version 3.0

Valid for NCVEC Technician Class Question Pool
July 1, 2018 to June 30, 2022

This book was conceived, written, and developed by Stu Turner, LLC. Stu Turner, Author. Copyright © 2018. All rights reserved.

Photography and Graphics Credit: All photographs, drawings, and graphics, unless otherwise credited, were produced by the Author as original materials, in some cases including components from copyright-free (open) and/or public domain sources. Cover design and art by *James Bucknall*.

All material is subject to US Copyright Law. Reproduction, publication, or duplication of this book, or any part thereof, in any manner, mechanically, electronically, or photographically, is prohibited without the express written permission of the Author. The Author, publisher, and seller assume no liability with respect to the use of the information contained herein.

Acknowledgements: Tremendous thanks to the following for their time and assistance with this book and with *HamRadioSchool.com*... You guys rock!

James Bucknall, KD0MFO, for webmaster support, layout advice, graphics support, reviews, and great friendship!

Bob Witte, K0NR, for technical review, suggestions, educational support, web site contributions, photos, gear, and for being the Elmer Supreme! Read Bob's blog at: ***k0nr.com/blog***

Steve Galchutt, WG0AT, for web contributions, the SOTA thing, photos, and *goatly* inspiration! Tha-a-a-a-a-a-nks, Steve!
See Steve at: ***youtube.com/user/goathiker***

Jürg Seyffer, K0POP, for photos, video support, and hamfest support.

Cole Turner, W0COL, Jake Turner, *W0JAK,* and Emma Turner, for allowing me to unabashedly use their images in embarrassing harebrained graphics.

W0TLM Tri-Lakes Monument Radio Association, for being a great radio club and providing the opportunity to try a hand at instructing amateur radio courses. ***w0tlm.com***

Liz, KT0LIZ, for putting up with the whole thing... again. Thanks honey!

Be sure to visit *HamRadioSchool.com* for:

- Additional multi-media learning content!
- Exam question pool review organized section-by-section!
- Practical advice, interesting articles, and fun things to do!
- *How-to* information on station set-up and ham activities!
- Sharing your comments, suggestions, and success story!

Technician Class and General Class Practice Apps
Section Quizzes & Practice Exams!

Study and practice exam questions on-the-go with your book and smart phone or tablet device!

HamRadioSchool.com

Teaching a ham class?

Check out our
Technician License Course
Instructor's Resources!

Use our ready-to-teach book and charts and just add your Elmering wisdom, demo's, and exciting classroom activities for an easy-to-teach and successful Technician License class!

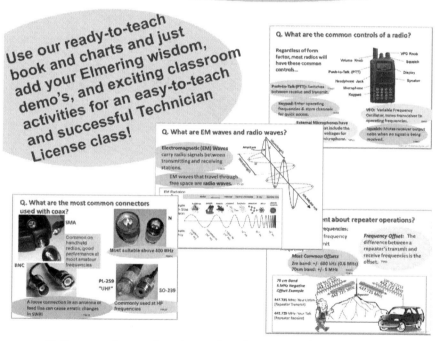

- Fully coordinated with our book, section-by-section.
- Loaded with colorful, instructional graphics.
- Highlights all exam question pool items.
- "Click-to-reveal" sequence of each chart's content.
- Includes animations and imbedded audio.
- Over 300 individual charts to guide your lessons.
- Pre-quizzes for students and video recommendations too!

Email: info@HamRadioSchool.com

Contents

	Preface		vi
	Using This Book and Passing Your Exam		ix
0.0	Before We Begin...		1
1.0	Operating Your Radio		9
	1.1	Transceiver Basics	9
	1.2	Ham Communication Basics	17
	1.3	Repeater Basics	25
2.0	FCC Rules & Regs		29
	2.1	The FCC and You	29
	2.2	Controlling Your Station	37
	2.3	Call Signs	41
	2.4	Talking to the World	47
3.0	Things To Do		53
4.0	Wavelength, Frequency, & Bands		61
	4.1	Wavelength and Frequency	61
	4.2	Bands, Band Plans, & License Privileges	69
5.0	Signal Propagation		75
6.0	How Radio Works		83
	6.1	Transmitting	84
	6.2	Receiving	97
	6.3	Bandwidth and Sidebands	103
7.0	Antennas		109
	7.1	Antenna Basics	109
	7.2	Standing Wave Ratio (SWR)	119
	7.3	Coax and Connectors	125
8.0	It's Electric!		129
	8.1	Electric Basics	130
	8.2	Ohm's Law and Power Law	133
	8.3	Making Electrical Measurements	141
9.0	Hamtronics		149
	9.1	Electronic Basics	150
	9.2	Transistors and More	157
10.0	Digital Modes		165
11.0	Space Contacts		173
12.0	Avoiding Interference		181
13.0	Safety		193
	13.1	Electrical Safety	194
	13.2	Antenna & Tower Safety	197
	13.3	RF Exposure Safety	202
	Index		211

HamRadioSchool.com

Preface

Congratulations on your decision to earn your FCC Technician amateur radio license and join nearly three-quarters of a million US hams! We're mighty happy to have you with us. We hope you find all the various facets of amateur radio fascinating and enjoyable, and we're here to help when you need it.

Why ham radio? Everyone has unique reasons for involvement with ham radio. Perhaps one of the most important is emergency preparation for your family. When an emergency arises – natural disasters like wildfire, tornados, hurricanes, earthquakes, or other man-made accidents or deliberate disruptions – cell phone networks are often overloaded or inoperative. Emergency responders are overwhelmed. Travel and access are frequently restricted. Throughout it all, ham radio remains operative and trustworthy, with robust, autonomous communication networks to keep you informed and to connect you with your family members when it really counts. This has been proven again and again around the world over decades of experience!

Many hams enjoy providing community service with their unique communications skills. Helping to coordinate and operate a parade, a foot or bicycle race, or a public community gathering with a group of fellow hams is an enjoyable and rewarding way to serve your community. Many hams also train and volunteer for deployment as public servants through emergency communications organizations that you will learn about in this book.

But for most amateur radio operators, ham radio is also a beloved hobby with a seemingly endless number of different aspects to investigate. From mountaintop peak operations to on-the-air group social gatherings to satellite and space station contacts to electronic circuit building to computer-digital communications to communicating around the globe, and much, much more, ham radio has an incredible array of activities to explore and enjoy. It can truly become a life-long hobby of fun and excitement for you and your family!

Is this book right for you? If you are interested in earning your Technician license, this book and its related web site are definitely for you, regardless of your background in science, technology, or math. If you have done nothing more than balance a checkbook since middle school math and you have replaced the batteries in an electronic toy, you are over-qualified to pass the Technician exam with help from this book and web site. If you are a professional engineer, a student of science, or a techno-whiz in your own right, you will likely speed through this book with enjoyment and enlightenment to license examination success in very short time.

Either way, this book will provide you fundamental understanding of radio along with the competence, and *confidence*, to get on the air with your first ham radio. Inside the book and on the web site you will find easy-to-grasp explanations of the technical topics using common examples and analogies to everyday things and experiences with which you are already familiar. You'll learn to use easy tools and techniques to help ensure your exam success. You will see ample pictures, graphics, and web-based multimedia that will help you intuitively comprehend everything from how radio electronics work to how to reach out and start a conversation on the air. You may even find it fun to read!

How is this book different? Unlike some other introductory ham radio books, this one does not pad its pages with the public domain questions from the exam question pool and try to "teach the test" by requiring you to memorize answers without understanding them. Rather, the pages are filled with relevant information that focuses you upon highlighted exam question content and that provides straightforward explanations so that you really comprehend radio. When you *really get it* you don't have to rely on mind-numbing memorization! Oh, and we provide you those public domain questions free, online at the *HamRadioSchool.com* web site, all organized by book section and accompanied by lots of additional content to help you learn very efficiently.

Yet other books are mind-numbingly technical and dry, filled with so much jargon and techno-speak that they seemingly require a Ph.D. in engineering to *really get it*. The goal of this book is to promote good, intuitive understanding of radio without *"going professorial"* on you. Simple explanations with a building-block approach will lead you to enjoyable learning, successful examination, and quickly getting on the air!

Get Going! Be sure you understand how to use this book as described in *Using This Book and Passing Your Exam* on the next page, and then start your learning both here and online at *HamRadioSchool.com*. If you have questions or comments for us, please contact us through the web site. We'll be glad to hear from you! *Good luck, and get going!*

With HamRadioSchool.com, passing your exam is easy.
More importantly, you'll *really get it!*
You'll really understand ham radio.
You'll be on the air quickly, with confidence!

Using This Book and Passing Your Exam

This *HamRadioSchool.com Technician License Course* book has been specially formatted to assist you with Technician license exam preparation! We recommend that you read this book's chapters in sequence first, then review material by topic, as necessary for your specific learning needs. We also recommend that you visit our web site, section-by-section, to take quizzes and to find additional materials that will make your learning experience an enjoyable one!

The *HamRadioSchool.com* web site provides additional learning tools organized section-by-section with the book. These enhanced learning tools may include video, audio, animations, graphics, photographs, or additional text explanations. You will also find the entire Technician Class exam question pool on the web site, with questions organized for ease of learning, section-by-section along with this book. You can also try out our quizzing and practice test app for mobile devices, containing all the quizzes and offering properly weighted practice exams anywhere, anytime. The combination of this book, the web-based learning tools, and the mobile app offers a powerful combination for really understanding ham radio.

Heavy Bold Text like this provides the answer to an exam pool question in *objective language* that mirrors the language of the question. All exam pool questions are covered this way in this book. The tab in the outer margin adjacent to the heavy bold text provides you the question identifier. You will find the exam questions and response options online, conveniently organized section-by-section, at *HamRadioSchool.com* under *Learning Material*. A page index of question identifiers is also included at the end of this book.

Example of Exam Question Objective Language Highlight and Exam Question:

> **Identification on the Air: An amateur station is required to transmit its assigned call sign at least every 10 minutes during, and at the end of, a contact.** `T1F03`

The margin tab identifies this as question T1F03. On the next page you will see the NCVEC question pool items T1F03 from which the boldface text above was derived. You'll find all the full exam pool questions at our web site for each section of this book.

T1F03 (D)   *Section 2.3, Page 41*
When is an amateur station required to transmit its assigned call sign?

  A. At the beginning of each contact, and every 10 minutes thereafter
  B. At least once during each transmission
  C. At least every 15 minutes during and at the end of a contact
  D. At least every 10 minutes during and at the end of a contact

We recommend that you read a book section, check for and review the section's online learning enhancements, and review the section's questions in exam pool format online or with our mobile app. As you get into later book chapters begin comprehensive practice tests online or with our app. When you are consistently passing practice exams you are ready for the real thing!

The Technician License (Element 2) Exam: The bottom line on passing the Technician exam is that you need at least 26 correct responses out of 35 total questions. That's about 74% correct answers to pass. There are 423 questions in the complete exam pool currently. Each question provides four multiple choice responses from which to choose. The order of the four question responses is not static -- their order will be scrambled on your exam among the "A B C D" designations.

Each exam will be comprised of questions drawn randomly from the exam pool, but with specific weighting applied by question topic. For example, the Technician exam must contain six exam questions from sub-element T1 that covers FCC rules, radio operator responsibilities, and related topics. The first two characters in a question's identifier specify its sub-element. The remaining exam weighting by sub-element are, with abbreviated descriptions:

T1	FCC Rules, Operator Responsibilities	6 questions
T2	Operating Procedures	3 questions
T3	Radio Waves and Propagation	3 questions
T4	Station Set Up & Practices	2 questions
T5	Electrical & Electronic Principles	4 questions
T6	Electronic Components & Circuits	4 questions
T7	Equipment, Problems, Troubleshooting	4 questions
T8	Modulation, Space Ops, Digital Modes	4 questions
T9	Antennas & Feedlines	2 questions
T0	Safety	3 questions

The third character in the question identifier specifies a topical group of questions within each sub-element. Each sub-element may have several groups of questions. The last two characters in the identifier specify a question from the group.

The Exam Session: All amateur radio exams are administered by Volunteer Examiners (VE). A VE is a licensed ham who volunteers to help administer the tests and develop new licensed operators. A minimum of three VEs must administer every exam. VE sessions are conducted regularly in every state.

The exam is most commonly administered on paper, so you will need a pencil (bring two, just in case one breaks), and you may use a conventional calculator with any and all memories cleared. Some VE teams now offer exams electronically, on computer, at a monitored exam session location. Either way, take your time and RTFQ! That is, *Read The Fine Question* carefully! Your exam will be graded immediately by the VEs, so you'll know right away if you have passed. If you have used the *HamRadioSchool.com* learning system well, we're confident you will succeed the first time through! Good luck!

Amateur radio VE examination sessions are regularly held all over the country. The VE exam typically utilizes "fill in the circle" paper response sheets, and a fee may be required. Volunteer Examiners are experienced hams who serve the amateur radio community by administering exams.

But, before we begin...

0.0 Before We Begin...

> **"** *Have I done the world good, or have I added a menace?* – Guglielmo Marconi

Since you are investing time with this book I believe it is safe to assume that your response to Marconi regarding his invention, radio, would be something like, *"Good. Much good indeed!"* (Caution: Following amateur radio licensing some spouse's opinions may vary.) While he stood upon the shoulders of scientific giants such as Hertz, Maxwell, Faraday, Tesla and others, we all owe Marconi a great debt of gratitude for his insight and innovation conducted around the turn of the 20th Century. But this is not a history book, so let's get on with that for which you opened the cover. Let's start learning about amateur radio!

But before we begin getting into the testable material, take a look at the list of terms below. If you are comfortable with most of these terms and understand their meaning, you can probably just read this chapter's paragraphs on the *Amateur Bands* and *License Classes*, and then skip right to Chapter 1. Go ahead if you want, and the rest of us will catch up to you shortly. Of course, you're welcome to continue with us and review these basic technical subjects to make sure we have a solid, common understanding.

Electromagnetic Waves	Modulation
Frequency	Alternating Current
Wavelength	Voltage

If the terms above are new to you, you are uncertain of their meaning, or especially if they strike fear into your heart, please continue with this section! While each of these terms will be discussed in more depth later in the book, it is important for readers who may not have a strong technical background to gain some fundamental knowledge of important technical topics in the easy-to-understand language and examples of this introductory chapter. Let's lay a solid foundation for these topics here, and the subsequent chapters' material will come much easier to you. Let's jump right into these terms.

Electromagnetic Waves: I am 100% certain that you have seen electromagnetic waves before. Light is comprised of a variety of electromagnetic waves that you perceive as various colors. These waves – we will call them EM waves for convenience – are made up of two different kinds of energy fields. As the name suggests, one of these energy fields is an *electric field* and the other is a *magnetic field*. You may have experienced an electric field by rubbing an inflated balloon on your hair to create a static charge that then pulls your hair toward the balloon. Every common magnet you have ever held creates a magnetic field that attracts many types of metal. All EM waves are made of those two kinds of invisible forces, or energy fields.

Why are they waves? The electric field and the magnetic field in EM transmissions vary in strength as they travel. Each energy field regularly increases and decreases in strength. We like to picture these fields rising and falling like water waves that are rolling along at the speed of light, as in Figure 0.1 below. As the wave travels past a stationary position, the electric field and the magnetic field smoothly increase and decrease in strength, or *amplitude*, as measured at the stationary position. Further, as indicated from the center axis of wave travel, the direction of each field reverses regularly, oscillating back-and-forth (up and down in the Figure 0.1) as observed from a stationary position. The distance the wave travels in one complete back-and-forth cycle is called the *wavelength*. You can imagine a wavelength as the distance from wave crest-to-crest, such as with a sequence of two regular ocean waves, or more conventionally where the axis of travel is crossed with one complete wave cycle.

Radio Waves: Like light, radio waves are EM waves too. They are different from light waves only in the rate at which their electric and magnetic fields

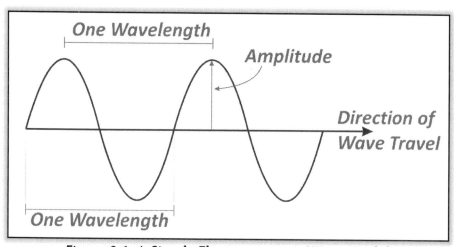

Figure 0.1: A Simple Electromagnetic Wave Model

wiggle back and forth as the wave travels past a stationary position. You may think of radio waves as being a bit lazier than light waves, wiggling the fields back-and-forth much slower than do light waves. But they still travel through space at the same speed as light waves, so that slower rate of wiggling makes for a lot longer distance covered in one of those back-and-forth cycles. In other words, radio waves have *longer wavelengths* than light waves.

Radio Frequency: The rate at which the electric field and magnetic field oscillate, stated as the number of completed cycles per second, is called the *frequency*. And remember, one back-and-forth cycle defines one wavelength of distance traveled. So frequency is also expressing the number of wavelengths per second that pass by as a continuous radio wave flies past you. The radio frequency to which you tune your radio – the radio in a car, the receiver of a stereo, or your new ham radio – is describing the number of cycles per second of the radio transmission. But instead of saying "cycles per second" all the time when discussing frequencies, we use the term *hertz* to mean cycles per second. Hertz is the unit of measure for radio frequency.

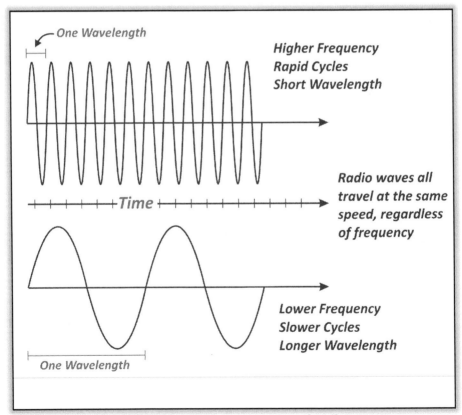

Figure 0.2: Comparison of Two EM Waves of Different Frequency

Modulation: *Modulation* is the process of placing an information signal into a radio wave by altering some characteristic of the wave. For example, we could simply turn the radio wave transmission on and off in distinct patterns to send a signal. *Morse Code signals* are like this, on and off patterns that represent letters, numbers, and punctuations. This modulation method is also called *continuous wave* (CW), because other characteristics of the waveform remain unchanged.

Instead of on-off patterns in the transmission we might change the frequency itself in a way that encodes a message. We could make the frequency shift higher or lower than a known reference frequency in patterns that carry a code of information. This is *frequency modulation*, or FM radio. The shifting FM frequencies often encode an audio voice signal, or music audio in the case of commercial FM radio.

We could vary the power level of the transmitted waves in a way that encodes a message. That is, we could manipulate the strength of the electric and magnetic fields as we transmit the wave. The energy level of the EM fields can be imagined as the height or size of the EM waves, and this is called the wave's *amplitude*. (Just like water waves, big tall waves have a lot of power, tiny short waves are weak!) Encoding a message by varying the EM field power or wave height is *amplitude modulation*, or AM radio. Again, the varying amplitude signal often will encode a voice audio signal. A special kind of AM used in

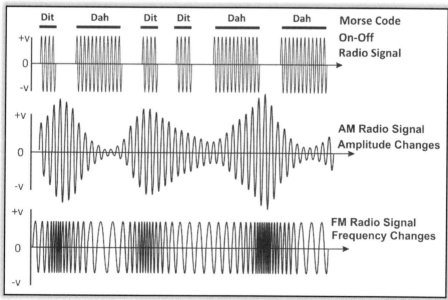

Figure 0.3: Comparison of Different Modulation Methods

amateur radio is called *single sideband* (SSB), and we'll discuss this more in Chapter 6.

In amateur radio we use different types of modulation, such as FM, AM, and SSB, to encode the sound of a voice or other forms of messages into the radio waves. Each modulation technique of sending a signal is called a *mode* of radio transmission.

Electrical Current: A radio transmitter uses electricity to produce radio waves. The way that electricity flows within wires or circuits, including antennas, helps to determine the frequency of the radio waves produced. Electricity is the movement of tiny charged particles called *electrons*. A measure of the amount of electrons moving through a wire is the *electrical current* – just like water current is a measure of the amount of water flowing down a river or through a pipe.

Voltage: *Voltage* is the force, or the pressure, pushing the electrons along through the wire. High voltage, like high water pressure, can really push the electrons forcefully through the wire in order that they can do a lot of work somewhere. Low voltage, like low water pressure, provides a less forceful push of the electrons along the wire. Also like water pressure in plumbing, voltage has a direction of force. It can push electrons this way or that in the wire, one direction or the other.

Direct and Alternating Current: When the voltage, or pressure, is pushing electrons in only one direction in a wire, we say that is *direct current* (DC). A typical battery produces one-way voltage resulting in direct current. However, other voltage sources such as the wall outlet of your home produce a constant back-and-forth pressure, effectively pushing-and-pulling the electrons in the wire. This kind of push-pull voltage creates *alternating current* (AC), with electrons accelerating in one direction in the wire, then slowing and reversing direction to accelerate the opposite way. This back-and-forth cycle of electron motion repeats continuously with alternating current, and we say that AC has a frequency of alternation, also expressed in hertz as the number of back-and-forth cycles per second.

Antenna Radiation: Notice that the back-and-forth current of AC is similar to the back-and-forth oscillation of energy in an EM radio wave. In fact, if you produce a rapidly alternating AC current – at rates equal to radio frequencies – and if you properly connect that AC current to an antenna, the antenna will convert some electrical energy into radio energy, radiating a radio wave with a frequency equal to the alternations of the AC electrical current. Radio frequency is determined by the AC frequency of back-and-forth electron motion

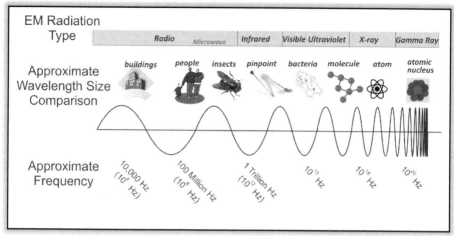

Figure 0.4: The Electromagnetic (EM) Spectrum

produced in a radio's electronic circuitry. Accelerating electric charge, like that surging back-and-forth in an antenna, produces EM waves in accordance with advanced laws of physics that we won't try to cover in this book!

EM Spectrum: The entire range of EM frequencies is very wide, and radio frequencies (RF) are on the low end of the range. In other words, in the spectrum of EM waves from radio waves to light waves to X-rays, RF has the slowest rates of EM field oscillations, and that also means the longest wavelengths. As EM frequency gets higher, the wavelengths get shorter and we move out of radio waves and up into light waves. The even higher frequencies with their very short wavelengths take us up into X-ray and Gamma Ray territory.

RF Spectrum: The radio frequencies include EM radiation up to a few hundred billion hertz. That is some mighty fast EM oscillation cycles, huh? Hundreds of billions of cycles every second! Most of the frequencies we will discuss for amateur radio use will be a few million to a few hundred million hertz. We will use the prefix "mega" to mean million, so megahertz (MHz) means "millions of cycles per second."

Scientists and engineers have named the different broad ranges of radio frequencies with some quite general names that you've probably heard before. In this amateur radio book we will be interested primarily in these frequency ranges:

    High Frequency (HF): 3 to 30 MHz
    Very High Frequency (VHF): 30 to 300 MHz
    Ultra High Frequency (UHF): 300 to 3000 MHz

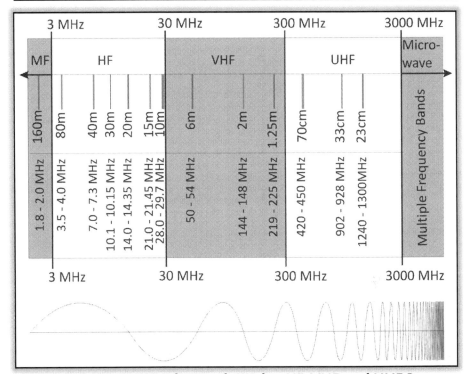

Figure 0.5: Amateur Radio Bands Within HF, VHF, and UHF Ranges

Amateur Bands: Within each of those very broad categories of HF, VHF, and UHF, several specific little ranges, or *bands*, of frequencies are reserved by law for amateur radio use. You may imagine each of these bands as being just like the commercial FM radio band that ranges from about 88 MHz to 108 MHz, and you can tune your radio across the band to pick up individual stations at different frequencies within the band. Compared to the entire radio spectrum these amateur bands are rather small, but they each contain from a few hundred thousand to a few tens of millions of hertz worth of frequencies, or *bandwidth*.

These amateur radio bands are identified by the frequency range they cover, but they are more commonly named by ham operators as the *approximate wavelength* of the band. Although each specific frequency in the band produces a slightly different wavelength, all of the band's wavelengths are "in the ballpark" near a rounded wavelength value that is used as the name of the band. For example, we will speak of the 10 meter band to identify radio frequencies from 28.0 to 29.7 MHz, all of which produce wavelengths that are near 10 meters (about 30 feet) in length.

Amateur License Classes: Currently only three different classes of amateur radio licenses are awarded in the United States: *Technician, General,* and *Extra.* The introductory license class is Technician and the highest available license class is Extra. As a radio operator progresses from Technician, to General, to Extra, more of the amateur radio bands are available to the license holder. The Technician is allowed to transmit on all bands in the UHF and VHF ranges, as well as limited segments and limited modes on some of the bands in the HF range. General class license holders are permitted to transmit by all modes on all Technician allocations plus large segments of each band in the HF range. Extra license holders have no restrictions, permitted to transmit on all amateur radio bands and with all modes. (Within established guidelines for use.)

Grandfathered License Classes: In earlier years the classes of amateur licenses and band privileges were parsed more finely, and six license classes were awarded in the US from 1978 to 2000. An introductory license with band privileges lower than Technician was called *Novice.* Above Technician was *Technician Plus.* Between General and Extra was a license class called *Advanced.* Although Novice and Advanced licenses are no longer granted, they are grandfathered classes, and many ham operators still hold these licenses and the band privileges that are associated with them. No Technician Plus licenses are held any longer by current FCC-licensed operators.

Now that you have a basic understanding of some radio-related technical topics, you are ready to begin your Technician license preparation. You will see each of those terms and topics again as you read through the book, along with some alternate descriptions of these concepts and some additional information about amateur radio operations. Be sure you have reviewed the *"Using This Book"* information in the introduction, then move on to Chapter 1.0 and start becoming a ham radio operator!

1.0 Operating Your Radio

> ❝ *Let's talk about the radio...*
> — Fern Moyse
> [The Hackensaw Boys]

Yes, let's talk about the radio, as Fern suggests! After all, that's why we're here.

In this chapter you will learn the practical basics necessary for the operation of any ham radio. In Section 1.1 we will cover a transceiver's common controls and components and introduce you to the different modes of transmitting and receiving signals. Section 1.2 is a summary of ham radio communication basics, including some common on-the-air procedures and terms, as well as an overview of the most common problems new hams have and how to solve them. Section 1.3 is all about amateur radio repeater stations and how you can use them to extend your radio's communications range. Ready?

Let's talk, starting with that new transceiver you're anxious to get.

1.1 Operating Your Radio — Transceiver Basics

Modern ham radios are a combination of a transmitter and a receiver, called a *transceiver*. A transmitter emits radio waves to carry your signal out to the world, while a receiver captures others' radio signals so you can hear them. **A transceiver** is a unit that does both jobs, **combining the functions of a transmitter and receiver,** and allowing easy two-way radio communication with one device.

All transceivers have some common basic parts.

Microphone: Converts sound into electrical signals, or audio signals, for the transmitter.

Transmitter: Encodes audio signals into radio frequency emissions. This encoding process is called *modulation*.

Antenna: Radiates radio frequency emissions during transmissions and detects radio frequencies during reception.

Receiver: Converts, or *demodulates*, radio signals back into audio signals.

Speaker: Transforms audio electrical signals into sounds.

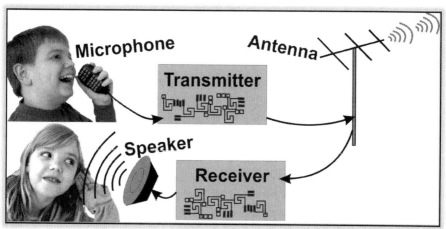

Figure 1.1: Transceiver Basic Components

Transceivers are manufactured in many sizes and forms, but most modern amateur transceivers fit into one of three common types.

Handheld Transceiver (HT): The HT radio is commonly the first type of ham radio that a Technician licensee will own. It is a small radio that fits in your hand and contains an integrated battery, an integrated antenna, and an integrated microphone. Although limited in output power it is very useful for portable communications. HTs usually transmit only *frequency modulated* (FM) signals in the VHF and/or UHF frequency ranges. **A handheld transceiver may be linked to an RF power amplifier to increase low power output.**

Mobile Station: A medium sized radio that typically uses either automobile battery power or a separate AC power supply. Mobile radios use an external antenna connected with coaxial cable and a separate handheld microphone. These radios are commonly installed in automobiles, but they may also be

1.1 Transceiver Basics

Figure 1.2: Transceiver Form Factor Types

used in homes as small base stations. Mobiles provide higher output power than HT radios, and some more capable models provide multiple operational modes and multiple frequency bands (Modes: FM, SSB, AM; Bands: HF/VHF/UHF).

Base Station: Larger in size and typically using an AC power supply or an extensive DC battery bank, these radios require external cable-connected antenna(s) and a separate handheld or desk microphone. A modern base station transceiver will usually provide higher output power and is frequently coupled with a separate component power amplifier. These radios typically provide multiple operational modes and multiple frequency bands. (Modes: FM, SSB, AM, CW; Bands: HF/VHF/UHF).

You probably noticed that some of these transceiver types offer multiple operational *modes* and *bands*. You may be wondering what that means. The start-up Chapter 0.0 provided some insight about modes and bands, and we'll learn more about amateur radio bands in Section 4.2, but let's get right to this matter of modes again. It's quite simple really!

Mode refers to the method of modulating a radio signal, or encoding information into the radio signal. So, the mode is the particular way that your voice (or other type of information) is put into the radio signal that your radio transmits. This is done by varying some characteristic of the radio waves with the variations of your voice, or other information type.

Let's just get introduced to some common ham radio modes for now. We'll examine these more closely in later chapters.

FM: *Frequency Modulation.* Frequency is the number of radio waves (cycles) per second a transmitter emits. In frequency modulation, small variations are made in the emitted radio frequencies that mirror the sound variations of your voice in the audio input signal. **FM is the mode most commonly used with VHF and UHF phone (voice) communications, including voice repeater stations that relay your signals. FM is also commonly used for VHF packet radio (digital) communications.**

[T8A02 T8A04]

AM: *Amplitude Modulation.* Every radio wave has a level of power, or wave height, known as the wave's *amplitude*. With AM, the power level of the emitted radio wave is varied to encode your voice audio signal (or other type of information) into the radio transmission.

SSB: *Single Sideband* mode is a special type of AM. The very efficient **SSB mode is often used for long distance or weak signal contacts on the VHF and UHF bands,** and it is very common on HF bands. **An advantage of SSB over FM for voice transmissions is narrower bandwidth,** meaning that a smaller portion of available radio spectrum is used. In other words, a smaller range or number of frequencies is necessary to carry the voice audio information. We'll examine more on bandwidth and sidebands in Section 6.3.

[T8A03 T8A07]

CW: *Continuous Wave* means that the transmitted signal is unchanging. No FM or AM modulation varies the signal. Rather, the signal transmission itself is interrupted in patterns over time to encode information. Morse Code is by far the most common code used by hams in CW mode. With Morse Code patterns of on/off radio transmissions represent letters, numbers, and punctuations.

Other modes are used by hams, particularly with a computer connected to the radio to create *digital signals* or to transmit images. We'll dig into that awesomeness a little later in Chapter 10.

Transceiver Controls: You may have seen some ham radios, or at least you have seen the examples in the pictures of this section, and you may be wondering what all those knobs and dials and buttons do and what other compo-

1.1 Transceiver Basics

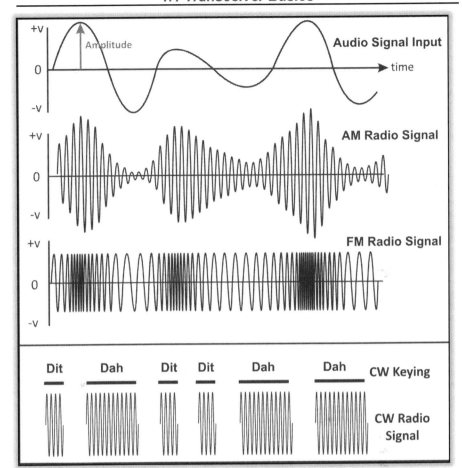

Figure 1.3: Modulation Methods

nents you may need to get on the air. Here are some basics about controls and components that will help you get started understanding your radio.

Push-To-Talk (PTT): The PTT button on a microphone or the side of an HT radio is used exactly that way -- You literally push to talk! Pushing the PTT button activates the microphone and radio transmitter, sending your signal to the world. **PTT switches between receive and transmit.**

Squelch: This control mutes the receiver output noise when no signal is being received. Commonly a rotary knob control, you can adjust the signal strength required to *open the squelch* and allow the receiver to create audio for you to hear. The squelch control cuts out random noise that you don't want to listen to in between radio transmissions. Newer transceivers often use a menu-selected squelch setting instead of an adjustable knob.

Variable Frequency Oscillator (VFO): This is the tuning control for your radio, used to scroll and **tune the transceiver to operating frequencies.** The VFO control is typically a rotary **knob** and may also be coupled with up/down arrow keys on a keypad. You will learn in Chapter 6 why it has that strange name.

Keypad: Most modern radios, particularly HTs, include an **integrated keypad with which you may enter operating frequencies, store favorite frequencies in channels to enable quick access,** program repeater channels and tones, and vary the functions of your radio. Modern radios may have multiple menu levels to control a wide variety of functions and set up features, and the keypad is the key to them all.

Headphones: Most radios support the use of headphones in place of a regular speaker. Headphones can help you copy signals in noisy areas, and most radios have connection ports for combination headphones-microphone assemblies. Some of these assemblies provide voice activated microphones, or *VOX*, in which PTT is activated by the relatively strong sound of your voice rather than a push-button.

Power Sources: Most HT radios will use an integrated battery that must be recharged or replaced over time. Larger radios commonly use a regulated power supply (AC-to-DC power supply) to provide a very stable voltage. However, almost all ham radios can be powered by external battery sources, and many hams keep a bank of back-up batteries on hand for emergency operations during power outages.

Antennas: Most HT radios are sold with a short integrated antenna referred to as a 'Rubber Duck' due to its rubberized molded exterior. **The Rubber Duck antenna does not transmit or receive as effectively as a full sized antenna, such as a quarter-wavelength antenna. A disadvantage of using a handheld VHF transceiver, with its integral antenna, inside a vehicle is its signals may not propagate well due to the shielding effect of the vehicle.** Larger radios will typically use external antennas that are sold separately from the radio. You may easily connect your HT to an external antenna by removing the rubber duck antenna and using coaxial cable and compatible connectors. Longer HT-mounted antennas for improved performance of handhelds are readily available also, supplanting the shorter rubber duck.

A great combination for the new ham is an HT radio and a magnetically mounted automobile roof antenna connected with a narrow cable that can slip through the door or window seal. That way you can connect your HT to the car external antenna for significantly improved performance when on the road, and use your rubber duck when on foot! *Quack, quack!*

1.1 Transceiver Basics

Congratulations! You have completed your first step toward your FCC amateur radio Technician License!

Now go to the *HamRadioSchool.com* web site and review the related questions from the technician question pool for **Section 1.1**.

www.HamRadioSchool.com/tech_media

Figure 1.4: Typical HT Transceiver Controls

1.2 Ham Communication Basics

Operating Your Radio
1.2 Ham Communication Basics

> **"** *The public airwaves provide a chance to affirm we want to be a good, decent people; a good, decent nation.* — Charles W. Pickering

You've got your license and new radio, you've got the transceiver control basics figured out, and you are ready to get on the air! What now? What do you say? How do you reach out to another ham? What frequency do you use? What cool ham phrases or terms should you use?

Don't worry, it's easy, and the ham radio community is jam packed with friendly folks – good, decent people – who will be happy to help a new operator get started. If you haven't been around ham radio very much and have not heard others talking on the air, it's probably a good idea to find a popular repeater station and just listen for a while. Then, when you're ready, use that PTT and make your first call! Here are some basic pointers to get your on-the-air communications off to a stellar beginning!

Simplex Communications: Transmitting and receiving on the same frequency, directly from radio to radio (as contrasted with repeater communications.) Your local area likely has coordinated specific frequencies for simplex communications on the VHF and UHF bands, and you should stick to these standard channels to help reduce interference. Ask an experienced ham about your local coordinated band plan, or use the national calling frequencies first to attempt to contact others in your area.

Repeater Communications: A repeater amateur station receives your signal on one channel (frequency) **and simultaneously retransmits it on a different channel.** So, repeater communications use more than one frequency: One frequency for transmitting and one frequency for listening. The repeater station is always the relay between you and others whom you may not be able to reliably reach by simplex communication. Your radio can be programmed to automatically switch from the repeater's "listen to" frequency to its "transmit to" or "talk" frequency when you PTT. That way, the practical use of repeaters is not much different from simplex operations. You will learn more about repeaters next in Section 1.3.

Station Identification: A transmitting station must properly identify, even when making on-the-air test transmissions.

Figure 1.5: Simplex vs. Repeater Communications

An amateur station must identify with its call sign every 10 minutes during, and at the end of, any set of transmissions of any kind.

T2A08 **CQ Contact: The procedural signal CQ means "calling any station."** More commonly used with noisier weak signal SSB communications than on FM repeaters or simplex, the CQ call will typically be repeated two or three times followed by the calling station's call sign. **T2A05 A station responding to a CQ call should repeat the other station's call sign followed by its own call sign.**

T2A12 When choosing an operating frequency for calling CQ, listen first to be sure no one else is using the frequency. You may also ask if the frequency is in use. Make sure you are in your assigned band as well, within your license privileges (see Section 4.2). **T4B13 You may also use the scanning function of an FM transceiver to scan through a range of frequencies to check for activity.**

1.2 Ham Communication Basics

Transmit your FCC call sign every 10 minutes and at the end of any set of transmissions!

While there is no requirement to identify your station at the start of a set of transmissions, most operators do that also.

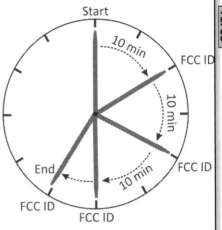

Figure 1.6: FCC Station Identification Requirements

Specific Station Contact: When you are calling a specific station whose call sign you know, you simply say the other station's call sign then identify with your own call sign. This applies to simplex and repeaters.

National Calling Frequencies: Standard frequencies on VHF and UHF bands reserved for making initial simplex contact with other stations. Once contact is established the communicating stations should move to another frequency in order to keep the calling frequency open for all stations' use.

2 meter band: 146.520 MHz is the national FM calling frequency.
70 cm band: 446.000 MHz is the national calling frequency.

Note that **the proper abbreviation for megahertz is MHz,** as used above.

Q-Signals: Abbreviations derived from Morse Code operations that are commonly used even in phone (voice) communications. Q-Signals help keep transmissions brief and efficient, and they are widely used by hams. A full list of Q-Signals is available on **HamRadioSchool.com**, but common Q-Signals include:

QRM: Interference from other radio stations
QRN: Static interference or atmospheric noise
QRP: Using low power; shall I reduce power?
QRQ: Send more quickly, send faster (CW speed)
QRS: Send more slowly (CW speed)

QRZ: Who is calling me?
QSL: Acknowledge receipt
QSO: A radio contact or conversation
QSY: Change of frequency
QTH: Location; what is your location?
73: Best regards (A procedural sign, not a Q-Signal, but commonly used)

Common Courtesy: No single radio amateur has sole privilege or rights to any amateur frequency, and common courtesy should prevail when two stations transmitting on the same frequency interfere with each other. If your station's transmission unintentionally interferes with another station, properly identify and move to a different frequency. Often a club or organization will have regularly scheduled on-air meetings called "nets," particularly on repeaters. Use common courtesy and move to another repeater or another frequency in such cases, and better yet, become familiar with the club and net schedules on repeaters that you use so that you may plan your use around scheduled events on the air. Even better still, inquire about joining in on nets of interest to you!

Self-Regulating Service: The amateur radio service prides itself on being a self-regulated, self-policed service under the FCC. As a licensed operator you should know the rules and follow them, encourage other operators in a positive way to uphold the same standards, and take pride in your on-air operations, making them efficient, enjoyable, and friendly.

Common Problems & Solutions: As you gain some experience with ham radio you will encounter some of the following common problems that limit or diminish your radio's performance. Most of these common problems have easy solutions. Let's wrap up this section with a look at seven common problems and how to solve them.

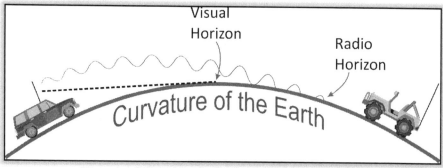
Figure 1.7: Radio Horizon vs. Visual Horizon

1.2 Ham Communication Basics

1. **Radio Horizon:** The distance over which two stations can communicate by direct path. This distance is somewhat further than the visual horizon, or visual line-of-sight, **because the earth seems less curved to radio waves than to light waves.** That is, radio waves are bent over the horizon a little more by the atmosphere and ground effects than are light waves. VHF and UHF signals are usually limited by the radio horizon, but repeater stations at a distance or in high locations help to resolve this limitation.

   T3C11

2. **Intermittent Signals: If another operator reports that your station's signals were strong a moment ago but are now weak or distorted, you may be experiencing random reflections and multi-path distortion.** In this situation your signal travels by more than one path to the receiving station and with varying distances or wave phase relationships among the signals. **Moving just a few feet** may resolve the reflections and improve your transmitted signal or your received signal if you are experiencing distortion in your audio. Inside buildings where many materials such as pipes and wires are inside walls, floors, and ceilings, moving just a few feet will often improve your signal if it is blocked or reflected by these hidden metal objects.

   T3A01

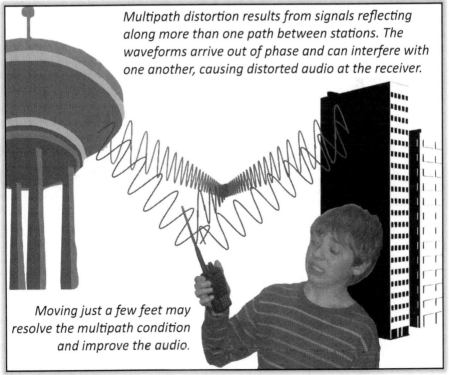

Multipath distortion results from signals reflecting along more than one path between stations. The waveforms arrive out of phase and can interfere with one another, causing distorted audio at the receiver.

Moving just a few feet may resolve the multipath condition and improve the audio.

Figure 1.8: Multipath Distortion and Random Reflections

3. **Picket Fencing: A rapid fluttering sound that is commonly heard from mobile stations that are moving while transmitting.** This is common with automobiles moving rapidly near metal signs, bridges, buildings, or other features in the environment that block or reflect the radio signals.

4. **Obstructions:** Buildings, hills, vegetation, or other natural or man-made features may block your direct line of sight path to a distant repeater or other station. **A directional antenna may be used to try and find a path that reflects your signals to the other station.** The directional antenna will allow you to focus most of the transmitted energy in the direction of the reflection path, thereby improving your signal strength along that indirect path.

5. **Antenna Polarization:** The physical orientation of both your antenna and the radio waves it emits. All electromagnetic (EM) waves, including radio waves, have a definite direction of oscillation of the intensity of electrical and magnetic fields that make up the wave, and that direction changes with your antenna's orientation. Specifically, **the orientation of the electric field of a radio wave is used to describe its polarization.** (See Figure 1.9.)

   a. **Identical polarization of the transmitting and receiving stations is best for signal strength,** usually either vertical antenna orientation or horizontal antenna orientation, **else signals will be significantly weaker.** (We will elaborate on this more in later sections.)

   b. **Vertical polarization**, where your antenna is vertical, is most common for FM simplex and FM repeater operations. Hold your HT antenna straight vertical for the best performance. The electric field oscillations will be vertical to the earth's surface, expanding and contracting up and down during each wave cycle.

   c. **Horizontal polarization, where your antenna elements are horizontal, is common for long-distance weak-signal operations using the VHF and UHF bands, particularly with CW and SSB modes.** The electric field oscillation is horizontal to the earth.

6. **Over Deviating:** Your FM signal is being driven too hard by your microphone's audio signal, causing distortion. **Talk farther away from the microphone if you are told your FM transceiver is over deviating.**

1.2 Ham Communication Basics

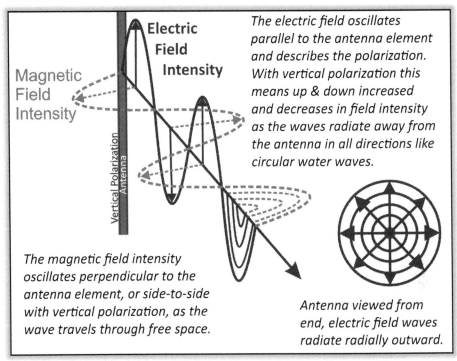

Figure 1.9 Vertical Polarization EM Wave Propagation

7. **Distorted or Unintelligible Signals:** This can be caused by several factors including **your transmitter being slightly off frequency, your batteries running low, or simply being in a bad location.**

T7B10

There you go! With these basics of ham communication under your belt you'll be ready to get on the air. Take a look at the related Technician test questions on **HamRadioSchool.com** for **Section 1.2.** I'll bet you can get most of them correct already!

www.HamRadioSchool.com/tech_media

Summary Table of seven Common Problems / Solutions

1.	Radio horizon blocks VHF/UHF signals and is the distance over which two stations can communication by direct path, but it is somewhat beyond the visual horizon (the earth seems less curved to radio waves).
2.	Multipath distortion and random reflections may be solved by moving your position just a few feet.
3.	Picket fencing is a fluttering noise often heard from mobile stations.
4.	You may be able to transmit "around" obstructions using a directional antenna to bounce signals off of terrain or structures.
5.	Polarization is the direction of electric field oscillations in the EM wave, and the best communications are with all stations having identical polarization, else your signals will be weak.
6.	Over deviating is when the audio signal is too strong, causing distortion in the modulated RF signal and received audio. Talk further away from the microphone to resolve over deviation.
7.	Distortion or unintelligible signals may be caused by a slightly off-frequency transmitter, low batteries, or poor location.

1.3 Repeater Basics

Operating Your Radio
1.3 Repeater Basics

> **"** There is no harm in repeating a good thing. — Plato

You have made your first simplex contact and a friendly fellow ham told you about a really cool repeater nearby on which a local group holds a new ham discussion net every Thursday night. That's exactly the kind of forum you'd like to get involved with! So, how do you get onto that repeater? How do you set up your radio for it? What are the QSOs like on a repeater?

Once again, the answers to these questions are not cosmic or complicated. A repeater is a good thing, so let's see how to utilize it.

Repeater: An amateur radio station that simultaneously retransmits the signal of another amateur station on a different channel or channels. Repeaters are often located on high terrain, on tall buildings, or on high towers, and they may retransmit at relatively high power levels, so the originating station's signal may be relayed over a much larger distance than is possible with the originating station alone.

Frequency Offset: The difference between a repeater's transmit and receive frequencies. All stations will monitor a repeater on its transmit frequency (your "listen" frequency). All stations will transmit to a repeater on its receive frequency (your "talk" frequency). Thus, when you use your "talk" frequency your signal is instantly repeated on the "listen" frequency for all other stations to hear. The difference between these two frequencies is the repeater *frequency offset*.

When you program a repeater channel into your radio, you'll select the proper offset value for the specific repeater.

- **Positive Offset:** Your talk frequency is higher than your listen frequency. (The repeater's receive is higher than its transmit.)

- **Negative Offset:** Your talk frequency is lower than your listen frequency. (The repeater's receive is lower than its transmit.)

Figure 1.10: Example of Repeater Offset Frequencies and Tones

- **2m Band Offset: A common 2m offset is 600 kHz (0.6 MHz), either positive or negative.**
- **70cm Band Offset: A common 70cm offset is 5 MHz, either positive or negative.**

When you program a repeater channel into your radio with an offset value it will automatically shift to the required "talk" frequency when you PTT. Most modern radios have the standard repeater offset values for the United States pre-programmed, including standards for positive or negative offset according to the portion of a band being utilized. However, not all US locations adhere to these standards and you may have to override the pre-programmed values to properly set up some repeater channels.

Tones and Squelch: Many repeaters require the use of a sub-audible tone in your transmission to activate the repeater. Although the tone is there and the repeater receives it, you do not hear it. If there is no tone in your transmission the repeater will ignore you! The tone is required to open the squelch of the repeater's receiver and allow your signal to be "heard" by the repeater. And there are other types of tones sometimes used for the same purpose, as listed on the opposite page.

When you program a repeater frequency pair into a radio channel you'll select the proper tone to be transmitted each time you push-to-talk, in addition to the offset value. The following is a summary of the various tone types that may be used to properly access a repeater, and a couple of related items about repeaters:

CTCSS: Continuous Tone-Coded Squelch System. This is the most common tone system used in the US, and it is also referred to as "PL Tone." **CTCSS**

1.3 Repeater Basics

uses the sub-audible tone transmitted with normal voice audio to open the squelch of the receiver. There are 42 standard CTCSS tone frequencies. [T2B02]

DCS: Digital Coded Squelch uses a stream of digital data to open the receiver's squelch.

Tone Burst: More common in Europe, a transmission of a 1,750 Hz audio tone at the beginning of each transmission used to open the receiver's squelch.

You might be unable to access a repeater whose output you can hear if you have an improper transceiver offset, or if the repeater requires a proper CTCSS or DCS tone from your transceiver that it is not transmitting. [T2B04]

Carrier Squelch: Only a radio frequency (RF) signal is required to break the squelch. Carrier squelch is the simplest type of squelch based on the presence or absence of a signal, and this is the same as the basic squelch circuit of your radio used in simplex operations.

Courtesy Tones: With repeaters you will often hear tones inserted by the repeater at the end of a repeated transmission. These courtesy tones have no squelch affect and are simply to help identify when another user has ended a transmission. And they sound cool!

Open/Closed Repeaters: By using tone squelch or other activation methods, some repeaters may be closed to public amateur use and reserved for only emergency, organizational, or club use. The majority of repeaters are open to use by all licensed amateurs. A good source of repeater information, including open/closed status, offset frequencies, and tone requirements, is a published repeater directory or an online description from the repeater operators.

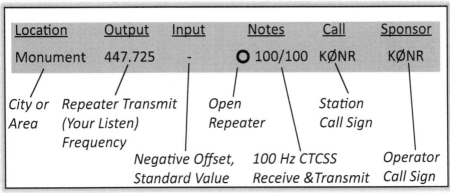

Figure 1.11: Sample Repeater Directory Listing

Calling for Contact: On repeaters, the CQ call is rarely used. Rather, **to indicate that you are listening and interested in a contact simply transmit your call sign.** As with simplex communication, if you know the call sign of another specific station you wish to call via a repeater, **say the other station's call sign then identify with your call sign.**

Repeater Coordination is conducted by regional **FrequencyCoordinators** who are **selected by amateur operators in the local or regional area whose stations are eligible to be repeater or auxiliary stations. The volunteer Frequency coordinator recognized by local amateurs recommends transmit/receive channels and other parameters for repeaters and auxiliary stations** to minimize interference between these stations and to ensure the most efficient use of the radio spectrum.

Linked Repeaters: Repeaters may be linked together using auxiliary stations and other methods. Linked repeater systems involving many repeater stations can provide very broad coverage of VHF and UHF signals. **A linked repeater network is a network of repeaters where signals recieved by one repeater are repeated by all repeaters.**

Simplex Instead? When stations can communicate directly without using a repeater, the operators should consider communicating via simplex rather than a repeater. You can easily check whether or not simplex communication is possible, and **most VHF/UHF transceivers have a convenient "reverse split" function to listen on a repeater's input frequency.** This way you can momentarily monitor the other stations' direct transmissions to hear if simplex communication is possible and, if so, free the repeater for others to use. Further, **if a station is not strong enough to keep a repeater's receiver squelch open, you might receive the station's signals by listening on the repeater input frequency** using the "reverse split" function.

Spectacular! Now you can dig into your radio's user manual, read the specifics of how to set up a repeater channel, and understand exactly what you are doing and what all the frequencies and tones are about. Repeater communications are fun and convenient, and you'll be using repeaters in no time.

Now, let's see what the exam question pool has in store for you regarding repeaters. Hit the Technician pool questions for **Section 1.3**.

www.HamRadioSchool.com/tech_media

2.0 FCC Rules & Regs

> *You have to learn the rules of the game. And then you have to play better than anyone else.* — Albert Einstein

Now you're radiating! Really, you're transmitting on repeaters, communicating simplex, and having a blast on the air. But, what rules do you have to follow regarding your transmissions? Are there things you cannot say on the air? Can you let your little brother talk on your ham radio, or Uncle Fred who has no license? Can you take your radio on vacation to Europe and transmit? And what about your license? How long does it last? Do you have to retest in the future? So many questions! But all the answers are right here. Don't fret.

This chapter is all about THE RULES. As a licensed amateur radio operator you are responsible for understanding and playing by the rules and regulations established by the **Federal Communications Commission (FCC), the agency that regulates and enforces the rules for the Amateur Radio Service in the United States.** Let's start *learning the rules of the game* with the relationship between the FCC and you that your amateur radio license will establish. [T1A02]

2.1 The FCC and You

Amateur Radio Service: The FCC sanctions the Amateur Radio Service for persons who are interested in radio technique solely with a personal aim and without pecuniary interest (that is, without profit or money-making intent). **One purpose of the Amateur Radio Service stated in FCC regulations is to advance skills in the technical and communication phases of the radio art.** In the spirit of this purpose, a permissible use of the Amateur Radio Service is allowing a person to conduct radio experiments and to communicate with other licensed hams around the world. [T1A01]

Part 97: The FCC rules and regulations that govern the Amateur Radio Service are contained in FCC Regulation Part 97. There are many sub-parts to Part 97 that provide guidelines on virtually every aspect of amateur radio. While Part 97 provides much spellbinding reading, it is not necessary for you to memorize it to become a ham radio operator. Simply be familiar with the most commonly applicable Part 97 rules and know that you can find guidance in Part 97 when you begin to venture beyond the typical amateur operations. However, be aware that **the FCC rules always apply to the operation of an amateur station** licensed by the FCC.

Rules Under Part 97: Most of the FCC part 97 rules are not hard to learn and are easy to comply with. The following list of SIX BIG RULES provides the most commonly applicable rules to amateur stations and operators. Learn them, know them, live them:

1. **FCC Inspection: You must make your station and records available to FCC inspection any time upon request by an FCC representative.** Inspections very rarely occur. Usually an FCC inspection will be initiated only in cases of repeated rules violations by a station. Rules violations are usually reported by other responsible amateur operators when violations occur multiple times with a known station. Additionally, the *American Radio Relay League* (ARRL) operates the *amateur auxiliary*, a volunteer organization that works in conjunction with the FCC to monitor activity on amateur radio frequencies and encourage amateur operators to self-police.

2. **Mailing Address: The license grantee must provide and maintain a correct mailing address with the FCC or revocation of the station license or suspension of the operator license may result.**

3. **Minimum Necessary Power:** Under normal, non-distress circumstances, an amateur should use the minimum transmitter power necessary to carry out the desired communication while not exceeding the maximum power permitted. This is difficult to judge sometimes, but as you learn you'll become comfortable with adjusting your radio power and requesting signal reports from other operators to better comply with this rule.

4. **Prohibited Transmissions:** The FCC, the *ARRL amateur auxiliary*, and most amateur operators don't take well to the following six prohibited activities:

   a. **Indecent or obscene words or language are prohibited in amateur transmissions.** There is no official list of prohibited foul terms, but you will probably know them if you hear them! Beyond individual obscenities, indecent language is also prohibited even

2.1 The FCC and You

if none of the typical obscenities are thrown into the mix. Transmit responsibly, even when others may not on rare occasions.

b. **Broadcasting: FCC rules define broadcasting as the transmission of information intended for reception by the general public. Amateur stations are authorized to transmit signals related to broadcasting, program production, or news gathering only where such communication is directly related to the immediate safety of human life or protection of property and no other communication means is available.** A "CQ" or other call indicates specifically to hams that you are listening or wish to initiate a QSO. It is *not* a one-way general public announcement. But this regulation denies broadcasting a "regularly scheduled radio show," for instance, to anyone listening to the airwaves, whether licensed hams or shortwave receiver enthusiasts.

FCC exceptions to this rule: **An amateur radio station may make one-way transmissions when transmitting code practice** (Morse code)**, information bulletins, or transmissions necessary to provide emergency communications.**

c. **The transmissions of messages encoded to hide their meaning are permitted only when transmitting control commands to space stations or radio controlled craft.** While CW Morse Code is approved, it is an open code that does not conceal meaning. You may not create your own secret code, verbal or otherwise, and transmit it on amateur radio frequencies.

d. **Music transmissions are authorized only when incidental to retransmission of manned spacecraft communications.** If you hear music from the International Space Station in a transmission or retransmission, that is no violation. However, if you hear Stu playing his banjo and singing on the amateur frequencies, remind him of this FCC regulation and politely encourage him to cease and desist immediately. No originals and no covers allowed.

e. **Harmful Interference:** That which seriously degrades, obstructs, or repeatedly interrupts a radio communication service operating in accordance with the radio regulations. Purposeful transmission on a frequency in use or with intent to block another legal operator's transmissions falls into this category. **At no time is willful interference to other amateur radio stations permitted!** Remember, no station has sole rights to any frequency, so be polite and willing to move to another frequency if conflicting opinions arise regarding frequency use.

Figure 2.1: Some FCC Prohibited Activities for Amateurs

    f. **Retransmission** of commercial, public, or entertainment radio or television stations is prohibited. Turn down that TV or radio in the background and never purposefully retransmit a broadcast service.

    g. However, **automatic retransmission of signals by a repeater, auxiliary, or space station** (including satellites) **is allowed**. For instance, you may hear on a repeater a retransmission of an ISS ARISS contact: *Amateur Radio on the International Space Station*. The ARISS program sponsored by the ARRL arranges amateur radio conversations between astronauts on ISS and earthly schools, museums, science centers, and community youth organizations. As a licensed Technician you may be able to arrange an ARISS contact for your school or organization!

5. **Sale or trade of equipment notifications may be transmitted as long as the equipment is normally used in an amateur radio**

2.1 The FCC and You

station and this activity is not conducted regularly. So, you cannot conduct *Bob's Radio Trade Hour* every Saturday afternoon at 1800 UTC, but you can occasionally notify others that you have some radio equipment for sale. Further, you should not be advertising your old truck for sale either – unless perhaps it comes free with the sale of a very nice mobile radio station that it happens to be wrapped around. (Just kidding – don't skirt the rules!)

6. **Payment or compensation for radio operation of a station may be received only by teachers being paid during communications incidental to classroom instruction at an educational institution.** Don't accept any money or gifts from your neighbor for making a regular radio contact with his son who is deployed to a remote island with few modern communication means. Do it simply because it is the neighborly thing to do, and be sure to reference *third party communications* in Section 2.4. However, if you are being paid as an instructor and use amateur radio communications as part of your lesson, you may receive your normal compensation for teaching.

Your License: Beyond the SIX BIG RULES just covered, FCC Part 97 also governs issuance of amateur radio licenses and their effective terms. As noted in the *Before We Begin* section, **the FCC currently makes available three new license classes: Technician, General, and Amateur Extra** classes. Your singular license grant is issued for the combination station and operator, and **any one person may hold only one operator/primary station license grant.**

Universal Licensing System (ULS): The FCC ULS contains all licensing information. It is accessible by internet and is an easily searchable database where you will find your license information.

License Effective Date: You may operate a transmitter on Amateur Radio Service frequencies as soon as your station/operator license grant appears in the FCC's license database. Following your successful licensing examination, your license will appear in the ULS usually within a few days. **The control operator's operator/primary station license appearing in the FCC ULS consolidated license database is proof of possession of an FCC-issued operator/primary license grant.**

T1C08 License Term: **Normally your station/operator license grant is issued for a 10 year term** that may be renewed without re-examination. No additional examination is required to renew your license as long as you do not wait too long to do it! Your license will expire after 10 years.

T1C09 T1C11 Expired Licenses: **You have a two year 'grace period' during which the license may be renewed without examination,** and after which the license and call sign are lost. **You may NOT TRANSMIT during the grace period. You must wait until the license renewal is shown on the FCC license database.**

How's it feel? Now you know some of the most important FCC rules about playing the ham radio game, so follow them to play well! But, there are still a few more things you must know before you are cut loose on your own to wield an amateur transceiver. Next we'll get at the issue of "control" of your station, and it has a specific meaning in ham radio.

But first, go whip through the exam questions for *The FCC & You*, **Section 2.1**.

www.HamRadioSchool.com/tech_media

2.1 The FCC and You

Summary Table of the SIX BIG RULES:

1.	You must make your station available for FCC inspection upon request.
2.	Maintain a correct mailing address with the FCC or your license may be revoked or suspended.
3.	Use the minimum necessary power to carry out the desired communication.
4.	Prohibited Activities: - Obscene or indecent language - Codes or ciphers hiding meaning - Harmful/willful interference - Retransmission of commercial broadcasts - General broadcasting (except code practice, bulletins, & emergencies) - Music transmissions (except incidental to manned spacecraft)
5.	Sale or trade of radio gear OK if not conducted regularly.
6.	No payment or compensation except for communications incidental to classroom instruction at an educational institution.

Summary Table of FCC License Term Provisions

1.	The FCC currently issues three classes of new amateur licenses: Technician, General, and Amateur Extra.
2.	You may operate on the air as soon as your name and call sign appear on the FCC ULS database, the proof of an FCC license grant.
3.	Normal amateur license issued for 10 year term.
4.	Two year grace period to renew after expiration of license.
5.	No transmitting allowed during 2 year grace period until license is renewed in FCC license database.
6.	Any one person may hold only one FCC Amateur Radio Service operator/primary station license grant.
7.	The control operator's operator/primary station license appearing in the FCC ULS consolidated license database is proof of possession of an FCC-issued operator/primary license grant.

When transmitting, an amateur station must have a control operator with license class privileges for the band and frequency of the transmission. Here Cole W0COL is a General Class control operator overseeing the transmissions of two Technician Class licensees, Kyle KY0HIP and Quentin KD0KGJ, who are trying their hands at 20-meter HF SSB operations during Boy Scout summer camp. Cole is the responsible station control operator, and Kyle and Quentin must use Cole's call sign in station identification. Let's get into station control and make sure you have a solid understanding of these regulations...

2.2 Controlling Your Station

FCC Rules & Regs
2.2 Controlling Your Station

> **❝** *I cannot trust a man to control others who cannot control himself.* — Robert E. Lee

Quite a few questions on THE RULES topic so far, huh? All those possible exam questions give you some indication how important it is to know and to follow THE RULES. There are a few more important regulations to know about some very practical things. For instance, who can use your radio? Can another licensed operator transmit with your station? If you're using your General licensed friend's radio, can you transmit on General class frequencies with your Technician license?

As the designated licensee for your station, you are responsible for the emissions from your radio station. Unless you have designated otherwise, you are the *control operator* for your station. **An amateur station is never permitted to transmit without a control operator.**

Control Operator: An amateur operator **designated by the licensee of an amateur station** to also be responsible for the emissions from that station. Only a person for whom an amateur operator/primary station license grant appears in the FCC database or who is authorized for alien reciprocal operation may be designated as the control operator by the station licensee.

The control operator may be the station licensee or another licensed operator designated by the licensee. However, the person whose name appears on the station license and FCC database, **the station licensee, is the control operator presumed by the FCC unless documentation to the contrary is in the station records.**

So, you can let your ham licensed buddy use your radio as long as he understands that he is assuming the role of control operator and is responsible for the transmissions. As the station's primary licensee, you have the power to determine who is in control of your station! **But when you give control operator responsibility to your buddy, both you (the station licensee) and he (the control operator) are equally responsible for proper operation of the station.** Be sure your buddy knows the rules, too, and that he will follow them! *Can you trust him to control himself?*

Repeater Control: Practically speaking, repeaters are dumb. Really dumb. They just automatically parrot back whatever is transmitted to them. Can the repeater or repeater operator be held responsible for repeating another station's rule violation? No! **The control operator of the originating station is accountable should a repeater inadvertently retransmit communications that violate the FCC rules.**

Frequency Privileges: Remember the question posed at the beginning of this section: If you're using your General licensed friend's radio, can you transmit on General class frequencies with your Technician license? No! **The class of operator license held by the control operator determines the transmitting privileges of an amateur station.** So if you're a Technician licensee and your friend is a General or Amateur Extra licensee, you may use his station as control operator only on Technician frequencies. But...

Figure 2.2: Third Party Communicator and Control Operator

A control operator may allow an unlicensed person (third party) to transmit on amateur bands, but the radio is still under control of the licensee whose FCC call sign is used to identify the station. Hams and Boy Scouts convene annually for Jamboree on the Air (JOTA), providing scouts a taste of ham radio excitement, including international contacts, by third party communication. Here Eric, KDØMUW, helps Garrett make his first ham radio contact on a local repeater.

2.2 Controlling Your Station

If your General licensed friend remains the control operator, present at the radio station's *control point* with you, you can transmit on General class frequencies under his supervision and using his station call sign. This is a fine point, but remember it depends on who is the designated control operator. **Under normal circumstances, a station operating in the exclusive** General **or Extra class operator segment of an amateur band may at no time have a Technician class licensee control operator.** It's all about the control operator's license.

Control Point: Note that your General class buddy has to be with you at the radio's **control point – that's the location at which the control operator function is performed.** For most stations the control point is going to be in front of the radio where the knobs and dials are located. Or with an HT, the control point is in the palm of your hand. 'Duh!' right?

Local Control: The control operator is at the station control point and can immediately manipulate the station operating adjustments. Handheld radios are almost always locally controlled.

Well, it's not always quite that simple because ham radio operators are clever and innovative types! Ham radios, such as some repeaters, can be operated from a distance through radio frequency controls. Others may be connected to the internet via a computer and operated from that wi-fi hot spot down at the coffee shop using a laptop. And then there are those automatic repeaters on a frozen mountain top with nobody around for miles. What then?

Remote Control: When the control operator is not at the station location but can indirectly manipulate the operating adjustments of the station from a remote control point, remote control is being used. This includes the radio link-controlled scenario. A common **example of remote control is operating the station over the Internet.** But all the control operator rules still apply, even if you're not physically in front of your radio -- **the control operator must be at the control point, a control operator is required at all times, and the control operator indirectly manipulates the controls.**

Automatic Control: The control operator is not present at a control point. Automatic Control is the only type of control in which it is permissible for the control operator to be at a location other than a control point. **Repeater operation is an example of automatic control.**

So, careful leaving your HT or car mobile station unattended where some self-proclaimed jokester can help you violate FCC regs! People are curious, after all. Explain the FCC rules and let them try it under your control, and help them become a licensed ham, too!

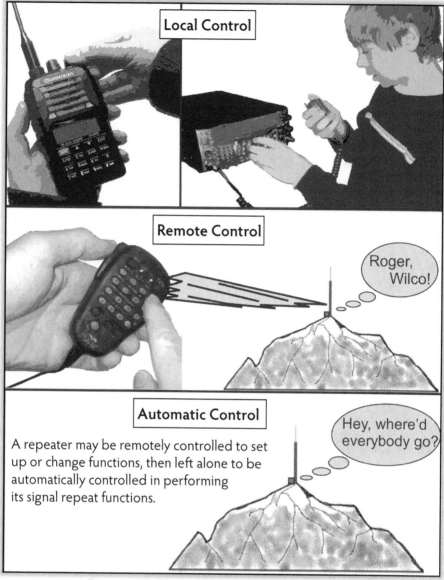

Figure 2.3 Three Types of Station Control

I hope that now you can control yourself! Or at least control your radio station properly. Always make sure there is a control operator for all your station's transmissions, and make sure those transmissions are legal for the control operator's license class. It's about that simple.

Let's hit the **Section 2.2** question pool! Last one in is QRN! ☺
www.HamRadioSchool.com/tech_media

2.3 FCC Rules & Regs — Call Signs

> *We all have such common ways to identify with each other... it's almost indescribable how it connects human to human... — Debby Boone*

Intertwined with the topic of control is the matter of identifying on the air, and hams have a common way of doing this with call signs. But with all respect to Debby, it's really not that difficult to describe how call signs connect us.

In most cases you'll be using your FCC-assigned call sign without modification to identify your station. But there are some special circumstances where you might need to make a slight modification or use another type of call sign altogether. And of course, you need to be familiar with FCC regulations governing call sign formats and use.

Call Sign: A unique alphanumeric identifier assigned by the FCC to a licensed operator-station pairing. No one else has your call sign – it identifies you and your station only. In the amateur service your license is granted for the pairing of operator and station, and your call sign points to both. Your call sign is you. Use it loudly and proudly!

Identification on the Air: We've covered this already, but it bears repeating: **An amateur station is required to transmit its assigned call sign at least every 10 minutes during, and at the end of, a contact.**

Use English or CW: The English language is the only acceptable language for use for station identification when operating in a phone (voice) sub-band. You may also use CW (Morse Code characters) to identify when transmitting phone signals, but this is uncommon except for repeater stations. Although, if you really want to whistle or toot out a little CW tone sequence instead of easily stating a few letters and numbers, you are in compliance doing so. Other hams will just think you're a little weird!

Phonetics: Papa, **H**otel, **O**scar, **N**ovember, **E**cho, **T**ango, **I**ndia, **C**harlie, **S**ierra! Those are standard phonetic alphabet characters. They come in handy in noisy

A – Alpha	J – Juliet	S – Sierra
B – Bravo	K – Kilo	T – Tango
C – Charlie	L – Lima	U – Uniform
D – Delta	M – Mike	V – Victor
E – Echo	N – November	W – Whiskey
F – Foxtrot	O – Oscar	X – X-Ray
G – Golf	P – Papa	Y – Yankee
H – Hotel	Q – Quebec	Z – Zulu
I – India	R – Romeo	

The International Telecommunications Union Standard Phonetic Alphabet

Figure 2.4: ITU Standard Phonetics

and weak signal conditions to help positively exchange call signs. **To ensure voice messages containing unusual words are received correctly, spell the words using a standard phonetic alphabet.** Although they are less frequently used on FM repeaters or simplex communications, phonetics are almost always used in the noisier HF SSB conditions. **The FCC encourages the use of a phonetic alphabet when identifying your Amateur Radio Service station using phone modes.**

Call Sign Formats: Call signs are formatted with sequences of letters and numbers. In the US, standard amateur radio station call signs must begin with A, K, N, or W, and they must have a single digit number that is preceded by one or two letters (the prefix) and followed by one to three letters (the suffix). In some special circumstances some additional self-assigned characters may be added after the suffix.

The following are the valid US standard amateur call sign formats. In the format templates below, the X's are alphabet letter places, and the Ø is the number placeholder for any digit 0 to 9.

2x3 Format: XXØXXX   Examples: KF5CLZ, KTØLIZ
May be held by any license class.
Must begin with KA – KZ or WA – WZ.

New Technicians are usually assigned 2x3 format call signs by the FCC from an alphabetical sequence. This will be you!

2.3 Call Signs

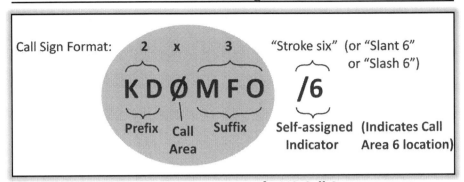

Figure 2.5: Dissection of a US Call Sign

1x3 Format: XØXXX   Example: W3ABC
May be held by Technician, General, Advanced, or Extra class licensees. Must begin with K, N, or W.

2x2 Format: XXØXX   Examples: KBØSA, WR1GL
May be held by Advanced or Extra class licensees.
Must begin with KA – KZ, NA – NZ, or WA – WZ for Advanced class.
May also begin with AA – AK for Extra class.

1x2 and 2x1 Formats: XØXX and XXØX   Examples: KØNR and AAØK
May be held only by Extra class licensees.
May begin with K, N, W, or AA – AK (with some specific exclusions)

1x1 Format: XØX   Example: W8M
Special Event Call Sign format, has a single letter in both prefix and suffix. It is temporarily issued for stations operating in conjunction with an activity of special significance to the amateur community. Effective term is usually not more than a few days.

Notice that for the zero digit in several of the example call signs here a 'slash zero' (Ø) character is used. This helps to easily differentiate zero from the letter 'O' and is common practice among the ham community.

Vanity Call Signs: A vanity call sign is a valid call sign for the license class specified by the amateur licensee. **Under the vanity call sign rules any licensed amateur may select a desired call sign** (subject to availability). **For example, K1XXX is a valid call sign for a Technician class amateur radio station** that an operator might select if it is not assigned to another station. This 1x3 vanity call sign could replace the 2x3 format call sign initially issued by the FCC to a new Technician Class licensee.

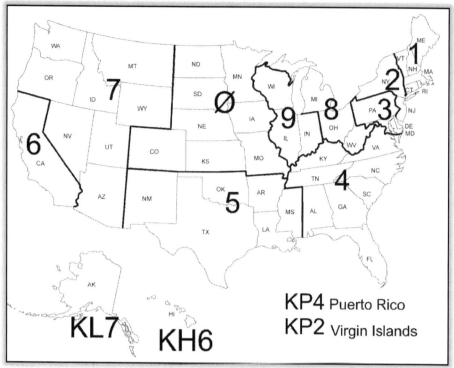

Figure 2.6: US Amateur Radio Call Districts

Call Areas or Districts: In the United States the single digit of the call sign separating the prefix and suffix indicates the geographic call area in which the license was awarded. These are also known as call *districts*. After a call sign is issued the call area number within it does not change even if the licensee permanently relocates to another call area, unless the licensee requests a new call sign be issued. As a result, call district indicators do not always match the registered transmitting location of a station.

Club Call Signs: The FCC will issue a unique call sign for organizations with a primary purpose of amateur radio service. **A club is required to have at least four members for the issuance of a club station license grant.** Club license grants must have a designated trustee who is responsible for the use of the call sign by the organization and who may select a vanity call sign for the club, if desired. The frequency privileges of a club call sign are determined by the privileges of the trustee, but all control operator regulations must still be followed when transmitting using a club call sign. So, as a Technician you cannot use your Extra class club's call sign to jump on the Extra class exclusive frequencies as a control operator! Nice try though.

T1F11

2.3 Call Signs

Tactical Call Signs: *"Roger Headquarters! Team Mole Rat has located the fox!"* These are tactical call signs, "Headquarters" and "Team Mole Rat." Tactical call signs typically describe a position, a responsibility, or an affiliation with an easy-to-understand name. "Parade Start, Announcer's Booth, or **Race Headquarters**" are additional examples. You and your group of hams can **use tactical identifiers, but you must still comply with the 10-minute and end-of-communication identification rules with your FCC assigned call sign.** So: *"Team Mole Rat is clearing off the frequency for lunch. WØSTU."*

Self-Assigned Call Sign Indicators: You can add some indicators to the end of your call sign to help avoid confusion and make clear your transmitting situation. For example, if you take your radio to another numbered call district and operate from there, you should make it known that you are operating from outside of your normal station call district by adding a self-assigned indicator. See the examples below.

There are **three different formats for stating a self-assigned call sign indicator on the air.** Take your pick. You can say:

"KL7CC **stroke** W3," "KL7CC **slant** W3," or "KL7CC **slash** W3"

They all mean the same thing, that KL7CC is visiting somewhere East, and not home in Homer, Alaska as usual. (The "W" is a standard used to indicate a US call area in the lower 48 states, in this example's case US call area 3.)

Similarly, when a new license privilege has been earned by CSCE, the FCC requires the operator to add indicators for the new license class until the upgraded license appears in the FCC license database: /KT, /AG, or /AE for upgraded Technician, General, or Extra.

"Dung Beetle to Book Reader – you've completed another section! Way to go! See how this tactical call sign connects us? Over."

You can have fun with your call sign, with a tactical call sign, or even just with the way you *say it with flare on the air!* I always enjoy adding just a little extra punch to my call sign, especially on days off work. Rattling off your new call sign will quickly become as easy and flowing as a slick nickname in no time.

"Book Reader – Now try the question pool items for **Section 2.3!** 73. WØSTU, clear."

www.HamRadioSchool.com/tech_media

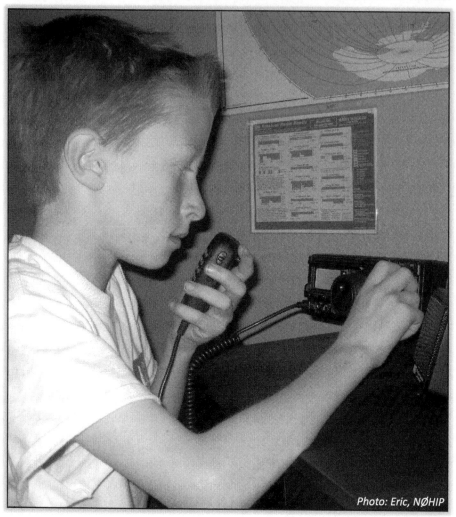
Photo: Eric, NØHIP

Ten is a lucky number for Brandon, KDØPWF. He earned his Technician license at 10 years old and immediately began working 10 meters. He quickly qualified for *10-10 International Net* membership, and within four months of licensing he had earned the *Worked All Continents* award, making radio contact with operators from every continent on earth. With his 10-meter Technician privileges, Brandon is really *talking to the world!*

Learn more about 10-10 International: www.ten-ten.org

2.4 Talking to the World

FCC Rules & Regs
2.4 Talking to the World

> ❝ It was impossible to get a conversation going, everybody was talking too much. — Yogi Berra

So you're howling your call sign comfortably, sticking to all the rules, and feeling good! Then you run out and purchase a SSB radio so you can reach out on the 10 meter band Technician frequencies and make contacts around the globe. Wow! That will be exciting, *talking to everyone so much!*

But, what are the rules for reaching out beyond the US national borders? Are there countries that are banned from amateur communications? Can you get into trouble literally *talking too much internationally?* What if you're interfering with stations outside the US? What if you're on a ship in international waters? Hrmmm.... Some more things to know about the rules, yes. Let's take a look at talking to the world.

Radio communications that can traverse the planet require a little coordination among nations. Otherwise we would all be interfering with one another and not making efficient use of the available radio spectrum. To help get things coordinated a **United Nations agency for information and communication technology issues has been established: The International Telecommunications Union, or ITU.**

ITU Regions: The ITU separates the world into three geographic regions for assigning and coordinating radio frequency use. These regions are depicted in Figure 2.7 on the following page. North American amateur stations are in ITU Region 2. Some US territories are located in ITU regions other than region 2, and frequency assignments are different from the 50 US states. An FCC-licensed station must abide by the frequencies assigned to the ITU region from which it operates.

International Waters: Within the international agreements made through the ITU, the FCC governs all spectrum use and radio stations inside the US, and **FCC licensed amateur stations may transmit from any vessel or craft located in international waters that is documented or registered in the United States.** So, as long as your US-registered yacht is out on the high seas outside of the international boundary of another nation, you can PTT with liberty and confidence under your FCC license.

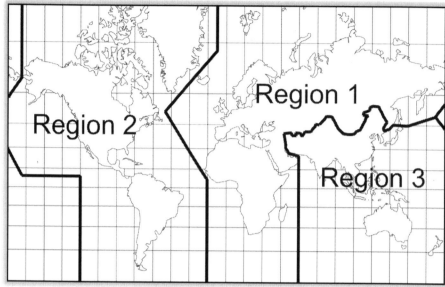

Figure 2.7: ITU Regions

Foreign Contacts and Communications: One purpose of the Amateur Radio Service as defined by FCC rules is that of enhancing international goodwill. But, foreign contacts and communications are limited by some nations and by agreements (or lack thereof) between nations. **FCC licensed stations are permitted to make international communications that are incidental to the purposes of the Amateur Radio Service and remarks of a personal character.** What's that mean? Normal chit-chat about life and work, discussions about radio, call sign exchanges of course. It is prudent to minimize political conversations in some nations. However, **FCC licensed stations are prohibited from exchanging communications with any country whose administration has notified the ITU that it objects to such communications.** Although no countries currently register such objections, a small number do not allow their citizens to use amateur radio. North Korea and Yemen are notable for this national policy.

Third-Party Communications: FCC Part 97.3 defines **the term "third-party communication" as a message from the control operator** (first party) **to another amateur station control operator** (second party) **on behalf of another person** (third party). Third party communication is also construed sometimes to be a non-licensed person transmitting on your radio under your licensed control operator supervision. Some countries get a little antsy about this sort of thing.

2.4 Talking to the World

Third-party communications of a non-emergency nature are authorized by the FCC with any foreign station whose government permits such communications. Check the international agreements before you allow international third-party communications using your station! **The foreign station must be one with which the US has a third-party agreement when a Technician Class control operator allows a non-licensed person to speak to the foreign station.** Completely within the US, have no worries about third parties. It's done all the time.

International Interference: We will discuss some technical methods for elimination of interference in Chapter 12, but your responsibility to eliminate interference extends even to foreign stations. On any band, if you learn that you are interfering with another radio station or another radio service altogether (commercial stations, radiolocation stations, military, etc.) outside of the US, you must stop operating or take steps to eliminate the harmful interference.

Radionavigation Service is protected from interference by amateur signals under all circumstances. As a Technician Class licensee with privileges in the 70-centimeter band (see Section 4.2), be aware that **the amateur service is secondary in all or some portions of some amateur bands (such as some portions of the 70 cm band), so US amateurs may find non-amateur stations in these portions and must avoid interfering with them.**

Operating in Foreign Countries: There are many reasons you may want to transmit from another country. Many hams enjoy the challenge and thrill of "*DXpeditions*," where operators travel to activate stations in foreign and possibly hard-to-contact geographical areas to help make DX radio contacts (distant contacts outside the US). However, **you may operate your amateur station in a foreign country only when authorized by that country.** Check the law of foreign nations well before traveling and transmitting! Many nations have *reciprocal agreements* with the US, allowing amateur stations to freely operate in each agreed nation with little or no red tape.

Standing International Agreements: The United States participates in a couple of international organizations in which reciprocal amateur radio communications licensing is recognized. However, be aware that the licensing requirements among participating nations do not align perfectly, so the reciprocity agreements are not applicable to all US license classes.

> **CEPT:** European Conference of Postal and Telecommunications Administrations (CEPT acronym is a French interpretation). CEPT is an organization of European nations and participating countries outside of Europe

Figure 2.8: Ham Radio Hardship — Caribbean Island DXpedition!

that share amateur radio licensing reciprocal requirements. Currently this reciprocity applies for FCC General class licenses and above, and there is no reciprocity agreement currently for FCC Technicians.

IARP: International Amateur Radio Permit. This permit may be issued to amateurs wishing to operate in member nations of *The Inter-American Telecommunications Commission* (CITEL). Many North and South American countries accept IARP, including: Argentina, Brazil, Canada, El Salvador, Panama, Peru, Trinidad and Tobago, United States of America, Uruguay, and Venezuela. There are two classes of IARPs, each with restrictions. Class 1 requires knowledge of international Morse Code, but carries all operating privileges. Class 2 does not require Morse Code, but is limited to 30 MHz and higher frequencies (10m – 70cm bands and higher).

2.4 Talking to the World

Most exchanges with foreign countries on the HF bands will probably be brief exchanges of call signs and perhaps light greetings and pleasantries. It's not that easy to get into trouble on the air, so don't fret. Still, make sure you understand your responsibilities according to the regulations and our international agreements. Your international contacts will be much more enjoyable and rewarding that way. *Capice?*

Konnichiwa! You have completed another advancement of your ham radio knowledge! Get online and try the **Section 2.4** questions for this section now, *hi hi.*

www.HamRadioSchool.com/tech_media

Buddipole's Chris, W6HFP, sets up a Mini-Buddipole on the east coast of 8P6/Barbados. Operations from foreign countries can be both rewarding and challenging! Photo by Steve, WG0AT; Courtesy Buddipole www.buddipole.com

Figure 3.0: James KDØMFO blends his hobbies of backpacking and amateur radio by competing in a VHF contest from a mountaintop location using a battery powered portable station. The contest goal is to make as many contacts a possible across as many geographic grid locations as possible within the contest's duration. You can contest from the comfort of your home shack or even from your car's mobile station, leaving the mountain climbing for another day! Contesting is just one of many intriguing *Things To Do* with amateur radio!

3.0 Things to Do!

> *Amateur Radio: The first technology-based social network. — Anonymous*

So, what kinds of things do ham radio operators do besides just jaw and be social? What kind of fun things and what kind of important things can you get involved with once you have your license? Are there contests? How can you be prepared to help with communications in an emergency?

Amateur Radio offers an incredible breadth of rewarding activities. Whether you are interested in amateur radio as a technical hobby, as an effective learning tool, for emergency preparedness, for community service, or for other reasons all your own, you are sure to find many of the facets of amateur radio intriguing, challenging, and addicting! The following descriptions barely scratch the surface of all the things you can do with ham radio, but these are some of the most common activities, and the ones for which exam questions are waiting!

Nets: A radio net is an on-air meeting of a group of amateur operators. Often a radio club or group with common interests will hold regularly scheduled nets. Repeaters or simplex frequencies may be used to convene a net. Nets usually have a designated **Net Control Station (NCS)** that is responsible for keeping the flow of transmissions from participants orderly, sequencing discussion topics like a meeting leader, and requesting responses station-by-station to avoid "doubles" where more than one station transmits simultaneously. As such, **an accepted practice for an amateur operator who has checked into a net is to remain on frequency without transmitting until asked to do so by the net control station.** Participating in an open net is a great way to get started practicing your new skills on the air with other friendly ham operators!

Traffic: A formal message exchanged by net stations during net operations. Often, near the beginning of a net and commonly combined with your check in transmission of your call sign and name, you will be asked to indicate whether or not you have traffic for the net. If you have an announcement that is of general interest to the group you should check in to the net "*with traffic*" and await recognition by net control to make your comments.

T2C06 **Priority or Emergency Traffic: An accepted practice during net operations to get the immediate attention of the net control station when reporting an emergency is to begin your transmission by saying "Priority" or "Emergency" followed by your call sign.** Although rarely implemented, this procedure is recognized universally as a means of getting quick response in handling an emergency, since a net is a structured conversation of multiple transmissions that may consume a significant amount of air time and make it otherwise difficult to break in.

Message Traffic Handling: One of the original and valuable services provided by amateur radio operators that is still used today is message traffic handling. Message traffic handling is particularly valuable during natural disasters when other means of communication are not operable. Formal message traffic handling uses a very specific format to help ensure the accuracy of relayed messages is preserved across multiple relay radio stations. T2C08 **Good traffic handling is characterized by passing messages exactly as received.** *Radiograms* may be addressed to anyone in the general public or to another

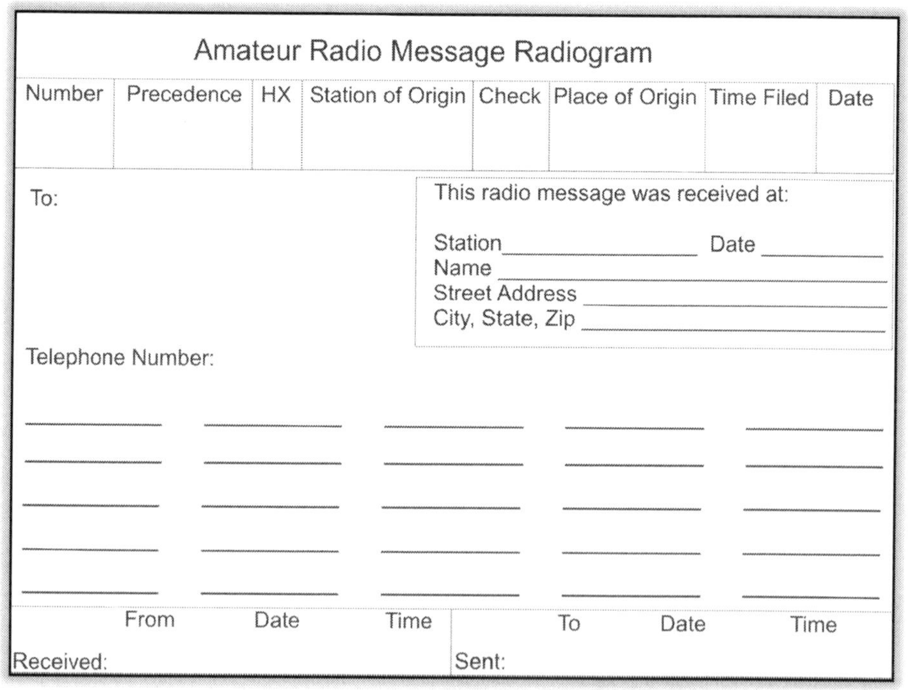
Amateur Radio Message Radiogram

Number	Precedence	HX	Station of Origin	Check	Place of Origin	Time Filed	Date

To:

This radio message was received at:

Station ______ Date ______
Name ______
Street Address ______
City, State, Zip ______

Telephone Number:

Received: From Date Time

Sent: To Date Time

Figure 3.1: A Typical Message Traffic Handling Radiogram Form licensed amateur radio operator. The radiogram is transmitted from station to station cross-country until the designated addressee is contacted. A couple of radiogram parts bear noting:

Preamble: The preamble of a formal traffic message is the information needed to track the message as it passes through the amateur radio traffic handling system. A preamble usually contains a message identification number, a message priority, the originating station, the date, and the place of origin, and a *check number*. Other optional handling instructions may also be provided.

Check: The check in reference to a formal traffic message **is a count of the number of words or word equivalents in the text portion of the message.** Radiogram messages are usually brief messages not longer than 25 words. The check helps ensure that the relayed message has been accurately received by a station for retransmission. The radiogram form of Figure 3.1 has spaces for five words per line to make word counting easy.

Contesting is an operating activity that involves contacting as many stations as possible during a specified period of time. Contests may specify the bands and modes allowed for contest contacts, as well as other rules. Contests are a great way to gauge the transmissions of your station for distance and quality.

Contest Contacts: A good procedure when contacting another station in a radio contest is to send only the minimum information needed for proper identification and the contest exchange. Check the contest rules for required information exchange before making contacts. Frequently the required exchange will include your geographic location, usually in terms of the Maidenhead Grid Square locator system. This minimum information transmission is a good policy since contesters are trying to make as many contacts as possible in a limited time and do not wish to "*rag chew*" (have an extended casual conversation).

Grid Locator: A grid locator, or Maidenhead Grid Locator, is a letter-number designator assigned to a geographic location. The basic grid square unit designated by a four character designator (two letters followed by two numbers) is a 1 x 2 degree area on the earth's surface. (See Figure 3.2.)

Hidden Transmitter Hunt are also known as "*foxhunts.*" **A directional antenna** or similar equipment **is used to locate a hidden transmitter** in this challenging and competitive activity. Foxhunts take many different forms and may require navigation by automobile, by foot, or by other means. Amateur radio clubs often sponsor foxhunts. You can get started in foxhunting with

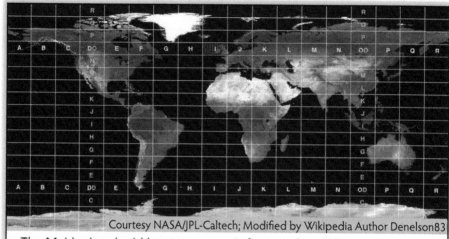

The Maidenhead grid locator system is frequently used to exchange geographic locations in radio contests. Two letters identify longitude-latitude grids by the matrix depicted above, and each grid is subdivided into smaller "squares" of 1x2 degrees, each designated by a pair of numbers following the grid letters. The author resides within DM79.

Figure 3.2: Maidenhead Grid Square Locator System

simple and inexpensive homemade or kit-built equipment combined with a common VHF or UHF HT radio.

Emergency Services: Amateur radio operators may provide emergency communication services in concert with public officials and organizations. **Two organizations having the common purpose of providing communications during emergencies are RACES and ARES.** In many areas RACES and ARES organizations will hold regular nets for the coordination of their volunteers, training, and equipment.

RACES: Radio Amateur Civil Emergency Service uses amateur frequencies and stations for emergency management or civil defense communications. RACES defines a protocol created by the FCC and by the Federal Emergency Management Agency (FEMA) for training and deploying volunteer radio operators in times of civil emergency. **RACES amateur operators are certified and enrolled by a civil defense organization** and may be activated by local, county, or state jurisdictions to assist with drills, exercises, and emergencies.

ARES: Amateur Radio Emergency Service consists of licensed amateurs who have voluntarily registered their qualifications and equipment with local ARES leadership for communications

3.0 Things to Do!

duty in the public service. Local level organizations determine the training requirements to participate fully in local ARES organizations.

Special Rules for Emergencies: When normal communications systems are not available **in situations involving the immediate safety of human life or the protection of property, amateur station control operators may operate outside the frequency privileges of their license class** and use any means of radio communication for essential communications. However, when using amateur radio simply at the request of public service officials, normal FCC rules still apply. The danger to human life or to property is the determining factor for deviating from any of the FCC rules.

T2C09

Now you understand just a few of the fun and important kinds of activities you can be involved with in amateur radio. Whether serving as a RACES or ARES emergency communications volunteer during a hurricane or wildfire evacuation, passing vital message traffic following an earthquake or tsunami, or helping local authorities manage communications outside the perimeter of a railway chemical spill, YOU can make a difference and serve your community.

Boy Scouts of Colorado Troop 6 compete in GeoFox around a mountain course. Finding a geocache using a GPS receiver gives a frequency for a hidden transmitter to be hunted with a directional antenna. The fox reveals the next geocache coordinate. Scout teams compete for best time completing a challenging course mixing foxhunting & geocaching.

Figure 3.3: Hidden Transmitter 'Foxhunt' with a GeoTwist

And after the emergency is passed you can tell your exciting emergency war story on the weekly net, enjoy a foxhunt, activate a SOTA peak (see Figures 3.5 and 3.6), or see how many contacts you can make in a radio contest! As a ham radio operator you can work hard, play hard, and love it all!

Go tackle the exam questions for **Section 3.0** at *HamRadioSchool.com* and think about all the things you'd like to do as a licensed amateur!

www.HamRadioSchool.com/tech_media

Figure 3.4: Colorado 14er Radio Event: Mountain Top Contacts!
Each August hams summit 14,000'+ mountains all across Colorado to make VHF and UHF simplex contacts. You can get incredible range from peak-to-peak! Here Randy, KNØTPC, and Andrew, KDØLLC, work 2m and 6m from Pikes Peak. Some peaks get activated with HF rigs as well and make worldwide contacts.

Figure 3.5 & 3.6: Summits On the Air (SOTA)

Steve, WGØAT, is frequently enlisted as control operator for his pet goats who really enjoy SOTA action. *www.youtube.com/goathiker*

SOTA is an award program for radio amateurs encouraging portable operation in mountainous areas. You don't have to climb even a small hill to participate!

Photos: Steve, WGØAT

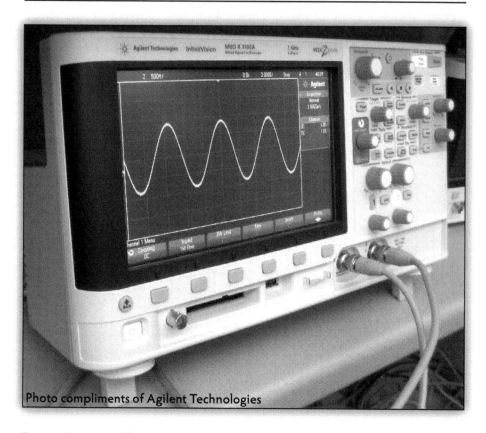

Photo compliments of Agilent Technologies

Figure 4.0: An oscilloscope is an electronic measurement instrument that can display an input voltage signal over time, allowing us to see waveforms in the time domain. It paints a dynamic picture of an AC waveform's voltage variations. The scope operator may change the range of time displayed across the horizontal extent of the screen to "zoom in or out" to inspect the waveform. The vertical voltage scale may also be adjusted to aid viewing. Oscilloscopes are very useful for evaluating the quality and characteristics of RF signals, including frequency, wavelength, and waveform consistency. They are often used to evaluate and troubleshoot transmitters and receivers. Let's learn more about these signals that the oscilloscope helps us visualize...

4.0 Wavelength, Frequency, & Bands

> ❝ *Can ye fathom the ocean, dark and deep, where the mighty waves and the grandeur sweep?* – Fanny Crosby

Aye, aye, Mate! This chapter is an introduction to the science of radio frequency emissions and the definitions of the amateur radio bands. When you have completed Section 4.1 you will have a solid introduction to radio wave characteristics. Section 4.2 describes how we use those characteristics in the identification of the frequency bands that are allocated by the FCC for amateur radio use. Let's start with a day at the beach *fathoming the ocean, dark and deep!* (There may be sharks.)

4.1 Wavelength and Frequency

Think about the ocean. Imagine yourself on the beach if you like, with the ocean waves rolling slowly in and crashing on the shoreline. Look out, that crab is about to pinch your toe!

Wavelength: Those ocean waves have a lot in common with radio waves. They have a characteristic *wavelength*, for instance. If you were bobbing out in the water you could get an estimate of the wavelength when you are carried up to the top of a wave and are able to see straight across to the crest of the next wave coming at you. That straight line distance crest-to-crest, top-to-top of two consecutive waves, from you to that shark fin, is the wavelength. The ocean wavelength may be 50 feet, for instance. That's a long wavelength by water wave standards, but not so huge for some radio frequency waves.

You could also measure the same way between the troughs, or bottoms of the swells, and you'd get the same distance. Or you could choose to measure from

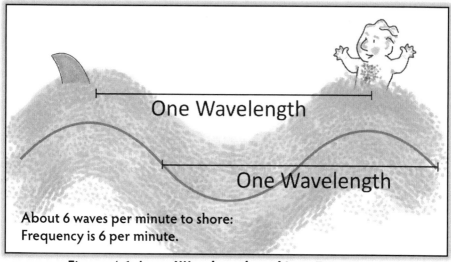

Figure 4.1: Long Wavelength and Low Frequency

exactly half way up each wave from the troughs and you would get the same measure of wavelength for regular repeating waves.

Now, you evade sharks, swim to shore, and walk over to a small tidal pool that is temporarily isolated from the great ocean waves. Only harmless minnows inhabit the little pool, *bright and shallow.* And an occasional crab, hungry for toes. Its surface is calm and still until you drop a pebble into the center of it. Miniature versions of those ocean waves ripple to the edges of the pool and you quickly estimate the distance between ripple crests to be about one inch. Those are quite short wavelengths as compared to the mighty ocean waves.

Frequency: How *frequently* do the waves come in? Looking back at the ocean waves you time their arrivals and find that about six waves roll into shore each minute. But with a pebble in the pool about 3 ripples reach the edge every second, so that would amount to 180 every minute if you continuously plopped pebbles into the water.

Those rates of wave arrival, or *frequencies* of the waves, are quite different: 6 per minute versus 180 per minute. The pool ripples arrive with higher frequency than do the ocean waves. The ocean waves are of lower frequency than the ripples. Now let's apply these characteristics of wavelength and frequency to our radio transmissions.

T3A07 **Electromagnetic Waves: EM waves carry radio signals between transmitting and receiving stations.** EM waves oscillate like the water waves, having a characteristic wavelength and frequency. But unlike the water waves, EM waves do not require any medium like water to flow within. Rather, EM

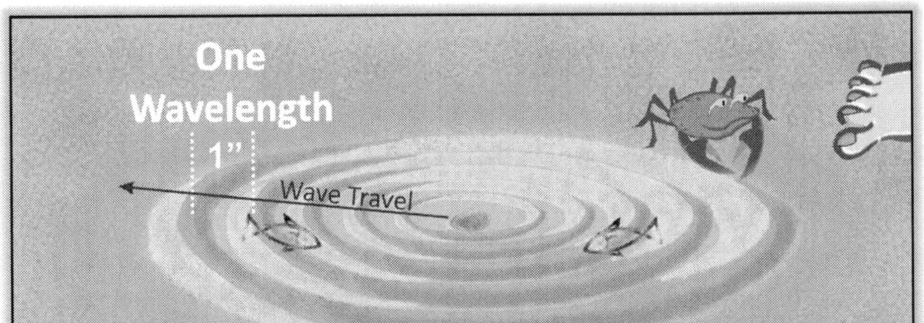

4.1 Wavelength and Frequency

One Wavelength 1"

Wave Travel

About 180 waves per minute to shore: Frequency is 180 per minute.

Figure 4.2: Short Wavelength and High Frequency

waves are oscillations of electric fields and magnetic fields that reinforce one another and sort of provide their own self-contained medium! **Radio waves are made up of electromagnetic energy.**

Light waves that we perceive with our eyes are one kind of EM wave. Radio waves are also EM waves, only of a much longer wavelength and lower frequency than light. Your doctor's X-rays are yet another, shorter wavelength and higher frequency EM wave.

Radio Waves: **As EM waves, radio waves have the two components, the electric and magnetic fields.** Like all EM waves in free space, **radio waves travel at the speed of light,** or an **approximate velocity of 300,000,000 meters per second** (300 million meters per second). This velocity does not change significantly in air or in vacuum. Good thing the ocean waves don't go that fast, huh?

Radio Frequency: Rather than measuring waves per minute like in the ocean and pool, radio frequencies are measured in waves (or cycles) per second, and this **unit of frequency is called hertz.**

Electromagnetic waves in the range of **radio frequency signals of all types are commonly referred to as RF,** meaning simply *radio frequencies*. RF transmissions that radiate from an antenna are originated in a transmitter with electrical currents that reverse direction in an electric circuit many times per second (alternating current, or AC). The number of AC reversals per second will generate an identical frequency RF signal from the energized antenna. **So, frequency is also used to describe the number of times that an alternating current reverses direction** in an electric circuit.

Radio Wavelengths: Just like the ocean and pool waves, radio waves will have a characteristic wavelength that is measured between equivalent wave positions of the electric or magnetic field oscillations – crest-to-crest, for instance. Because the waves are moving through space it is easy to consider that **the distance a radio wave travels in the completion of one cycle** (one complete wave oscillation) **is its wavelength.**

T3B01

Radio wavelengths are typically expressed in the unit of meters. Described this way, **the approximate wavelength of radio waves is often used to identify the different frequency bands.**

T3B07

So, you will hear hams discussing the "*2 meter band*" or the "*6 meter band*" or the "*10 meter band*." This does not mean that all of the wavelengths transmitted in the 2 meter band are exactly two meters long, but rather they are *approximately* two meters in wavelength. In fact, the 2 meter band's wavelengths vary from longest to shortest over a span of about 5.5 centimeters, or about 2.25 inches, but all pretty close to two meters.

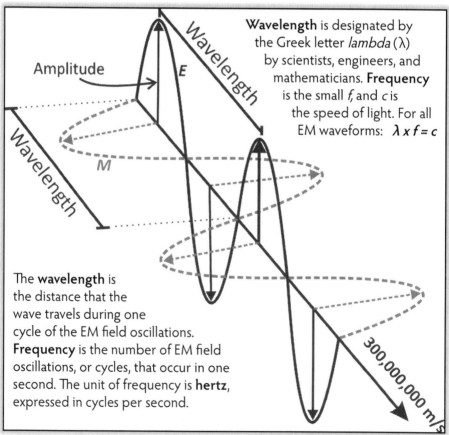

Figure 4.3: Electromagnetic Wave Wavelength and Amplitude

4.1 Wavelength and Frequency

Wavelength-Frequency Relationship: Because radio signals travel at a constant speed, a special relationship arises between wavelength and frequency of waves. **As the wavelength gets shorter, the frequency gets higher, or increases** in hertz. Conversely, as the wavelength gets longer, the frequency gets lower, or decreases in hertz.

Think back to the water waves: Those giant ocean waves had long wavelengths and low frequency, rolling into shore only a few times each minute. The pool ripples had short wavelengths and arrived with high frequency of well over a hundred times each minute. Radio waves work in a similar way: *long and low, short and high.*

A simple mathematical **formula** relates wavelength and frequency for all radio waves, and it is **used for converting frequency to wavelength in meters.** It is also used the other way, converting wavelength to frequency. The following equations are always true for radio signals:

Wavelength (in meters) = 300 ÷ frequency (in megahertz)
Frequency (in megahertz) = 300 ÷ wavelength (in meters)

To use this simple relationship, the wavelength must always be expressed in meters and the frequency in millions of hertz, or "megahertz." The prefix mega means one million.

Examples: Suppose you want to know the specific wavelength for a frequency in the 2 meter band that is displayed on your radio: 146.52 MHz, the national calling frequency. Since the frequency is already provided in megahertz (MHz), it is really easy to calculate the wavelength:

Wavelength (in meters) = 300 ÷ 146.52 MHz
So, Wavelength = 2.0475 meters

You can see that this is pretty close to two meters, hence **146.52 MHz is in the "2 meter band."**

What if you wished to determine the frequency of a wavelength 21.0 meters long? No sweat:

Frequency (in MHz) = 300 ÷ 21.0 m
Frequency = 14.286 MHz

And yes, that frequency is squarely in the *"20 meter band"* in the HF range. We'll explore more about all those bands in the next section.

Math Prefixes and Conversions: Sometimes for convenience frequencies will be expressed in other multiples of hertz besides mega, or one million. Some other common mathematical prefixes include:

> kilo = 1000　　　as in...　kilohertz (kHz) = 1000 Hertz
> Giga = 1 Billion　as in...　Gigahertz (GHz) = 1,000,000,000 Hertz

You can convert between these prefixes by moving the decimal point left or right three places for each step: Hz, kHz, MHz, GHz. To convert from a lower prefix to higher prefix, such as kilohertz to Megahertz, move the decimal left three positions (adding left zeros if needed). To convert from higher prefix to lower, such as Gigahertz to Megahertz, move the decimal right three places. To convert between greater prefix differences, such as from Gigahertz down to kilohertz, you'll have to make more than one of these step conversions -- GHz to kHz requires two decimal-moving steps, or a total of six digit positions. Let's try some examples!

Examples:

Converting low to high (Hz to kHz to MHz to GHz)
1,500,000 Hz = **1,500 kHz** = **1.5 MHz** = **0.0015 GHz**
(Move the decimal 3 places left for each prefix step.)

Converting high to low (GHz to MHz to kHz to Hz)
0.003525 GHz = **3.525 MHz** = **3,525 kHz** = **3,525,000 Hz**
(Move the decimal 3 places right for each prefix step.)

I like to remember this with a goofy little rhyme that refers to the prefix as either being large & hefty (like MHz or GHz), or small and slight (like kHz or Hz):

From hefty to slight, dot moves right.
From slight to hefty, dot's a lefty.

Use the examples above to see how that goofism works! The first example is hefty to slight prefixes. The second example is slight to hefty prefixes. Try a couple more from the question pool:

Covert **28,400 kHz** to megahertz (MHz). *Hint: slight to hefty, one step!*
Move the decimal left three places: **28,400 kHz = 28.400 MHz.**

Convert the **frequency display 2425 MHz** to **Gigahertz.**
Move the decimal left three positions: **2425 MHz = 2.425 GHz.**

We'll revisit this kind of math prefix conversion and decimal shifting in Section 8.3 with some electrical measurements, so keep that goofism handy!

4.1 Wavelength and Frequency

Amplitude: Remember when you were out in the ocean at the start of this section, bobbing up and down as the waves and sharks rolled by? Your position at the high point of the wave or at the low trough, as measured from the middle height of the wave, is the *amplitude* of the wave. You can think of amplitude in two ways: 1) it is the height of the wave as measured from the middle, or the maximum "size" of the electric or magnetic field; and 2) it is the *power* of the radio signal. Hence, a low amplitude represented by a short waveform means low signal power. A high amplitude, or tall waveform, represents high signal power. Radio wave power, or amplitude, can be varied to encode a signal, and that is *amplitude modulation*, or AM radio as we saw way back in Section 1.1. (Refer to AM or SSB modulation, Figure 1.3 on page 13.)

Polarization: Also as noted before, a radio wave's electric field component and magnetic field component oscillate with the wave in a specific orientation, or direction. Radio wave polarization refers to the direction of oscillation, and the electric field direction is the reference used. Remember, identical polarization is important for strong signal reception, as a pair of "cross polarized" antennas are not very efficient. Vertical, horizontal, circular, and random polarizations are used in amateur radio. (Refer to polarization, Figure 1.9.)

Phase Relationships: In the course of one wavelength an exact position within the up-down or side-to-side cycle is called the phase of the wave. In mathematics the phase is described as an angle between 0 and 360 degrees, just like a circle. Beginning at the axis of propagation with 0 degrees, the wave increases to maximum amplitude at 90 degrees, returns back to the axis half way through the cycle at 180 degrees, continues to the most negative value (below the axis) at 270 degrees, and finally completes the cycle back up to the axis at 360 degrees – where it starts all over again with the next wave cycle. (See Figure 4.4 on the next page.)

Two waveforms of equal wavelength have a *phase relationship* with one another that is described in terms of the difference in degrees between the two waves. For instance, one wave may be considered "behind" another wave by 180 degrees if the two waves are oscillating exactly opposite directions of one another. If this occurs, the electric field of the first wave will be positive when the second wave's field is a negative (opposite direction) value of the same magnitude. If the waves' electric fields are added together, such as when an antenna detects both waveforms simultaneously, the net signal strength at the antenna will be zero! The perfectly out-of-phase waves cancel out one another. Other phase relationships result in different field strength sums. Phase relationships are important to understanding many concepts in radio wave propagation.

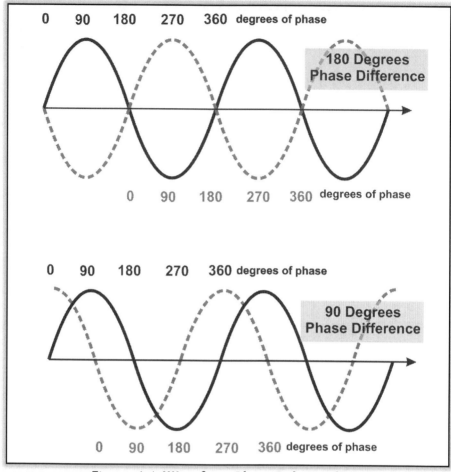

Figure 4.4: Waveform Phase Relationships

Figure 4.4 illustrates the 180 degree "out of phase" relationship and a 90 degree phase relationship.

Shazaam! That's pretty cosmic stuff, huh? Don't hesitate to reread this section a few times if the concepts of electromagnetic waves and frequencies are foreign to you. When you're at least semi-comfortable with it, get online and try the question pool's **Section 4.1** exam questions. They're not as scary as sharks and they're less sneaky than crabs! Good luck, and get going!

www.HamRadioSchool.com/tech_media

4.2 Bands, Band Plans, & License Privileges

Wavelength, Frequency, & Bands

> *Have you considered that if you don't make waves, nobody including yourself will know that you are alive?* – Theodore Isaac Rubin

One reason all that wavelength and frequency stuff is important is because that is how the FCC defines the various segments of the radio spectrum on which hams are allowed to transmit, and because hams use those designations in every-day discussion. And even within an FCC designated frequency band there are *sub-bands*, again defined by the frequency range, in which only certain modes of transmission are allowed or in which some license classes are prohibited. Commonly, detailed band plans are locally coordinated to define frequency ranges for specific operations, such as simplex voice, repeater frequency pairs, digital modes, and even for experimental purposes.

So, in order to understand such *band plans*, the limitations of your license privileges, and to avoid accidentally interfering with other stations, you should understand the FCC amateur radio band plan and your local frequency coordination band plans. **Beyond the privileges established by the FCC, a band plan is a voluntary guideline for using different modes or activities within an amateur band.** That is, the FCC band plan is regulation, while locally coordinated plans are voluntary recommendations.

I know, it sounds complicated, but you'll warm up to band plans quickly once you begin using your radio. Study the Amateur Band Plan extracts presented in this section and the full FCC amateur plan on our web site, and it'll begin to make more sense to you. Then you can *make waves* properly, *feeling alive* and letting it be known to everyone else on the air!

HF, VHF, UHF: The broadest categories of the most common amateur RF transmissions are *High Frequency* (HF), *Very High Frequency* (VHF), and *Ultra High Frequency* (UHF). Each is a specific range of frequencies.

        HF: 3 to 30 MHz
        VHF: 30 to 300 MHz
        UHF: 300 to 3000 MHz

Notice how these are each bounded by a '3' number, only with different quantities of zeros following. It is easy to remember that way; just adding zeros behind the 3's to get the boundary of each range of frequencies. And all are in units of megahertz (MHz).

You should be aware that there are several additional categories, from extremely low frequency (ELF) to *extremely high frequency* (EHF). Amateurs do have privileges from low frequency (LF) to EFH, but HF, VHF, and UHF are, by far, the most commonly used ranges.

Amateur Frequency Bands: Within each of the broad categories of HF, VHF, and UHF are narrower ranges of frequencies that have been allocated for amateur use. These are the bands that amateurs tend to identify by the approximate wavelength associated with the band frequencies. Remember, you can calculate a frequency from a wavelength, and vice versa, as we did in the last section. Using the calculation you can usually narrow down what band a frequency belongs to, but you need to have a little more knowledge of the band plans for some exam pool questions, like this one:

Q. Which frequency is within the 6 meter amateur band?

    A. 49.00 MHz   **B. 52.525 MHz**
    C. 28.50 MHz   D. 222.15 MHz

Performing the calculation 300 ÷ 6 = 50.0 MHz. But the closest answer, 49.00 MHz, is incorrect! The 6 meter band ranges 50.0 to 54.0 MHz. So, it pays to be familiar with the boundaries of the bands.

Sub-Bands: There are several questions in the pool about sub-bands, and while you can always look them up on a chart you have to know them for the exam. In particular you should familiarize yourself with which Technician license bands have *mode restricted sub-bands*. Mode restricted means that you may use only certain transmission modes in those sub-bands, such as CW-only or digital-only modes. Be sure you are familiar with the CW-only and data-only (digital mode-only) sub-bands are located within the Technician bands. For instance, **in the HF bands only the 10-meter band has frequencies available to the Technician Class operator for RTTY and data transmissions.** (28.0 - 28.3 MHz, as depicted in Figure 4.6.)

Technician License Privileges: In accordance with the FCC amateur band plan, each license class has specific frequency privileges. License privileges expand with the higher license classes, General and Amateur Extra. However, your Technician license privileges provide a tremendous breadth of opportunities to experience the variety of activities available in amateur radio. Refer-

4.2 Bands, Band Plans, & License Privileges

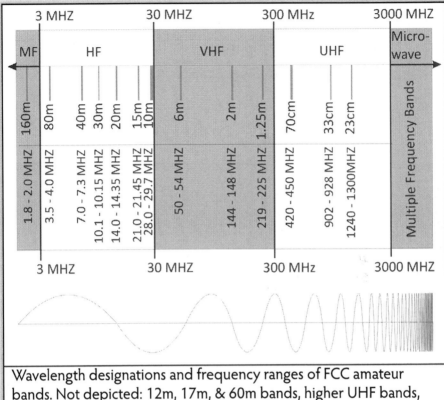

Wavelength designations and frequency ranges of FCC amateur bands. Not depicted: 12m, 17m, & 60m bands, higher UHF bands, and detailed microwave bands. Note upper/lower frequency scale is logarithmic (10x).

Figure 4.5: Amateur Bands within HF, VHF, & UHF Regions

ence Figure 4.6 page as you read about the Technician license phone, CW, and digital/data privileges.

Technician Phone (voice) Privileges: As a Technician licensee you have phone mode privileges in VHF and UHF equivalent to those of General and Amateur Extra licensees. There are no Technician restrictions beyond the FCC plan except for your locally coordinated band plans, but these local band plans are important to understand. For instance, FM phone **simplex channels are designated in VHF/UHF band plans so that stations within mutual communications range can communicate without tying up a repeater.** And you don't want to interfere with a repeater's signals either, so using those designated simplex channels is good amateur practice.

Referencing Figure 4.6, you have full phone access to: 6m band, 2m band, 1.25m band, 70 cm band, and higher frequency bands. (Note: Technicians also

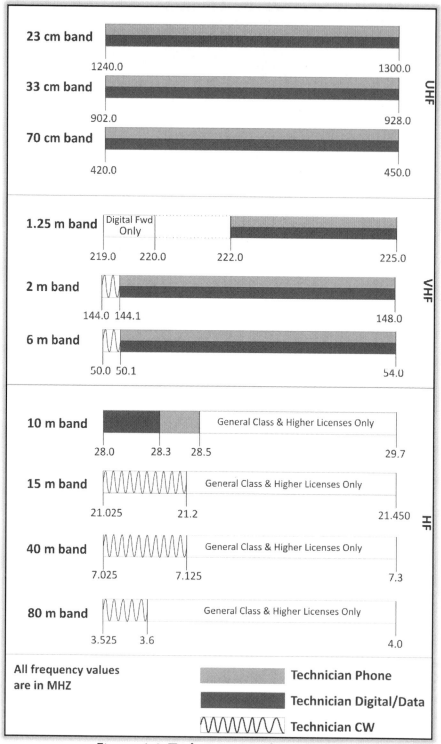

Figure 4.6: Technician Band Privileges

4.2 Bands, Band Plans, & License Privileges

have privileges in higher UHF and microwave bands that are less commonly used and are not depicted in Figure 4.6.)

While most phone privileges in the VHF and UHF bands implies FM voice mode, you should be aware that **single sideband (SSB) phone mode may be used in at least some portion of all amateur bands above 50 MHz** (6 meter band and higher frequency bands). Locally coordinated band plans will usually designate sub-bands for SSB operations separate from FM operations. Because of its efficient use of power, SSB is a popular mode for contesting in VHF and UHF bands. (More on SSB coming in Chapter 6.)

In the HF bands Technicians have phone privileges in the 10m band only, and specifically a 200 kHz sub-band between 28.300 – 28.500 MHz. On the lower HF frequency bands, 12m to 160m, Technicians have no phone privileges. Upgrade to General license to use those bands!

Technician CW Privileges: Technician licensees have CW privileges in the VHF 6m and 2m bands, and in the low frequency portions of 10m, 15m, 40m, and 80m bands. On the 6 meter band **emissions are limited to CW-only** in the mode-restricted sub-band **50.0 – 50.1 MHz.** Similarly on 2m band **emissions are restricted to CW-only** in the sub-band **144.0 – 144.1 MHz.** Notice that CW sub-bands are all in the lowest frequency part of each band, and each a 100 kHz bandwidth for 6-meter and 2-meter bands.

Technician Digital / Data Privileges: Technicians may use digital transmission modes all across the VHF and UHF bands, such as 6m, 2m, 1.25m, 70cm, and higher bands, except where CW-only restricted. (Check your locally coordinated band plan for additional restrictions on digital / data transmissions.) Additionally, Technicians may use digital or data modes in the lowest frequencies of the HF 10m band, 28.000 – 28.300 MHz. Note that a unique data-only emission mode sub-band exists **between 219 and 220 MHz** in the 1.25m band **for fixed digital message forwarding systems only** (email, APRS, etc. – See Chapter 10).

Technician HF Power Limitation: Technicians operating in the HF bands have a stricter power limitation than do General or Extra class operators. **Technician class operators using their assigned portions of the HF bands have a maximum peak envelope power** (PEP) **of 200 watts.** But don't worry... you can communicate around the globe with much less! And **when using frequencies above 30 MHz, the maximum PEP for Technician class operators is 1500 watts, except for some specific restrictions.** Most operators never approach this power limit in these VHF, UHF, and microwave ranges.

Secondary Privileges: Some bands or sub-bands may be available for amateur use only on a *secondary basis*. **Amateur service is secondary in some portions of the 70 cm band. This means that amateurs may find non-amateur stations in the bands and must avoid interfering with them.** Avoid transmitting near frequencies in use by primary users and leave the frequency or cease your operations if requested by a primary user. (Also, see the FCC Amateur Radio Band Plan notes regarding the 160m, 60m, 40m, and 30m bands.)

Study the ARRL FCC band plan chart on the web site and focus on the Technician privileges that are designated by the 'T' in the letters to the right of each band. And pay attention to the color or pattern codes, noting phone, data, and CW privileges. It won't take long to see the pattern of mode use and license privileges, even if the frequency values are not second nature yet. Give it time and that will come. You'll be spouting off bands and frequencies like an old elmer in no time!

And remember: When you are just getting started with FM operations and you are using 2m, 1.25m, or 70cm repeaters or simplex channels, you are safely within your license privileges and coordinated band plan usage. Have no fear! Make lots of waves!

Time for questions! Log on, check out the FCC band plan chart, and tackle the questions for **Section 4.2**. Good luck!

www.HamRadioSchool.com/tech_media

5.0 Signal Propagation

> **❝** *The electromagnetic waves are literally skyscrapers in as much as they touch the ionosphere and are reflected from it.* — Peter Redgrove

Up to now we've focused quite a lot on VHF and UHF communications with simplex or repeater operations via strong signals. Now we're going to jump into a topic that still applies to the VHF frequencies, but is absolutely the heart and soul of HF communications around the world where we are transmitting and receiving weak signals. So, we're going to climb upon those *electromagnetic skyscrapers* now and stretch your radio horizons!

Propagation refers to the spreading or traveling of radio waves through the atmosphere or free space. Different RF frequencies have different propagation characteristics, being affected by the atmosphere and environment in different ways. The various characteristics of propagation may be typed roughly along the HF, VHF, and UHF frequency categories, so we will consider each frequency range in turn and examine the factors impacting propagation.

HF Propagation

Ionosphere: The high frequency bands (160m – 10m) are readily bent or refracted by layers of electrically charged particles called ions high in the atmosphere. Collectively these layers are known as the ionosphere. The strength of this bending effect varies with frequency and with the densities of the ionosphere's different layers. **An advantage of HF vs VHF and higher frequencies is that long distance ionospheric propagation is far more common on HF.**

Sky Wave or Skip: Signals that are bent back to earth by the ionosphere are sometimes called "sky wave" propagation or "skip." **The ionosphere enables the propagation of radio signals around the world** with multiple reflections between the ionosphere and earth. Generally, longer wavelengths (lower frequencies) are refracted more readily than shorter wavelengths (higher frequencies). The ionosphere bends lower frequency signals more than it bends higher frequency signals.

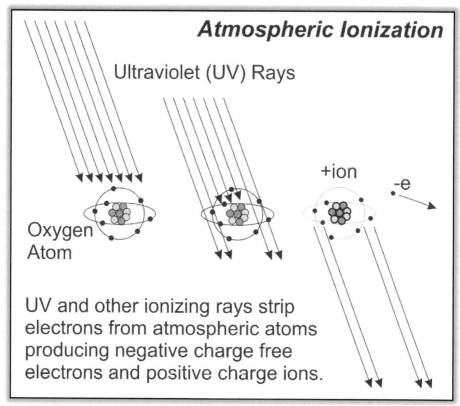

Figure 5.1: Atmospheric ionization, primarily by ultraviolet radiation from sunspots, creates the ionosphere.

Skip Signal Polarization: As a radio signal moves into the ionosphere the electromagnetic field of the waveform is affected by the ionosphere's charged particles and by the earth's magnetic field. Imagine the nicely oscillating waveform, as depicted in Figures 1.9 and 4.3, beginning to rotate around as it propagates forward. The polarization of the wave, normally defined by the direction of the electric field oscillation, is now changing from moment to moment as the waveform twists along like a corkscrew! This spinning polarization resulting from propagation through the ionosphere is called *elliptical polarization*. **The result is that either vertically or horizontally polarized antennas may be used for transmission or reception of these elliptically polarized signals refracted from the ionosphere.** The polarization of skip signals becomes randomized and essentially irrelevant, and they will be weaker than signals well-matched to antenna polarization.

Signal Fade: Also common with skip propagation is **irregular fading of signals received by ionospheric reflection.** This fluctuation in signal

5.0 Signal Propagation

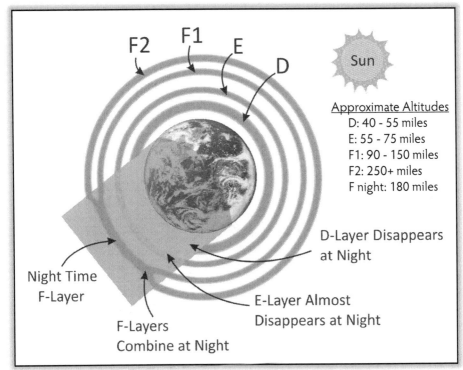

Figure 5.2: Diurnal Cycle of the Ionosphere

strength is **caused by random combining of signals arriving via different paths,** thereby causing them to interfere in constructive or destructive ways, as the phase relationships shift among the multiple paths.

Ionosphere Diurnal Cycle: The ionosphere's charged particles are created by the sun's radiation when high energy light rays strip electrons from atoms high in the atmosphere. More sunlight and more sunspot activity results in more ions, or a denser and more effective ionosphere. The density and arrangement of layers of the ionosphere change with the day-night cycle of the earth (diurnal cycle), with a general reduction in density and effectiveness for bending radio signals at night.

Layers of Ionosphere: The ionosphere exhibits four distinct layers designated from low to high altitude as: D Layer, E Layer, F1 Layer, and F2 Layer. On the night side of the earth, while in darkness, the high F1 and F2 layers merge into a single F Layer. The E Layer weakens significantly at night, and the low altitude D Layer typically disappears entirely at night. These daily cyclical changes cause variations in the skip propagation behavior of different HF frequencies.

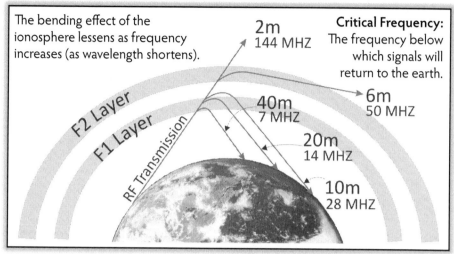

Figure 5.3: Ionosphere Effects by Frequency

Upper HF Bands: The higher HF frequency bands such as 10m, 12m, 15m, 17m, 20m, will be bent most significantly by the dense F1 and F2 Layers, which are the highest altitude layers. Thus, these shorter wavelength bands tend to propagate long distances due to the high altitude of the layers from which they are typically reflected, particularly in daylight hours when the F layers are dense and highly activated. However, the E layer will sometimes also bend the higher frequencies when it is activated, particularly the 10m band.

Lower HF Bands: The lower frequency HF bands such as 40m, 60m, 80m, 160m, tend to be absorbed by the ion charges of the D layer. As a result, these bands do not achieve good skip propagation during the day. When the D Layers dissipate at night these low frequency HF bands may then be bent very effectively by the high altitude combined F-layer that endures through the night. So, at night the low frequency bands reach higher ionospheric layers where the skip distances are greater and their long distance propagation is enhanced.

Solar Cycles and Effects: The ionosphere is ionized to various degrees by the variable output of the sun and by the day-night cycle. Sunspots are regions on the face of the sun that produce a lot of ultraviolet radiation (UV), and UV radiation produces ions in the earth's ionosphere. Thus, the ionosphere is most densely charged with ions during periods of high sunspot activity and especially on the daylight side of the earth. Sunspots vary in number and intensity over an 11-year cycle of the sun. This has big effects on radio skip propagation!

For instance, because the 10m band is the highest frequency HF amateur band, the ionosphere's bending effect on its frequencies is weaker than for the lower bands. The ionosphere density is not always sufficient to bend 10m signals back to earth. **Generally, the best time for long-distance 10 meter band propagation via the F layer is from dawn to shortly after sunset during periods of high sunspot activity. During the peak of the sunspot cycle, 6m band and 10m band may provide long distance communications** by skip propagation.

Of course, 10m is of great interest to all Technicians since this is where the license provides HF phone privileges! In the mornings during high sunspot activity you will be able to skip to the east better, so European stations will be within reach from the US. In the afternoon the west opens up and the Pacific nations are popular. The longer skip distances tend to be up to 2,500 miles per bounce, and closer stations *inside the bounce* may not be heard.

Beacons: A beacon is an amateur station transmitting communications for the purposes of observing propagation or related experimental activities. You can often judge HF propagation conditions by listening for beacons whose Morse code IDs will provide their locations. Lists of beacons are easy to find via online search.

VHF Propagation

The VHF bands (6m, 2m, 1.25m) are less susceptible to the ionosphere's bending effects because signal frequencies are higher than HF. Usually, VHF signals are *above the critical frequency*, meaning that they are not bent sufficiently to return them to the earth's surface. But occasionally VHF signals are bent back to earth when the E-Layer is very active with charged particles. VHF frequencies may also be affected by other atmospheric phenomena besides the ionosphere, carrying your signals long distances!

Multi-mode Radio: Signals propagating over long distances become weak, and some operating modes work better than others for VHF weak signal communications. Single sideband mode is one popular VHF weak signal mode, and CW's narrow bandwidth works particularly well. Multi-mode transceivers will typically provide FM, SSB, and CW modes, and such a transceivers may be combined with a VHF power amplifier to provide greater range. Be sure to match transceiver and amplifier operating mode: **The function of the SSB/CW-FM switch of a VHF power amplifier is to set the amplifier for proper operation in the selected mode.**

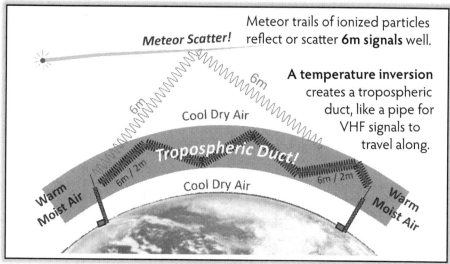

Figure 5.4: Tropospheric Ducting & Meteor Scatter

Sporadic E: The ionosphere E-Layer effect is very dynamic or sporadic, often changing significantly in strength or effect in a matter of seconds to minutes. Patches of the E-Layer can become quite dense with ions and be very effective with even relatively short VHF wavelengths. Thus, when the E-Layer is very active **strong over-the-horizon signals on 10m, 6m, and 2m are most commonly associated with E-Layer signal refraction called "Sporadic E."**

Tropospheric Ducting: When warm air masses move above cool air masses in the lowest layer of the atmosphere to create **a temperature inversion in the atmosphere,** an effective pipe or "duct" is formed in the troposphere that may propagate VHF frequencies. **Tropospheric ducting allows over-the-horizon VHF and UHF communications to ranges up to 300 miles on a regular basis.**

Tropospheric Scatter: Some VHF (and UHF) signals may be randomly scattered near the top of the troposphere. This weak signal scatter is cause by small particles high in the troposphere such as water, volcanic ash, or dust.

Auroral Propagation: The Northern Lights or aurora, are also charged particles in the atmosphere that can bend VHF signals back to the earth. Aurora are very dynamic, and **the characteristic of VHF signals received via auroral reflection is rapid fluctuations of strength and often sound distorted.** The 6m band tends to be most effective for aurora reflection.

Meteor Scatter: The 6m band is best suited to communicating via meteor scatter, in which signals are reflected off of the atmospheric ionization that trails behind meteors as they enter the atmosphere. These communications are usually a very brief exchange of call signs that last for only a few seconds until the meteor's ionized trail dissipates.

Vegetation: Live trees and other vegetation have been shown to absorb VHF and higher frequencies. **The range of VHF and UHF signals might be greater in winter due to less absorption by vegetation.**

UHF and Microwave Propagation

The ultra high frequency bands (70 cm – 23 cm and higher) are usually not reflected by the ionosphere. UHF signals are rarely heard from stations outside your local coverage area. UHF frequencies may be affected by tropospheric scatter, as noted under VHF Propagation.

Knife Edge Diffraction: Can cause radio signals to be heard despite obstructions between the transmitting and receiving stations. Signals are partially bent around solid objects exhibiting sharp edges. Knife edge effects around buildings or over mountain peaks can help direct radio signals over the horizon or around obstacles.

Weather Considerations: Lower frequencies of the HF and VHF ranges are not significantly impacted by meteorological conditions such as moisture. For

Figure 5.5: Radio signals in the 6-meter band are well suited for auroral propagation, affecting long distance communication over the poles.   Photo courtesy KØPOP

T3A12 instance, **fog and light rain will have little effect on the 10 meter and 6 meter bands,** but moisture begins to have greater effect at frequencies above VHF/UHF, and particularly into the microwave range. **Precipitation** **T3A13** **decreases range at microwave frequencies** due to absorption of these higher frequencies. Consider your microwave oven that heats food primarily through the absorption of microwave energy by water in the food.

Like I said, *stretching your radio horizons.* Get it? Once you have your Technician license you can get on 10m band and try your hand at ionospheric skip. You can make contacts around the globe, sometimes with just a few watts of power. It's a great HF band, and with the sun very active and firing up the F layers, it is a load of fun!

Sporadic E can be very exciting as well, if less reliable. Sporadic E tends to become more common about twice during the year, in June and in January. Listen for those sporadic E opportunities and capitalize on some long distance contacts. VHF contesting gets really fun with sporadic E!

But for now, go snag those exam pool questions for **Section 5.0.**
www.HamRadioSchool.com/tech_media

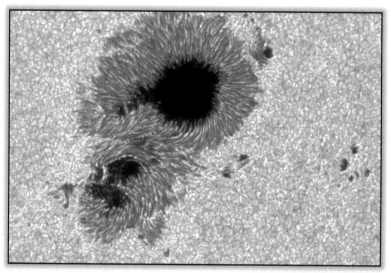

Figure 5.6: Sunspots increase solar ultraviolet radiation that helps to create the earth's ionosphere and provide long-distance, over-the-horizon skip propagation. The broad perimeter of sunspots like this one shines bright with UV radiation!

Photo courtesy NASA/JPL-Caltech

6.0 How Radio Works

> **Knowing how things work is the basis for appreciation, and is thus a source of civilized delight. — William Safire**

I know you have a burning question within you, begging for a sane and sensible response in common language we can all understand: *How does radio really work?*

This chapter will temporarily sate your thirst for knowledge of radio's inner workings. *Temporarily*, because once you have digested this introduction to radio's secrets it will likely make you crave even more detailed understanding of RF magic. Ready yourself for major infusion of civilized radio delight!

This chapter contains some challenging technical concepts, but we will tackle them with simplified explanations and build one thing upon another. A greater amount of background explanation is provided here than in other chapters, but this extra background will provide a solid foundation for comprehending the innards and functions of your radio. It will also help make the exam questions about these topics seem delightfully easy!

The Big Picture: Here is an overview of the big picture we will paint in the three sections of this chapter:

1. Your voice is made of many different sound tones that form a band of sonic frequencies. (A continuous range of frequencies.)
2. The radio microphone converts the band of sound frequencies into an equivalent band of audio electrical signals that contain the sound wave information of your voice.
3. The audio electrical signals are used to shape, or modulate, an equivalent band of radio frequency (RF) signals so that they contain the audio signal information within them.
4. The band of RF signals is sent from the transmitter to be radiated into space by the antenna.
5. A receiving antenna captures the RF band signals and sends them to the receiver electronic circuits.

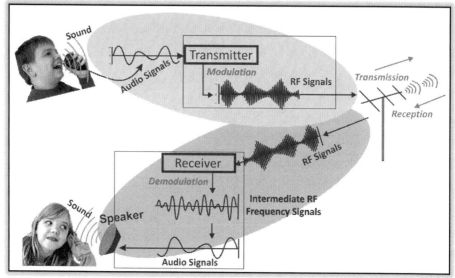

Figure 6.1: Transceiver Big Picture

6. The receiver circuits recreate the audio band signals from the modulated RF band signals in a series of steps that convert the higher radio frequencies into lower radio frequencies and finally into even lower frequency audio electrical signals. (Demodulation process.)
7. The extracted (demodulated) audio signals are fed to a speaker to recreate the original voice sounds.

Quite a lot of detail can be unfolded from that series of events that describes exactly how your radio works. Let the unfolding begin!

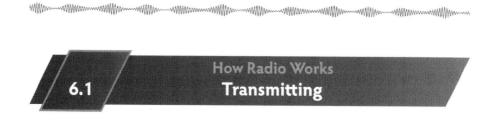

How Radio Works
6.1 Transmitting

CW Transmission: The simplest transmission mode is CW, or continuous wave transmissions. Recall that CW uses only an unmodulated steady signal that is interrupted in patterns to convey a message, and Morse Code is the most common 'pattern' used in amateur radio with CW mode.

A simple CW transmitter has these components as shown in Figure 6.2:

6.1 Transmitting

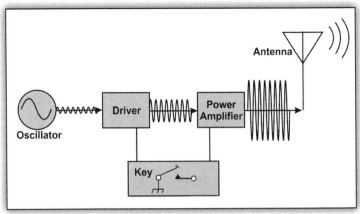

Figure 6.2: CW Transmitter Block Diagram

- **Oscillator: The oscillator is a circuit that generates a signal at a specified frequency,** perhaps many megahertz. Remember, this signal is an electrical alternating current surging back and forth, and it is routed to the driver component of the CW transmitter.

- **Driver:** The driver is a type of amplifier that boosts the amplitude (power) of the relatively weak RF signal generated by the oscillator.

- **Power Amplifier:** The power amplifier receives the oscillating signal from the driver, boosts its power further, and outputs the signal to the antenna.

- **Key:** The key, or telegraph key, is a switch that controls whether the continuous wave signal is passed or interrupted between the driver and power amplifier. The key is the control an operator uses to send the patterns of Morse Code.

- **Antenna:** As the strongly amplified alternating current (AC) surges back and forth in the antenna much of its power is converted into electromagnetic radiation of a frequency equal to the AC frequency.

Thus, an RF signal is transmitted from the antenna when the key is closed, completing the circuit and allowing the alternating electrical current to energize the antenna. On the other end of the communication another antenna will be energized by the radio waves impinging on its elements, converting them back into alternating electrical currents that are conducted down the antenna feedline (cable). A radio receiver will convert these recreated AC signals into an audio frequency signal that is emitted by a speaker as a consistent tone. This way, the Morse Code signal can be heard by the receiving radio operator as a pattern of tones. That is basic transmission, but there's a lot more! Now let's see how your voice is included in a transmission.

Modulated Phone Transmission: Phone modes transmit the sound of your voice by radio waves. When you push-to-talk you power up the microphone and you activate the transmitter. The sound waves detected by the microphone are encoded into radio frequency transmissions. This encoding process is called *modulation*. Let's start our modulation journey with some important background about sound and microphones.

Sound: Sound is our perception of mechanical waves in the air. Just as ocean waves need the medium of water to travel, sound needs the medium of air.

Sound waves are the *compression* and *rarefaction* of air molecules moving across a distance. The molecules get squeezed tightly together in the compressions and they get spread far apart in the rarefactions. A loud sound will have densely compacted air compression areas and thinly populated air rarefaction areas. A soft sound will have only mild differences in the density of molecules across the wave. We say these variations in molecule densities are variations in air pressure, or *sound pressure*. The magnitude of the difference in a wave's sound pressure is its amplitude.

Voice: Your voice is a blend of many different sound frequencies. Depending on your individual vocal chords the low vowel sounds, such as the 'o' sound at the end of the word 'radio,' may contain frequencies around 200 Hz.

The hard consonant sounds such as those of D, T, P, or Ch, contain much higher frequencies, perhaps near 2,500 Hz or higher. And there are many more in between. Most voices can be clearly produced with a continuous range of about 3,000 different sound frequencies, or 3,000 Hz.

Microphone: Your radio microphone detects a range of sound frequencies made by your voice and converts those into AC electrical signals, usually called *audio* signals. These audio frequency signals will vary in voltage the same way the sound waves vary with your voice: Make a loud sound and the amplitude of the voltage signals becomes greater; make the pitch of your voice go high and the frequencies of the voltage signals get higher too (shorter wavelengths). Figure 6.3 illustrates sound waves converted into audio electrical signals by a microphone. The microphone performs this conversion for the many different frequencies of your voice all at once, creating many different audio electrical frequency signals simultaneously.

Notice in the figure that the electrical audio signals produced by the microphone are depicted as squiggly waveforms in which the voltage oscillates from +v to –v. The pointing arrow of the horizontal axis represents the passage of time; as you move along the axis you are seeing different points in time. Every point on the squiggly waveform represents the direction and magnitude

6.1 Transmitting

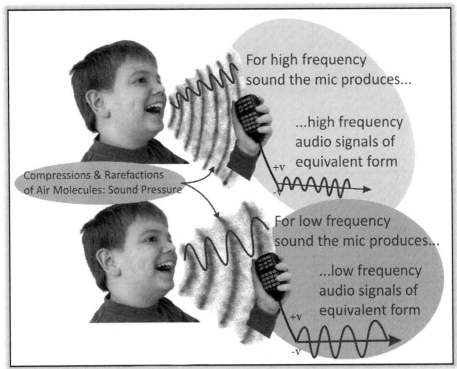

Figure 6.3: Sound Converted to Audio Electrical Signals

(strength) of the signal voltage at the given point in time on the axis. The +v and −v voltages simply indicate opposite directions of the voltage force in the microphone's AC signal.

The voltage force pushes electrons in the '+' direction up to some +v maximum force, then it reduces in strength back to zero at the axis. The voltage continues by reversing its force to the '−' direction, again reaching a maximum force of −v, then subsiding back to zero again at the axis. Repeat. Repeat. Repeat. This back-and-forth voltage occurs with the same regularity as the sound frequency of your voice that it is representing – the same as the air wave compressions and rarefactions produced by the sound of your voice. Note, these AC signals are of much lower frequency than RF, hundreds or thousands of hertz rather than the millions or hundreds of millions of hertz we have considered in the amateur radio frequency bands.

A depiction like the squiggly line electrical signals of Figure 6.3, in which time runs along the horizontal axis and the signal strength is depicted as up-and-down squiggly lines, is a "time domain" view of a signal. (Keep that in mind, and we will examine a different but related view in a moment!)

Audio Band: Remember, the microphone is creating a varying voltage signal like the time domain depiction for each of the many different frequencies of your voice. As depicted in Figure 6.4, you may imagine the microphone's audio signals as a set of about 3,000 waveforms, low to high frequency, each with a rapidly alternating voltage level over time, and the set of them accurately copying the variations among the 3,000 sound waveforms of your voice.

We call this set of electrical signals representing your voice the *audio band*. Because it is comprised of a band of about 3,000 frequencies we say it has a bandwidth of 3,000 Hz (or 3.0 kHz). In the 3D view of Figure 6.4 you can imagine viewing straight down the frequency axis and getting a time domain view, like the squiggly microphone waveform depiction of Figure 6.3.

Alternatively, if you view down the time axis straight onto the band of frequencies, you will get a "frequency domain" view. The frequency domain view depicts the amplitude (height) of each waveform in the band from low to high frequency values. The amplitude represents the power (or sound loudness) for each frequency in the band. You may have seen an audio stereo equalizer display like this in which the display indicators jump up and down across the band of frequencies as music is played. That equalizer display is a frequency domain view. (Note: Since it would get a little crowded trying to depict almost

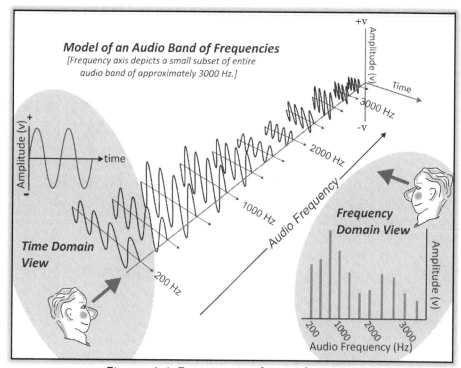

Figure 6.4: Envisioning the Audio Band

6.1 Transmitting

3,000 frequencies of the audio band, an interval subset of audio frequencies is depicted in our frequency domain view of Figure 6.4.)

We will use both time domain and frequency domain views throughout this chapter and on the *HamRadioSchool.com* web site to describe how radio works, so study these graphs closely!

Microphone Gain: For each of the frequencies in the audio band the microphone produces a small squiggly voltage signal that is proportional to the sound pressure levels. These low power signals are delivered to a signal amplifier that boosts them to greater voltage levels that can be used by the radio transmitter. The ratio of increase in the signal levels produced by the microphone amplifier is the microphone's *gain*. You can imagine that the amplifier could really boost the signals a lot and produce very large changes in the oscillating voltages of the signals (high gain), or it could increase them only slightly to produce mild proportional increases in the signal amplitude (low gain).

If a transmitter is operated with the microphone gain set too high, the output signal might become distorted. *Clipping* of the audio signal is one type of distortion possible from too high gain, as depicted in Figure 6.5. A signal is clipped when the maximum output voltage level of the microphone amplifier is reached before the microphone's input signal has achieved its maximum amplitude.

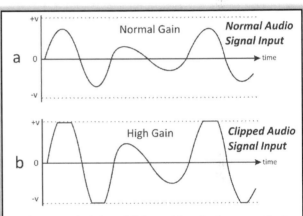

Audio signals 'a' and 'b' are identical except that 'b' is of greater amplitude due to high microphone amplifier gain. In 'b' the maximum output signal limit is reached, "clipping" the signal peaks and distorting the audio.

Figure 6.5: Excessive Microphone Gain

If a repeater user says your transmissions are breaking up on voice peaks you might be talking to loudly. Back off the microphone or the voice volume a bit and try again. You'll find the sweet spot.

Amplitude Modulation (AM): The encoding of information into radio frequency signals is *modulation*. In a phone mode the information to be encoded is the sound of your voice, now represented by the audio band electrical signals, boosted by the microphone amplifier. The radio transmitter must now create radio signals that represent these audio band signals.

Remember, the radio frequency signals are typically many millions of hertz (MHz), while the audio signals are typically only a few hundred to a few thousand hertz. The much higher frequency (shorter wavelength) RF signals can be "shaped" to mimic the much lower frequency (longer wavelength) audio signals. In AM, the amplitude of an RF signal is shaped to mimic the amplitude of an audio signal. The following is a somewhat simplified version of how this is done by the transmitter so that the many various frequencies of your voice are carried by the radio waves.

Audio Band to RF Band: Each of the approximately 3,000 audio band frequencies is assigned a unique radio frequency counterpart to represent it. There is a one-to-one matching of audio-to-RF frequencies. So, when you PTT you are transmitting a band of a few thousand different radio frequencies that are near the frequency to which you have tuned the radio. You are not transmitting just that single tuned frequency!

The tuned frequency value on the radio display is called the *carrier frequency*. The carrier is a reference frequency value that is used to calculate a unique RF band counterpart frequency for each of the audio band frequencies delivered from the microphone. Figure 6.6a depicts a frequency domain view of the one-to-one matching of the audio band frequencies to an RF band's frequencies within the 10m amateur band (28 MHz range). This RF domain depicts one AM *sideband,* meaning that this RF band of counterpart frequen-

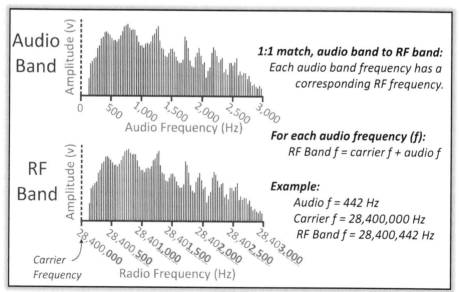

Figure 6.6a: Correspondence of Audio and RF Band Frequencies

cies is all on one side of the carrier frequency – in this example, the sideband frequencies are all higher than (above) the carrier frequency of 28.4 MHz.

Notice that in the RF sideband of Figure 6.6a each RF frequency is calculated by adding the counterpart audio frequency to the carrier frequency value. Performing this simple addition for each of the approximately 3,000 audio frequencies determines the band of RF frequencies that will be transmitted in this sideband. Notice also that the amplitude of each RF sideband frequency mimics the amplitude of its counterpart audio frequency. So, the shape of the frequency bands is identical, with the RF band copying the audio band over the time of transmission. If these were two stereo equalizer displays they would be dancing in synchrony, only different in frequency values by a few million hertz! Now let's see how that dancing act is accomplished for each one of the nearly 3,000 frequencies in the bands.

Envelopes: Now reference the Figure 6.6b time domain depiction of a single frequency out of the 3,000 Hz band. The audio signal shape and its amplitude mirror image are used to control the '+v' and the '–v' values of its much higher radio frequency counterpart. The enclosing "shape" of the audio signal amplitude, called the *envelope,* is imposed on the radio frequency amplitude over time. The amplitude of the RF signal increases and decreases over the

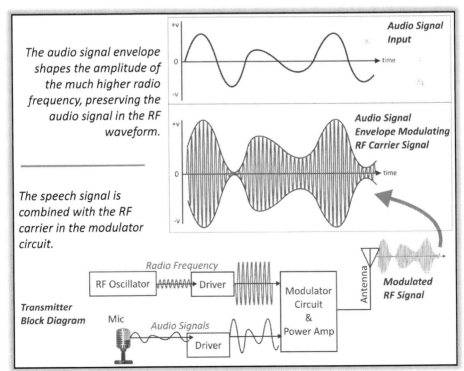

Figure 6.6b: Modulating RF Signals with an Audio Envelope

transmission time exactly as dictated by its audio signal counterpart, even though the RF oscillates at a much higher frequency "inside the envelope." But unlike the low audio frequency, the higher RF may be radiated and effectively transmitted through space, carrying the audio waveform information along. An identical process occurs for each of the nearly 3,000 Hz of audio frequencies and each uniquely calculated counterpart RF band frequency. Thus proceeds the amplitude modulation dance!

Modulator Circuit: The lower portion of Figure 6.6b depicts an amplitude modulation transmitter block diagram. Notice that the upper path of the transmitter sequence is almost identical to the CW transmitter of Figure 6.2. The oscillator circuit produces the RF carrier signal that is combined with your audio signals in the amplitude modulation process. The lower path in the block diagram represents the audio signal creation, amplification, and combining with the RF carrier signal. **Modulation, described by the combining of your speech with an RF carrier signal,** is accomplished in the modulator circuit part of the transmitter as shown in the block diagram.

AM Transmission: Finally, the entire band of amplitude modulated RF signals is radiated from the antenna as in Figure 6.6c, but this band is not alone! With true AM, a sideband above the carrier is transmitted just as in our example, but another entire sideband of frequencies *below* the carrier is also transmitted, and the carrier frequency itself is transmitted. The sideband

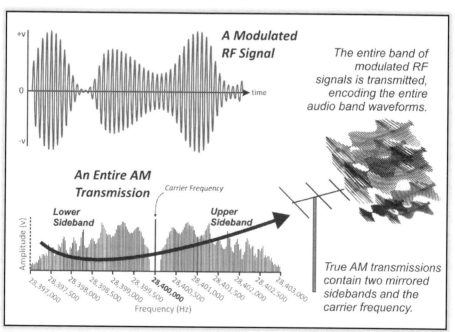

Figure 6.6c: Transmitting the AM Band of Modulated RF Frequencies

6.1 Transmitting

frequencies below the carrier are calculated by subtracting each audio frequency from the carrier value rather than adding to it, as in our previous 10m band example of Figure 6.6a. This results in a mirror image sideband on the lower side of the carrier doing the modulation dance too! True AM is a robust, if dual-redundant and somewhat power-inefficient, phone mode.

We will examine AM transmission and its skinny dancing cousin, *single sideband transmission*, a bit more closely in Section 6.3. For now let's venture briefly into the world of frequency modulation (FM) transmission.

FM Phone Modulation: Frequency modulation works differently than AM. Rather than making changes to the amplitude of RF signals to encode the audio signals, the frequency of an RF signal is changed as dictated by the audio band signal amplitude. You were introduced to the FM mode basic concept back in Section 1.3.

Deviation: Notice in the FM time domain depiction of Figure 6.7 the RF carrier frequency increases (shorter wavelengths) as the audio signal amplitude increases, and the RF carrier frequency decreases (longer wavelengths) as the audio amplitude decreases. When the audio signal amplitude is at zero, the associated RF carrier frequency value is known as the *resting frequency*. The change in the RF carrier frequency from its resting frequency is called the frequency *deviation*. The amount of deviation of an FM signal is determined by the amplitude of the modulating audio signal.

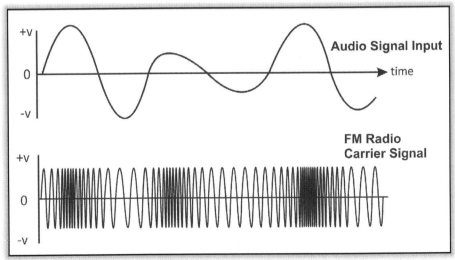

Figure 6.7: Revisiting Frequency Modulation

FM Spring Model: I like to think of the FM carrier waveform as a spring that has a preferred state of intermediate stretch (resting frequency). The carrier spring may be stretched further out than its preferred state, extending the distance between coils (deviated to a lower frequency, longer wavelength form). The spring may also be compressed tighter than its preferred state, squeezing the coils closer together (deviated to a higher frequency, shorter wavelength form).

During FM transmission the carrier spring is constantly jittering back and forth between different amounts of extension or compression – variable magnitudes of frequency deviation from the resting frequency. As noted before, the amount of the extension and compression of the spring deviation is determined by the amplitude of the audio signal, as in Figure 6.8. So, speaking loudly into the microphone increases the audio signal amplitude and drives a large FM carrier deviation – big spring extensions and compressions. Remaining silent leaves the FM carrier at its resting frequency, with no deviation at all. Other sound levels in between these extremes produce intermediate levels of FM carrier deviation – intermediate magnitudes of extensions and compressions during the spring jittering.

FM Bandwidth: This leads to an interesting characteristic of FM transmission: As the deviation of an FM transmitter is increased its signal occupies more bandwidth. Remember, bandwidth is the range of the set of frequencies used in the transmission. As you speak louder the carrier frequency deviates across a wider range of frequencies, thereby using more bandwidth. FM uses variable amounts of bandwidth depending upon the loudness of your voice! (We will compare mode bandwidths in Section 6.3.)

FM Transmission: Now, let's take the spring model one step further. Each frequency in the audio band, from about 200 Hz to 3,000 Hz, is going to make the spring jitter at a rate equal to each of those different audio frequencies. For instance, the 200 Hz audio frequency is going to jitter the carrier spring at 200 times per second – the spring is extended and compressed 200 times each second. Similarly, the 2,500 Hz audio signal is going to extend and compress the spring 2,500 times each second. With FM, this is how the band of audio frequencies is represented, with a commensurate band of carrier spring jittering rates (a band of audio deviation frequencies).

6.1 Transmitting

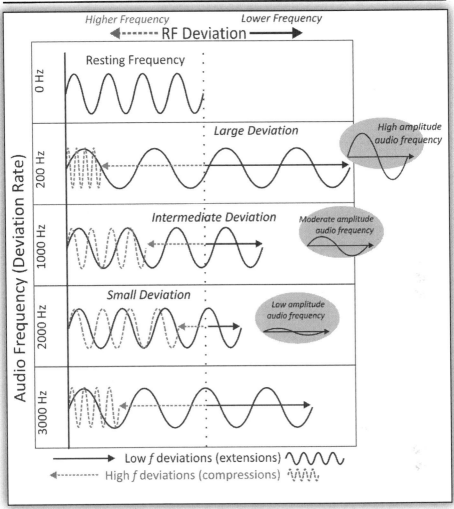

Figure 6.8: Spring Model of FM Carrier Deviation

Bringing it all together, each audio frequency is represented by the frequency of deviation of the RF carrier signal (the spring jitter rate), and an audio frequency's amplitude is represented by the magnitude of that deviation (the amount of extension and compression). So, you may think of the FM transmission as a set of carrier springs lined up in parallel as in Figure 6.8, each spring jittering at a different audio frequency, and each spring deviating by an amount proportional to the audio frequency amplitude, or loudness.

Keep in mind that like the previous AM description, the FM spring model is a simplification that omits some complex mathematics that more precisely describe the FM transmission signal. With FM the transmission signal gets very complicated, with all the various audio jittering frequencies piled upon one another in a wild and complex modulation dance. We have avoided both *Fourier Transforms* and *Bessel Functions* to gain a more intuitive way of thinking about AM and FM modulation. However, be aware in any more advanced learning about RF modulation you undertake that our intuitive models have limitations and do not precisely represent physical reality. They're a good start to really getting it, however!

The question pool items for *Section 6.1* are combined with those for Section 6.2. So, press on to the next section – Receiving. You'll catch up on the question pool practice after that.

6.2 How Radio Works — Receiving

> **"** No man would listen to you talk if he didn't know it was his turn next. – Edgar Watson Howe

You can have your turn any time you want. But for now I hope you will continue receiving. The second half of radio communication story is just as spellbinding as the first half! Again we will examine AM first, followed by FM receiving. Let's see how things are going following transmission…

AM and SSB Receiving: When we last left our hero, *Audio Band*, he was trapped and hopelessly entangled within AM waveforms of radio frequencies being hurdled through space at the speed of light with no particular destination known! Is all hope lost for our hero? Will Audio Band ever again be free to vibrate the molecules of air as audible sound? Is there any chance he will be received and freed through the incredible power of demodulation?

But of course! It's *Superheterodyne* to the rescue!

Frequency Mixing: We interrupt this story to bring you the following hot background information that will help you comprehend the incredible demodulation power of Superheterodyne. The Superheterodyne receiver is well practiced in the art of *frequency mixing*, allowing it to convert high frequency radio signals into lower frequency signals while preserving any enveloping modulating signal, such as Audio Band! With this power, Superheterodyne may free Audio Band from his RF bondage!

When two signals of different frequencies are combined, or mixed, a lower frequency product signal results. (A higher frequency product also results that we will disregard, or filter away.) If one of the mixed frequencies contains modulation information, such as a modulating envelope of audio signals, that envelope of modulation will still shape the amplitude of the lower frequency product signal. That is, the amplitude modulation information is preserved. A component called **a mixer is used to convert a radio signal from one frequency to another.** [Visit the *HamRadioSchool.com* Section 6.2 learning media to find out more about frequency mixing.]

T7A03

Superheterodyne: The superheterodyne is just a fancy way of referring to a receiver that uses frequency mixing to begin extracting Audio Band from his RF prison. A superheterodyne receiver uses a mixer to shift the incoming signal to an intermediate frequency. That is, the received RF signal is mixed with another unmodulated RF signal of a different frequency, and a considerably lower frequency, still-modulated, RF signal results. We call this lower RF frequency the *intermediate frequency* (IF) because it is in between the originally received higher RF frequency and the much lower audio frequency that remains trapped in the modulating envelope of the IF signal.

More than one mixing stage may be used by a receiver to convert the modulated signal to lower frequencies. Once the modulated signal is converted low enough, the enveloping audio band signals may be extracted from it by electronic filtering. Figure 6.9 is a block diagram of a single-conversion superheterodyne receiver. It is a superheterodyne because it uses a mixer circuit to produce an intermediate frequency (IF) for the IF amplifier. It is a single-conversion type because it uses only one intermediate frequency step and, thus, it has only one IF amplifier.

Figure 6.10 is an elaborated version of Figure 6.9 illustrating the sequence of signal demodulation steps in a superheterodyne receiver. Follow along...

1. The modulated RF signal is mixed with the oscillator frequency.

2. The mixer produces the intermediate frequency with audio modulation information preserved in the IF signals.

3. The IF signals are amplified and sent to another mixing circuit (product detector).

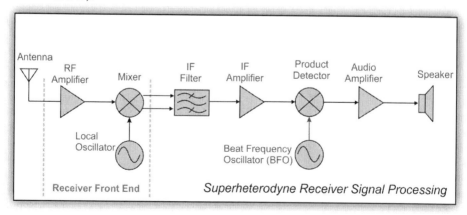

Figure 6.9: Single-Conversion Superheterodyne Block Diagram

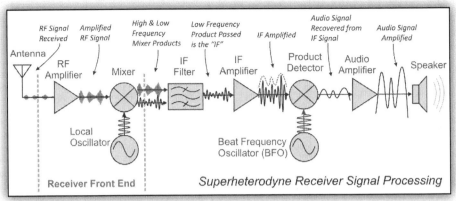

Figure 6.10: Superheterodyne Signal Demodulation Sequence

4. Mixing with the Beat Frequency Oscillator signal results in an even lower output frequency in the audio frequency range, allowing the preserved original audio band signal to be output to an audio amplifier.

5. The audio band signals are sent to a speaker where they are transformed into the original sound of your voice.

Voila! Audio Band is freed from his RF chains to grace the ears of another operator with the sound of your voice! With that big picture in mind, let's take a bit closer look at some receiver components and their functions.

RF Preamplifier: In many receivers **an RF preamplifier will be installed between the antenna and receiver** to boost weak RF signals before any mixing or demodulation is accomplished. This helps provide the mixer with stronger initial RF signals.

Product Detector: The second mixer in the path of Figure 6.11 is referred to as the *product detector* because it begins the process of identifying audio signal products that are encoded in the IF signals (the modulation envelope information). The function of a product detector is to detect CW and SSB signals, and to begin the conversion of IF signals to lower frequencies for audio demodulation. **The ability of a receiver to detect the presence of a signal is called *sensitivity*.** The product detector's output results from mixing the IF with an unmodulated signal from the beat frequency oscillator.

Oscillator: In Figure 6.10 two oscillator blocks are depicted in the processing path. The first oscillator provides the first mixer circuit an unmodulated

RF frequency to mix with a received RF signal to produce the intermediate frequency (IF) signal. This first oscillator in the path is a variable one, able to produce a wide range of frequencies for mixing with the received signal.

The ability to vary its mixing frequency is a very important function of this oscillator. And this oscillator is connected to your radio's tuning knob. This is the *variable frequency oscillator* (VFO) that you learned about in Section 1.1. When you tune your radio, this oscillator's frequency is adjusted so that it provides exactly the right mixing frequency to produce a single, constant IF value as the output of the mixer. The IF value always remains the same, and the VFO becomes a means of selecting the desired receive frequency from among all the various signals resonating on the antenna.

For instance, suppose you want to demodulate a 28.400 MHz signal as in our previous transmission example. The VFO is adjusted to provide a mixing frequency that combines with 28.400 MHz (and its RF band containing your voice signals) to produce the very specific IF for which the receiver has been specially designed to further process into audio frequencies. The frequency of 455 kHz (0.455 MHz) is a commonly used IF. All the other RF frequencies input from the antenna are also mixed with the VFO frequency and produce a variety of lower output frequencies, but only the specially selected IF signal of 455 kHz is processed beyond the mixer. All those other undesired mixer products are ignored and filtered away.

If you shift the VFO frequency to another value, the exact same IF (455 kHz) will result from VFO signal mixing with a different received frequency. So, in effect, the VFO allows you to select the received RF signals from your antenna that you wish to have mixed down to the IF value. This is how you tune your receiver to various selected frequencies.

Beat Frequency Oscillator: The second oscillator in the path, the *beat frequency oscillator* (BFO), serves a similar mixing function in a lower frequency range. It provides a mixing frequency to create even lower frequencies from the IF amplifier signals. These low products are the audio frequency envelope signals that feed the speaker and reproduce the sound of a transmitted voice.

RIT / Clarifier: The BFO may also be varied somewhat using a receiver control called **RIT (Receiver Incremental Tuning),** also known as the *clarifier*. By tweaking the BFO mixing frequency the demodulated audio signals can be adjusted slightly in sound frequency alignment. Every transceiver in the world is not calibrated perfectly, and sometimes the receiver's signal processing will not be aligned quite right with the proper audio output frequencies, even

6.2 Receiving

though your receiver display indicates that you are perfectly tuned to the carrier value.

For instance, the entire audio band may be processed a couple of hundred hertz high, making all the audio signals produce sound frequencies 200 Hz higher than the original voice frequencies. The received voice will sound artificially high pitched, perhaps a bit like Mickey Mouse! The RIT control allows you to vary the BFO slightly to adjust only the receiver's late stage processing and ratchet down those frequencies by 200 Hz to where the voice will sound correctly pitched. **The receiver incremental tuning, or receiver RIT is the control to use if the voice pitch of a single-sideband signal seems too high or too low.**

[T4B06]

Note, with RIT only the receiver is adjusted, leaving the transmitter frequency to remain unchanged – you don't want to vary your transmitted frequency as your contact is dialing in your signal. If you try to correct the received pitch by retuning the transceiver (including transmission frequency), the two of you will chase each other around the dial trying to get your respective sound corrected! Use the RIT / clarifier, and leave your transmitter on one frequency.

Automatic Gain Control (AGC): Used to keep received audio relatively constant, the AGC in a superheterodyne receiver is a kind of feedback circuit. The AGC measures the output of the IF amplifier and adjusts the gain of preceding processing stages. As a result, the output amplitude of each signal processing stage is kept within the designed input range of the subsequent stage, avoiding distortion due to over-driving amplifiers or other circuits.

[T4B11]

FM Receiving: Demodulating FM signals uses somewhat different techniques than the AM and SSB case, and there are several different varieties of FM demodulators. Demodulators are electronic circuits designed to evaluate the frequency deviations of the FM carrier and output signals with voltage variations that represent the frequency deviations. These voltage varied signals contain the original audio band information and drive the receiver's speaker to produce sound.

Take a look at Figure 6.11 on the next page and follow the path of FM receiver blocks. Like AM and SSB receiving, FM receivers will commonly use a preamplifier to boost RF signals right after the antenna. A mixer circuit with oscillator is followed by specially tuned filters to produce an intermediate frequency

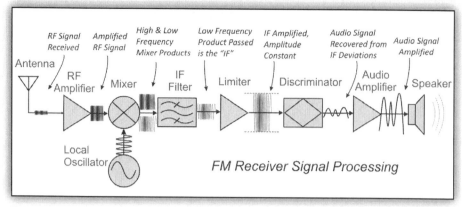

Figure 6.11: The FM receiver signal processing begins the same as the SSB superheterodyne, but a limiter circuit ensures a constant IF amplitude and a discriminator circuit recovers the audio signal from the IF deviations.

that is then amplified. The significant differences in the signal processing path from AM and SSB demodulation then follow.

Limiter: The *limiter* is a circuit that limits the amplitude of the FM signals going into the next stage demodulator circuit. The FM demodulator stage works best with a constant amplitude level, so the limiter helps keep the amplitude smoothed to a consistent level. Remember, the modulated voice information is contained in the frequency deviations, so limiting the amplitude of the signal does not impact the modulated information.

Discriminator: A *frequency discriminator* is one common type of FM demodulation circuit. A discriminator demodulates FM signals, extracting the audio signals from the frequency deviations. Only FM receivers have a discriminator. The discriminator evaluates the intermediate frequency deviations from resting state and translates them into variable amplitude audio signals for the speaker. Once again, your voice is decoded from a modulated RF signal and reproduced for the receiving radio operator!

Get to the questions on Receiving, **Section 6.2**. Next up we will compare bandwidth used by the various modes of transmission, along with a closer look at those "sidebands."

www.HamRadioSchool.com/tech_media

6.3 Bandwidth and Sidebands

> **How Radio Works**

> **❝** *I'd really love to take that on, but I just don't have the bandwidth right now. – The Engineer's Excuse*

With all of the transmitting and receiving concepts under your belt you should now have the bandwidth to discuss a few very practical considerations regarding the small RF bands that are transmitted and received by your radio.

Bandwidth: Bandwidth implies capacity. In radio the bandwidth of a signal is the amount of spectrum used. Generally, the more bandwidth available the more information can be communicated per unit of time. With greater bandwidth of signals you can squeeze in more audio information and produce a higher quality sound. With narrow bandwidth the quality of sound may suffer, and the amount of information transmitted per unit of time is reduced. Each mode uses a unique amount of bandwidth. Let's see how they match up!

AM vs. SSB: We noted in an earlier section that **single sideband mode is a form of amplitude modulation,** or AM. We also noted that its primary advantage for voice transmission was its narrow bandwidth.

As we have seen, voice modulation requires a band of radio frequencies to carry the information of the audio band signals produced by the microphone from your voice. In our example we considered a band of about 3,000 frequencies, or a bandwidth of about 3.0 kHz (3,000 Hz). **That is the approximate bandwidth of a single sideband (SSB) voice signal: 3 kHz.** But why is it called "single sideband," and how does it compare with those other voice modes like AM and FM, or with CW?

In Section 6.1 we introduced the concept that a true AM signal is redundant, producing two RF bands – one above the carrier frequency and a second below the carrier frequency. Figure 6.12 compares AM to SSB with frequency domain views. The upper band, or upper sideband (USB), is assigned by the transmitter by adding the audio frequency values to the carrier frequency,

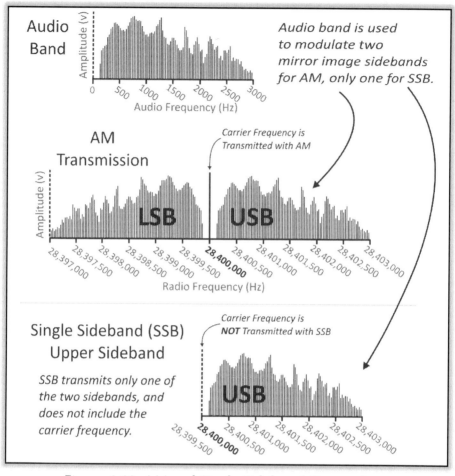

Figure 6.12: AM and Single Sideband Comparison

just as in the example of Section 6.1. The lower sideband (LSB) is assigned by subtracting the audio frequency values from the carrier frequency value.

Both sidebands carry the exact same information, a redundant encoding of the voice audio band. The two sidebands are like mirror images of one another. This redundancy provides AM with a robust signal and improved reliability, but it consumes a lot of bandwidth, approximately 6 kHz, or about twice that used by SSB.

SSB mode uses only one of the two AM sidebands, and it does not transmit the central carrier frequency. So, SSB is truly a single sideband. Your receiver artificially reproduces the carrier frequency as a reference point so that all the individual sideband frequencies may be recovered.

6.3 Bandwidth & Sidebands

Which sideband does your radio use, upper or lower? The answer is, "it depends!" The standard worldwide agreed convention for SSB voice is to use upper sideband for bands 30m and higher frequency. So, **the upper sideband is normally used for 10 meter HF, VHF and UHF single sideband communications.** The lower sideband is normally used in the lower frequency bands of HF for SSB phone (40m through 160m bands).

FM Bandwidth: Recall that FM bandwidth changes with the amplitude of the audio signal driving the frequency deviations. Louder sound means greater audio signal power (greater amplitude) that is converted into greater frequency deviations in the FM transmitted RF band. **FM phone bandwidth, such as a VHF repeater signal, is typically between 10 and 15 kHz.** So, FM requires up to five times the bandwidth of SSB, but it offers the advantages of clear, robust audio.

CW Bandwidth: CW is the type of emission that has the narrowest bandwidth. Since CW is transmitting only a single carrier wave for tone production, **the maximum bandwidth required to transmit is very narrow, typically around 150 Hz.** That's only 5% of SSB bandwidth!

With CW and many digital modes that use narrow bandwidth, low power operation (QRP) is very popular. Long distance contacts can be made on just a few watts of power since the transmitted power is condensed into the very narrow band of frequencies, not spread out over thousands of hertz of frequencies as in phone modes. You can get a lot of signal 'punch' with CW!

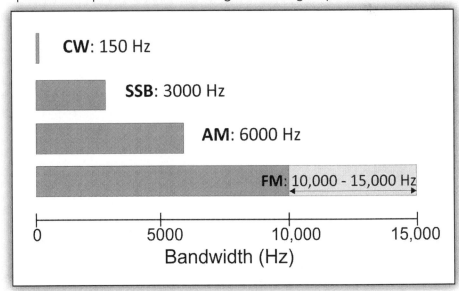

Figure 6.13: Comparison of Approximate Bandwidths by Mode

Edge of Band Considerations: Look back to Section 4.2 at the FCC amateur band plan that defines the limits of Technician license privileges. Obviously there are edges to the bands where your technician privileges will end. You are not allowed to transmit beyond those edge limits with even a single hertz in your small transmitted band of RF frequencies! Take note...

> **Transmitter frequency displays have calibration error that you must allow for.**
>
> **Transmitter frequency can drift over time.**
>
> **Your modulation sidebands must not extend beyond the band edge.**
>
> **For all these reasons you should not set your transmit frequency to be exactly at the edge of an amateur band or sub-band.**

(T1B09)

For example: Suppose you are operating on 10m phone, properly using the upper sideband (USB). What is the highest frequency that you should tune to so that you avoid transmitting outside of your Technician privileges?

Examine Figure 6.14. The Technician 10m phone privileges extend up to 28.500 MHz. Your USB signal is about 3 kHz wide, extending above your tuned carrier frequency shown on the radio display. At the very least you should not transmit when tuned above a frequency 3 kHz below 28.500 MHz.

28.500 MHz − 0.003 MHz = 28.497 MHz   (3 kHz = 0.003 MHz)

So you should not transmit in SSB mode above 28.497 MHz because your 3 kHz bandwidth USB signal may extend above the Technician limit of 28.500 MHz. But keep in mind the drift and calibration error as well.

It may be prudent to cut that maximum by another few hertz, just to be sure! Maybe 28.496.500 MHz max, giving you a 500 Hz buffer for drift and calibration error.

Transverters: A transverter allows you to extend your radio's capabilities into higher RF bands. **A transverter converts RF input and output of a transceiver to another band** entirely. For example, a transverter could take the output of a low-powered 28 MHz SSB exciter (the signal from your transceiver) and produce a 222 MHz output signal, retaining the modulated information across the frequency conversion. If you should get into trans-

(T7A06)

6.3 Bandwidth & Sidebands

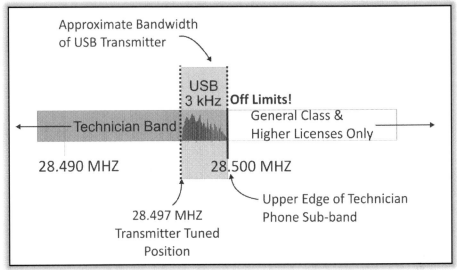

Figure 6.14: Edge of Band Tuning Considerations for Bandwidth

verting, perhaps to transmit in the microwave frequency bands allocated to amateur use, take great care to ensure your transmissions remain within the privileges of your license.

Whew! Take a deep series of breaths. Congratulations! You made it through some of the most challenging material of this book. If you didn't quite get it all, don't worry. You will over time, as your amateur radio bandwidth expands, and even if some of your understanding comes after you've got your Technician license hanging in your ham shack. Zero-in on those highlighted test question topics and reread this chapter's three sections a little at a time. Check out the web site for additional materials about the workings of radio. You'll be glad you did!

And while you're at it now, keep the book handy and go work through the questions for **Section 6.3**. You're on your way to really getting it!

www.HamRadioSchool.com/tech_media

Note: *FM bandwidth in the amateur radio practice is commonly greater than the 10 to 15 kHz range stated in the exam question pool material and in this section. You may experience bandwidths greater than 15 kHz in practice.*

Beautiful antenna farm of Frank, K7SFN, overlooking snowy Nevada mountains.   *Photo courtesy of K7SFN*

7.0 Antennas

> **Invisible airwaves crackle with life**
> **Bright antennae bristle with the energy**
> — *The Spirit of Radio, Neil Peart [Rush]*

Nothing inspires awe, appreciation, and fun projects among hams more than a well-crafted, highly effective antenna! There is just something about gleaming aluminum and copper, wire and welds, connectors and coax all coming together to bristle with the energy and radiate information across the vast landscape. It's a fact: Antennas are fascinating and very cool.

Antennas are sort of like the filaments of light bulbs! They receive electrical energy and radiate much of it as electromagnetic energy. Where a light bulb filament radiates visible light EM (and a fair amount of infrared heat), your radio antenna radiates radio frequency EM. But unlike the light bulb your antenna's EM emissions may be detected around the world!

In this chapter we will start with some basics about antenna characteristics and designs. In Section 7.2 we will learn about standing wave ratio (SWR) and how to get the most out of your antenna system. Section 7.3 wraps up the antenna admiration with practical considerations about coaxial cable and connectors.

7.1 Antenna Basics

Resonance: Antennas radiate best when they resonate with the frequency of transmission. Think of pushing someone on a swing, where you can time your pushes so that the swing continues to go back and forth with only a slight reinforcing shove each back-and-forth cycle. The oscillating period of the swing and your timed pushes are in resonance with one another, and you can keep the swing going very efficiently with little effort.

The oscillating period of the swing is determined by the length of the rope or chain by which it hangs – a long rope produces a long period back-and-forth, while a short rope results in quick back-and-forth. The period of an antenna's oscillation, or its resonant frequency, is determined largely by the antenna's physical length. The timing of the pushes the antenna gets is determined by the radio frequency fed into it by the transmitter.

So an antenna should be trimmed to the proper resonant length for the frequency it is intended to radiate in order for it to radiate efficiently and not waste your transmitter's energy to heat.

Lower frequency bands where wavelengths are long will need a longer antenna. High frequencies with short wavelengths resonate with shorter antennas. You can change the resonant frequency of an antenna by lengthening or shortening its conductive element. **For instance, to change a dipole antenna to make it resonate on a higher frequency, you would shorten it.** (See dipole antenna type later in this section.)

T9A05

The resonant length of an antenna is a multiple of the wavelength it is intended to radiate, and fractional multiples such as ½ or ¼ wavelength are very common. In general, longer antennas such as ½ wavelength provide very good performance, while antennas of less than ¼ wavelength (like that short rubber duck on an HT) will be less effective radiators of RF.

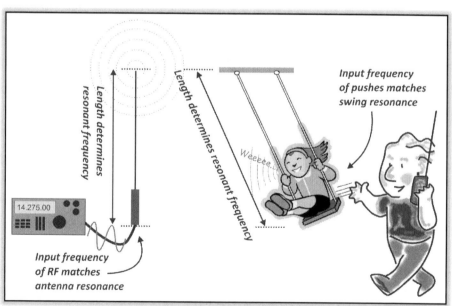

Figure 7.1: Concept of Resonance

7.1 Antenna Basics

Antenna Types: The names of basic antenna types tend to tell a lot about the antenna. Usually the name has been derived from the physical form, the orientation, the length, or the effects of the antenna type. Here are some relevant examples.

Vertical Antennas: A simple antenna oriented vertically to the earth's surface. Regarding EM field polarization, a vertical antenna produces an electric field that is perpendicular to the earth.

Quarter Wave Vertical: A commonly used vertical antenna is the ¼ wave vertical, meaning its height is ¼ of its resonant frequency wavelength. As you can easily calculate, a ¼ wave antenna for the 2 meter band will extend approximately 2m x 0.25 = 0.5m, or about 1.5 feet. A ¼ wave vertical for the 40m band would stand about 10m high, or about 30 feet. We'll get into calculating antenna lengths more a bit later in this section.

Ground Plane: A ¼ wave vertical works best when it has a ground plane. A ground plane is a conductive surface perpendicular to the antenna that acts like a mirror for RF purposes. A car's metal rooftop can serve as a very effective ground plane for a VHF or UHF ¼ wave vertical antenna. The ground plane's RF mirror essentially creates another virtual ¼ wave antenna as a mirror image of the real ¼ wave vertical, and electrically the real and virtual antennas complement one another to act much like a longer and more efficient ½ wave antenna. Way cool, huh?

A collection of radially oriented wires extending from the base of a ground mounted vertical may serve as a ground plane, and some antennas will have abbreviated ground planes made from three or four short radials angled down slightly from the base of a vertical. For an indoor VHF or UHF antenna, mounting it on a metal cookie sheet or a plane of aluminum foil can really improve performance.

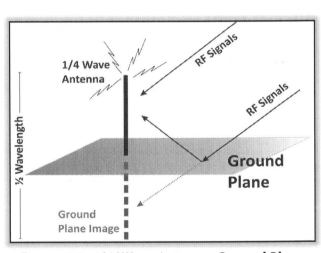

Figure 7.2: 1/4 Wave Antenna Ground Plane

Dipole Antenna: The dipole is another simple antenna. You may think of the dipole as two ¼ wave antennas placed end-to-end, almost like having the virtual ground plane image of a ¼ wave antenna turned physically real. A dipole is typically ½ wavelength long, with two conductors (frequently copper wires) extending in opposite directions. One of the conductors is attached to the RF conducting side of the feedline from the transceiver, such as the center wire conductor of a coaxial cable. The other conductor is attached to the ground side of the feedline, such as the braided shield portion of a coax cable.

A half-wave wire dipole is a common and inexpensive way to radiate the long wavelengths of the HF bands. For erecting convenience, a lengthy wire **simple dipole is oriented parallel to the earth's surface, and is a horizontally polarized antenna.** The dipole is also said to be a *center fed antenna* because the feedline from the transceiver attaches at the center point and each of the conductors is of equivalent length.

Radiating Pattern: **A half-wave dipole antenna radiates the strongest signals broadside to the antenna.** In other words, the strongest RF emissions come out radially away from the dipole's conductors, or wires. The radiating strength pattern looks a bit like a big donut with the wire running

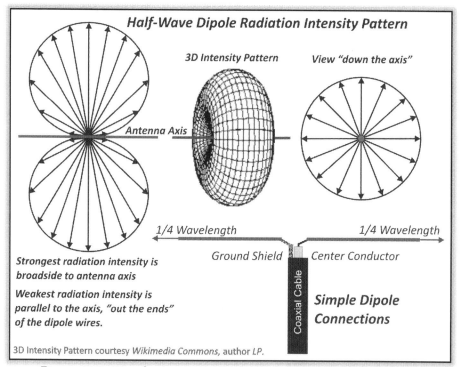

Figure 7.3: Dipole Antenna Radiating Pattern in Free Space

7.1 Antenna Basics

right through the donut hole. The poorest RF emissions are directly out the ends of the dipole's wires.

RF Coupling: The dipole antenna pattern on the preceding page has no objects nearby the antenna, as if it is far above the ground – at least several wavelengths of distance. (The perfect model dipole has infinite space around it, but of course that is just a model.) This is important is because of an effect called *RF coupling*. Radiating antennas are affected by surrounding conductors, such as metal and the ground. The antenna's pattern of radiation and its resonant frequency can be significantly altered by surrounding conductors and by its height above the ground. Directional antennas leverage this effect.

Beam or Directional Antennas: Beam antennas are designed to concentrate signals in one direction. The physical design of beam antennas is more complex than verticals or dipoles, and many types of beam antennas will have multiple elements (active and passive conductor components) to take advantage of the effects of RF coupling to shape the radiating pattern. **Examples of directional antennas include the quad, Yagi, and dish** antenna types.

Antenna Gain: Directional or beam antennas are said to have gain in the direction of the concentrated signals. **Gain is the antenna's increased signal strength in a specified direction compared to a reference antenna.** The dipole antenna discussed earlier is a common standard reference for comparison, as is the isotropic (radiating evenly in all horizontal directions) vertical antenna.

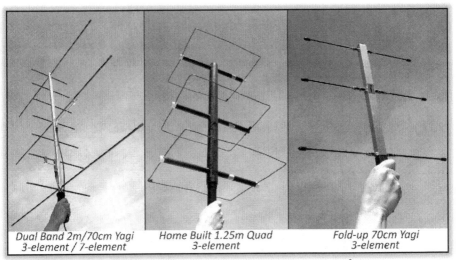

Figure 7.4: Three Different VHF/UHF Directional Antennas

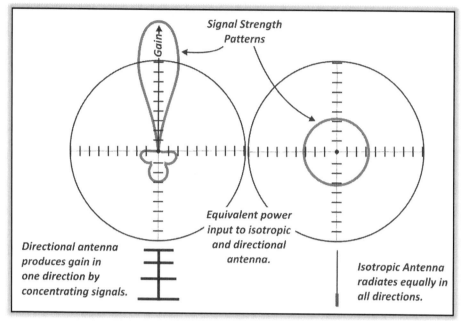

Figure 7.5: Gain Pattern of a Directional Antenna

Think about gain this way: The reference antenna spreads the power of the transmitter evenly in all directions, more or less. Imagine you use an RF field strength meter to measure the transmitted electric field strength 100 feet away from the antenna. Suppose you get a reading of 1.0 in this case. (Just a relative measure; we'll discuss units of RF field strength later.) Then you switch to a beam antenna and measure in the direction of concentrated emissions, again 100 feet away from the antenna. This time your field strength meter reads 6.0.

In the direction of the beam your antenna is providing signal gain of a 6:1 ratio. However, if you measure behind the beam or to the side, you will find the RF field strength to be less than that of the reference antenna, perhaps a reading of 0.1 or less. All of the energy that the isotropic reference antenna spread around has been pointed in one direction to provide gain. Essentially, the evenly distributed isotropic signal that works equally well in all directions has been traded for much improved performance in one direction. With antennas, everything is a trade-off.

Dummy Load: A *dummy load* is not an antenna. Rather, it is a non-emitting substitute for an antenna. From the transmitter's electrical point of view the dummy load looks like an antenna, but it merely dissipates the transmitted energy into heat instead of radiating RF energy. **The purpose of a dummy load is to prevent transmitting signals over the air when making**

T7C01

7.1 Antenna Basics

tests of your transmitter. A dummy load may be a small, ceramic module for low power use, or a large can of mineral oil with an antenna connector integrated onto it for very high power absorption. Technically speaking, **a dummy load consists of a non-inductive resistor and a heat sink,** which means that in use it does not create undesirable electronic effects and it can dissipate the heat generated by the RF. (Resistors and inductance topics coming in Chapter 9.)

Antenna Length: The actual length of an antenna's conducting element is usually slightly less than its wavelength multiple due to some complex electrical dynamics of finite length radiating element. Still, a close approximation of ideal antenna length can be calculated with simple formulas.

To calculate approximate antenna length in meters, multiply the resonant frequency's wavelength by the antenna multiple (1/4 wave, 1/2 wave, etc.) as illustrated earlier in this section. To calculate approximate antenna length in feet or inches, use the following formulas:

For ½ Wavelength Antennas
468 ÷ frequency in MHz = Length in Feet

For ¼ Wavelength Antennas
234 ÷ frequency in MHz = Length in Feet

To convert to inches, multiply Length in Feet x 12.

Example 1: **Approximate length, in inches, of a quarter-wavelength vertical antenna for 146 MHz is...**

234 ÷ 146 = 1.60 feet;
1.60 x 12 = 19 inches

The approximate length is 19 inches.

Example 2: **Approximate length, in inches, of a half-wavelength 6 meter wire dipole antenna is...**

468 ÷ 50 = 9.36 feet   (Note: 6m frequency is 50 MHz)
9.63 x 12 = 112 inches

The approximate length is 112 inches. Notice in this example that it was first necessary to convert 6m into its commensurate frequency of 50 MHz. Remember from Section 4.1, Wavelength & Frequency:

300 ÷ wavelength = frequency in MHz
So, 300 ÷ 6 = 50 MHz

The values 468 and 234 come from conversions between the use of feet and the use of meters for wavelength measurement, plus a 5% length adjustment. Notice that the ¼ wavelength dividend, 234, is exactly one-half the ½-wavelength dividend, 468. It is easy to remember that these numbers are sequential counting numbers (2, 3, 4) and sequential even numbers (4, 6, 8).

Mobile Antennas: Antennas used with mobile stations, such as in motor vehicles, require a little special consideration due to the unique requirements of a mobile station. For instance, mobile antenna length is limited by safety practicality, and a mobile station does not have a static environment from which it transmits consistently.

Mobile antennas are often mounted in the center of the vehicle roof because that normally provides the most uniform radiation pattern. The flat roof acts as a ground plane for the vertical antenna, and an uneven ground plane results in uneven performance patterns for the antenna. Still, good (if uneven) antenna performance can result from other mounting positions on a vehicle.

The radiation pattern of a vertical antenna is also affected by the antenna length, and a greater variety of vertical antenna lengths is available beyond the common 1/4 and 1/2 wavelength discussed earlier in this section. **For VHF or UHF mobile service a properly mounted 5/8 wavelength antenna has a lower radiation angle and more gain than a 1/4 wavelength antenna,** usually providing improved coverage. The improved gain of the 5/8 wavelength antenna comes from concentrating the signals more horizontally than the 1/4 wavelength antenna. But, if you wish to operate in areas where VHF or UHF repeaters are at high vertical angles to your traveling route, such as below nearby repeaters positioned upon mountaintops or skyscrapers, the higher vertical radiation angles of a 1/4 wave antenna may provide better performance. Remember, every antenna is a trade-off.

T9A12

Loading: Because mobile antennas cannot be physically long enough to be at least 1/4 wavelength radiators for most of the long-wavelength HF bands (10 to 160 meter bands), electronic tricks are used to make shorter antennas behave like longer antennas. These tricks are called *loading* the antenna, and loading makes the antenna seem electrically longer than it is physically. So, a

7.1 Antenna Basics

relatively short antenna on a vehicle can be made to radiate frequencies much lower than its physical length allows in the non-loaded case.

One common loading method is to insert a conductive coil into the antenna. These coils are called *inductors*, and they impact the flow of AC in the antenna. We will explore the effects of inductors more in Chapter 8, but **one type of loading when referring to an antenna is inserting an inductor in the radiating portion of the antenna to make it electrically longer.** [T9A02]

An inductor may also be used along with other loading components, such as a *capacitor, or capacitance hat*. This may be a disk or spoked ring added to the antenna's radiating element, and it can further enhance the low frequency radiating ability of a physically short antenna, helping the antenna circuit to resonate at the lower frequencies.

Figure 7.6: An inductor loaded mobile antenna.

Photo: Paul, AAØK
High-Q-Antennas

What's the trade-off with loaded antennas? Most full-sized antennas will radiate very effectively across a wide range of frequency values either side of the specific frequency for which its length is cut. So, you can use one antenna length to get good performance across the entire 20-meter band, for instance, a bandwidth of over 300 kHz. However, as you load an antenna and physically shorten it, the range of frequencies over which the antenna radiates efficiently becomes narrower. A physically short, highly loaded 20-meter antenna may perform well over only 100 kHz or less, depending on the amount of loading.

Don't run out to make invisible airwaves crackle with life just yet! There's more to know about antennas, about confirming resonant performance, and about feedlines and connectors. Read on, but first try the online questions for **Section 7.1** and make sure you've really got it!

www.HamRadioSchool.com/tech_media

Bob, KØNR, readies a 6m Yagi directional for VHF contesting.

7.2 Standing Wave Ratio (SWR)

> **"** An antenna is just an electromagnetic fishing pole. – Anonymous Ham

Once you have an approximate length for your antenna element you may want to trim its length more precisely in order to achieve the best resonance performance feasible. You'll catch more RF fish that way.

You can gauge your antenna's proper trim length by measuring how well it resonates across the frequencies of the band for which it is designed. By trimming the length you can alter the resonant frequency for the antenna to be higher or lower in the band. One way to gauge the resonant frequency in an antenna system is by evaluating the *standing wave ratio*, or SWR.

Standing Wave Ratio (SWR)

SWR: SWR is the ratio of the electrical voltage in the forward direction to your antenna with the electrical voltage of reflections in the reverse direction back toward the transmitter. This ratio of forward and reverse voltages indicates how well your antenna, feedline, and transmitter are electrically *matched* with one another. Voltage levels directly impact the power directed into an antenna system, and electrical mismatches create power reflections in the system. Optimally, all electrical power sent forward to the antenna will be radiated and zero power will be reflected, but such perfection is rarely achieved in an antenna system. Although SWR is a voltage ratio, it is most often calculated from measurements of power in each direction.

SWR may be calculated like this: $SWR = \dfrac{\sqrt{Fwd\ Pwr} + \sqrt{Refl\ Pwr}}{\sqrt{Fwd\ Pwr} - \sqrt{Refl\ Pwr}}$

Notice in this calculation that the very best condition, where all power is moving forward toward the antenna and zero power is reflected back, results in a 1/1 voltage ratio, or 1:1. As reflected power increases, the ratio begins to increase. For instance, imagine you measured in your transmission line a forward power of 81 watts and a reflected power of 9 watts. The SWR would be 2:1, calculated like this:

$$SWR = \frac{\sqrt{81}+\sqrt{9}}{\sqrt{81}-\sqrt{9}} = \frac{9+3}{9-3} = \frac{12}{6} = \frac{2}{1} \text{ or } 2:1$$

You can see from these calculations that a low SWR ratio like 1:1 is very good, meaning that little power is reflecting back from your antenna. And a high SWR ratio, say 4:1, is poor because it means quite a lot of transmitter power is being reflected back from the antenna instead of being radiated. Much of that power is being wasted.

In general terms, **SWR is a measure of how well a load is matched to a transmission line.** In most cases the load is an antenna. The word "matched" in this definition means *impedance* match.

Impedance: Impedance is a measure of the opposition to AC (alternating current) **current flow in a circuit.** You may think of it much like resistance to the flow of electrons back and forth in the circuit. (We'll cover this more in Section 8.1, *Electric Basics*.) **A unit of impedance is the ohm.**

Impedance Matching: In antennas and antenna feedlines, it is important to ensure that impedance is matched, or the same, throughout the system from the transceiver to the antenna. The antenna, the feedline, and the transmitter should all have equivalent characteristic impedance. When the system is matched like this, the reflected power will be minimized and the antenna radiation will be greatest. The antenna resonant frequency, in large part determined by antenna length, is one factor affecting an antenna's impedance.

Impedance Mismatch: If the components of your antenna system are not impedance matched, power will be reflected where impedance changes exist, and SWR will rise. This may occur due to any of the following reasons:
- Improperly trimmed antenna length for frequency
- Different, unmatched impedance feedline segments or connectors
- Loose antenna or feedline connectors
- Open or shorted feedline or antenna conductors
- Moisture in a coaxial cable feedline
- Metal conductors near the antenna affecting impedance
- Antenna height above ground insufficient
- Other factors

7.2 SWR

50 Ohm Impedance: Most modern amateur radios are engineered to use 50 Ohm impedance coaxial cable and connectors. **The impedance of the most coaxial cables used in amateur radio installations is 50 ohms.**

Antenna Tuner: The major function of an antenna tuner (antenna coupler) is that it matches the antenna system impedance to the transceiver's output impedance. This device commonly used with HF transceivers uses electronic networks to artificially adjust the apparent impedance of the antenna system (feedline, connectors, and antenna) as "sensed" by the transceiver. *What's the point?*

An antenna tuner can help boost the power sent to a poorly matched antenna system. **To protect the output amplifier transistors, most solid-state** (non-tube type) **transmitters reduce output power as SWR increases.** While the tuner cannot actually change the inherent impedance of the feedline and antenna, it can present the transceiver with an impedance near its designed value (usually 50 ohms) to avoid the automatic power reductions, and then safely handle the reflected power so it does not damage the amplifier transistors. More power will be radiated by the antenna simply because the transceiver power reduction is avoided, but the impedance mismatch and associated power reflections are not eliminated by the tuner.

Measuring SWR: There are a couple of different ways to measure SWR in your antenna system. Usually you will position a measuring device between the transceiver and feedline, or connect a measurement device to your feedline without connecting to your transceiver. Usually an antenna and feedline system SWR is not measured with an antenna tuner in the circuit.

SWR Meter: An external SWR meter is properly located in series with the feedline, between the transmitter and antenna. It will display the SWR by measuring forward and reflected power simultaneously. Usually a direct readout of SWR is provided. Frequently these meters will provide "cross needle readout" whereby forward power is indicated by one needle, reverse power by a second needle, and the crossing position of the two needles indicates SWR on a separately printed scale on the meter face. See Figure 7.7.

Directional Wattmeter: A directional wattmeter reads power in only one direction at a time, allowing for separate measurements of forward power and reflected power. A manual calculation of SWR may then be undertaken as described earlier in this section. **A directional wattmeter could be used to determine if a feedline and antenna are properly matched, if an SWR meter is not available.**

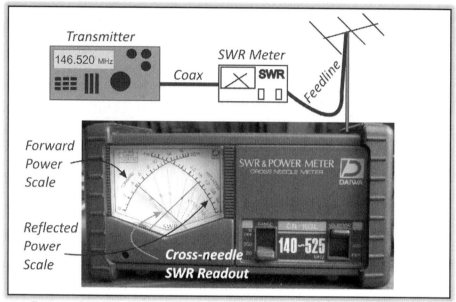

Figure 7.7: Typical Cross Needle SWR Meter and Connection

Antenna Analyzer: An antenna analyzer is an instrument that can be used to determine if an antenna is resonant at the desired operating frequency. The analyzer connects to the antenna system without the transceiver and sends variable frequency signals to the antenna system. These signals allow rapid measurement of SWR across a broad band of frequencies. Minimized SWR readings indicate resonant frequencies for the antenna system, and those frequencies are indicated on the analyzer display.

SWR Ratios: What SWR ratio should you expect from your antenna system? The ratio of 1:1 is best, as we've noted, since **a 1:1 reading on an SWR meter indicates a perfect impedance match between the antenna and the feedline,** and no reflections or loss of power. A well-constructed and well-trimmed antenna can usually achieve 1.5:1, or lower.

Here are some additional guidelines about SWR ratios:

2:1 is the approximate SWR value above which protection circuits in most solid-state transmitters begin to reduce transmitter power.

3:1 SWR is the value above which many lower capability antenna tuners will no longer be able to provide the transmitter a matching impedance. **4:1 SWR reading means an impedance mismatch.**

7.2 SWR

Generally, you should strive for low SWR in your antenna system. Most VHF and UHF commercially manufactured antennas will have pre-set SWR trims that are well below 2:1, and further trimming is unwarranted. If you choose to construct your own antennas, a challenge that many hams love to take on, you will surely want to thoroughly check and trim your creations.

Most wire dipoles applied to HF operations will require trimming of length to achieve good SWR values, since an antenna's resonant frequency is one significant factor affecting its impedance. Depending on design and environmental circumstances, it may be desirable to tweak the trim of a wire dipole such that the minimum SWR is in the portion of the amateur band where your license privileges apply.

For example, because the 10 meter band is quite wide, extending for 1.7 MHz of bandwidth, it is sometimes difficult to maintain low SWR across the entire band of frequencies with a single dipole design. However, the Technician privileges are in the lowest 0.5 MHz (500 kHz) of the 10m band. So, you may wish to trim the length of your 10m dipole to minimize SWR near the lower part of the 10m band, perhaps with an optimum frequency near 28.300 MHz. That way, it is likely that a single dipole will provide good SWR across the 500 kHz of Technician frequencies.

SWR Curves: An SWR curve of your antenna system performance may be plotted as is Figure 7.8 on the next page. You may measure SWR with one of the instruments discussed in this section and plot the results of SWR across a band of frequencies. A typical SWR curve will be U-shaped or V-shaped, and it will move up or down the frequency spectrum as you trim, or make changes in the length of the dipole antenna. Generally, trimming the dipole shorter will move the SWR curve to the right and match your antenna to higher frequencies. Lengthening the dipole has the opposite effect, moving the curve to the left and matching the antenna to lower frequencies. By properly trimming your dipole antenna you may center the best SWR performance in the portion of the band where you expect to operate your station the most.

SWR Bandwidth: The range of frequencies for which an antenna provides a desired value of SWR or lower is referred to as the SWR bandwidth. For example, in the "Middle Antenna Trim" of Figure 7.8 the "2:1 SWR bandwidth" is indicated to be approximately 28.020 MHz to 28.560 MHz. That is the band for which the SWR is 2:1 or lower. This is a 2:1 SWR bandwidth of 540 kHz (0.540 MHz). Harkening back to the loaded antenna topic of Section 7.1, the SWR bandwidth will become narrower as antenna loading is implemented to allow operation with substantially shortened antenna physical lengths.

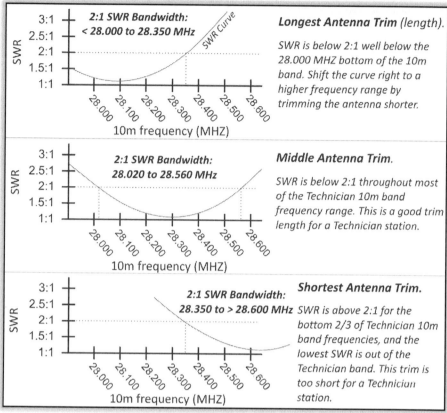

Figure 7.8: SWR Curves Changing with Antenna Trim Length

Now you can make sure you are casting efficiently and effectively with your electromagnetic fishing poles. You won't have to worry about SWR adjustment with most purchased HT vertical antennas or rubber ducks, nor with most VHF and UHF mobile antennas used on your car or in your home. But soon, when you start creating your own gleaming lovelies or purchasing a commercial wire dipole, you'll want to make sure you've done your due diligence with trimming, and drive that SWR as low as possible in the frequency ranges you plan to use.

Good luck with those future endeavors and with the fishing, but study the questions for **Section 7.2** first!

www.HamRadioSchool.com/tech_media

7.3 Coax and Connectors

> *Many a live wire would be a dead one except for his connections.* – Wilson Mizner

The SWR of your antenna system is a vital consideration for effective RF emissions. **It is important to have a low SWR when using a coaxial cable feedline to reduce signal losses.** In this section we will take a close look at the characteristics of coaxial cable because it is very commonly used by amateur operators, and we'll examine the connectors that *keep it live*.

Coaxial Cable: Coaxial cable is the most common feedline selected for amateur radio antenna systems because it is easy to use and requires few special installation considerations.

Physical Features: Coaxial cable, or *coax*, has a center conductor (typically copper) that may be solid or multi-stranded wire. The center conductor is surrounded by a tubular dielectric insulator, such as a plastic like polyethylene. A metallic shield or braid surrounds the insulator and center conductor, helping to reduce RF interference. **The use of shielded wire prevents coupling of unwanted signals to or from the wire.** A plastic or rubber jacket forms the exterior of the coax, protecting against moisture penetration and helping maintain the integrity of the cable.

Electrical Features: No RF feedline provides perfect, lossless transmission of power. Each type of coax has unique impedance and RF signal loss character-

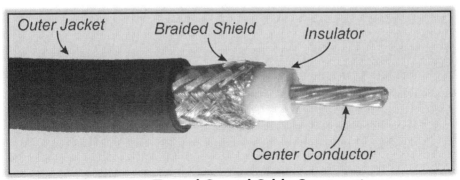

Figure 7.9: Typical Coaxial Cable Construction

istics. These electrical features are affected by the physical dimensions of the cable and the type of materials used. The diameter of the cable and the type of dielectric insulation material are two of the more common physical features of interest that impact both impedance value and loss characteristics.

Skin Effect: Radio frequency signals tend to travel on the outside surface of conductors, including the center conductor of coaxial cable. Megahertz range RF electric signals with frequencies much higher than standard alternating household current (a mere 60 Hz) do not penetrate deeply into the conducting material. This is referred to as *skin effect*. Since the electromagnetic fields tend to flow near and around the skin of the wire conductor, the materials immediately surrounding the conductor affect the electrical signal transmission speed and the signal loss. The diameter of the conductor also has an effect, since more surface area provides less impedance to electron flow.

Feedline Loss: Power lost in a feedline is converted into heat. Generally, as the frequency of a signal passing through coaxial cable is increased the loss increases. Generally, electrical loss will be greater with narrower gauge coaxial cable and loss will be less with larger cable. (Example: Larger diameter **RG-8 cable has less loss at a given frequency than RG-58 coax** that has a much narrower diameter.) **For VHF and UHF frequencies, air-insulated hard line has the lowest loss characteristics.** As the name implies, air insulated cable uses simply air between the center conductor wire and the surrounding shield.

Moisture Contamination is the most common cause for failure of coax cable.

1. **Air core or air insulated coax requires special techniques to prevent water absorption, as compared to more common foam or solid dielectric types.** Air core must be carefully sealed at connectors and other precautions taken, and **this is a disadvantage** of air core.

2. **Ultraviolet light can damage the outer jacket material allowing water to enter the cable, so the outer jacket should be resistant to ultraviolet light.** All types of coax can be damaged over time by the sun's ultraviolet rays.

3. **Coax connectors exposed to the weather should be sealed against water intrusion to prevent increased feedline loss.**

7.3 Coax & Connectors

Connectors for coaxial cable have unique form factors and sizes that are intended for use with specific cable diameters and for various frequency applications.

PL-259 Connector is commonly used at HF frequencies. It imposes some significant signal loss at higher frequencies, particularly in the UHF range. Still, this is one of the most commonly used connectors for all applications. The female matching connector to the PL-259 is designated the SO-239 connector.

[T9B07]

Type N-Connector is most suitable for frequencies above 400 MHz. The N-connector is commonly used for UHF applications and many operators prefer their lower loss characteristics for VHF frequencies as well.

[T9B06]

SMA Connector is a small diameter coax connector that has become very popular for HT radio use in recent years. The SMA connector offers good performance at VHF and UHF frequencies.

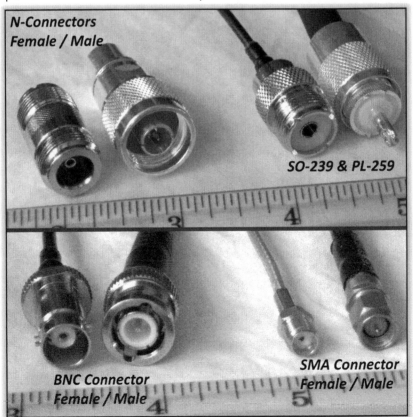

Figure 7.10: Common Coaxial Cable Connector Types

BNC Connector is a common connector on HT radios, particularly older models. It is still widely used, it is a sturdy connector option for smaller diameter coax, and it offers good performance for VHF and UHF frequencies.

Care and Maintenance: A loose connection in an antenna or feedline, usually at a connector, **can cause erratic changes in SWR readings.** Carefully mount connectors to coax and properly solder the connections for both center conductor and shield. Seal connectors well if they will be exposed to the weather. Check the condition of your coax outer jacket for cracks, stiffness, or other indications that moisture may be able to penetrate.

Be aware that there are many different varieties of coaxial cable suitable for amateur radio use. The best cable to use often depends upon the specific application, the length of the cable run, and your budget. Before you design an antenna system for your ham shack, take some time to investigate the signal loss values and costs of various feedline options, as well as factors such as flexibility and power handling capacity.

Prefabricated coaxial cables can be purchased from vendors in lengths that you specify, or in standard precut lengths, and with or without connectors of your choosing attached and soldered into place. You may prefer to learn how to attach and solder connectors yourself, saving dollars and taking pride in a more hand-crafted system with which you will have familiarity for maintenance and repair purposes.

There are other types of feedlines with different characteristics. Flat twin lead cable and "ladder line" is quite popular and used for many applications. Twin lead offers no shielding like coax, so it is more susceptible to electronic and RF noise interference than coax, but its low loss electrical characteristics are very desirable for some types of antenna applications.

I hope that you can keep your radio's wires live with solid connections using what you've learned in this section. But before you run out to run cable to your bristling antenna farm, try the questions for **Section 7.3**. I think you'll find them rather easy now!

www.HamRadioSchool.com/tech_media

8.0 It's Electric!

> **❝** *Electricity is really just organized lightning. – George Carlin*

The little slivers of lightning within your radio are indeed highly organized, performing many precision tasks! Understanding of the organization and the nature of the radio's electrical tasks starts with the basic characteristics of organized lightning. Let's strike!

In this chapter we will first examine the basic characteristic of electricity in Section 8.1 and introduce a water flow model that will help us think about how electricity works. Voltage, current, resistance, and the units of measurement for each are simply defined and explained in terms that are almost exactly like water flowing in pipes.

In Section 8.2 we will learn two fundamental laws of electricity: Ohm's Law and the Power Law. These laws describe the basic behaviors of electricity. We will expand the water flow model and use some easy-to-remember tools for calculating electrical values with these laws. We will also introduce the decibel and describe how power relationships are defined using the decibel as a measure of comparison between power values.

Section 8.3 discusses equipment and proper methods for making basic electrical measurements, again taking advantage of the water flow model for ease of understanding. We will also learn a simple method of shifting electrical numerical values back-and-forth between all those confusing math prefixes, like milli-, micro-, mega-, and others. You'll be able to keep all those prefixes straight after Section 8.3 and shove pesky decimals around with great confidence!

HamRadioSchool.com

8.1 It's Electric! Electric Basics

Electricity in a Circuit is much like water flowing in plumbing. Instead of water molecules flowing in a pipe, electricity is electrons flowing in a conductor such as a wire. The basic measures of electricity can be likened to characteristics of water.

Voltage (E) is the electrical term for the electromotive force (EMF) that causes electrons to flow. *Voltage is like water pressure* in plumbing. High pressure pushes water current strongly through pipes; high voltage pushes electrons strongly through electrical conductors like copper wire.

Volt (v): The unit of electromotive force, a measure of the "electron pressure." For instance, **a mobile transceiver typically requires about 12 volts to operate.**

Battery: A battery may be thought of as the water pump causing the electron pressure and inducing a flow of current, and higher voltage batteries provide higher pressure (voltage) just like a stronger water pump.

Current (I) is the name for the flow of electrons in an electric circuit, just as water current is the flow of water particles through a pipe or down a river.

Ampere (A): The basic unit of electrical current is the Ampere, or Amp (A). **Electrical current is measured in units of Amperes.**

Direct Current (DC): Current that flows in only one direction in a circuit. Direct current is typical of current flowing from a battery in which the electrons consistently move in one direction through a closed circuit.

Alternating Current (AC): Current that reverses direction on a regular basis in a circuit. The number of times per second that AC reverses direction is its frequency, in units of hertz. Alternating current is typical of that from a household wall outlet. In the US, standard AC frequency is 60 hertz. In RF oscillators, alternating current for the production of radio signals will reverse direction many millions of times

8.1 Electric Basics

each second to produce megahertz range frequencies of HF, VHF, UHF, and higher.

Conductors / Insulators: A good electrical conductor, such as copper, allows electrons to flow readily through it. **A good electrical insulator, such as glass,** allows no flow of electrons through it. Most electronic circuits use a combination of conductors, insulators, and *semi-conductors* (partially conducting materials whose conductivity may be changed in a controlled way).

Resistance (R) is the opposition to the flow of direct current (DC) in a circuit. You may think of resistance as a constriction or partial blockage in a water pipe and also as a device that forces the water to do work with the current, such as a water wheel driving a mill.

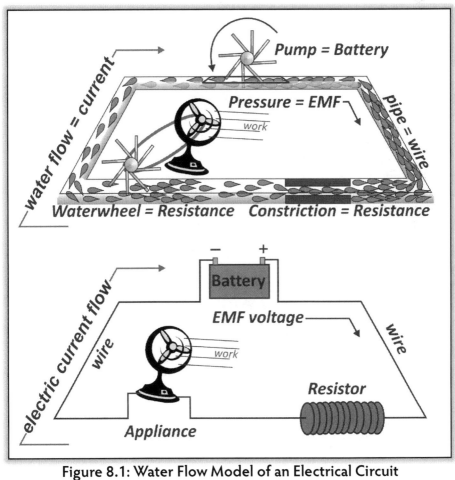

Figure 8.1: Water Flow Model of an Electrical Circuit

Ohm (Ω): The unit of resistance (and impedance).

Appliances: All electrical appliances, such as light bulbs, heating elements, motors, or RF transmitters offer electrical resistance in the course of performing some work, just as the waterwheel offers resistance to water flow while doing its mechanical work.

Resistor: An electronic component that opposes the flow of electrical current through it, reducing the current flow (given a constant voltage) and transforming electrical energy from the resisted current into waste heat. A resistor is like a narrowing of the water pipe, or an obstacle in the pipe, constricting the allowable flow of current.

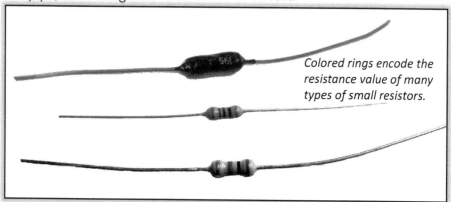

Colored rings encode the resistance value of many types of small resistors.

Figure 8.2: Example Resistors

Impedance: A measure of the opposition to the flow of alternating current (AC) in a circuit, expressed in **units of ohms.** Similar to resistance, impedance may be thought of as a blockage in the water pipe, or a device on which work is done by the alternating current. Since many RF circuits, such as the circuit comprised of your transmitter, feedline, and antenna, utilize alternating current at HF, VHF, and UHF frequencies, impedance has a significant impact on the operation of these circuits. (See Section 7.2, *SWR*.) However, as you will learn as your electronics studies progress, impedance is more complex than simple resistance, comprised of multiple unique effects of AC electronic components.

Are you getting a jolt from this organized lightning? Electricity in circuits is really more like water in pipes than wild flying bolts. More fun with electron flow is coming next, but try the **_Section 8.1_** questions first. You may be *shocked* by how much you've already learned!

www.HamRadioSchool.com/tech_media

8.2 Ohm's Law and Power Law

It's Electric!

> **"** *Ohm found that the results could be summed up in such a simple law that he who runs may read it, and a schoolboy now can predict what Faraday then could only guess at roughly.* – Oliver Heaviside

Gee, you can read it even while running by. Must be pretty simple! And it really is. Two fundamental laws of electricity are key to understanding many aspects of your radio, from the way electronic circuits work to determining the capacity needed from your power supply or batteries. Ohm's Law defines a simple relationship among EMF (voltage), current, and resistance. The Power Law defines a relationship among electrical power, current, and EMF (voltage). If you can multiply and divide you are overqualified to apply these two laws.

Ohm's Law: E = I x R   Used to calculate voltage in a circuit.

E is electromotive force (EMF), in volts.
I is current, in amps.
R is resistance, in Ohms.

With some very simple algebra you obtain the alternate forms of this relationship:

I = E ÷ R   and   **R = E ÷ I**

[T5D05] [T5D06] [T5D07] [T5D08]
[T5D09] [T5D10] [T5D11] [T5D12]
[T5D02] [T5D01] [T5D03]

So, if you know any two of these quantities you can easily calculate the third. There are several questions in the Technician question pool about this relationship. Here is an easy visual tool to help you keep Ohm's Law straight and guarantee you answer the questions correctly:

Draw a capital 'T' inside a triangle to make three divisions and place the letters E, I, and R inside, like this. When an exam question asks for the value of one of these quantities, either

EMF, current, or resistance, it will always provide the other two quantities you need.

To use the Ohm's Law Triangle, cover the quantity being asked for and examine the two remaining ones. If the two remaining quantities are side-by-side, multiply them together for the answer. If the two quantities are one-above-the-other, divide the top one by the bottom one to get the answer. Here are a couple of examples right from the question pool.

Q. What is the resistance of a circuit in which a current of 3 amperes flows through a resistor connected to 90 volts?

    A. 3 ohms   C. 93 ohms
    B. 30 ohms   D. 270 ohms

R (resistance) is asked for, so cover R in the triangle. Note that E (volts) and I (current in amperes) remain and are one-over-the-other, E / I. Divide:

    90 v ÷ 3 amps = **30 ohms**

The correct answer is 'B.'

Q. What is the voltage across a 10-ohm resistor if a current of 2 amperes flows through it?

    A. 8 volts   C. 12 volts
    B. 0.2 volts D. 20 volts

Voltage (v) is asked for, so cover the E. Note that I (current in amps) and R (resistance in ohms) remains, and they are side-by-side. Multiply:

    2 amps x 10 ohms = **20 volts**

The correct answer is 'D.'

The same method applies for all Ohm's Law questions. If current is asked for, cover the I and divide: E ÷ R … That's 'volts ÷ ohms' to get current in amperes. Don't let variations in question wording trick you! Practice.

Ohm's Law Water Analogy: Think about Ohm's Law with the water analogy that we introduced in the last section. Remember that EMF (voltage) is like

8.2 Ohm's Law & Power Law

the water pressure pushing water through the plumbing pipes, while current (amperes) is like the quantity of water that flows through the pipes, perhaps in gallons per minute. Resistance (ohms) is like the diameter of the pipe, or the reduced room to flow if obstacles are in the pipe.

One expression of Ohm's Law is: I = E ÷ R. So the amount of water flowing (water current) is equal to the water pressure divided by the pipe resistance.

> If the water pressure is high, the amount of flow is high.
> If the water pressure is low, the amount of flow is low.
> If the pipe is wide open with tiny resistance, current is high.
> If the pipe is narrow and clogged, current is low.

This makes sense to anyone who has ever tried to take a shower while the dishwasher is running, the clothes washer is filling, and the kids are outside with the hose washing the dog. The water pressure is very low, so your shower is a dribble. But when the dishes and the dog are clean and the clothes washer completes its cycle, you get a blast of water with the increased pressure... Unless, of course, the corrosion in the pipes has plugged up the shower head offering high resistance. In that case you still get only a little water out. Bad day for a shower.

The Power Law is just as easy to use as Ohm's Law, and there is a handy visual tool for it, and a water analogy, too! Let's go there.

Power: the rate at which electrical energy is used. Electrical power is measured in units of watts.

Power Law: P = I x E   Used to calculate power in a DC circuit.

T5A10 T5A02 T5C08 T5C10

> P is power, in watts.
> I is current, in amps.
> E is electromotive force (EMF), in volts.

Just as with Ohm's Law, you can rearrange the relationship to be:

> E = P ÷ I   and   I = P ÷ E

Again like Ohm's Law, if you know any two of these quantities you can easily calculate the third. There are a few questions in the Technician question pool about this relationship also, and you can use the same kind of visual tool to remember the relationships:

Draw the same triangle form with divisions, but place the letters P, I, and E inside this time, with P up top. When an exam question asks for the value of one of these quantities, either power, current, or EMF, it will always provide the other two quantities you need.

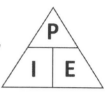

The same technique applies for using the Power Triangle: Cover the quantity being asked for, then multiply or divide the remaining two quantities depending on their position. If they're side-by-side, multiply. If one is over the other, divide the top by the bottom value. A couple of examples from the question pool never hurt…

Q. How much power is being used in a circuit when the applied voltage is 13.8 volts DC and the current is 10 amperes?

    A. 138 watts   **C. 23.8 watts**
    B. 0.7 watts   **D. 3.8 watts**

Power is asked for, so cover P, leaving I x E:
10 amps x 13.8v = **138 watts**

The correct answer is 'A.'

Q. How many amperes are flowing in a circuit when the applied voltage is 12 volts DC and the load is 120 watts?

    A. 0.1 amperes   **C. 12 amperes**
    B. 10 amperes   **D. 132 amperes**

Amperes is asked for, the unit of current (I).
Cover the I and divide P / E.
120 watts ÷ 12v = **10 amperes**

The correct answer is 'B.'

Power Water Analogy: The Power Law can be easily comprehended with a water analogy also. Power is a measure of how much work can be done over time by the electricity, or the water. The P = I x E relationship says that power is the result of multiplying the amount of water (current, I) by the water pressure (voltage, E).

8.2 Ohm's Law & Power Law

A large volume of water (high current) can do a lot of work even if it is under low pressure (low voltage). Imagine an ocean wave slowly washing past you, shoving you back to shore, perhaps landing you on your bottom. The ocean current is not under high pressure, but it can sure do a lot of work pushing you around because the current is huge! Similarly, a lot of electrical current, such as that from a heavy duty automobile starting battery, can do a lot of work under the relatively low EMF of 12 volts.

On the other hand, imagine a fire hose blasting into your chest with a quick burst, putting you down on the ground a few feet backward, just like that ocean wave. Ouch! That's not a lot of water compared to the big wave, but it is under a lot of pressure, so it can do the same work as the wave. High voltage with relatively few electrons of current moving can have a big effect. Shuffle your rubber slippers across the carpet during a dry winter day then reach out for a grounded light switch or metal doorknob. ZAP! That static discharge may result from an EMF of several thousand volts, but the electrical current is tiny. It still will get your attention!

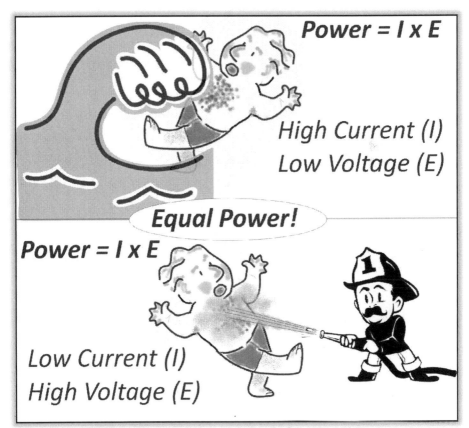

Figure 8.3: A Water Analogy for Power Law

Power Changes in decibels: A common calculation in RF applications involves determining power change, such as the change in the power of a signal received from another station. An indication of this is provided on a radio's signal strength meter, or "S-meter." As a rule of thumb, one unit of change on an S-meter is approximately 6 *decibels* of power change.

Uh… so what's a decibel?

Decibel (dB): A fractional logarithmic unit indicating a ratio of power or intensity relative to a reference level. A logarithmic scale for power is convenient because power values vary over a very wide range, and a logarithmic scale allows for easy comparisons, or ratios, across such a broad range.

A logarithmic scale means that each equally spaced unit on the scale changes in absolute measure by a factor of 10, such as the lower scale of Figure 8.4. The bel is a seldom used logarithmic ratio unit equating to a 10:1 ratio. Each increasing unit on the logarithmic scale equates to an increase of 1 bel.

"Deci" means 1/10, or 0.1. The decibel is 1/10 of a bel. So 10 decibels represents one bel, or one logarithmic unit of change, or a comparison ratio of 10:1 between two power values. This can be a little confusing if it has been a while since high school math, so here are two simple of rules of thumb that you can use to interpret power changes in decibels:

1. A doubling or halving of power (watts) is equal to a change of approximately 3 decibels. [3 dB = 2x, or 2:1 ratio]
2. A 10x change of power (watts) is equal to a change of 10 decibels. [10 dB = 10x, or a 10:1 ratio]

A couple of exam pool questions will help drive home how to use these rules of thumb.

Q. What is the approximate amount of change, measured in decibels (dB), of a power increase from 5 watts to 10 watts?

    A. 2 dB   **C. 5 dB**
    B. 3 dB   **D. 10 dB**

Check decibel rule #1: Power going from 5 watts to 10 watts is a doubling of power. A doubling of power is an increase of **3 dB**. The correct answer is 'B'. Remember, it is the comparison, or the ratio of the two values that counts in determining decibels, and not any absolute numerical value!

8.2 Ohm's Law & Power Law

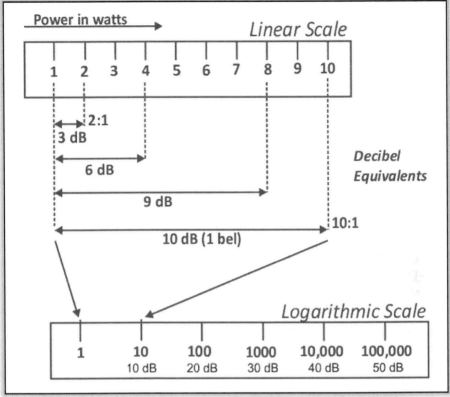

Figure 8.4: Relationship of Linear Scale to Logarithmic Scale

Q. What is the approximate amount of change, measured in decibels (dB), of a power decrease from 12 watts to 3 watts?

A. -1 dB   C. -6 dB
B. -3 dB   D. -9 dB

This one is a little trickier. Again, apply decibel rule #1 like this: A halving of 12 watts is 6 watts; that's one 3 dB reduction, or -3 dB. A halving of 6 watts is 3 watts; that's another -3 dB change. The total decibel reduction from 12 watts to 3 watts is two "halving" steps, or two changes of -3 dB each, or **-6 dB** total change. The correct answer is 'C.'

Q. What is the amount of change, measured in decibels (dB), of a power increase from 20 watts to 200 watts?

A. 10 dB   C. 18 dB
B. 12 dB   D. 28 dB

Check decibel rule #2: Power changing from 20 to 200 watts is a factor of 10 increase (20 watts x 10 = 200 watts). That is a **10 dB** increase. The correct answer is 'A.'

Like I said, if you can multiply and divide numbers you are overqualified to apply Ohm's Law and the Power Law as a ham radio operator. Figuring out decibel logarithmic power changes isn't much tougher.

You can also apply the principles of these laws in making decisions about your ham shack set-up. For example, let's apply Ohm's Law to a power supply for a base station transceiver. **Why should wiring between the power source and radio be heavy-gauge wire and kept as short as possible?**

Suppose your lengthy power cable from the DC supply to the transceiver has a total resistance of 0.1 ohm, and suppose you are drawing 20 amps of current with your transceiver during transmit times. By Ohm's Law the EMF voltage will drop by 2.0 volts across that power cable (E = I x R), and that can impact the operation of your transceiver. That would drop your power supply voltage from 13.8 volts to 11.8 volts! **Keep the wire as short as possible to avoid voltage falling below that needed for proper operation.**

Using the Power Law (P = I x E) you can calculate the electrical current a transceiver will need from a power supply and thereby ensure you use a proper capacity supply. **You must consider the following to determine the minimum current capacity needed for a transceiver power supply:**

- Efficiency of the transmitter at full power
- Receiver and control circuit power
- Power supply regulation and heat dissipation

If the transmitter is only 50% efficient, you'll need 100W of electrical power to transmit 50W of RF signal! The receiver and control circuits will require additional power beyond that. And the supply's regulation and heat dissipation capabilities may impact the power it can provide. After examining the total power needs, Power Law can tell you the current capacity needed (I = P ÷ E).

One more section to go regarding things electrical! First, go *run* by the **Section 8.2** question pool for this section. *Ohm my!* You're developing some *powerful* number skills now!

www.HamRadioSchool.com/tech_media

8.3 Making Electrical Measurements

> *Benjamin Franklin may have discovered electricity, but it was the man who invented the meter who made the money.* – Earl Wilson

If you are ever going to apply any of the electrical knowledge you have accumulated so far, you should be able to properly measure electricity. It's a good skill to have that will come in handy in many situations. We can use the water analogy of electricity to reason out how to make some electrical measurements, and we can use the goofy little rhyme learned back in the Section 4.1, *Wavelength and Frequency*, to switch between different magnitudes and prefixes used with electrical measures.

First, let's take a look at the various types of instruments used to measure the basic electrical characteristics we have learned about.

Instruments: Each of the electrical quantities in Ohm's Law – EMF (in volts), current (in amperes), and resistance (in ohms) – can be measured with a unique electrical instrument.

Voltmeter: An instrument used to measure electrical potential or electromotive force is a voltmeter. Using the water analogy, we can see that **the correct way to connect a voltmeter to a circuit is in parallel with the circuit.** Think of the voltmeter allowing just a little of the water from a high pressure location to squirt through the measuring device and flow out to a lower pressure position in the circuit, as in Figure 8.5 on the next page. If there is a water pressure difference between the 'inflow' location and the 'outflow' location, the water will surge through the measuring device and cause it to register the pressure difference, or in this case, the electrical potential difference or EMF. **Take precaution when measuring high voltages that the voltmeter and leads are rated for use at the voltages to be measured,** or the voltmeter may be damaged and the leads may overheat!

Ammeter: An instrument used to measure electrical current is an ammeter. Again, the water analogy shows the correct connection technique:

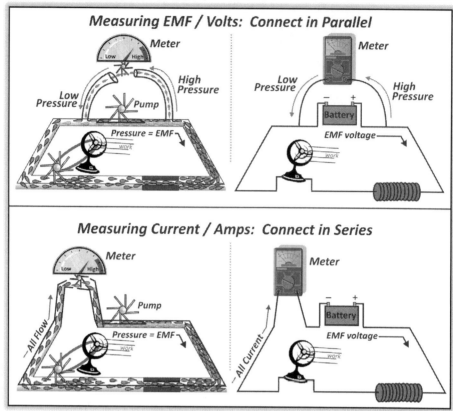

Figure 8.5: Measuring EMF / Volts vs. Current / Amps

T7D03 **A simple ammeter is usually connected to a circuit in series with the circuit.** Since you are measuring current, or the amount of water that is flowing, you have to let all the water flow through the measuring device or you will miss some of it! So, connect in series such that all the flowing electrons are routed through the ammeter.

T7D05 Ohmmeter: **An instrument used to measure resistance is an ohmmeter.** An ohmmeter is usually connected across the resistive element, whether a simple resistor or an appliance being driven within the circuit. You may think of the ohmmeter as squirting a little water of a specific pressure (voltage) through the resistive element and measuring how much current gets through it. Then, using Ohm's Law where $R = E \div I$, resistance in ohms is calculated from the known voltage (E) and the measured current (I). (Note: An ohmmeter may also use the reverse technique of a known input current and measured voltage drop to compute resistance.)

T7D11 Ohmmeter Precautions: You may have already realized from that last paragraph that **when measuring circuit resistance with an ohmmeter you**

8.3 Making Electrical Measurements

should take precaution to ensure that the circuit is not powered. This makes sense because the ohmmeter relies upon its own known input voltage for accurate resistance measurement. If there is another voltage applied to the circuit the measurement will be erroneous.

The situation above can also happen if electric charge is stored in the circuit within a component called a *capacitor*. We will learn more about capacitors in the next section, but think of it like a small battery that can temporarily store electrical energy, and when the circuit is completed it discharges the current into the circuit. **If an ohmmeter is connected across a circuit and initially indicates a low resistance and then shows increasing resistance with time, what is probably happening is that the circuit contains a large capacitor** that is discharging through the ohmmeter. The extra current and voltage of the capacitor fools the ohmmeter into thinking its own provided current is flowing quite freely with very low resistance, and as the capacitor's charge is exhausted the ohmmeter corrects to the higher resistance reading that results from only its own stable current through the resistor.

Multimeter: A common instrument available at any hardware store is the *multimeter*. As the name implies, it provides the capability of measuring multiple electrical characteristics. **A multimeter is commonly used to make measurements of voltage and resistance,** as well as current (amperage).

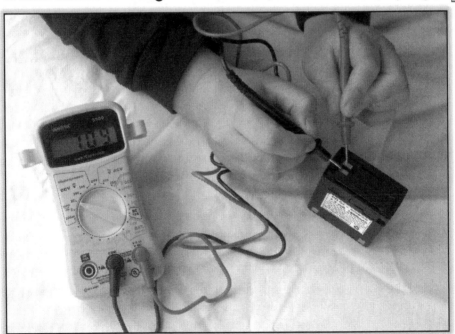

Figure 8.6: Measuring Radio Battery Voltage with a Multimeter

A multimeter allows the user to select the type of measurement to be made, usually with a simple dial or push-button control. But some caution is warranted when using a multimeter to make sure you have selected the correct measurement setting for the type of measurement you intend to make. **A multimeter might be damaged by attempting to measure voltage when using the resistance setting.** This scenario might allow high current to flow through sensitive circuits in the multimeter that are designed to measure only the small, instrument-provided currents for resistance measuring, just as with an ohmmeter. Putting higher voltage pressure behind those circuits and pushing a lot of current through them may result in an electronic component burning out!

Units and Prefixes: Just as with the broad range of radio frequencies, the breadth of electrical measurement magnitudes require that we use prefixes for convenience to denote thousands, millions, or billions of units, or on the smaller side of one, thousandths, millionths, billionths, or even trillionths of units. As noted at the start of this section, that extremely cheesy little rhyme can help us here, too:

From hefty to slight, dot moves right. From slight to hefty, dot's a lefty.

Now learn prefixes from hefty to slight, left to right,
And slather rhyming cheeses on the Tech pool teases!
Sling that techno-speak like a savvy geek,
And measure electricity with simplicity!

Uh, geez, sorry, that just slipped out. It won't happen again. I promise. I have no future as a hip-hop rap star, huh?

Less than One: Where values get smaller than one, the prefixes and their meanings are as follows, slight (smaller) to hefty (larger):

pico	one trillionth	1/1,000,000,000,000	0.000000000001
nano	one billionth	1/1,000,000,000	0.000000001
micro	**one millionth**	1/1,000,000	0.000001
milli	one thousandth	1/1,000	0.001
	unity		1

8.3 Making Electrical Measurements

More than One: Where values get big, you will recognize these prefixes and their meanings from previous sections. Continuing in slight to hefty sequence, picking up at unity value (1):

	unity	1
kilo	**one thousand**	1,000
mega	one million	1,000,000
giga	one billion	1,000,000,000

That's about as far as we need to go, as these are the most common prefixes you will encounter in amateur radio. Be aware, there are more, greater and smaller.

You may want to create your own mnemonic phrase to remember this sequence, slight to hefty, as presented above. Or, you can use my *assassin shopping* mnemonic, with apology for the violent imagery an inelegance:

Pick from **Nan, Mic,** or **Milli, One** to **Kill Meg** & **Gigi.**

I'm sure you will pick right up on the sequence represented as pico-nano-micro-milli-one-kilo-mega-giga. This includes unity, or 1, to help keep straight that important positional relationship. However, I really don't advocate violence against anyone named Meg or Gigi.

Now, from Pick-to-Gigi, let's slather some of that rhyming cheese and solve a few examples directly from the Technician question pool.

Q. How many milliamperes is 1.5 amperes?
 A. 15 milliamperes   **C. 1500 milliamperes**
 B. 150 milliamperes   **D. 15,000 milliamperes**

Always place the known quantity on the left before slathering cheese, just to keep your brain straight. Like this: *1.5 amperes = ? milliamperes*

Ampere is the unity value 1, and milliamperes is smaller (slighter) than 1. Just like before, we move the decimal point in the proper direction 3 places for each prefix step. There is only one step between unity (1) ampere and milli-ampere (one thousandth). That's from 'One' to 'Milli.'

You may now apply the cheese:
 From hefty to slight, dot moves right! Right 3 places, like this:
  1.5 amperes = 1,500 milliamperes
  The correct answer is 'C.'

Q. How many microfarads are equal to 1,000,000 picofarads?
A. 0.001 microfarads   C. 1000 microfarads
B. 1 microfarad   D. 1,000,000,000 microfarads

Again, the known quantity to the left, then determine the number of prefix steps and size relationship, and last the glorious cheese:

1,000,000 picofarads = ? microfarads
Pico to micro is 2 prefix steps, or 6 places, from smaller to larger.
From slight to hefty, dot's a lefty! (Move decimal left 6 places.)
1,000,000 picofarads = 1 microfarad   Answer 'B' is correct.

One more, just for fun:

Q. If an ammeter calibrated in amperes is used to measure a 3000-milliampere current, what reading would it show?
A. 0.003 amperes   C. 3 amperes
B. 0.3 amperes   D. 3,000,000 amperes

Don't let the framing of the question trick you. It is a basic conversion. Follow the same procedure, starting with the known quantity:

3,000 milliamperes = ? amperes
Milli to unity (1) is one prefix step, smaller to larger.
From slight to hefty, dot's a lefty!
3,000 milliamperes = 3 amperes.   'C' is correct.

Almost done… Just one last thing… Kind of a leftover electrical topic…

Battery Types: Before we depart from our electrical discussion, we must address a few points about batteries. Virtually every HT radio uses batteries, and most ham radios can be operated on battery power. This is one of the advantages of ham radio for emergency preparedness, after all. We don't need no stinkin' power grid!

Carbon-Zinc: *Carbon-zinc* and the closely related *alkaline* batteries are what you probably think of as just plain old generic batteries – nothing special, and they drain pretty quickly. Carbon-zinc is an older battery technology now infrequently utilized in amateur radio. **Carbon-zinc batteries are not rechargeable,** nor are their alkaline cousins.

8.3 Making Electrical Measurements

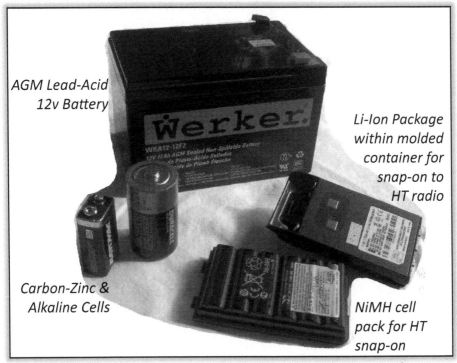

Figure 8.7: Various Battery Types Used in Amateur Radio

Nickel-Metal Hydride (NiMH): These batteries and the older, similar nickel-cadmium (NiCad) cells **are rechargeable batteries** still in common use with many amateur radios. Most NiMH batteries are sealed packages containing multiple individual cells. They are well suited for amateur radio use because they can provide high surge currents for transmitting power.

Lithium-Ion: *Lithium-ion* cells are becoming very popular due to their high charge densities, or ability to store larger amounts of energy than other battery types. This allows them to be smaller and lighter than other cell types for the same capacity or time of use. Many modern HT radios employ *Li-ion* batteries. **Lithium-Ion batteries are rechargeable.**

Lead-Acid: Although very old technology, **lead-acid is a rechargeable battery type** still commonly used. Variations known as '*gel cells*' or *AGM* (absorbent glass mat) are frequently used in amateur radio for portable operations, for emergency backup power, or as a primary power source. Lead-acid cells provide excellent surge currents for transmitting power. They are also very cost effective, but lead-acid batteries have a relatively low energy-to-weight ratio; they're heavy, but they are reliable.

T6A10

The *Absorbent Glass Mat* (AGM) battery holds the electrolyte in glass matting rather than a flowing liquid like common lead-acid cells. This helps make the cells safer if damaged, less prone to leakage or spilling, and essentially maintenance free except for charging. AGM batteries are more expensive than liquid electrolytic lead-acid cells, and they require "smart charger" technology to avoid overcharging that will cause the AGM cell to fail prematurely. The smart charger senses the battery charge level and adjusts the charging current to an optimized profile over the charge time, ending with a maintenance "trickle charge" to keep the battery at maximum charge state without damaging it.

Time now to measure your electrical success. Work through the questions for **Section 8.3** and then come back for some electronic wonderment in the next section. If you have never understood what those little components in your electronic devices actually do and how they work, we are going to begin to absolve you of that innocence next!

www.HamRadioSchool.com/tech_media

Bonus Question from the Tech Pool:

T5B05

Q. Which of the following is equal to 500 milliwatts?
    A. 0.02 watts   **C. 5 watts**
    B. 0.5 watts   **D. 50 watts**

    500 milliwatts = ? watts
    Dot moves 3 places left. (Going slight to hefty one step.)
    Correct answer is **0.5 watts** (B).

9.0 Hamtronics

> *When I was a teenager in the late 30's and early 40's, electronics wasn't a word. You were interested in radio if you were interested in electronics.* – Ken Olson

Electronics remain at the heart of radio today. Many radio amateurs enjoy wielding a hot soldering iron to piece together electronic components on a printed circuit board. One of the FCC's stated purposes in Part 97 for establishing the Amateur Radio Service is to expand the reservoir of trained electronics experts [Part 97.1(d)]. Although it isn't absolutely necessary for daily radio operations to comprehend the incredible manipulation of electrons taking place in the palm of your hand, it is good to be familiar with the basics of electronics for troubleshooting, for safety, and simply for expanding your understanding of radio.

And then there is the Technician question pool in which about 12% of the 420+ questions relate to electronics and electronic concepts. You will typically encounter about four electronics questions on your exam, so let's get at this topic with gusto! With the knowledge you have accumulated in the last few sections it will be a piece of cake.

In Section 9.1 we will discuss basic electronics concepts and learn the names, symbols, and elementary functions of some of the most common electronic components such as *resistors, capacitors,* and *diodes*. We will examine the effect that each of these components has on the flow of electrons in a circuit.

In Section 9.2 we will expand the discussion to a special electronic component called the *transistor,* and we will consider a couple of basic electronic circuits constructed from the various components learned in Section 9.1. We will also cover a couple of basics about soldering these components together to form circuits.

9.1 Hamtronics Electronic Basics

The Big Picture: Radio electronics are comprised of individual electronic components linked together to form complex circuits in which electron flow is manipulated. Each component is precision manufactured with specialized materials, most commonly *semiconductors*, and each component serves a unique function in the manipulation of voltage, current, resistance, impedance, and other electrical waveform characteristics.

[16D09] **A device that combines several semiconductors and other components into one package is called an integrated circuit** (IC). An integrated circuit may perform a wide variety of tasks, including transmitting and receiving radio signals.

Semiconductor: One of several types of material with electrical conductivity in between that of a conductor and that of an insulator. These materials are used to create a variety of electronic components such as transistors, diodes, resistors, and others. Sometimes the term 'semiconductor' is used to refer generally to the class of electronic components made from these materials, as in the highlighted text above.

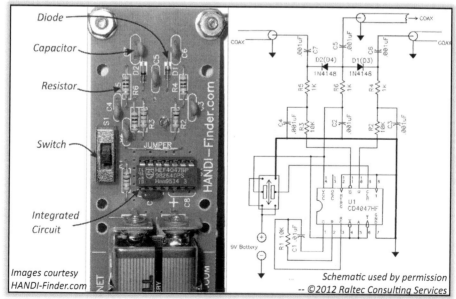

Figure 9.1: Printed Circuit Board with IC and Schematic Diagram

9.1 Electronic Basics

Schematic: An electrical wiring diagram that uses standard component symbols is a schematic. The symbols on an electrical schematic represent electrical components. Electrical schematics accurately represent only the way components are interconnected. The connecting wire lengths shown in a schematic diagram are not usually accurate, and the symbols do not depict a true physical appearance of the electronic components.

Electronic Components manipulate the flow of electrons, or current, in a circuit as well as the EMF or voltage across portions of the circuit. Some electrical components are combined in specific ways to change AC current to DC current, to produce radio frequency AC current oscillations, to alter the amplitude, frequency, or phase of an RF signal, and to perform other functions that make radio communications possible. Some electrical components simply emit light and serve as a visual indicator on your radio, such as a "Power On" light. Electronic components include *resistors, capacitors, inductors, diodes* and more! Let's take a closer look at some of these.

Resistor: An electrical component that opposes the flow of current in a DC circuit is a resistor. Given a constant voltage, resistors reduce current flow in accordance with Ohm's Law (Section 8.2).

Potentiometer or Variable Resistor: An electronic component in which the amount of resistance it provides in a circuit may be varied across a specified range of values. The change in the value of a potentiometer is often accomplished by physically manipulating a control. **A potentiometer is often used as an adjustable volume control** on a radio, for instance. **A potentiometer controls resistance.**

Symbols: The symbol for a simple resistor is a zig-zag line. An arrow added to the zig-zag line and pointing into it is the symbol for a variable resistor.

Resistor   *Variable Resistor*

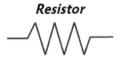 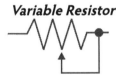

Capacitor: An electrical component that stores energy in an electric field is a capacitor. A capacitor consists of two or more conductive surfaces separated by an insulator. The ability to store energy in an electric field is called capacitance, and the basic unit of capacitance is the farad.

Symbols: The symbol for a capacitor is two lines separated a short distance and oriented perpendicular to the circuit wiring connections. Usually, but not always, one of the lines is curved slightly. A variable capacitor with which capacitance may be adjusted to different values will typically have an arrow depicted angled over the capacitor symbol.

Capacitor   *Variable Capacitor*

Structure and Behavior: A capacitor may consist of metal foils separated by a layer of insulating film. When a voltage is applied across the conducting surfaces a static electric field builds up across the insulating layer and causes a positive charge to collect on one conductor and a negative charge on the other conductor. A capacitor tends to oppose DC currents because it is effectively a gap or opening in the circuit, and DC current will cross the insulated gap only if the charge builds up and the electric potential across the gap is great enough to cause a 'jump' of charge. Capacitors tend to offer reduced opposition to AC currents since the static electric charges it creates on each conductor can build and drain repeatedly as the current reverses direction each cycle.

Inductor: An electrical component that stores energy in a magnetic field is an inductor. An inductor is usually constructed as a coil of wire. The ability to store energy in a magnetic field is called inductance, and the basic unit of inductance is the henry.

Symbols: The symbol for an inductor is a 'humped' line reminiscent of a coil. A variable inductor with which inductance may be adjusted to different values will add an arrow pointing into the inductor symbol.

Inductor   *Variable Inductor*

Structure and Behavior: An inductor is composed of a coil of wire, frequently coiled around a metal core or a toroid that provides enhanced performance. As current flows through the coil a magnetic field is induced around the coil, and the expansion or contraction of the magnetic field imposes some opposition to current flow since the expansion and contraction of the field does work. Inductors tend to oppose AC currents because the reversal of current direction causes repeated expansion and

9.1 Electronic Basics

contraction of the magnetic field with alternating directions of magnetic field lines (magnetic field directionality depends upon current direction). Inductors tend to offer little or no opposition to DC currents following the initial current flow's build-up of the magnetic field since with DC current the magnetic field is stable.

Diode: An electronic component that allows current to flow in only one direction is a diode.

Symbol: The symbol for a diode is a triangle with a straight line across the triangle point that lies on the wiring line.

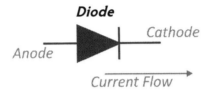

Structure and Behavior: A diode has two electrode leads called the anode and the cathode. Current is allowed to flow in the direction of anode-to-cathode, but not in the opposite direction. **The cathode lead of a semiconductor diode is often marked on the package with a stripe** around the component's circumference that is mirrored in a schematic diagram by the line on the diode's symbol.

Light Emitting Diode (LED): A special diode that emits light when 'forward biased' or when current flows in its allowable direction. **LEDs are commonly used as visual indicators** on displays or electronics.

Symbol: The symbol for a light emitting diode (LED) is a diode symbol with small arrows added that point away from the triangle at an angle, reminiscent of rays of light emitted from the diode. The small arrows may be straight or "zig-zag" style.

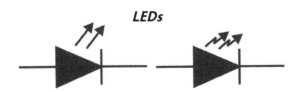

Series and Parallel Circuits: Electronic components like the ones we have examined in this section can be arranged in two basic circuit configurations: series configuration or parallel configuration. Complex circuits can be constructed with various combinations and nestings of series and parallel configurations. Let's take a look at some fundamental laws of voltage and current that apply to series and parallel circuit configurations.

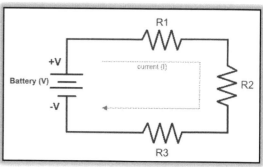

A series configuration of resistors with a battery is depicted in Figure 9.2. Current flows from the battery through each resistor in sequence and back to the battery's opposite terminal. Keeping in mind our water analogy, it is easy to reason that **in a series type circuit the current is the same through all components.**

Figure 9.2: Series circuit example.

Whatever current flows out of the battery must flow through each component equally in order to return to the battery. Considering the point of connection between any two resisters, or the *junction* of two components, we can clearly state that **the current at the junction of two components in series is unchanged** from the current anywhere else in the circuit.

The story is different for the voltage measured across these resistors. Keeping in mind our water pressure analogy for voltage (or EMF), **the voltage across each of two components in series with a voltage source** (battery) **is determined by the type and value of the components.** So, in our simple resistor series circuit of Figure 9.2 the voltage drop across any of the three resistors will be dependent upon the resistance value of each resistor, and these may be different from one another or they may be identical. Other types of components such as diodes, capacitors, or inductors will have similar variable effects on the voltage.

In a parallel configuration like that of Figure 9.3, current and voltage behave in a somewhat inverse manner to the series configuration. **In a parallel type circuit, the voltage is the same across all components.** The EMF 'pressure' is equally divided among the

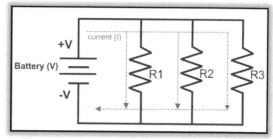

Figure 9.3: Parallel circuit example.

9.1 Electronic Basics

multiple parallel paths and components in the circuit. **The voltage across each of two** (or more) **components in parallel with a voltage source is the same voltage as the source.** If the battery in the figure is a 12-volt source, the voltage measured across any of the three resistor paths will also be 12 volts.

Instead, it is the current that varies through the parallel paths. **At the junction of two** (or more) **components in parallel, the current divides between them dependent on the value of the components.** So, in our parallel resistor circuit of Figure 9.3 the current through each of the three parallel paths would vary. If resistor R1 has a high value of resistance compared with R2 and R3, less current will flow through the R1 path than through R2 and R3 paths. The current seeks the path(s) of least resistance, quite literally.

Keep these relationships in mind. They apply to series and parallel configurations of electronic components no matter how complex a circuit becomes.

Circuit Type	Equivalent	Variable
Series	Current	Voltage
Parallel	Voltage	Current

There are more electronic components and more schematic symbols to learn, including a little about how some components can work together to perform specific jobs. Check out the summary chart on the next page, and then take a break and make sure you have absorbed everything so far by hitting the question bank for **Section 9.1**. We'll pick up with the topic of transistors and additional component symbols in the next section.

www.HamRadioSchool.com/tech_media

Summary of Electronic Components from Section 9.1

Component	Parameter	Functions	Example
Resistor	Resistance (R) unit ohm	Opposes the flow of current in a DC circuit	
Potentiometer or Variable Resistor	Resistance (R) unit ohm	Commonly used as an adjustable volume control	
Capacitor	Capacitance unit farad	Stores energy in an electric field	
Inductor	Inductance unit henry	Stores energy in a magnetic field	
Diode	No unit of measure; leads are anode and cathode	Allows current to flow in only one direction	
LED: Light Emitting Diode	No unit of measure; a special type of diode	LED is commonly used as a visual indicator	

9.2 Hamtronics: Transistors and More

> *We believe that electricity exists, because the electric company keeps sending us bills for it, but we cannot figure out how it travels inside wires.* – Dave Barry

Of course, we really have figured out how electricity travels inside wires and we have learned to control it pretty well. One of the most useful electronic components for controlling electricity traveling in wires is the *transistor*, and we will focus on it in the first part of this section. We will also briefly review some more commonly known electronic components and their schematic symbols, such as switches, fuses, and lamps. We will finish up our electronic exploration with some odds and ends about groups of components that make circuits and some facts about soldering.

Transistor: A class of electronic components that uses a voltage or current signal to control current flow. A transistor can be used as an electronic switch or as a signal amplifier. Amplification occurs when a controlling signal is input into the transistor such that it allows a larger current flow to continue through the transistor. However, a controlling signal may also be input that allows no current at all to flow, thereby making the transistor an electronic switch to turn on or off another electric current routed through the transistor.

Structure and Behavior: A transistor can consist of three layers of semiconductor material. The specific types of semiconductor materials are N-type that promotes an excess of negative charge accumulation, and P-type that promotes an excess of positive charge accumulation. These materials are sandwiched in PNP or NPN layers to create a transistor, and when currents are applied to the individual layers their charge interactions produce the unique transistor behaviors.

A transistor has three *electrode leads*, or *terminals*, for connecting each of the layers in a circuit. A voltage or a current applied to one of the terminals controls the current flowing via the other two terminals. In other words, the current flowing through the transistor varies in magnitude as dictated by the controlling signal. The power of the controlled current can be much greater than the power of the controlling current, so a transistor

T6B11
T6B10

effectively amplifies a signal that is used as the controlling signal. **A transistor's ability to amplify a signal is called gain.** (The concept of gain applies to transistors as well as to antennas, although in this case there is no 'directionality' of signal propagation as that producing antenna gain.) **A transistor can be the primary gain-producing component in an RF power amplifier.**

Water Analogy: Yep, our old friend the water analogy applies to the action of transistors too, as in Figure 9.4 below. You may think of a transistor as an in-line plumbing valve that controls a large, high pressure flow of water in a pipe. Your manipulations of the valve, very weak in comparison to the power available in the strong flow of water, are like the low power controlling signals sent into the transistor. You can change the volume and power of the water flowing over time by making changes to the valve position over time. Imagine that you quickly open and close the valve several times in sequence – your weak valve signals are amplified into similar pulses in the powerful flow of water current through the pipe.

Two types of transistors are commonly used:
1) Bipolar Junction Transistor (BJT) and 2) Field Effect Transistor (FET).

Bipolar Junction Transistor (BJT): The BJT, arrangement, has three terminals (or electrodes) that are called:
1. Base – the electrode to which a controlling current is applied.
2. Collector – one of the electrodes through which larger current flow occurs

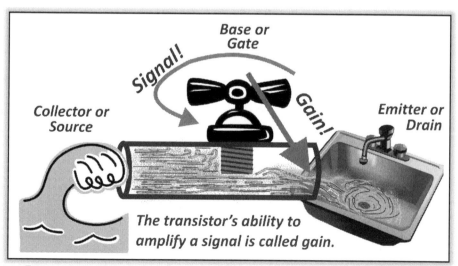

Figure 9.4: Water Analogy Applied to Basic Transistor Function

9.2 Transistors & More

3. Emitter – one of the electrodes through which larger current flow occurs, and through which the base controlling current is also routed.

BJT Symbol: A transistor symbol is a circle with three lines extending from it to represent the three electrode connections, and a "pi-like" symbol within the circle. The BJT internal symbol typically depicts slanted legs of the pi-like symbol inside the circle.

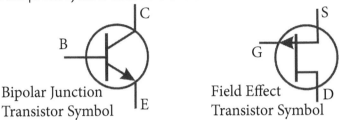

Bipolar Junction Transistor Symbol

Field Effect Transistor Symbol

Field Effect Transistor (FET): The FET uses an electric field to vary the size of a channel in its P-type and N-type semiconductor materials. Current flow is varied according to the channel's size or width. Different from the BJT, a controlling voltage signal is applied rather than a controlling current signal. The FET has three electrodes that are called:
1. Gate – the electrode to which a controlling voltage is applied.
2. Source – one electrodes through which larger current flow occurs.
3. Drain – one electrodes through which larger current flow occurs.

More Components and Symbols: Let's take a look at some additional electronic components that are probably a little more familiar to you, along with their schematic symbols.

Lamp: A simple filament based bulb that emits light when a current is passed through it.

Battery: A chemical based source of electrical power.

Antenna: The RF radiating element of a radio system. The symbol resembles an inverted coat hanger.

Lamp

Battery

Antenna

Switch: A component used to connect or disconnect an electrical circuit. The simplest switch is termed "*single-pole, single-throw*" meaning that there is only one contact for the switch to make when closed (single pole) and only one lever to move (single throw). More complex switch designs may

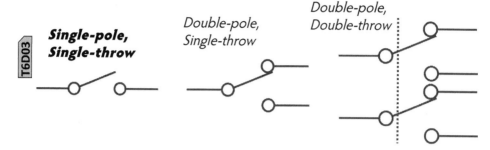

incorporate multiple contacts or multiple levers, as illustrated in the schematic symbols below.

Relay: An electrically controlled switch, usually thrown by providing or removing current from an electromagnet's coil. As discussed in Section 9.1, a coil, or *inductor*, creates a magnetic field when current flows through it. This magnetic effect can be employed as an electromagnet to open or close a switch with magnetic force. This switch arrangement is called a *relay*.

Fuse: Used to protect other circuit components from current overloads. If excessive current flows through the fuse, a narrow conductor or wire within the fuse will overheat and break, stopping the flow of current through the fuse.

Fuse

Meter: Used to display an electrical quantity as a numeric value. Meters may include a needle pointer and scale or an electronic digit readout using LED or *liquid crystal display* (*LCD*) numerical characters.

Regulator: A type of circuit that controls the amount of voltage from a power supply. A *regulated power supply* helps protect sensitive circuits in your radio from spikes and variations of voltage.

Transformer: Used to convert from one voltage to another in a circuit. **Commonly used to change 120v AC house current to a lower AC voltage for other uses.** A transformer uses two coils (inductors) of different numbers of wire windings, each usually with metal core bars. Magnetic induction from one coil induces a current in the other with a voltage change proportional to the difference in winding numbers between the coils. The symbol for a transformer is a simplified representation of its physical form with inductors and core bars.

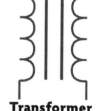
Transformer

Integrating Components Into Circuits: By combining the components listed in this section and the last, many useful

9.2 Transistors & More

circuits or circuit portions may be constructed. Here are three good examples for your consideration.

1. Rectifier: A device or circuit that changes an alternating current into a direct current signal. A rectifier uses multiple diodes to make the conversion from AC to DC current. Diodes are arranged in a circuit to provide two one-way paths for current such that both AC current directions result in current moving in only a single direction for output or application to a load (appliance). Compare the arrow paths of figure 9.5 depicting the two directions of AC current through the rectifier circuit.

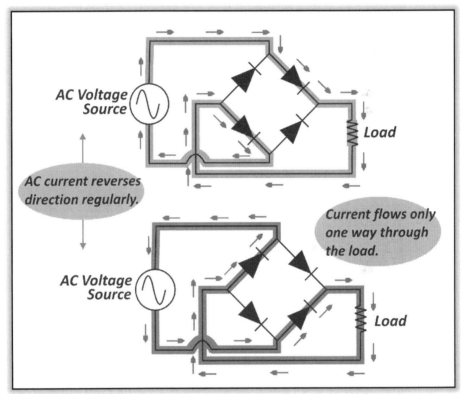

Figure 9.5: Two AC Current Paths of a Diode Rectifier Circuit

2. Tuned Circuit: An inductor and a capacitor connected in series or parallel to form a filter is a resonant or tuned circuit. A *tuned circuit* allows current to flow back and forth between the inductor and the capacitor, alternatively storing and releasing energy as a magnetic field (inductor) and an electric field (capacitor). The values of inductance and capacitance in the components of the tuned circuit may be selected so that the back-and-forth oscillations of AC current occur at a desired frequency, such as a specified RF frequency. Tuned circuits may form the basis of RF oscillators in a radio, or they can be used to filter or select for only certain ranges of frequencies. The frequency of oscillation for a tuned circuit is called its *resonant frequency*, or *frequency of resonance*.

Figure 9.6 is a simplified diagram of a tuned circuit for receiving RF signals. The antenna sends signals received to the circuit. The tuned circuit has a variable capacitor whose value may be changed to select a resonant frequency for the circuit. With only a little RF signal from the antenna at the tuned frequency value, the circuit will begin to resonate, sending current alternatively clockwise and counterclockwise, building up the capacitor's electric field and then discharging to build up the inductor's magnetic field, repeatedly. This resonating signal can then be tapped by the demodulating circuit of the receiver for signal processing, as discussed in Section 6.2, *Receiving*.

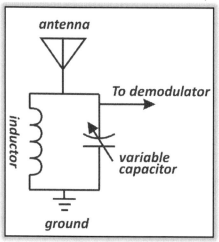

Figure 9.6: Simple Tuned Circuit

3. Control Circuit: Many different arrangements of components are used to form circuits for the control of devices. One simple circuit uses a transistor to control the brightness of a lamp, as shown below from the Technician question pool Figure T1.

The E-shaped symbols facing downward are electrical ground, so you may consider those positions all commonly connected. The V-shaped symbols on the far left indicate connections to other sources or circuits – in this case providing a controlling current through **resistor #1** to transistor #2's base electrode. **The BJT transistor, component #2, functions to control the flow of current** from the battery #4, through the **lamp #3,** and ulti-

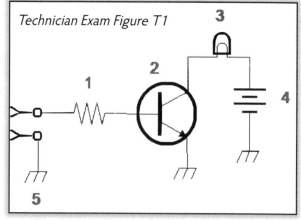

Figure 9.7: Control Circuit for a Lamp

9.2 Transistors & More

mately through its collector and emitter electrodes out to electrical ground. As the controlling current is varied on the transistor the current allowed through the lamp varies commensurately, thereby controlling the lamp's brightness.

Printed Circuit Boards: Electronic circuits are commonly constructed on *printed circuit boards* (*PCBs*) where the electrode wires or leads of components are mounted in contact with a pattern of conducting material that has been printed onto the board. The thin printed pattern of conductive material serves the same function as wires connecting the components together in the manner prescribed by a schematic diagram. A common method of mounting components onto a PCB is by inserting the component terminal wires through small holes in the PCB and *soldering* the wires to the opposite side of the board in contact with the conductive pattern printed there.

Solder: *Solder* is a metal blend that melts at relatively low temperatures and provides excellent electrical conductivity. Common solder blends include the metals lead and tin, and frequently a small amount of silver. Solder is used to join conductors (wires, components leads, PCB pads) by heating the conductors briefly with a small iron, thereby causing the solder to melt, and then cool to solidify firmly around the conductors.

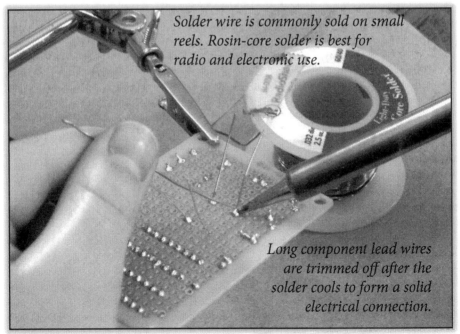

Solder wire is commonly sold on small reels. Rosin-core solder is best for radio and electronic use.

Long component lead wires are trimmed off after the solder cools to form a solid electrical connection.

Figure 9.8: Soldering Components "Through-the-Hole" on a PCB

Rosin-Core Solder is best for radio and electronic use. A center core of *rosin* spreads around the solder joint and helps reduce oxidation that erodes the integrity of a soldered joint over time.

Cold Solder Joint: A grainy or dull surface on a solder joint is characteristic of a "cold" solder joint, and it indicates that the solder joint did not form properly, warranting removal, cleaning, and resoldering of the joint to ensure a solid electrical connection. A good solder joint is usually smooth and shiny.

And that's how electricity flows through wires, under complete control by a bunch of electronic components just like the ones we've learned about in these last two section. If you have followed most of the discussion in these two sections, you now are more educated about electronics than 95% of your fellow citizens. Congratulations! Now go prove your 5% status with the rest of the Technician questions about electronics for **Section 9.2**. Good luck!

www.HamRadioSchool.com/tech_media

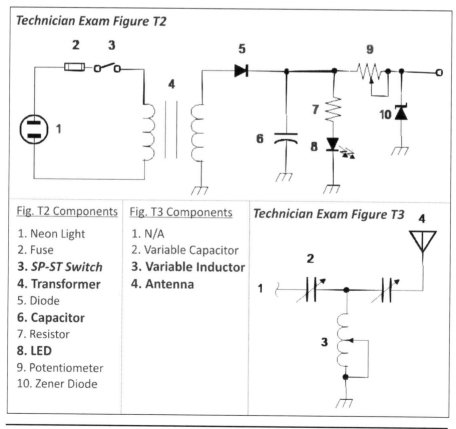

10.0 . Digital Modes

> **❝** *I do not fear computers. I fear the lack of them.* – Isaac Asimov

Do not fear a computer in your ham shack! Ham radio and computers go together like ham and eggs. **A computer may be used as part of your amateur station for logging contacts and information, for generating and decoding digital signals, and even for sending and receiving CW!** Indeed, you should fear the lack of a computer connected to your rig, or at least realize you're missing out on some very cool ham action without one.

Digital Mode: A digital mode in amateur radio is one of several methods of communication in which information is encoded into digital form for transmission. Amateur radio **digital communication modes include packet radio, IEEE 802.11, JT65,** automatic packet reporting (APRS), PSK31, and even good ol' Morse Code. And more that you'll learn about in this section! Digital form may be thought of as a sequence or pattern of on/off signals or discrete signal changes representing binary characters (as in 1 / 0 sequences).

International Morse Code is used when sending CW in the amateur bands. This first-ever digital mode transmits a binary code via continuous wave (unmodulated) transmissions. Any of the following equipment may be used to transmit CW in the amateur bands:

> **Straight Key:** A vertical spring-lever arm that may be finger tapped or pressed to make an electrical contact for the transmission of CW signals.

> **Electronic Keyer:** Devices that electronically produce CW signals of consistent duration and tone for the "dit" (dot) and the "dah" (dash) of Morse code. **An electronic keyer is a device that assists in manual sending of Morse code.** Keyers are often used with paddle or touch key input devices, facilitating separate operator input actions for dit or dah via a pair of paddles or touch sensitive contacts. The electronic keyer outputs dits and dahs of consistent duration and timing in response to operator keying input, helping improve the quality of code transmitted.

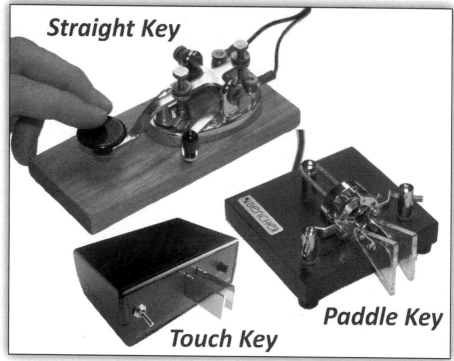

Figure 10.1: Example Morse Code Keys for CW Transmitting

Computer Keyboard: With a proper computer interface, keyboard keystrokes may be converted into CW Morse Code signals for transmission. Similarly, software may be used to translate received Morse Code into on-screen computer text.

Packet Radio: Packet Radio is a digital communication method used commonly with FM modulation on VHF and UHF bands to transmit digital data including email, text, and position-reporting messages. Information is transmitted in groups of discrete packages, or packets, that are received and assembled for decoding.

Terminal Node Controller (TNC): Typically a hardware 'box' connected between a transceiver and a computer in a packet radio station to control the transmission and reception of digitally encoded messages. A TNC is much like a computer MODEM that connects one computer to another or to the internet, only the TNC connects via a radio transceiver.

PSK31: Phase Shift Keying 31 is a low-rate data transmission mode for keyboard-to-keyboard text messaging that works well in the noisy environment of single sideband HF operations. This digital communications mode encodes messages by rapidly shifting the phase of an audio signal waveform

10.0 Digital Modes

between two states to form sequences of binary character codes. The two waveform phase states serve the same function as two different tones or on/off transmission states. The PSK31 tone sounds like a whining whistle, and a sound card interface connects the computer and radio so that software may control the transmission and reception of PSK31 signals. PSK31 uses a very narrow bandwidth and is effective for QRP (low power) transmissions.

Sound Card Interface (SCI): When conducting digital communications, a computer's sound card provides audio to the radio's microphone input and converts received audio to digital form for computer processing of messages. The sound card interface translates between audio signals used by the radio and digital signals used by the computer. **The computer sound card microphone or line input port is connected to the transceiver's headphone or speaker output for operating digital modes.** This way the radio's received signal audio is provided to the SCI for decoding on-screen.

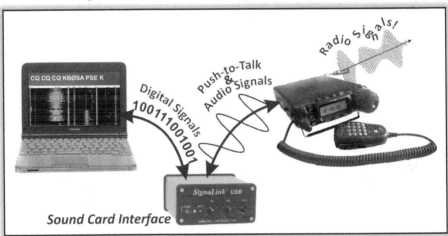

Figure 10.2: PSK31 Sound Card Interface Functionality

Whether by TNC or SCI, **the connections between a voice transceiver and a computer for digital operation usually include receive audio, transmit audio, and push-to-talk (PTT).**

WSJT Suite: A very popular set of digital modes well suited for very weak signal operations, the WSJT suite was developed by Joe Taylor, K1JT. Several specific modes comprise the suite, including the popular JT65 and FT8 modes. **Moonbounce, or Earth-Moon-Earth, weak signal propagation beacons, and meteor scatter are all supported by the digital mode software in the WSJT suite. FT8 operates in low signal-to-noise conditions with transmissions on 15-second intervals.**

Automatic Packet Reporting System (APRS) is a digital mode that **can send automatic position reports from a mobile amateur radio station using data provided to the transmitter by a Global Positioning System receiver** (GPS receiver). Position coordinate information (and other digital packet information) is transmitted via *digipeaters*, or digital repeaters, that relay packets to a receiving network or internet gateway.

Figure 10.3: HT with Built-In GPS and TNC

One application of APRS is to provide real-time tactical digital communications in conjunction with a map showing the location of stations. Such a mapping function can be affected in a locally implemented computer network or, when received by an internet gateway, station position reports may be posted on a web server map that is publicly accessible, such as the APRS.fi web site.

Internet Radio Linking Project (IRLP): IRLP is a technique to connect amateur radio systems, such as repeaters, via the Internet using Voice Over Internet Protocol (VoIP). **VoIP is a method of delivering voice communications over the Internet using digital techniques.** Two repeaters may be joined so that all transmissions received and repeated locally by either station are also repeated by the other station in a different geographic location. That is, each station not only transmits RF locally, but also sends a digitally converted VoIP signal through the Internet to the other repeater where reconversion to RF signals occurs and an identical transmission is made from the linked repeater station.

Gateway: The name given to an amateur radio station that is used to connect other amateur stations to the Internet is a gateway. Thus, an IRLP repeater station is a gateway station. Two major linking systems use VoIP: IRLP and Echolink. While these two systems operate similarly, there are some differences. EchoLink allows amateur operators to use a personal computer as an EchoLink gateway, connecting the computer with microphone and audio capability to any other Echo-Link node, whether that node is a computer or a repeater gateway station. **Before you may use the EchoLink system to communicate using a repeater, you must register your call sign and provide proof of license.**

10.0 Digital Modes

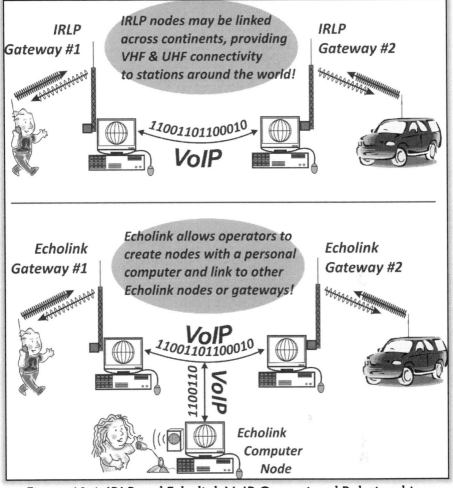

Figure 10.4: IRLP and Echolink VoIP Operational Relationships

Specifying IRLP Nodes: When connecting to an IRLP gateway, you may select a specific IRLP node using the transceiver's keypad to transmit the IRLP node ID. Such **access to some IRLP nodes, and control of repeaters linked by IRLP, is accomplished using DTMF signals.** DTMF tones are like those transmitted over telephone when you push-button tone dial a number.

Repeater Information: A list of active nodes that use VoIP may be obtained by subscribing to an online service, from online repeater lists maintained by the local repeater frequency coordinator, or from a repeater directory. A repeater directory can

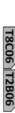

be obtained in book form from most ham radio distributors, and IRLP or Echolink listings may also be found through an Internet search.

Other Digital Modes: Some radio manufacturers have implemented highly capable digital modes unique to their radio brand. The Icom *D-Star* digital voice (DV) mode is one popular example, and Yaesu's *System Fusion* another. Voice audio is digitized to be transmitted and received as a digital RF stream of data, eliminating any RF analog signal in transmitting and receiving. An Internet-linked network of voice and data digital repeaters supports worldwide communications with digital voice and data.

Digital Mobile Radio (DMR) has become a very popular DV option offering a similar open standardized digital voice specification. **DMR uses a technique for time-multiplexing two digital voice signals on a single 12.5 kHz repeater channel,** enhancing the efficiency of band utilization. A feature of DMR is "talk groups." **A talk group on a DMR digital repeater is a way for groups of users to share a channel at different times without being heard by other users on the channel. You can join a digital repeater's talk group by programming your radio with the group's ID or code.**

Figure 10.5: HT with DV capability and GPS data. Icom ID-31A

Broadband-Hamnet (TM) **or high-speed multi-media network is an amateur radio-based data network using commercial Wi-Fi gear with modified firmware.** It establishes a "local area network" (LAN) over a wide area using Wi-Fi frequencies that overlap with amateur microwave bands and typically implements the IEEE 802.11 LAN communication standard.

Errors in Digital Transmissions: Because digital transmission rely upon series of discrete signals, it is somewhat easy for a packet of digits to be incorrectly interpreted if only one of the hundreds or thousands of digits transmitted is omitted or incorrectly decoded.

Any of the following error checking methods may be included in a packet transmission to help insure correct receipt:

Check Sum: A value **included in a packet transmission to permit error detection,** the check sum is a mathematical tool for checking the integrity of the data transmission. Essentially, the received check sum in the packet must match a calculated summation of the data bits received in order for the digital packet to be confirmed valid and error free.

Header: Data **included in a packet transmission** at the beginning of a packet that **contains the call sign of the station to which the information is being sent,** time stamp, IP address, check sum, sending station ID or call sign, and other information.

Automatic Repeat Request (ARQ): Included in a packet transmission in case of error, this is a digital scheme whereby the receiving station detects errors and sends a request to the sending station to retransmit the information.

[T8D11]

BER: The *Bit Error Rate* is a count of the number of omitted or altered data bits in a reception due to noise, interference, distortion, or faulty synchronization. **Error rates are likely to increase if VHF or UHF data signals arrive via multiple paths,** thereby arriving at the receiving station with slightly different time or phase and causing multipath interference, as discussed for phone mode in Section 1.2, *Ham Communication Basics.*

[T3A10]

Radio Remote Control: Radio control of model vehicles, such as airplanes, boats, or rockets, may use amateur digital signals. **Transmitting signals to control a model craft is the only circumstance an amateur station may transmit without on-the-air identification.** An ID sticker required on the maximum 1-watt transmitter substitutes for the on-air ID.

[T1D11]

Amateur Television: Although not really a digital mode, television transmissions with amateur radio utilize unique data transmission formats and the equipment frequently involves a computer interface for the video source. Two basic amateur TV signal types are *slow-scan television* (SSTV) and *fast-scan television* (FSTV).

Slow-scan TV: SSTV uses only about 3 kHz of bandwidth, similar to SSB phone mode. Thus, it can be transmitted on the HF bands. However, a single frame image typically requires several seconds to a couple of minutes to transmit.

Fast-scan TV: FSTV is nearly identical in quality to broadcast television because it utilizes the same transmission standard as commercial broadcasting and because it uses much greater bandwidth than SSTV. The lowest frequency practical for FSTV due to bandwidth considerations is the UHF 70 cm band. **The typical bandwidth of analog FSTV transmissions on the 70 centimeter band is about 6 MHz.** With this bandwidth FSTV can produce broadcast quality video and sound.

Analog fast-scan color TV signals utilize a type of transmission indicated by the term "*NTSC*," which is a TV transmission format standard established by the *National Television System Committee*.

With a video camera, a computer, and amateur TV software, you can get started experimenting with amateur television as a new Technician!

In spite of some of the technical methods used to make digital modes come to life, implementing them with your radio is really very easy. For most digital modes just a software installation and perhaps an electronic box connected between radio and computer will get you started in the world of digital communications over the amateur bands. No need to fear computers at all, especially in the ham shack. Try the Technician question pool items for **Section 10.0**, then come back for a journey into the final frontier!

www.HamRadioSchool.com/tech_media

Summary Table of Digital Modes and Characteristics

Digital Mode	Description	Hardware/Comments
CW	Uses International Morse Code	Electronic keyer assists with manual sending of Morse cod
PSK31	Phase Shift Keying 31	Uses sound card interface (SCI)
APRS	Automatic Packet Reporting System	Uses GPS receiver data for position reports
WSJT (FT8)	Weak signal modes	Uses timed inteval transmissions
IRLP & Echolink	Uses VoIP internet link called "gateway"	Controled by DTMF tones; Echolink requires registration
DMR	Time-multiplexed voice signals, 12.5 kHz	Facilitates "talk groups" by programming DMR radio
FSTV	Fast-scan television	NTSC signal, 6 MHz bandwidth, on 70cm band (or higher freq.)
Radio Control Craft	1-watt maximum power	Only conditions no on-air ID is required (sticker on transmitter)

11.0 Space Contacts

> *That's one small step for a ham, one giant leap for hamkind.* – Anonymous

With your Technician license, a handheld 2m/70cm transceiver, and a directional antenna, you can make long distance contacts using orbital satellites as repeaters and you can even talk to astronauts on the International Space Station! Let's learn how to take this small step.

Space Station: By FCC Part 97 definition, a space station is an amateur station located more than 50 km above the earth's surface. [T1A07]
Multiple amateur radio satellites reside in *low earth orbit* (LEO) that are essentially repeaters in space.

As one of these amateur radio satellites passes over your position you can talk to amateur radio operators in other countries, or stations hundreds of miles away, via the satellite-based repeater that will relay your UHF/VHF signals across a wide area. You may also be able to contact amateur operator astronauts onboard the International Space Station (ISS). Using a handheld beam antenna with your HT you can manually track the satellite across the sky and get very good results with 5 watts of power or less!

Figure 11.1: Early Morning ISS Contact

Orbit and Path: Amateur satellites may be in one of several different types of orbits, or maneuvers about the earth in circular or elliptical paths.

LEO is low earth orbit, meaning that a satellite or space station is orbiting up to a few hundred miles above the earth. (This may be compared to a geostationary orbit in which a satellite is about 22,800 miles above the earth's equator such that it orbits once per 24 hours, thereby remaining over one position on the earth's surface. Amateur radio satellites are not usually lifted into geostationary orbits.)

Polar Orbit: LEO amateur radio satellites will commonly be placed in *polar orbits* in which the satellite passes over or near the north and south geographic poles of the earth. In this way the satellite will pass within contact range of virtually every position on earth over the course of several orbits, as the earth turns beneath it. If the satellite is moving south-to-north over your position it is said to have an *ascending approach* or orbit. If it is moving north-to-south, it is said to have a *descending approach* or orbit.

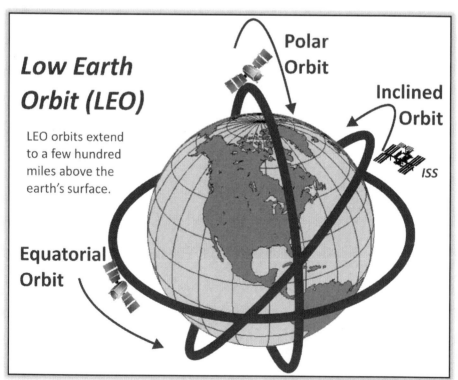

Figure 11.2: Comparison of Basic Low Earth Orbit Paths

11.0 Space Contacts

Contact Time: The duration of a satellite's pass over your location will depend significantly upon its height above the horizon. Passes near the horizon will result in brief contact periods. Passes directly overhead will provide the longest contact periods, typically up to several minutes as the satellite moves from horizon to horizon.

Because the satellite window is brief, and because its coverage may extend over an area of hundreds of thousands of square miles, satellite contacts must be conducted with great efficiency. Many operators may be attempting to use the satellite simultaneously, and usually there is only one repeater frequency pair available. Most contacts will consist simply of call sign and grid square location exchanges.

Satellite Tracking Program: To determine the time period during which an amateur satellite or space station can be accessed you may use a satellite tracking program with your personal computer. **Such programs use the satellite's Keplerian elements as input,** along with the correct time and your station location to calculate the time and precise path of a satellite pass overhead. The Keplerian elements mathematically define a satellite's orbit.

Tracking programs, multiple internet sites, and even mobile device apps provide regularly updated satellite orbit information. With many of these resources you can simply identify your location by postal zip code, by grid square locator, or by latitude-longitude coordinate and obtain a customized report of upcoming satellite passes within your horizon. These customized reports and **tracking programs will provide maps showing real time position of the satellite track over the earth,** as well as **the time, azimuth and elevation of start, maximum altitude, and end of pass. The apparent frequency of the satellite transmission, including effects of Doppler shift,** may also be included in a report. (See forward paragraph on Doppler shift, this section.) With all of this information you can readily track the bird's path across your local sky. See Figure 11.3, next page.

Uplink / Downlink: The *uplink frequency* is the frequency used to transmit to the satellite. The *downlink frequency* is the frequency used to receive the satellite's transmissions. **Transmission modes commonly used by amateur radio satellites include SSB, FM, CW/data,** and others.

Split Channel: Commonly a *split channel* arrangement – a UHF and a VHF frequency pair or *duplex* channel – will be used for the satellite uplink/downlink pair. This is much like a normal repeater offset in which your radio automatically shifts to the transmit frequency when you PTT, only in this case the offset is between two different bands, the 2m (VHF) and

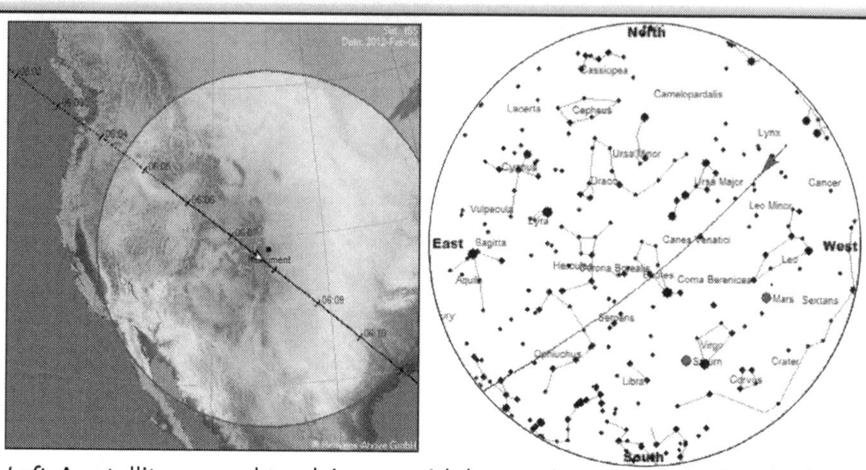

Left: A satellite ground track image with hour:minute time depicted. The circle indicates the position where the satellite will be 10 degrees above the horizon for the user-selected observation position on earth.

Right: A star chart indicating the path of the selected satellite pass relative to constellations, planets, and the moon. *Courtesy of Heavens-Above.com*

Figure 11.3: Example Online Satellite Tracking Products

70cm (UHF) bands. Refer to your radio user's manual for setting up a split frequency or duplex channel, sometimes called an "*odd split*." You should note the satellite mode to find the specific frequency split arrangement for a given satellite. (Note: The ISS also tends to use split channel operations for phone contacts with astronaut amateurs.)

Mode: The uplink / downlink frequency split arrangement is referred to as the satellite *mode*. (This should not be confused with earthbound transmission modes that instead refer to the method of modulating the signal, such as FM, SSB, or CW.) For example, **if the satellite is said to be operating in "mode U/V," this means that the satellite uplink is in the 70 centimeter band (UHF) and the downlink is in the 2 meter band (VHF).** Hence, "U/V." Mode "V/U" would be the opposite, where uplink is on 2m band and downlink is on 70cm band.

License Privileges: Any amateur whose license privileges allow them to transmit on the satellite uplink frequency may be the control operator of a station communicating through an amateur satellite or space station. Most satellites and the ISS use UHF and VHF amateur frequencies. **Any amateur holding a Technician or higher class license may make contact with an amateur station on the**

11.0 Space Contacts

International Space Station (ISS) using 2 meter and 70 cm band frequencies.

Power Requirements: Like any amateur communication, the transmitter power used on the uplink frequency of an amateur satellite or space station should be the minimum amount of power needed to complete the contact. Usually you will need no more than the typical 5W of a modern HT radio, coupled with an appropriate directional antenna pointed at the satellite, to make reliable contacts. **The impact of using too much effective radiated power on a satellite uplink is blocking access by other users,** and that's just rude. Some types of satellite receivers that can receive multiple signals simultaneously over a wide frequency band will be desensitized to weaker signals if one received signal is really strong.

Telecommand: By FCC Part 97 definition, a telecommand is a one-way transmission to initiate, modify or terminate functions of a device at a distance. Amateur satellite controllers must use telecommands sent from earth to the satellite station to operate the satellite station. Controllers of earthbound repeater stations may also use telecommands to change remote repeater station functions, especially if the repeater is located in a difficult to reach area, such as a mountain top.

Telemetry: By FCC Part 97 definition, telemetry is a one-way transmission of measurements at a distance from the measuring instrument. **Anyone may receive the telemetry signal from a space station.**

> **Satellite Beacon: A transmission from a satellite that contains status information is called the beacon. Satellite beacons typically transmit information about the health and status of the satellite. A good way to judge whether your uplink power is too low or too high is that your signal strength on the downlink should be about the same as the beacon** signal strength. This is because most satellites will adjust downlink signal power to be commensurate with the power of the received uplink signal. The beacon is a good stable reference against which you can adjust your signal strength. If the downlink signal is much stronger than the beacon, reduce your uplink power.

Common Transmission Effects: Due to the motion of satellites and space stations, you may experience some unique audio effects with space contacts that are not typical of other amateur communications.

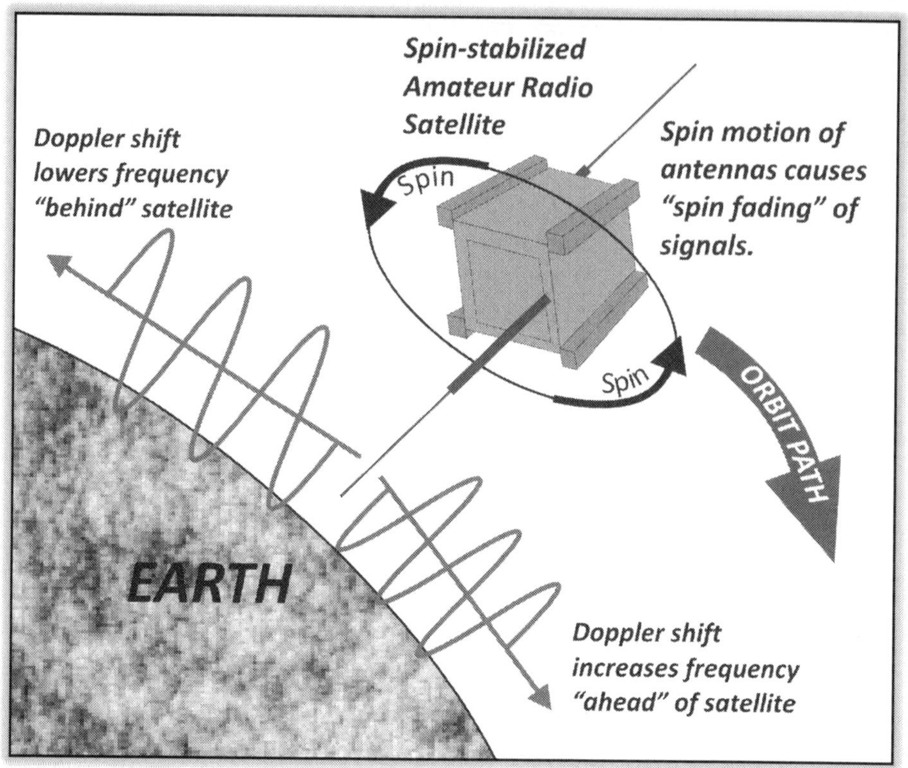

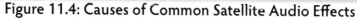

Figure 11.4: Causes of Common Satellite Audio Effects

Spin Fading: Satellites are often rotating to provide stability. **Rotation of the satellite and its antennas causes spin fading of satellite signals,** which is a fluctuation of signal strength or quality as the satellite spins and its antenna polarization changes with the spin.

Doppler Shift: An observed change in signal frequency caused by relative motion between the satellite and the earth station is Doppler Shift. You will notice Doppler Shift as a gradual change in the tone of satellite signals, from higher to lower tone, because the satellite is moving fast enough to cause minor compression of RF frequencies as it approaches your position, and minor rarefaction (lowering) of RF frequencies as it moves away from your position. This is the same effect with sound waves that causes a swiftly passing train's whistle or horn to sound higher pitched as it approaches and shift to a lower pitch as it passes by and moves away. Usually with FM ops this does not disrupt communications, and it can be alleviated with minor receiver tuning changes over the period of the satellite pass, if desired. With SSB mode, Doppler effects are much more significant, requiring tuning changes during the pass.

11.0 Space Contacts

Amateur radio satellites really are a giant leap for hams. Getting VHF and UHF signals spread across such a vast area is a rare treat, and satellite contacts are really fun. And while the crew of the International Space Station has had sporadic activity with amateur operators onboard over the years, making contact with another human being in space is a delight I guarantee you will never forget!

We are approaching the final frontier of our initial amateur radio expedition! Only a couple more topics to blast off into. Beat up the **Section 11.0** Technician questions on Space Contacts and we'll take a look at issues of radio interference.

www.HamRadioSchool.com/tech_media

Figure 11.5: ISS Commander Doug Wheelock, KF5BOC
Courtesy NASA/JPL-Caltech

Astronaut Douglas Wheelock, Colonel, US Army, was very active on amateur radio from orbit during his long-duration stay aboard the International Space Station, June - November 2010. Numerous earthly hams were thrilled to make contact with him, collecting a rare and coveted prize in amateur radio. The author and his son, WØJAK, were each lucky to make contact with Colonel Wheelock on the morning of October 13, 2010, using an HT radio and a dual-band handheld Yagi antenna, as shown in Figure 11.1. Thank you, sir!

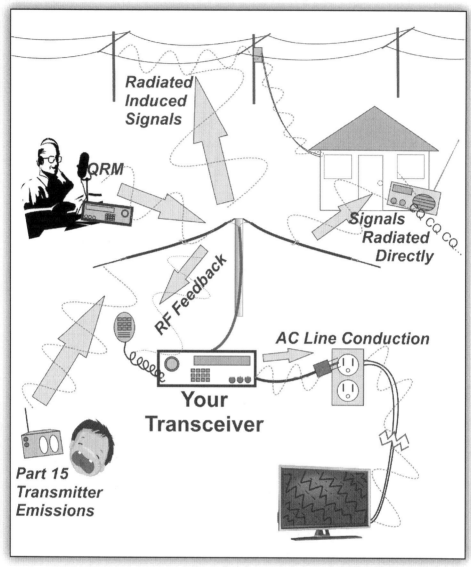

Figure 12.0: Interference! Signals from your station may be radiated directly to other devices or conducted along AC power lines to other devices. Radiated signals may induce currents on cables or wires to be conducted into other devices. Your radio may even inadvertently receive its own signal transmissions via the microphone cord behaving like an antenna. Other amateur radio station transmissions on nearby or overlapping frequencies may interfere with your communications, and non-licensed emitters such as Part 15 devices may cause noise on your received audio. Good amateur practice and common filtering techniques can reduce or eliminate most interference problems. Let's see how...

12.0 Avoiding Interference

> **"** *The radio makes hideous sounds.* – Bob Dylan

Interference happens. Sometimes your radio will indeed make hideous sounds due to the effects of other radio stations or transmitters. Your radio may impose some hideous sounds or images of its own on other electronic devices as well. As a licensed amateur radio operator it is your responsibility to have familiarity with the FCC regulations regarding interference and with the common methods of resolving interference when it rears its hideous head. Nobody wants an ongoing argument with a neighbor over a few flying frequencies. Keep it cool with the following good information.

Interference is the undesirable reception of RF signals produced either properly or improperly by another electronic device. Interference may be received by your radio station from other sources, or interference may be produced by your radio station and affect other devices. Usually, interference problems can be easily solved with one or more standard approaches. Filtering at the offended or receiving device is the most common resolution approach. Let's first consider the case of your ham radio transmissions causing interference with other devices.

Ham Interference to Other Devices: Your station transmissions may interfere with other electronic devices, including other radio receivers and devices never intended to receive radio signals at all. Your RF signals may travel from your transmitter to other devices by two different ways, and possibly both ways simultaneously:

Radiated Signals: The wires associated with other devices can act as antennas to inadvertently receive your station's radiated signals. Wiring such as power cords, speaker wires, TV antennas and cables, component connecting cables, or even internal wiring within electronic devices may pick up your RF signals.

Conducted Signals: In addition to radiating RF via your station antenna, your transmitter may also output signals onto household AC wiring, or such wiring may have RF signals induced on it, and these signals are conducted into other powered equipment to impose interference.

We'll consider some simple methods of filtering these signals out of the other devices in a moment, but first let's take note of some troublesome types of **RF emissions that can cause radio frequency interference: Fundamental overload, spurious emissions (including harmonics),** and RF feedback into your transmitter.

Fundamental Overload: Interference in a radio receiver caused by very strong signals. You may experience fundamental overload with your station if another station is transmitting a strong signal very nearby, especially in the same band. With fundamental overload the receiver fails to reject these undesired signals that overload the receiver circuitry and may cause distorted, unintelligible audio, and override any other weaker signals you may desire to receive. Your station may cause fundamental overload of a telephone, television, or commercial radio receiver if you are transmitting very strong signals. For instance, **a broadcast AM or FM radio may receive an amateur radio transmission unintentionally because the receiver is unable to reject strong signals outside the AM or FM band.**

Spurious Emissions: Undesired radio frequency emissions not deliberately transmitted by a radio transmitter are called spurious emissions. A spurious emission is any radio frequency transmission outside of the intended and assigned bandwidth for the operating mode being used. Two of the more common types of spurious emissions are harmonics and splatter.

Harmonics: Emissions that are frequency multiples of the intended (or 'fundamental') frequency of a transmitter are called harmonics. Virtually all transmitters produce some harmonics at low power levels. [Typically the 2nd harmonic (double the fundamental frequency) or 3rd harmonic (triple the fundamental) are the strongest harmonic frequencies, but other multiples may also cause interference with devices.] Harmonics generated by your station may lie outside of the amateur bands and cause interference in non-amateur radio receivers and electronic devices. Harmonics are one type of spurious emission, as depicted in Figure 12.1.

12.0 Avoiding Interference

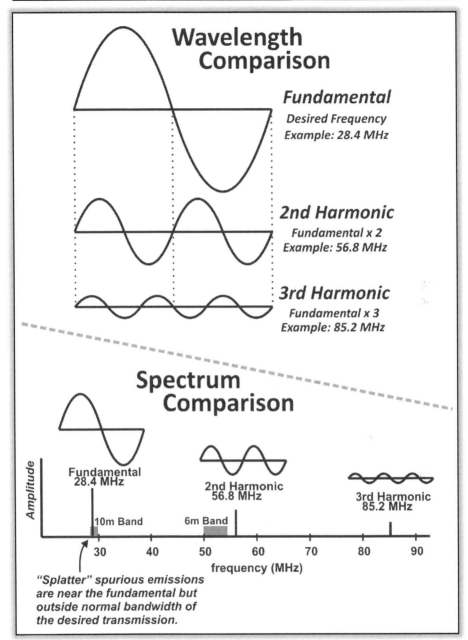

Figure 12.1: Spurious Emissions - Harmonics and Splatter

Splatter: Transmissions of excessive bandwidth. For instance, if your SSB transmitter is emitting 20 kHz worth of frequencies, you are emitting about 17 kHz of spurious emissions outside of the necessary and proper 3 kHz bandwidth for SSB mode. Splatter will not make friends on the air. Check your transmitter for off-frequency operation or spurious emissions if you receive a report that your station's transmissions are causing splatter or interference with nearby frequencies!

RF Feedback: A garbled, distorted, or unintelligible voice transmission is a symptom of RF feedback. This is caused by your own transmitted signal being fed back into your transmitter unintentionally. For example, if your microphone and its cable act as an effective antenna for the frequency on which you are operating, your signal will be fed back into your transmitter. RF feedback can usually be alleviated by increasing the separation of the transmitter and antenna, or by adding a simple filter to the microphone cable. (See ferrite choke, below.)

Alleviating Interference with Filters: No matter the specific type of RF emissions causing interference to another device, easy-to-implement and inexpensive filters placed on the receiving device will usually work to reduce or eliminate the interference caused by your station. Snap-on ferrite chokes, low-pass and high-pass filters, band-reject and band-pass filters may all be useful in correcting a radio frequency interference problem. When an interference problem arises with a neighbor, a combination of cordial communication, polite investigation, and sound technical fixes usually helps maintain friendships and the enjoyment of amateur radio. Let's explore a few common types of friendship-saving filters.

Ferrite Choke: One of the simplest and cheapest filtering solutions for audio devices is the ferrite or magnetic choke (also known as snap-on chokes). A ferrite choke will reduce RF current flowing on the shield of an audio cable (the cable being an "inadvertent receiver" antenna). Assist your neighbor in snapping one or two ferrite chokes on audio cables such as speaker lines to help avoid destroying his music listening enjoyment with your ham radio transmissions. Additionally, **distorted audio caused by RF current on the shield of a microphone cable may be cured using a ferrite choke.**

RF Filters: A type of low-pass filter, RF filters allow lower frequency signals such as audio signals to pass, while blocking higher frequencies such as RF. **Interference from an amateur transmitter to a nearby telephone can be reduced or eliminated by putting an RF filter on the telephone.** These filters are readily available as small plug-and-forget modules that fit into standard telephone jacks. If you hear your radio transmissions through the phone, try one of these inexpensive modules first.

12.0 Avoiding Interference

Other RF filters are designed to pass and block specific frequency ranges. Low-pass or high-pass filters allow the passing of frequencies above (high-pass) or below (low-pass) a specific frequency value, while blocking all others. A band-pass filter allows a range of specified frequencies (the band) to pass, while blocking all frequencies above and below the pass band. The inverse type of filter is called a band-reject filter, blocking a specified band of frequencies while allowing all others to pass. For instance, **a band-reject filter can reduce overload to a VHF transceiver from a nearby FM broadcast station** by rejecting the broadcast band frequencies. The 6 meter band tops out at 54.0 MHz, the 2 meter band begins at 144.0 MHz, and the commercial FM band to be rejected with a filter is nestled in between from 88.0 to 108.0 MHz. REJECT the FM jocks, QSO with your pals.

Although sometimes requiring careful consideration, these types of filter devices may be purchased or created to solve almost any type of RF interference. For example, **overload of a non-amateur radio or TV receiver by an amateur signal may be reduced or eliminated with a**

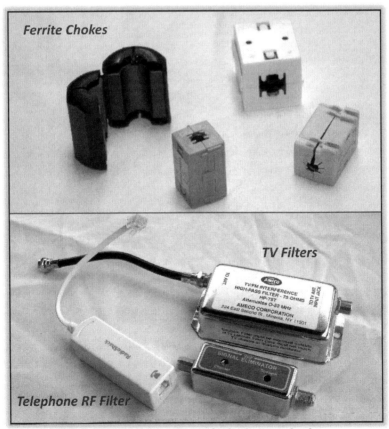

Figure 12.2: Examples of Chokes and Filters

filter at the antenna input of the affected receiver, blocking the amateur signal while allowing desired signals to pass.

Non-filtering Considerations: Before jumping to a filter fix, it's a good idea to check some other basic things first. For instance, poor connectors on interfered device cables can sometimes promote interference. **The first step to resolving cable TV interference from your ham radio transmissions should be to ensure all TV coaxial connectors are installed properly.** You can also conduct some other simple investigations: **If a neighbor tells you that your station's transmissions are interfering with their radio or TV reception, make sure that your station is functioning properly and that it does not cause interference to your own radio or television when it is tuned to the same channel** as your neighbor's device.

Other Device Interference to Ham Stations: Sometimes other devices, either intentional or unintentional emitters, may cause interference to your station. You will usually hear this type of interference in your receive audio. The source of the interference could be from a nearby faulty power line, from an electric motor or other device, or from another electronic device that emits RF intentionally. It could even be from intentional jamming of RF signals. Often, the nature of the noise will be a sufficient clue to the source of the interference. It may be necessary in some cases to track down the source of interference using radio direction finding.

Radio direction finding is a method used to locate sources of noise interference or jamming. A simple directional antenna on a mobile receiver such as an HT radio is often sufficient to track down troublesome sources of interference such as electrical noise. The S-meter of the receiver may be a sufficient index to get a fix on an offending RF source, as it will show increased signal strength as the directional antenna is pointed in the direction of the RF source.

Interference from Neighbors: If something in a neighbor's home is causing harmful interference to your amateur station, you should:

1. **Work with your neighbor to identify the offending device.**
2. **Politely inform your neighbor about the rules that prohibit the use of devices that cause interference.**
3. **Check your station and make sure it meets the standards of good amateur practice.**

12.0 Avoiding Interference

Part 15 Devices: Many modern household electronic devices are intentional transmitters: Baby monitors, remotely controlled toys, wireless computer routers, cordless phones, and many others. Most of these are classified by the FCC as a **Part 15 device, an unlicensed device that may emit low-powered radio signals on frequencies used by a licensed service.** It is possible for Part 15 devices to cause interference with your station, and operators of such devices are required to avoid use that imposes such interference. Still, common courtesy and polite negotiation should be the approach should someone else's device be a source of trouble.

Mobile Station Interference Problems: Mobile stations in automobiles require some specific implementations to avoid interference from an automobile's electrical systems.

Alternator Whine: The source of a high-pitched whine that varies with engine speed in a mobile transceiver's receive audio is the alternator. The car's alternator generates AC power and produces this broadband interference. If another operator reports a variable high-pitched whine on the audio from your mobile transmitter, noise from the vehicle's electrical system is being transmitted along with your speech audio. Usually, alleviating transmitted electrical system noise will require a suppression technique applied to the offending vehicle source, such as spark plug suppressors or repair or replacement of the alternator or computer controller module generating the noise.

Noise Blanker: Turning on the radio's noise blanker can help reduce ignition interference to the receiver or to remove power line noise. The noise blanker is a special type of filter designed to reduce broadband noise of a regular frequency or pulse, like that created by the engine's electric ignition system or power line hum. Most modern radios will have a noise blanker filtering option available in the setup menu structure. The noise blanker effects only the receive audio and will not alleviate transmitted electrical system noise from your mobile station.

Battery Connections: A mobile transceiver's power cable negative return connection should be made at the battery or engine block ground strap. Using direct and dedicated power connections from the car battery, with in-line fuses and avoiding all use of any automobile wiring, will help avoid electrical system interference and potential electrical hazards.

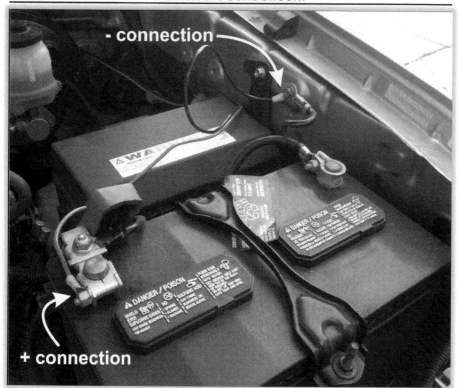

Figure 12.3: Route mobile station power connections directly to battery terminals or engine block ground strap.

Grounding: Grounding your mobile radio to the automobile chassis may help reduce ground loop interference. Grounding your base station to conductive rods driven into the earth may help alleviate the same type of undesirable currents. *Ground loop* currents are caused by variations in the ground voltage level among different components of a radio station. A single-point ground connection, as illustrated in Figure 12.4 and pictured in Figure 12.7 at the end of this section, is best to eliminate ground loop currents. Use of a flat strap conductor is best for RF grounding, such as wide copper strap. **Flat strap provides the lowest impedance to RF signals** due to the greater surface area on which RF currents can flow. Low impedance will help stray currents find their way to ground instead of to other trouble-making paths through you or your radio gear.

T4A08

Rejecting QRM: *QRM*, or interference from other amateur stations transmitting on nearby frequencies, may be rejected by varying your radio's receive filter, if available. **Having multiple receive bandwidth choices on a multimode transceiver is an advantage that permits noise or inter-**

T4B08

12.0 Avoiding Interference

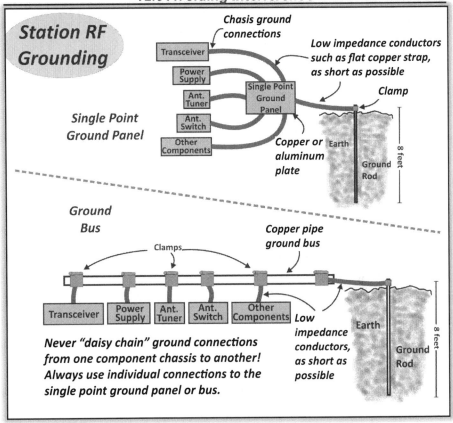

Figure 12.4: Station Single Point Grounding Options

ference reduction by selecting a bandwidth matching the mode. That is, you may select a filter that passes only enough RF bandwidth for the mode you are using and rejects frequencies outside that mode's normal bandwidth. [Review mode bandwidths in section 6.3, *How Radio Works*.]

Selectivity: The term that describes the ability of a receiver to discriminate between multiple signals is selectivity. Your selected receive filter bandwidth is one factor that determines your receiver's selectivity. Other factors, such as the intermediate frequency conversion system, will also affect selectivity. Selectivity is an important metric defining the quality of a receiver. [T7A04]

SSB Filtering: For single sideband mode an appropriate receive filter to select to minimize noise and interference is 2400 Hz (2.4 kHz). Since a typical SSB signal may be up to 3000 Hz (3.0 kHz) wide, this filter selection will reject noise or QRM on adjacent frequencies while [T4B09]

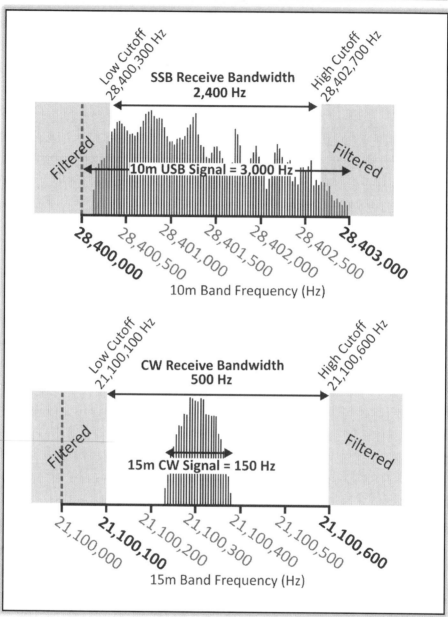

Figure 12.5: Matching Filters to Bandwidth for QRM Rejection

allowing sufficient bandwidth for good audio to pass through to your receiver. This scenario is illustrated in Figure 12.5 with a 10m band example.

CW Filtering: For CW reception an appropriate receive filter to select to minimize noise and interference is 500 Hz. A typical CW signal may be about 150 Hz wide, but filters narrower than 500

12.0 Avoiding Interference

Figure 12.6: Example of HF Station Filter Bandwidth Selection

Hz are less common. A 500 Hz filter is usually sufficient to reject adjacent frequency noise or QRM and isolate the desired CW signal. (This filter is also suitable for PSK31 mode, as the signal bandwidth is about 300 Hz.) A CW example is illustrated in the lower part of Figure 12.5.

Filtering Other Modes: Similarly for other modes (PSK31, AM, various digital modes), select a filter that matches the bandwidth of the mode in order to best reject noise and interference on nearby frequencies. Many modern radios provide convenient operator manipulation of filter bandwidths by digital signal processing and other methods.

Figure 12.6 depicts one base station filter selection example. The high and low cutoff frequencies of the desired receive band are adjusted with two rotary knobs at the lower left. The audio band corresponding index values for the cutoff frequencies are displayed as "LOCUT" and "HICUT." The resulting receive bandwidth is graphically displayed by a curved line scale that lengthens or shortens with receive bandwidth. Independent adjustment of the low cutoff and high cutoff frequencies allows easy operator control of the bandwidth and positioning of the receive band in order that QRM or other interference may be rejected.

Dealing with interference promptly and correctly is much easier than dealing with irate neighbors, irate amateur operators, or hideous sounds. You may notice some fundamental overload when operating in close proximity to other stations with your FM HT radio or mobile station, and you'll surely get QRM to reject once you get started with the 10 meter band using SSB mode. You might even discover that you have some offending emissions coming from sources in or near your home creating noise on your SSB receiver. These can be frustrating at times. The best policy as a new ham when faced with a vexing interference problem is to remain calm and seek the sage advice of an experienced ham, or "Elmer," who is eager to help. Together you will usually be able to reduce or eliminate the interference problem.

Don't forget to practice the questions from the pool for Avoiding Interference, **Section 12.0**!

www.HamRadioSchool.com/tech_media

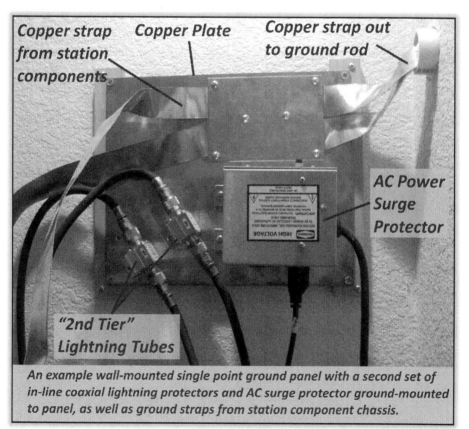

An example wall-mounted single point ground panel with a second set of in-line coaxial lightning protectors and AC surge protector ground-mounted to panel, as well as ground straps from station component chassis.

Figure 12.7: Example base station single soint ground panel as depicted in Figure 12.4.

13.0 Safety

> *" I could tell that my parents hated me. My bath toys were a toaster and a radio. – Rodney Dangerfield*

Most ham radio operations and station installation activities are not quite as hazardous as Rodney's childhood radio experience. And most ham shacks do not include toasters at all. However, because stations that are more elaborate than an HT will require some electrical power connections, will perhaps involve exterior antennas and towers, and typically will provide higher RF power transmission, safety becomes paramount. In this chapter we will examine potential hazards and safe practices that can help you avoid injury or equipment damage.

In Section 13.1 we will address basic electrical safety. It is important that you understand the sources of electrical shock associated with your station, as well as practical precautions for avoiding it. You should also be aware of hazards that batteries present and know how to safely charge, discharge, and store your batteries.

Section 13.2 highlights common sense precautions to take when erecting and operating tall antennas and towers. From proper climbing gear to grounding for lightning strikes, you will learn how to stay alive and uninjured to transmit another day.

Exposure to radio frequency emissions is the subject of Section 13.3. As an amateur station operator you should be able to estimate the RF exposure to humans that your station imposes, and you should know how to take action to reduce exposure levels when warranted by exposure guidelines.

Let's examine these common sense measures for keeping ourselves, our friends and neighbors, and our families safe while we enjoy amateur radio.

13.1 Safety
Electrical Safety

Electrical Safety involves avoiding electrical shock through knowledge of potential dangers and taking proper precautions.

Dangerous Electric Shock: The commonly accepted value for the lowest voltage that can cause a dangerous electric shock is about 30 volts, but it is the electrical *current* that flows and causes health hazards. **Current flowing through the body causes health hazards by:**

- **Heating tissue** (burns)
- **Disrupting the electrical functions of cells** (nervous system disfunction or loss of consciousness)
- **Causing involuntary muscle contractions** (including stopping the heart and inability to control body movements)

Typical household AC voltage of 120 volts is more than enough to be deadly. Even 12v batteries, such as high capacity lead-acid cells, can provide fatal currents especially when multiple cells are connected in series such that higher voltages result. Be very careful that you do not come into contact with bare wires connected to power sources or with unprotected battery terminals that may send a surge of current through your body. Also, because currents passing through your body are seeking a path to electrical ground, it is a good idea to always wear shoes so that some insulation between you and earth ground is afforded. Your bare feet will provide a low resistance pathway directly to ground. It pays to be conscientious around any source of current, regardless of voltage levels.

Sources of Electric Shock: Power supplies, even when turned off and disconnected, may still present a hazard of electric shock from stored charge in large capacitors. Allow ample time for capacitors to discharge before touching any part of the circuits. It is also feasible to carefully discharge capacitors through resistors, safely dissipating the energy into heat, if the circuit has been constructed with such a safety feature. If you are not sure, take no chances. Any equipment while powered from 120 V AC circuits presents a significant hazard. Batteries, while usually below 30 V, may still deliver a painful and dangerous shock.

13.1 Electrical Safety

Electrical Precautions: **Guard against electrical shock at your station by:**

- **Using three-wire cords and plugs for all AC powered equipment**
- **Connecting all AC powered station equipment to a common safety ground**
- **Using a circuit protected ground-fault interrupter (GFI) electrical outlet)**
- **Placing a fuse or circuit breaker in series with the AC "hot" conductor on any home-built equipment powered from 120V AC circuits**

Safety Ground: **In the United States, the green wire in a three-wire electrical AC plug is connected to the equipment ground.** *Green to ground!* The equipment ground, usually connected to the chassis or cabinet of a piece of radio gear, helps shunt any stray current to ground, reducing the risk of electrical shock and overloads in circuits.

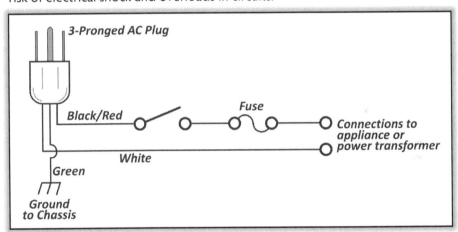

Figure 13.1: Wiring Diagram of Common 3-Pronged AC Plug

Fuses: **In an electrical circuit fuses interrupt power in case of overload** and help prevent electrical shock and fire hazards. **Never install a higher ampere rated fuse than is called for in a circuit or excessive current could cause a fire.** The whole purpose of a fuse is to break and disconnect the circuit any time excessive current is drawn through the wire by accident. If the fuse is not in place or if it is rated too high, excessive current will heat the wires, possibly melting insulation, burning or shocking you, and possibly starting a fire. Fuses are cheap. Fires and funeral are expensive. Use fuses.

Figure 13.2: In-line Fuses in a Radio Power Cable

Batteries may cause painful shock and present additional hazards when charging or discharging. When recharging a battery, take all precautions and ensure the procedure you use is correct for your battery type. Become familiar with the manufacturer's recommendations for recharging your batteries.

Explosive Gas: Hydrogen, an explosive gas, may be discharged and collect in the area around a conventional 12V storage battery if not properly vented. This problem is lessened with sealed batteries, but vented and liquid electrolyte batteries should be stored outside to avoid dangerous gas build up or acid spill in your radio shack.

T0A10 **Charging/Discharging Too Quickly: A lead-acid storage battery can overheat, give off flammable gas** (hydrogen), **or explode if it is charged or discharged too quickly.** Check manufacturer's recommendations for charging and discharge rates, and utilize a manufacturer-recommended smart charger to adjust the charging voltage profile for AGM or gel cell type lead-acid batteries. Battery explosions can be fatal to anyone nearby!

T0A01 **Shorting the terminals of a 12-volt storage battery can cause burns, fire, or an explosion.** Be very careful to avoid any conductor contacting across the two battery terminals! Protect the battery terminals.

And beyond all that, do not play with your radio in the bathtub. Next we'll consider precautions when working with antenna towers, but first take a look at the questions associated with electrical safety, **Section 13.1**.

www.HamRadioSchool.com/tech_media

13.2 Antenna & Tower Safety

> *The lofty pine is oftenest shaken by the wind; High towers fall with a heavier crash; And the lightning strikes the highest mountain.* – Horace

Although the ancient Roman poet probably wasn't a ham operator, Horace clearly knew a thing or two about hazards with antennas and towers. My amateur radio station is one of many with an antenna perched up in a lofty pine that is often shaken by the wind. Other stations more well accoutred than mine have high towers erected and maintained by safety conscious hams who seek to avoid a heavy crash and to mitigate a lightning strike! Here we shall learn some basic safety precautions with antennas and towers that all hams should know and heed.

Antenna Tower Safety involves understanding potential dangers associated with erecting, operating, and maintaining any type of tower, mast, or antenna, and taking proper precautions to avoid injury or damage.

Climbing antenna towers presents multiple hazards that can cause injury or death.

Hard Hat & Safety Glasses: Members of a tower work team should wear a hard hat and safety glasses at all times when any work is being done on the tower. Tools or other objects dropped from heights represent significant hazards for head and eye injury. A set of pliers through the skull or a screwdriver through an eye socket is a poor way to enhance your ham radio experience.

Photo: Perry Jager NØWMZ
Pictured: Dave Novotny WA6IFI

Figure 13.3: Climbing Safety Gear Includes a Hardhat, Safety Glasses, & Climbing Harness

Climbing Harness: A good precaution to observe when any work is being done on a tower is to put on a carefully inspected climbing harness (fall arrester) and safety glasses. A harness, properly attached to the tower structure, helps avoid accidental falls. Better to be strung up than flung down to the ground.

Observer: It is never safe to climb a tower without a helper or observer. In the case of an injury, a fall, or a complication on the tower an observer or helper can provide immediate assistance, first aid, or seek additional emergency help.

Erecting a Tower or Antenna must be done carefully and with consideration for surrounding obstacles.

Overhead Electrical Wires are deadly when contacted directly or indirectly with a conductor such as a metal tower or mast. **Look for and stay clear of any overhead electrical wires.**

Minimum safe distance from a power line: When installing an antenna of any type, the minimum safe distance from a power line is enough so that if the antenna falls unexpectedly, no part of it can come closer than 10 feet to the power wires. This is an important safety rule for any antenna system. Don't take the chance – keep your antenna away from power lines.

Utility Poles: Utility poles should not have antennas attached to them since the antenna could contact high-voltage power lines. Although it might seem like a convenient mast to use, the risk to life and equipment is not worth it. Additionally, power lines are common incidental RF emission source, inducing noise in your receiver.

Guy Lines: Many types of vertical antenna mounts will require guy lines to secure the vertical mast. Guy lines should be evenly tensioned using turnbuckles. **Prevent lossening of the guy line from vibration using a safety wire through the turnbuckle.**

Gin Pole: A gin pole, used to lift tower sections or antennas, can help avoid strain or injury of workers installing the tower or antenna. When using a gin pole keep in mind the same safe distance precautions from power lines as noted above.

Crank-Up Towers: *Crank up towers* are a great way to get a high performance antenna high in the air for a short time. These towers typically have

13.2 Antenna & Tower Safety

mechanically lifted segments that telescope or raise up with a manual or motor-powered crank in a matter of minutes. They can be a real convenience in areas where permanent antenna structures are prohibited. However, **never climb a crank-up tower unless retracted or mechanical safety locking devices have been installed.** These portable or temporary towers may collapse or fall if climbed while extended. If your fingers, arms, legs or other body parts are in the way as the tower collapses, you will be severely injured or killed by the collapsing parts, if not from the fall and impact with the ground. *Remember, crank it down first!*

Grounding Towers and Antennas: It is good practice to protect against lightning strikes and the potential of lightning energy being routed into your radio shack by properly grounding your external antenna or tower.

Local Electrical Codes: **Grounding requirements for amateur radio towers or antennas are established by local electrical codes.** You should make sure that you comply with all local electrical codes with any antenna system or tower.

Grounding for Lightning: **For towers, a proper grounding method is to use separate eight-foot long ground rods for each tower leg, bonded to the tower and also to each other. Tower ground wires installed for lightning protection should be short and direct. Sharp bends must be avoided.** Usually, broad conductor strap, such as copper strap, is best for grounding connections since it

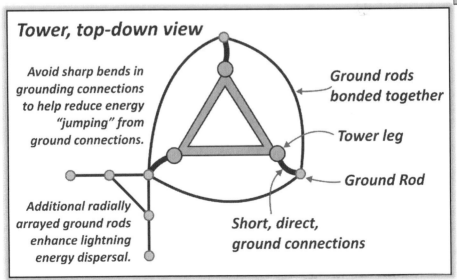

Figure 13.4: Top-down View of Tower Grounding Arrangement

provides greater surface area for current flow than wires. Sharp bends or creases in the grounding strap increase resistance and encourage lightning to depart from the conductor and "jump" to nearby objects.

For any station earth grounding, **all external grounding rods or earth connections should be bonded together with heavy wire or conductive strap.** Don't skimp on the ground rods! They help dissipate lightning energy into the earth when a strike occurs. Rods should be separated by twice their in-earth depth to promote lightning energy dispersal and to avoid saturating the ground with that energy – if the local surface ground cannot dissipate the lightning the energy will seek other routes to a ground level voltage, such as through your shack and equipment.

Coaxial Cable Feedline Lightning Protectors: Lightning protectors, also called *lightning tubes*, typically use common coaxial connector interfaces (N-connector or PL-259) so that they may be inserted in-line in coaxial antenna feedlines. If an electrical surge due to a lightning strike flows down the coax, the lightning tube is designed to break like a fuse very rapidly, significantly reducing the surge currents continuing down the coaxial feedline toward the shack and instead directing the energy safely to the ground.

Commonly such lightning protectors will be mounted and grounded onto a conductor plate (copper or aluminum) mounted on an external radio shack wall so that the plate may be easily grounded (See Figure 13.5). **Mount all coaxial cable feedline lightning protectors on a metal plate that is in turn connected to an external ground rod** (such as an 8-foot or longer ground rod inserted into the earth). If you do not ground the protectors the lightning energy will not have a safe route to ground and may jump to other nearby conductors such as housing wires, pipes, computers, refrigerators, or anything conductive.

With proper precautions you can survive even the worst antenna and tower calamities predicted by Horace and live to erect a better system another day. While most cases of simple wire or small vertical antenna erection present relatively little hazard, take no chances. Be certain of your environment and your local codes, always wear proper safety equipment, and always have an observer to assist you. Be safe, not sorry!

The questions! Practice the questions for **Section 13.2.**

www.HamRadioSchool.com/tech_media

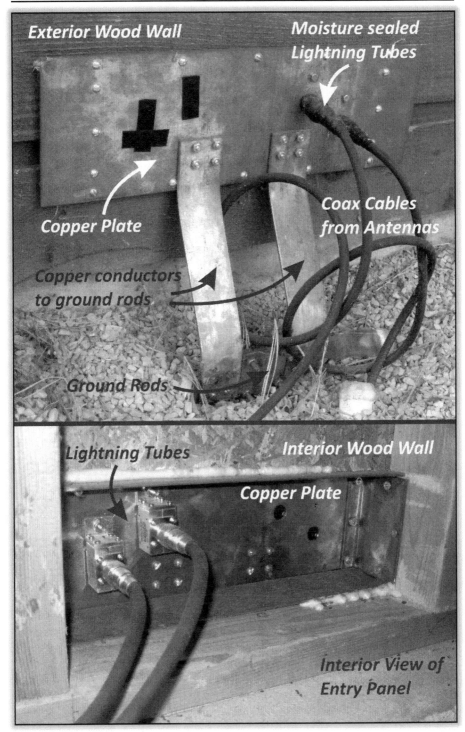

Figure 13.5: Lightning Protected Exterior Cable Entry Panel

13.3 RF Exposure Safety

> *It's not true I had nothing on, I had the radio on.* – Marilyn Monroe

Each time you push-to-talk, you expose yourself... to RF energy, I mean. And you are exposing others around you as well. How much radio exposure is safe? How do factors of frequency, power, or distance make a difference to exposure limits? How can you be sure your station is within safe limits? Should you put on aluminum foil coveralls before operating your station?

RF Exposure Safety involves understanding the FCC RF exposure limits and how to apply them with your station, ensuring that your station does not expose any person to levels of RF energy that exceed recommended levels. In most amateur stations RF exposure is not a great concern, but as an amateur operator you should be familiar with limits and requirements to evaluate exposure to assure safe operations for yourself, your family, and your neighbors.

Figure 13.6: Typical RF Aluminum Coveralls

Non-Ionizing Radiation: **UHF, VHF, and HF emissions are non-ionizing radiation.** This means that the RF emissions do not strip electrons from atoms like *ionizing radiation,* such as ultraviolet rays and X-rays. **As non-ionizing radiation RF radiation does not have sufficient energy to cause genetic damage** or biological molecular changes.

RF Heating of Tissues: RF emissions are absorbed by tissues in our body causing heating of those tissues. With excessive RF exposure tissue damage can occur due to the body's inability to dissipate the heat delivered. Think of the way a microwave oven works – a great amount of microwave RF energy is delivered inside the oven, rapidly cooking the items placed there that have no way of shedding the absorbed energy and resultant heat. Regarding the

13.3 RF Exposure Safety

human body, a relative lack of blood flow to help dissipate excess heat makes our eyes and the male's testes most vulnerable to RF heating.

RF Burns: RF burns are painful and may happen if a person accidentally touches your antenna while you are transmitting, allowing RF electrical currents to flow through the body to ground. Unlike conventional heat burns, RF burns are from the flow of electrical current and may extend deep below the skin surface, requiring long healing times. RF burns are not a significant hazard with HT radios emitting 5W or less, but take care to ensure that no person touches your mobile or fixed station transmitting at higher power levels.

Power Density is the measure of RF power over area. Typically this is expressed as *milliwatts per square centimeter* (mW/cm^2). RF exposure limits recommended by the FCC, or the *Maximum Permissible Exposure* (MPE), are expressed in these units for each frequency band. Several factors affect power density and the resulting human exposure.

Factors Affecting RF Exposure: Each of the following affect the RF exposure of people near an amateur station antenna:

- **Frequency and power level of the RF field**
- **Distance from the antenna to a person**
- **Radiation pattern of the antenna**
- Duty Cycle of transmissions

Frequency: Exposure limits vary with frequency because the human body absorbs more RF energy at some frequencies than at others.

The greatest absorption, and thus **the lowest Maximum Permissible Exposure (MPE) limit,** is found for the VHF band of 30 to 300 MHz. **Note that this includes** the popular 2m band (near 144 MHz) and the 6m band **(near 50 MHz).**

Power Level: Greater power output increases the power density of the RF field. **The maximum power level that an amateur radio station may use at VHF frequencies** (1.25m, 2m, 6m bands) **before an RF exposure evaluation is required is 50 watts PEP at the antenna.** If you are outputting 50 watts with your transmitter you will likely have a little less than 50 watts at the antenna due to feedline loss. If your antenna is some distance above and away from people, you are safe. However, if you increase your power above 50 watts or if your antenna is nearby, such as inside your home or right outside the 2nd story bedroom, you must evaluate exposure levels.

PEP: *Peak Envelope Power* is the average power supplied to the antenna during an RF cycle at the peak of the amplitude of the RF signal's envelope. Most power meters have a PEP setting that allows an amateur operator to make measurements of PEP via a power meter on the feedline.

Distance from Antenna: RF energy spreads out as distance from the antenna increases, reducing the power per unit area. Specifically, power levels fall off as the square of the distance, so doubling the distance from the antenna reduces your exposure by a factor of four (1/4). Thus, **relocating antennas is one of the most common actions an amateur might take to prevent exposure to RF radiation in excess of FCC-supplied limits.**

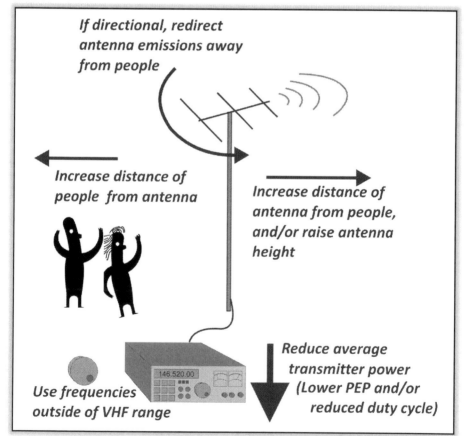

Figure 13.7: Factors Affecting RF Exposure and Mitigation

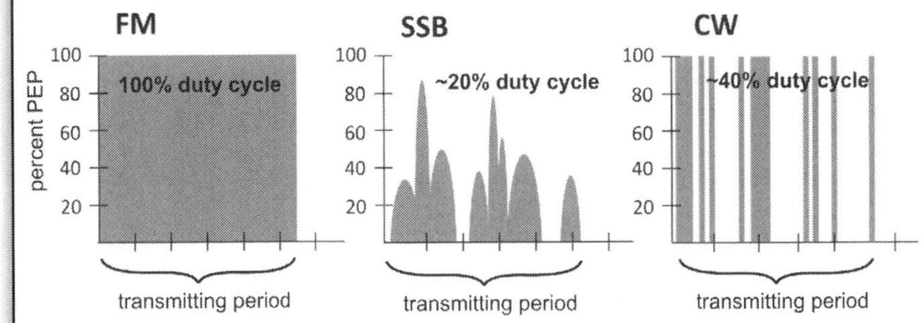

13.3 RF Exposure Safety

The duty cycle of transmission modes is determined by transmitter "on air" time and percent PEP within any single transmission. For 100% PEP modes (FM, CW) duty cycle is simply the ratio of "on air" time to total operating time. Multiple transmitter operating periods and receiver "listening periods" may comprise a standard averaging period of 6 or 30 minutes for estimating RF exposure levels.

Figure 13.8: Duty Cycle of a Transmitter

Antenna Radiation Pattern: As we learned in Section 7.1, directional antennas will concentrate power in one direction, while isotropic antennas and dipole antennas distribute radiation more equally in all directions. Assessing RF exposure should take into consideration the power gain of any directional antennas used by the station.

Duty Cycle: Duty cycle affects the average exposure of people to radiation, so it is a factor used to determine safe RF radiation exposure levels. During an averaging time for RF exposure (6 or 30 minute measurement period), **duty cycle is the percentage of time that a transmitter is transmitting.** Thus, if the duty cycle is 50% across an averaging period, the power density may be doubled. **In a 6 minute averaging time, 2 times as much power density (mW/cm^2) is permitted if the signal is present for 3 minutes and absent for 3 minutes, rather than being present for the entire 6 minutes.**

More generally, duty cycle estimation should vary with the mode of transmission you are using. FM signals transmit at 100% power for the entire PTT transmission time. SSB signals vary in power with your audio signal amplitude, dropping to near zero power between words and sentences, and causing the duty cycle to be reduced.

Complying with Limits: If your station requires an exposure evaluation, you may conduct it yourself or with help from a fellow amateur by any of the following **acceptable methods of determining compliance:**

- **By calculation based on FCC OET Bulletin 65**
- **By calculation based on computer modeling**
- **By measurement of field strength using calibrated equipment**

Note: **You can make sure your station stays in compliance with RF safety regulation by re-evaluating the station whenever an item of equipment is changed.**

Practical Advice on RF Exposure Compliance: Most new ham stations are not going to require an evaluation. But if you plan to use power levels above 50 watts (especially in 6m, 2m, and 70cm bands), if you plan to use a directional antenna with substantial gain figures, or if your antenna must be in close proximity with people, it is your responsibility to ensure your station is not exposing humans to RF levels in excess of the Maximum Permissible Exposure (MPE) limits defined in FCC OET Bulletin 65.

The FCC Office of Engineering and Technology (OET) Bulletin 65 from August 1997 contains more information than most new hams are likely to absorb in a short time. However, the tables and graph of MPE from the bulletin's appendix A is quite useful. Armed with a computed estimate of exposure in mW/cm^2 (milliwatts per square centimeter), you can use these tables to make a good estimate of whether or not your station is complying with MPE limits.

How can you easily make such a computation, you ask? The internet comes to the rescue! In addition to commercial and freeware computer software programs, several good internet sites are now available to estimate exposure levels using basic information that is easily known to you about your station and the exposure environment. Most of these sites utilize the formulas given in FCC OET Bulletin 65, but research sufficiently to be sure these are used. An internet search of "RF Exposure Calculator" will turn up multiple options. You will also find links to online exposure calculators in the Section 13.3 learning media at *HamRadioSchool.com*.

In most MPE calculator cases using the FCC formulas, you will need to enter the following types of information:

- **Average PEP** power at the antenna. This should be very close to your transmitter power, and you may measure close to your antenna with a power meter on the feedline. You may also need to adjust the power value for the duty cycle that is typical of your operational mode.

13.3 RF Exposure Safety

- **Gain** of your antenna in the direction of interest, or the isotropic gain.
- **Distance** to the area of interest for your measurement. That is, how far from your antenna to the living room or to your neighbor's house.
- **Frequency** of transmission, usually in MHz.

To use the FCC tables:

1. Make your estimates of exposure power density in mW/cm^2, perhaps using an online calculator as described earlier in this section.

2. Reference the frequency range in megahertz in the left column of the OET Bulletin 65 table (included at the end of this section):
   - For 6m and 2m bands the 30 – 300 MHz row applies.
   - For 70cm band the 300 – 1500 MHz row applies.
   - For 10m, the 3.0 – 30 MHz row applies.
   - Go across the rows to the Power Density column to read the MPE.

   Note that MPE for 6m and 2m is 1.0 mW/cm^2 for controlled exposure (you, the operator) and 0.2 mW/cm^2 for uncontrolled exposure (other people), and note that the other two ranges require a simple calculation based upon the specific frequency of exposure.

3. Compare your computed exposure level for your station with the MPE values in the table to determine if your station is exceeding the MPE.

4. If you find your station is exceeding the MPE, take steps to reduce the exposure.

Congratulations! You have completed all of the testable material for your FCC Technician VE Exam. Review the last set of questions from **Section 13.3**, take practice exams, and go get your license!

www.HamRadioSchool.com/tech_media

Please give us some feedback and let us know how you are doing by visiting the *HamRadioSchool.com* web site!

Good luck! I hope to hear you on the air soon. 73. WØSTU, clear.

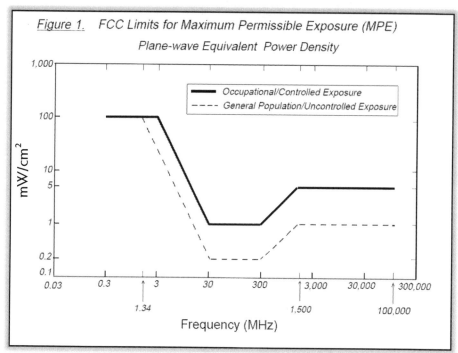

Figure 13.9: OET Bulletin 65 Chart of MPE (mW/cm^2) by Frequency.

Note that the lowest allowable MPE is in the VHF range, 30 - 300 MHz. The human body absorbs VHF more readily than other frequency ranges, hence the allowable exposure is lowest for VHF. The VHF exposure limit is 1.0 mW/cm^2 for controlled exposure (operators) and 0.2 mW/cm^2 for uncontrolled exposure to the general population. (See notes 1 and 2 of the FCC OEM Bulletin 65 extract on the next page.)

13.3 RF Exposure Safety

Table 1. LIMITS FOR MAXIMUM PERMISSIBLE EXPOSURE (MPE)

(A) Limits for Occupational/Controlled Exposure

Frequency Range (MHz)	Electric Field Strength (E) (V/m)	Magnetic Field Strength (H) (A/m)	Power Density (S) (mW/cm^2)	Averaging $|E|^2$, $|H|^2$ or S (minutes)
0.3 - 3.0	614	1.63	(100)*	6
3.0-30	1842/f	4.89/f	(900/f^2)	6
30-300	61.4	0.163	1.0	6
300-1500	--	--	f/300	6
1500-100,000	--	--	5	6

(B) Limits for General Population/Uncontrolled Exposure

Frequency Range (MHz)	Electric Field Strength (E) (V/m)	Magnetic Field Strength (H) (A/m)	Power Density (S) (mW/cm^2)	Averaging $|E|^2$, $|H|^2$ or S (minutes)
0.3-1.34	614	1.63	(100)*	30
1.34-30	824/f	2.19/f	(180/f)*	30
30-300	27.5	0.073	0.2	30
300-1500	--	--	f/1500	30
1500-100,000	--	--	1.0	30

f = frequency in MHz   *Plane-wave equivalent power density

NOTE 1: *Occupational/controlled* limits apply in situations in which persons are exposed as a consequence of their employment provided those persons are fully aware of the potential for exposure and can exercise control over their exposure. Limits for occupational/controlled exposure also apply in situations when an individual is transient through a location where occupational/controlled limits apply provided he or she is made aware of the potential for exposure.

NOTE 2: *General population/uncontrolled* exposures apply in situations in which the general public may be exposed, or in which persons that are exposed as a consequence of their employment may not be fully aware of the potential for exposure or can not exercise control over their exposure.

Figure 13.10: FCC OEM Bulletin 65 Table of MPE Limits

Index

Index of Terms

Ø (slash zero) 43
alternating current (AC) 5, 130
alternator whine 187
amateur bands 7, 69-74
ammeter 141
ampere (amp) 130
amplitude 2, 67
amplitude modulation (AM) 4, 12, 89
anode 153
antenna 5, 10, 14, 109-128
antenna analyzer 122
antenna tuner 121
APRS 165, 168
ARES 56
audio band 88, 90
auroral propagation 80
automatic gain control (AGC) 101
automatic repeat request (ARQ) 171
averaging time (RF exposure) 205
band plan 69-74
bands 69-74
bandwidth 103-107
base station 11
batteries 146-148, 159, 196
beam antenna 113
beat frequency oscillator 99
bipolar junction transistor (BJT) 158
bit error rate (BER) 171
BNC connector 127-128
Broadband Hamnet 170
call districts (US) 44
call sign formats 42-43
call signs 41-45
calling frequency 19
capacitor 143, 151
cathode 153
check (radiogram) 55
check sum 171
clarifier 100
climbing harness 198
clipping 89
club call signs 44
coaxial cable (coax) 125-128
conductor 131
connectors (coaxial cable) 127

contesting 55
continuous wave (CW) 4, 12, 84, 105, 165
control (station) 37-40
control circuit 162
control operator 37
control point 39
courtesy tones 27
CQ 18
crank-up tower 198
cross needle SWR meter 121-122
CTCSS 26
current 5, 130
cute XYL 16
DCS 27
decibel (dB) 138
deviation (FM) 93
digital mobile radio (DMR) 170
digital mode 165-172
digital transmission errors 170
diode 153, 156
dipole antenna 112
direct current (DC) 5, 130
directional antenna 113
directional wattmeter 121
discriminator (FM) 102
Doppler shift (satellite) 178
dummy load 114
duty cycle 205
DXpedition 49
Echolink 168
electric shock 194
electrical precautions 195
electrical safety 194
electromagnetic spectrum 6
electromagnetic wave 2, 62
emergency services 56
entry panel 200-201
envelope (modulation) 91
exam (license) xii-xiii
farad (unit) 151
fast-scan TV 172
FCC 29
FCC Rules 29-51
feedline loss 126
ferrite choke 184
field effect transistor (FET) 159

211

filters   184-186
foxhunt   55
frequency   3, 62-64
frequency modulation (FM)   4, 12, 91, 101
fundamental overload   182
fuse   160, 195
gain (antenna)   113
gain (transistor)   158
gateway (internet)   168
gin pole   198
global positioning system (GPS)   168
goats   59
grid locator   55-56
ground plane   111
grounding (lightning)   199
grounding (RF)   188
grounding (towers, antennas)   199
harmonic emissions   182-183
henry (unit)   152
hertz   3, 63
High Frequency (HF)   6, 69
HT   10, 15
identification   17, 19, 41, 45
impedance   118, 132
inductor   117, 152
insulator   131
integrated circuit   150
interference   180-192
international agreements   49-50
international interference   49
ionizing radiation   202
ionosphere   75-78
IRLP   168-169
ITU   47
ITU regions   47-48
KØNR   118
KDØKGJ   36
KDØLLC   58
KDØMFO   52
KDØMUW   38
KDØPWF   46
KF5BOC   179
KNØTPC   58
KTØLIZ   16
KYØHIP   36, 57
Keplerian elements   175
key (CW)   165-166

keyer (electronic)   165
keypad   14
knife edge diffraction   81
lamp   159, 162
LED (light emitting diode)   153
license classes (amateur)   7, 33
license provisions, term   33
lightning protectors (tubes)   200-201
limiter (FM)   102
linked repeater   28
loaded antenna   116-117
low earth orbit (LEO)   174
Maidenhead grid locator   55, 56
math prefixes, converting   66, 144
maximum permissible exposure   203-206
measurements (electrical)   141
message traffic handling   54
meteor scatter   80
meter (display)   160
microphone   10, 86-87
mixing (frequencies)   97
mobile antennas   117
mobile station   10, 117, 187
mode (modulation)   12
mode (satellite)   176
modulation   4, 86-95
modulator circuit   92
Morse Code   4, 12, 41, 85, 165
multimeter   143
multi-mode transceiver   79
multipath distortion   21
N-connector   127
net   53
noise blanker   187
non-ionizing radiation   202
NTSC signal   172
OET Bulletin 65   206-209
offset frequency   25
ohm   132
ohmmeter   142
Ohm's Law   133
oscillator   85
packet   166
Part 15 device   187
Part 97   30
peak envelope power (PEP)   204
phase relationship (waveform)   67-68

Index

phonetics 41
picket fencing 22
PL-259 connector 127
polarization 22, 23, 67, 76
potentiometer 151
power density (RF) 203
power law 135
power supply 14
preamble (radiogram) 55
preamplifier (RF) 99
printed circuit board (PCB) 163
product detector 99
prohibited activities 30-32
propagation (signal) 75-82
PSK31 166
push to talk (PTT) 13
Q signals 19
QRM (rejecting) 188-191
RACES 56
radio horizon 20
radio waves 2, 63
radiogram 54
radionavigation interference 49
receiver 10
receiving 97-102
rectifier circuit 161
regulator circuit 160
relay 160
remote control vehicles 171
repeater coordination 28
repeater directory 169
repeater station 17, 25-28
resistance 129
resistor 132, 151
resonance 109
RF burns 203
RF coupling 113
RF exposure 202-209
RF exposure calculations 206-207
RF feedback 184
RF filters 184-186
RF heating 202
RF spectrum 6
RIT (receiver incremental tuning) 100
rubber duck antenna 14
safety ground 195
satellite beacon 175

satellite tracking programs 171
scatter (tropospheric) 80
schematic symbols 151
secondary privileges 74
selectivity (receiver) 189
self-assigned indicator 45
semiconductor 150
sensitivity (receiver) 99
signal fade 76-77
simplex operations 17
single point ground 188-189
single sideband (SSB) 4, 12, 97, 103
skin effect 126
skip propagation 75
sky wave propagation 75
slow-scan TV 171
SMA connector 127
snap-on choke 184-185
solder 163
Summits On The Air (SOTA) 59
sound card interface (SCI) 167
space contacts 173-179
space station (Part 97) 173
speaker 10
spin fading 178
splatter 183
sporadic E 80
spurious emissions 182
squelch 13
standing wave ratio (SWR) 119-124
subelements (exam pool) x
superheterodyne receiver 98
switch 159-160
SWR bandwidth 123
SWR curve 123-124
SWR meter 121
tactical call sign 45
talk group (DMR) 170
telecommand 177
telemetry 177
television (amateur) 171
terminal node controller (TNC) 166
third party 38, 48
tone burst 27
tower safety 197
traffic 53
transceiver 9

transformer   160
transistor   157-159
transmitter   10
transmitting   84-95
transverter   106
tropospheric ducting   80
trustee (club)   44
tuned circuit   161
Ultra High Frequency (UHF)   6, 69, 81
utility poles   198
vanity call sign   43
variable frequency oscillator (VFO)   14
variable resistor   151
vertical antenna   111
Very High Frequency (VHF)   6, 69, 81
volt   130
voltage   5, 130
voltmeter   141
WØCOL   21, 36, 40
WØJAK   10, 84, 87, 119, 173, 202, cover
WØSTU   xii, 32, 173, back cover
WA6IFI   197
WGØAT   59
W6HFP   51
wavelength   2, 61-63
WSJT Digital Modes   167
Yagi antenna   113

Index

Element 2 Technician Exam Pool Question and Page Index

EL. T1		EL. T2		EL. T3		EL. T4	
T1A01	29	T1D01	48	T2A01	26	T3A01	21	T4A01	140
T1A02	29	T1D02	31	T2A02	19	T3A02	81	T4A02	165
T1A03	42	T1D03	31	T2A03	26	T3A03	22	T4A03	140
T1A04	33	T1D04	31	T2A04	19,28	T3A04	22	T4A04	167
T1A05	33	T1D05	32	T2A05	18	T3A05	22	T4A05	121
T1A06	79	T1D06	30	T2A06	17	T3A06	22	T4A06	167
T1A07	173	T1D07	32	T2A07	25	T3A07	62	T4A07	167
T1A08	28	T1D08	33	T2A08	18	T3A08	76	T4A08	188
T1A09	28	T1D09	31	T2A09	28	T3A09	76	T4A09	184
T1A10	56	T1D10	31	T2A10	69	T3A10	171	T4A10	187
T1A11	31	T1D11	171	T2A11	17	T3A11	75	T4A11	187
				T2A12	18	T3A12	82		
T1B01	47	T1E01	37			T3A13	82	T4B01	89
T1B02	176	T1E02	176	T2B01	28			T4B02	14
T1B03	70	T1E03	37	T2B02	27	T3B01	64	T4B03	13
T1B04	19,65	T1E04	38	T2B03	28	T3B02	22	T4B04	14
T1B05	73	T1E05	39	T2B04	27	T3B03	63	T4B05	187
T1B06	73	T1E06	39	T2B05	89	T3B04	63	T4B06	100
T1B07	73	T1E07	37	T2B06	169	T3B05	65	T4B07	100
T1B08	49,74	T1E08	39	T2B07	170	T3B06	65	T4B08	188
T1B09	106	T1E09	39	T2B08	20	T3B07	64	T4B09	189
T1B10	70	T1E10	39	T2B09	170	T3B08	69	T4B10	190
T1B11	73	T1E11	37	T2B10	19	T3B09	69	T4B11	100
T1B12	73			T2B11	20	T3B10	69	T4B12	187
		T1F01	30	T2B12	71	T3B11	63	T4B13	18
T1C01	33	T1F02	45	T2B13	73				
T1C02	43	T1F03	19,41	T2B14	28	T3C01	81		
T1C03	48	T1F04	41			T3C02	75		
T1C04	49	T1F05	41	T2C01	30	T3C03	80		
T1C05	43	T1F06	45	T2C02	53	T3C04	80		
T1C06	47	T1F07	49	T2C03	42	T3C05	81		
T1C07	30	T1F08	48	T2C04	56	T3C06	80		
T1C08	34	T1F09	17,25	T2C05	53	T3C07	80		
T1C09	34	T1F10	38	T2C06	54	T3C08	80		
T1C10	33	T1F11	44	T2C07	53	T3C09	79		
T1C11	34			T2C08	54	T3C10	79		
				T2C09	57	T3C11	21		
				T2C10	55				
				T2C11	55				
				T2C12	56				

Continued...

EL. T5		EL. T6				EL. T7			
T5A01	130	T5D01	133	T6C01	151	T7A01	99	T7D01	141
T5A02	135	T5D02	133	T6C02	151,162	T7A02	9	T7D02	141
T5A03	130	T5D03	133	T6C03	162	T7A03	97	T7D03	142
T5A04	130	T5D04	134	T6C04	159	T7A04	189	T7D04	141
T5A05	130	T5D05	133	T6C05	159	T7A05	85	T7D05	142
T5A06	130	T5D06	133	T6C06	152	T7A06	106	T7D06	144
T5A07	131	T5D07	133	T6C07	153	T7A07	13	T7D07	143
T5A08	131	T5D08	133	T6C08	151	T7A08	92	T7D08	164
T5A09	130	T5D09	133	T6C09	160	T7A09	79	T7D09	164
T5A10	135	T5D10	133	T6C10	152	T7A10	10	T7D10	143
T5A11	130	T5D11	133	T6C11	159	T7A11	99	T7D11	142
T5A12	63,130	T5D12	133,134	T6C12	151			T7D12	141
T5A13	154	T5D13	154	T6C13	151	T7B01	22		
T5A14	154	T5D14	155			T7B02	182		
		T5D15	154	T6D01	161	T7B03	182		
T5B01	145	T5D16	155	T6D02	160	T7B04	184		
T5B02	66			T6D03	160	T7B05	185		
T5B03	145	EL. T6		T6D04	160,162	T7B06	186		
T5B04	144	T6A01	151	T6D05	160,162	T7B07	185		
T5B05	148	T6A02	151	T6D06	160	T7B08	186		
T5B06	146	T6A03	151	T6D07	153	T7B09	187		
T5B07	66	T6A04	151	T6D08	161	T7B10	23		
T5B08	146	T6A05	151	T6D09	150	T7B11	184		
T5B09	138	T6A06	152	T6D10	162	T7B12	186		
T5B10	139	T6A07	152	T6D11	161				
T5B11	139	T6A08	159	T6D12	125	T7C01	114		
T5B12	66	T6A09	160			T7C02	122		
T5B13	66	T6A10	147			T7C03	120		
		T6A11	146			T7C04	122		
T5C01	151					T7C05	121		
T5C02	151	T6B01	157			T7C06	123		
T5C03	152	T6B02	153			T7C07	126		
T5C04	152	T6B03	157			T7C08	121		
T5C05	63	T6B04	157			T7C09	126		
T5C06	63	T6B05	157			T7C10	126		
T5C07	63	T6B06	153			T7C11	126		
T5C08	135	T6B07	153			T7C12	115		
T5C09	136	T6B08	159						
T5C10	135	T6B09	153						
T5C11	136	T6B10	158						
T5C12	120,132	T6B11	158						
T5C13	120,132	T6B12	154						
T5C14	19								

Index

EL T8		EL T9		EL. TØ	
T8A01	103	T8D01	165	T0A01	196
T8A02	12	T8D02	168	T0A02	194
T8A03	12	T8D03	168	T0A03	195
T8A04	12	T8D04	172	T0A04	195
T8A05	105	T8D05	168	T0A05	195
T8A06	105	T8D06	166	T0A06	195
T8A07	12	T8D07	170	T0A07	200
T8A08	103	T8D08	170	T0A08	195
T8A09	105	T8D09	165	T0A09	200
T8A10	172	T8D10	167	T0A10	196
T8A11	105	T8D11	171	T0A11	194
		T8D12	170		
T8B01	177	T8D13	167	T0B01	197
T8B02	177	T8D14	165	T0B02	198
T8B03	175			T0B03	198
T8B04	175			T0B04	198
T8B05	177	EL. T9		T0B05	198
T8B06	175	T9A01	113	T0B06	198
T8B07	178	T9A02	117	T0B07	199
T8B08	176	T9A03	112	T0B08	199
T8B09	178	T9A04	14	T0B09	198
T8B10	174	T9A05	110	T0B10	199
T8B11	177	T9A06	113	T0B11	199
T8B12	177	T9A07	14	T0B12	199
		T9A08	115	T0B13	198
T8C01	186	T9A09	115		
T8C02	55	T9A10	112	T0C01	202
T8C03	55	T9A11	113	T0C02	203
T8C04	55	T9A12	116	T0C03	203
T8C05	55			T0C04	203
T8C06	169	T9B01	125	T0C05	203
T8C07	168	T9B02	121	T0C06	205
T8C08	168	T9B03	125	T0C07	203
T8C09	169	T9B04	121	T0C08	204
T8C10	168	T9B05	126	T0C09	206
T8C11	168	T9B06	127	T0C10	205
		T9B07	127	T0C11	205
		T9B08	126	T0C12	202
		T9B09	128	T0C13	205
		T9B10	126		
		T9B11	126		

HamRadioSchool.com
General License Course

*Complete Element 3 Exam Preparation
and more,
to help you really understand ham radio!*

by
Stu Turner
WØSTU

Bob Witte KØNR, Technical Editor

Third Edition: Version 3.0

This book was conceived, written, and developed by Stu Turner, LLC. Stu Turner, Author. **Copyright © 2019. All rights reserved.**

Photography and Graphics Credit: All photographs, drawings, and graphics, unless otherwise credited, were produced by the Author as original materials, in some cases including components from copyright-free (open) and/or public domain sources.

HamRadioSchool.com logo, cover art, and cover design by James Bucknall. Cover photography by Stu Turner, LLC. Author photo by Dan Oldfield Photography.

All material is subject to US Copyright Law. Reproduction, publication, or duplication of this book, or any part thereof, in any manner, mechanically, electronically, or photographically, is prohibited without the express written permission of the Author. The Author, publisher, and seller assume no liability with respect to the use of the information contained herein.

General Class practice app for quizzes & exams!

Study and practice exam questions on-the-go with your book and smart phone or tablet device!

Check your smart phone store for the *HamRadioSchool.com* quizzing & exam app!

- Take short quizzes focused on just the exam questions from your current book section, for *step-by-step* learning ease!

- Take properly weighted and randomized full 35-question practice exams to test your readiness for VE examination!

- Let the app ensure you see *all the questions* and retake questions that you got wrong in previous practice exams!

- Let the app track your performance by book section so you always know where to focus your review!

- Intuitive and easy-to-use app lets you review topic knowledge and practice for your exam anywhere, anytime!

Acknowledgements: Tremendous thanks to the following for their time and assistance with this book and with *HamRadioSchool.com*... You guys rock!

Bob Witte, KØNR, for technical editing, suggestions, educational support, web site contributions, photos, gear, and for being the Elmer Supreme! Thank you Mr. Editor, I could not have done it without you.

James Bucknall, KDØMFO, for cover art, webmaster support, classroom support, layout advice, and great friendship!

Paul Swanson, AAØK, for photos, educational support, and classroom support! Thanks Paul!

Eric Worley, WØRLY, for photos and classroom support! Thanks Eric!

Steve Galchutt, WGØAT, for photos and *goatly* inspiration! Tha-a-a-a-a-a-nks, Steve!

Ham Radio Outlet, Denver, Colorado, for photography subject matter, for carrying the books, and for being **THE** ham radio retailer in Colorado.

Agilent Technologies, for oscilloscope measurement images and photographs of scopes and other electronic measurement devices.

Cole Turner, WØCOL, and Jake Turner, WØJAK, for being splendid models for illustrative photographs and for the cover art.

Joyce Witte, KØJJW, for photos, classroom support, positive encouragement, always a kind word, and very tasty treats at our local class offerings!

Dan Oldfield, NØOLD, for great photography and friendship! Thanks Dan!

WØTLM Tri-Lakes Monument Radio Association, for being a great radio club and providing the opportunity for me to try a hand at instructing amateur radio courses!

Liz, KTØLIZ, for putting up with the whole thing... *again!* Thanks honey!

Be sure to visit *HamRadioSchool.com* for:

- Additional multi-media learning content
- Exam question pool review organized section-by-section
- Practical advice, interesting articles, and fun things to do
- *How-to* information on station set-up and ham activities
- Asking questions or sharing your success story with us

With HamRadioSchool.com's Integrated Learning System you will

Really Get It!

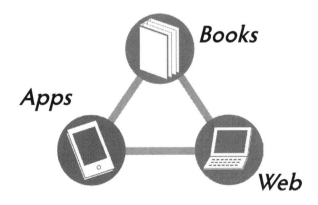

Teaching a ham class?

Check out our Instructor's Resources!

Use our ready-to-teach book and charts, and just add your Elmering wisdom and demos for an easy-to-teach and successful license class!

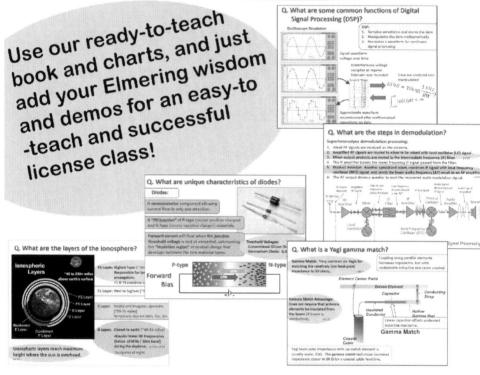

- Technician & General Class Materials
- Fully coordinated with our books, section-by-section
- Loaded with colorful, instructional graphics
- Highlights all exam pool question items
- "Click-to-reveal" sequence of each chart's content
- Includes animations and imbedded audio
- Over 300 individual charts per course
- Quizzes, video recommendations, and more!

Email: info@HamRadioSchool.com

Contents

	Preface	**226**
	Using This Book and Passing Your Exam	**227**
0.0	**Before We Begin...**	**231**
1.0	**Rules and Regs**	**239**
	1.1 Bands and Privileges	240
	1.2 Special Services	247
	1.3 DX and Details	253
2.0	**Operating Your Radio**	**261**
	2.1 Good Amateur Practice	261
	2.2 Operating Techniques	269
	2.3 CW	277
	2.4 Digital Mode Basics	283
	2.5 More Digital Modes	291
3.0	**Propagation**	**297**
	3.1 Solar Activity	297
	3.2 Ionosphere & Magnetosphere	303
	3.3 Operational Impacts	311
4.0	**How Radio Works**	**317**
	4.1 AM and SSB	318
	4.2 FM	335
	4.3 Signal Processing	345
5.0	**Antennas**	**359**
	5.1 Theory & Principles	363
	5.2 Directional Antennas	383
	5.3 SWR & Impedance Matching	393
6.0	**Hamtronics**	**403**
	6.1 Power and Principles	404
	6.2 Components	415
	6.3 Series & Parallel Component	433
	6.4 Impedance & Reactance	441
	6.5 Power Sources	449
	6.6 Amps & Tubes	461
	6.7 ICs and Computers	469
	6.8 Measurement	479
	6.9 Avoiding Interference	483
7.0	**Safety**	**491**
	7.1 Electrical & Antenna Precautions	491
	7.2 RF Exposure	503
	Topic Index	**512**
	Question Index	**515**

Preface

Congratulations on your decision to upgrade your FCC amateur radio license to General Class! You will really enjoy the added privileges that you will receive on the HF bands, with greatly expanded capability to make long distance contacts. The General Class ticket really opens up a whole other world of amateur radio coolness.

In this book you will learn all you need to not just pass your General Class VE exam, but to become a competent and safe ham radio operator. We really believe in preserving the quality of operations that uncountable proud amateurs have developed and maintained over the decades. We want you to really understand ham radio and keep with the tradition of *doing ham right!*

Is this book right for you? If you are interested in earning your General Class license, this book and its related web site are definitely for you, regardless of your background in science, technology, or math. This book will provide you fundamental understanding of radio along with the competence, and *confidence*, to get on all the HF bands. Inside the book and on the web site you will find easy-to-grasp explanations of the technical topics using common examples and analogies to everyday things and experiences with which you are already familiar. You will see ample pictures, graphics, and web-based media that will help you intuitively comprehend everything from how radio electronics work to how to set up your first HF station.

How is this book different? Unlike some other intermediate ham radio books, this one does not pad its pages with the public domain questions from the exam question pool and try to "teach the test" by requiring you to memorize answers without understanding them. Rather, the pages provide relevant information that focuses you on the right content while providing straightforward explanations so that you really comprehend radio. When you ***really get it*** you don't have to rely on mind-numbing memorization! Oh, and we provide you those public domain questions free, online at the *HamRadioSchool.com* web site, all organized by book section and accompanied by lots of additional content to help you learn very efficiently.

Get Going! Be sure you understand how to use this book as described in ***Using This Book and Passing Your Exam*** on the next page, and then start your learning both here and online at *HamRadioSchool.com*. If you have questions or comments for us, please contact us through the web site. We'll be glad to hear from you! *Good luck, and get going!*

Stu
WØSTU

Using This Book
and
Passing Your Exam

This *HamRadioSchool.com General License Course* book has been specially formatted to assist you with General license exam preparation. We recommend that you read this book's chapters in sequence first, then review material by topic, as necessary for your specific learning needs. We also recommend that you visit our web site section-by-section to take quizzes and to find additional materials that will make your learning experience an enjoyable one!

The *HamRadioSchool.com* web site provides additional learning tools organized section-by-section with the book. These enhanced learning tools may include video, audio, animations, graphics, photographs, or additional text explanations. You will also find the entire General Class exam question pool on the web site, with questions organized for ease of learning, section-by-section along with this book. The combination of this book and the web-based learning tools offers a powerful combination for really understanding ham radio.

Heavy Bold Text like this provides the answer to an exam pool question in *objective language* that mirrors the language of the question. All the exam pool questions are covered this way in this book. The tab in the outer margin adjacent to the heavy bold text provides you the question identifier. You will find each complete exam question with all response options online, conveniently organized section-by-section, at *HamRadioSchool.com*. A page index of question identifiers and topics is also included at the end of this book.

Example of Exam Question Objective Language Highlight and Exam Question:

> Book text: **A license revocation disqualifies a third party from participating in stating a message over an amateur station.**
>
> Question Item: **G1E01** (A)   *Section 1.3, Page 30*
> Which of the following would disqualify a third party from participating in stating a message over an amateur station?
>   A. The third party's amateur license has been revoked and not reinstated
>   B. The third party is not a U.S. citizen
>   C. The third party is a license amateur
>   D. The third party is speaking in a language other than English

G1E01

We recommend that you read a book section, check for and review the section's online learning enhancements, and review the section's questions in exam pool format online or with our app. As you get into later book chapters, begin comprehensive practice tests online or with our app. When you are consistently passing practice exams you are ready for the real thing!

The General License (Element 3) Exam: The bottom line on passing the General exam is that you need at least 26 correct responses out of 35 total questions. That's about 74% correct answers to pass. There are 457 questions in the complete exam pool. Each question provides four multiple choice responses from which to choose. The order of the four question responses is not static -- the order will be scrambled on your exam among the "A B C D" designations.

Each exam will be comprised of questions drawn randomly from the exam pool, but with specific weighting applied by question topic, or sub-element. The exam sub-elements and question quantities drawn from each on a typical VE exam follows:

G1	FCC Rules	5 questions
G2	Operating Procedures	5 questions
G3	Radio Wave Propagation	3 questions
G4	Amateur Radio Practices	5 questions
G5	Electrical Principles	3 questions
G6	Circuit Components	2 questions
G7	Practical Circuits	3 questions
G8	Signals and Emissions	3 questions
G9	Antennas & Feedlines	4 questions
G0	Safety	2 questions

The third character in each question identifier specifies a topical group of questions within the sub-element. Each sub-element may have several groups of questions. The last two characters identify the question from the group.

The Exam Session: All amateur radio exams are administered by Volunteer Examiners (VE). A VE is a licensed ham who volunteers to help administer the tests and develop new licensed operators. A minimum of three VEs must administer every exam. VE sessions are conducted regularly in every state. Check with your local club or online for sessions near you.

The exam is usually administered on paper, although some computer-hosted exams are now implemented. With the paper exams you will need a pencil, and a calculator. Take your time and RTFQ! That is, *Read The Fine Question* carefully! Your exam will be graded immediately by the administering VEs, so you'll know right away if you have passed. If you have used the HamRadioSchool.com learning system well, we're confident you will succeed the first time through! Good luck!

Turn the page and start your preparation for General Class today!

But, before we begin...

0.0 Before We Begin...

Before we begin our trek into the General Class topics and exam questions, let's review a few important themes from Technician Class material and beyond. Technical backgrounds and familiarity with the Technician Class material are likely to vary quite a lot across the population of potential readers seeking to upgrade to General Class license, so it's a good idea to make sure we all have some common foundational understanding before getting into the thick of the General Class material. That's what this little prelude chapter is all about.

If you have recently earned your Technician Class license with the *HamRadioSchool.com Technician License Course*, you've probably got a solid background for proceeding. If it has been a while since you have practiced or even thought about that material much, or if you are one of the many thousands who *memorized without comprehension* to pass your Technician VE Exam, this chapter is especially for you. You may also want to snag a copy of the *HamRadioSchool.com Technician License Course* book as a reference as you work through the General Class material. It will help you to *really get it*, and you'll be a more competent, safer, and overall happier ham by really understanding amateur radio. And don't fret if you don't have total recall of all topics briefly reviewed here. We'll cover each in more depth throughout the book.

Some of the topics on which we'll refresh ourselves in this chapter include:

- What's different about operating on HF?
- Modes
- AC signals and RF signals
- Interpreting time domain and frequency domain signal representations.
- Oscilloscopes
- Decibels
- Impedance matching and SWR
- Oscillator circuits and resonance

Fire up your neurons, here we go!

What's different about operating on HF? The bulk of on-air experience for most folks with a Technician Class license is VHF and UHF FM operations – simplex or repeater QSOs with a handheld transceiver or mobile/base FM station. With a General Class ticket the world of HF privilege really opens up to you, and the typical HF band operations are significantly different from those on VHF and UHF FM.

Single sideband (SSB) operations are most popular for voice communication on the HF bands. Being a special form of amplitude modulation, SSB is more subject to electrical noise than FM, such as that produced by lightning or some electronic devices. The quality of audio with SSB does not usually match that of local FM signals. You'll find SSB sometimes scratchy, noisy, weak, and inconsistent due to atmospheric and transmission path effects. The frequencies of the HF bands are commonly bent back to earth by the ionosphere, so HF SSB signals can travel far over the horizon, unlike the typical "radio line of sight" limits of VHF and UHF bands. Since SSB signals travel great distances they become quite weak, sometimes making the reception of distant stations challenging, but all the more rewarding.

Unlike typical VHF/UHF FM local operations, the HF band plans do not identify specific *channels* for use. There are no designated repeater paired frequencies or simplex frequency channels to skip among with pre-defined proper spacing to avoid interference. Rather, the HF bands allow contiguous tuning across the band, with any frequency available to any operator with the license privilege for it. Combined with the fact that HF signals can skip over the horizon great distances, contiguous band tuning makes the potential for interference between stations much more likely. This has two main implications for HF ops: 1) You need to be polite and willing to share the spectrum of the bands with your fellow hams, else chaos ensues, and 2) You must be very aware of your transmitted signal's bandwidth to help ensure you are not interfering with other communications on the band.

All of these factors and others require that phone operations on HF SSB proceed somewhat differently than FM. For instance, the use of a phonetic alphabet is much more prominent to ensure positive exchanges because of the poorer signal quality. Operators will often "set up shop" on a specific frequency to which they have meticulously tuned their rig and amp and call "CQ" until found by other operators surfing across the band. Many operators will specifically seek only stations in foreign countries by calling "CQ DX." (DX = Distant stations, outside of the calling country.) And often there will be interference between stations on a busy band, with transmissions overlapping with various power levels, requiring the careful adjustment of receiver filters to isolate the desired signal.

Before We Begin...

The HF bands have sub-bands dedicated to particular modes of operating. Below the phone sub-bands you'll find digital operations with beeps and chirps and mournful droning. Further down is usually CW, with various speeds of Morse Code exchanges. You must take care to transmit only in the sub-bands designated for the General License Class operator, too! The higher license classes of Advanced and Extra have sub-bands exclusively for their use.

But you will learn about all of these factors of HF in the coming chapters and sections, and with just a little practice on the air it will all become second nature to you. No need to worry. Let's move on for now...

Modes: We have already touched on the matter of modes. Single sideband, digital, and CW are modes, each referring to a type of signal modulation. The matter of modes can get a bit complicated, and I will refer you to the HamRadioSchool.com web article *Loads of Modes* to help disentangle it all. Generally, there are two connotations to the term *mode*: Operating Mode and Modulation Mode.

> *Operating mode* refers to what the operator is doing to send and receive signals. Common examples are phone mode (voice ops), or digital mode (use of a computer connected to the radio).

> *Modulation mode* refers to the specific method by which information is encoded into the radio emissions. Single sideband is a modulation mode, as is FM, CW, and PSK-31 digital.

Sometimes this terminology gets combined and mixed together, and it can be confusing. Keep in mind that SSB is a phone mode (SSB = modulation type, and phone = operating technique). "FM phone" is a similar combination of modulation and ops description. Packet radio is a digital mode (Packet = modulation type, digital = operating technique). And there are others, of course. Some modes are more popular on certain bands than on others. Single sideband is very popular on the HF bands due to its narrow bandwidth efficiency. FM is more popular on the VHF/UHF bands due to the greater bandwidth available on those higher bands, as FM requires greater bandwidth for each transmission. Some digital modes perform quite well on the HF bands, while others need the greater bandwidth available on VHF and higher frequencies.

AC and RF Signals: You probably realize that the oscillating radio frequency (RF) signals that radiate from your station's antenna are the result of alternating electric currents (AC) flowing back and forth rapidly in the antenna. The oscillations of the RF signal's electric field, or *cycles*, equal the frequency of the back-and-forth AC frequency in the antenna. Frequency is measured in *cycles per second*, whether referring to AC electrical cycles in a circuit or RF electric field cycles flying through the air. The unit of one cycle per second is one *hertz*, and frequency is defined in hertz, kilohertz (thousands of hertz), megahertz (millions of hertz), etc.

We represent each of these types of cycles with a sine wave. For electrical AC in a circuit the sine wave's up-and-down flow represents the direction and magnitude of the electric voltage that is the force, or pressure, shoving the electric current back and forth in the circuit. Above the zero line the voltage is pushing one direction in the circuit, and below the zero line the voltage is pushing the opposite way. We call these two directions of flow positive and negative (+ and -), and the magnitude of the voltage is represented on the vertical dimension, or the vertical axis, in units of volts. Time is represented on the horizontal axis, or the zero line, left to right.

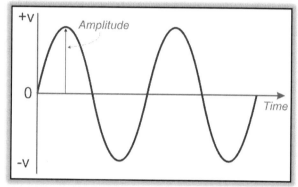

Figure 0.1: A sine wave signal time domain view.

With radio wave signals, the sine wave represents how the electric field of the radio signal is oscillating as it travels through free space. The field extends itself in two opposing directions from the axis of propagation. The zero line is again a measure of time, and also represents the axis of propagation – the direction the wave is traveling at the speed of light as the electric field changes back and forth at radio frequency.

The height of the sine wave at its peak is called the amplitude of the signal, and amplitude is a measure of the signal strength, or power.

Time Domain and Frequency Domain Views: The sine wave view of a signal described above is a *time domain view*. This is because the horizontal axis is depicting the progression of time. The time domain view defines how the signal voltage is changing over time, defining both the frequency and the amplitude of the signal. However, a typical radio transmission is comprised of a small band of many contiguous frequencies, defined as some *bandwidth*. A sine wave in the time domain view is usually depicting only one frequency out of a few thousand hertz of frequencies in a transmitted band. To depict the entire band we use a *frequency domain view*.

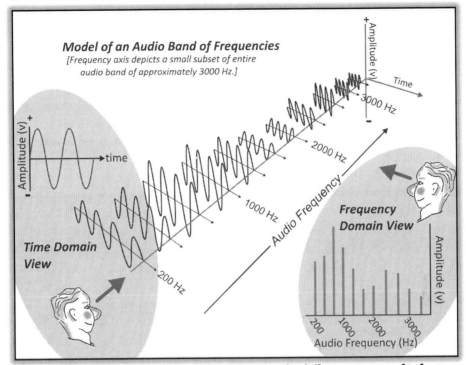

Figure 0.2: Two related views of signals provide different types of information. The horizontal axis represents either time or frequency, depending on the view.

The frequency domain view has frequency (in hertz) on the horizontal axis, and amplitude on the vertical axis. This depiction provides a definition of the band of frequencies comprising a signal, and it defines the amplitude of each frequency across the band. This is much like an audio equalizer display in which the power of the various audio frequencies is indicated over time by a set of vertical LEDs or LCD segments that dance with the music frequencies in electronic display.

Figure 0.2 illustrates how the frequency domain view and time domain view are related: You can imagine the time domain view as taking a slice of the frequency domain view and turning it 90 degrees to its side. Alternatively, you can imagine the frequency domain view as the entire band of time domain frequency slices aggregated together and turned 90 degrees to look across all frequencies. The time and frequency domain views can depict audio frequencies, such as the signals generated by a microphone to serve as modulating signals, or they may depict radio frequencies, such as a band of transmitted RF signals. We will use both time domain and frequency domain depictions of signals and bands throughout this book.

Oscilloscopes: An oscilloscope is an electronic measurement device that allows us to measure and view signals in the time domain (and other views, depending upon the device capabilities). With an oscilloscope we may tap into an electric circuit and get a dynamic picture of the voltage variations ongoing inside the circuit. A typical oscilloscope will display time across the horizontal dimension and voltage on the vertical, just like the time domain view of waveforms. The amount of time displayed in total across the screen can be varied, and the scale of voltage can be altered to view a wide range of signal strengths. With RF signals the oscilloscope may be set to display only a few microseconds (millionths of a second) or nanoseconds (billionths of a second) in order that we can view and measure a few cycles of waveforms in great detail as they rapidly oscillate. We will refer to oscilloscope measurements in several sections of this book.

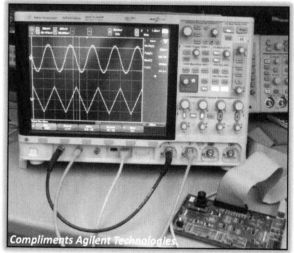

Figure 0.3: An oscilloscope displaying a time domain view of two different signals.

Decibels (dB): The decibel is used to compare two measures, much like a ratio of two numbers. In amateur radio a common comparison using decibels is power changes. For example, you might observe with the signal strength meter on a receiver that the strength of a received signal has increased by 6 dB or decreased by 3 dB. Notice that these measures indicate nothing about the absolute power value of the signal – there is no quoting of watts or any other absolute unit of power. Notice also that the measure is meaningful only in comparison to the previous power level – an increase in power or a decrease in power as related by the size of the decibel change.

The decibel is a logarithmic unit. This means that it is based on factor of 10 changes. The "bel" is a unit indicating change by a factor of 10, or 10X. For instance, a power increase from 10 watts to 100 watts could be characterized as a 1 bel increase – a factor of 10 increase. But the bel is usually too coarse of a unit, so the decibel is more typically used. The decibel is 1/10 of a bel.

You may recall from your Technician Class studies some useful rules of thumb equating decibels to relative change values. For instance, a doubling or halving of power equates to a change of 3 dB, either increased (doubling) or decreased (halving). Put another way, a 2X change equals a 3 dB change. So, an increase in power from 50 watts to 100 watts is a 3 dB increase. Double again to 200 watts and that is a 4X increase, or 6 dB. Another rule of thumb alludes to the bel as 10 dB. A 10X change equates to 10 dB. Our example above, going from 10 watts to 100 watts, is a 10 dB increase. We will use these simple rules for decibels again in our General Class studies.

Impedance Matching & SWR: Impedance (Z) in an electrical circuit is the opposition to the flow of alternating current (AC). The unit of impedance is the ohm (Ω). Every AC circuit, including RF *transmitter / feed line / antenna* circuits, will have some impedance due to the components comprising the circuit and their impact on AC. Maximum power transfer occurs when all of the components have identical impedance. For instance, to get the most power transferred to an antenna for transmission of RF energy the transmitter circuit, the feed line, and the antenna feed point should be matched in impedance.

When components of a circuit do not match in impedance, some of the power in the circuit will be reflected from the position of the mismatch. For instance, if your transmitter and feed line are each 50 Ω, but your antenna feed point is 100 Ω, you will have an impedance mismatch and some of your transmitter's power will be reflected from the antenna feed point back down the feed line toward the transmitter. The poorer the impedance match the greater the magnitude of reflected power. A ratio comparison of the forward voltage with the reflected voltage is called SWR, or standing wave ratio. We will examine SWR more closely in Chapter 5, *Antennas*.

Oscillator Circuits and Resonance: Much of radio functioning is based upon the concepts of oscillator circuits and resonance. An oscillator circuit produces the very rapid AC that is necessary for the generation of RF signals. A common oscillator circuit will include electronic components called capacitors and inductors.

A capacitor is like two parallel conductive plates separated from one another. When AC flows back and forth in a circuit with a capacitor, the capacitor plates rapidly charge and discharge, with positive and negative electrical charges building up alternatively on opposite sides of the capacitor with each reversal of AC. A capacitor will allow high frequency AC to flow freely, but it impedes low frequency AC or DC current. So, a capacitor will increase impedance for low frequencies but not for high frequencies. This capacitive contribution to a circuit's impedance is called *capacitive reactance* (X_c).

An inductor is a coil of wire that creates a magnetic field about itself when current flows through it in one direction, just like an electromagnet. The direction, or polarity, of the magnetic field is determined by the direction of electric current flow. When an inductor is in an AC circuit, the inductor builds a magnetic field first with one polarity, and as the current reverses the magnetic field is collapsed and rebuilt with opposite polarity. All of this building, collapsing, and building again with each AC cycle causes the inductor to impede AC also. But, exactly opposite of the capacitor, the inductor impedes high frequency AC and allows low frequency AC or DC current to pass easily. The inductor's contribution to a circuit's impedance is called *inductive reactance* (X_L).

Inductive reactance, capacitive reactance, and regular old electrical resistance combine and total to a circuit's overall impedance. We will discuss the concept of reactance in several sections.

In circuits containing both capacitors and inductors, a special state of AC flow may arise called resonance. Resonance means that energy can be transformed between different states very easily, or with very little loss of energy during transitions. In this case, energy is easily shifted from electric charge (capacitor) to magnetic field (inductor), with great efficiency. Resonance occurs in LC circuits (circuits containing an inductor, L, and a capacitor C) when the inductive reactance and capacitive reactance are equal. This equality will occur only at a specific AC frequency in the circuit, and the frequency of resonance is determined by the values of capacitance and inductance of the LC components in the circuit.

So, we can select inductors and capacitors to build LC circuits that will become resonant at a desired AC frequency. Or, we may use variable components to build LC circuits that will resonate at variable frequencies. In this way oscillators are constructed to generate RF frequencies of alternating current for radio tuning operations.

In the chapters that follow we shall see more on how capacitance, inductance, and each type of resulting reactance effects circuit behavior, and particularly how it impacts antenna circuit performance.

With this concept review under our belts, let's move on to become General Class Amateur Radio Operators! We now begin, in earnest, with a look at General Class rules and regulations. Good luck with your studies!

~ Stu WØSTU

1.0 Rules & Regs

> **❝** *Radio is called a medium because it is rare that anything is well done.* — Fred Allen

OK, so we are indeed *amateur* radio operators, by FCC designation. And we all learn and improve as we proceed along in our various efforts. But contrary to Fred's sentiments amateur radio can, and should, be *well done*! All amateur license classes should strive to conduct their on-air operations with a pride of competence, within the rules and regulations established by the FCC. Especially now that you endeavor to upgrade your license to General Class, I hope that you will seek to make your station operation as well done as a crispy, blackened burger forsaken on a blazing grill!

In Section 1.1 we will examine all the new frequency band privileges that you'll have as a General Class operator. The HF bands really open up to you now! In Section 1.2 you'll get a peek at some "special services" that you may want to become involved with as a General Class licensee. In Section 1.3 we will expand on a few more detailed rules and regulations that are particularly relevant to the more advanced operator.

Before we dive into the rules and regulations with which you should comply to keep your operation crisp, let's see just how your General Class adventure will begin. First you need a CSCE for General Class.

CSCE: The *Certificate of Successful Completion of Examination* is awarded to you immediately when you pass your General license examination, and **it is valid for exam element credit for 365 days,** one full year. You will rarely need that long of proof, as your upgraded license will usually appear on the FCC ULS within days of your successful examination. The *Universal License System* (ULS) is the FCC database of issued licenses and applications that has a web-based interface for your convenience.

The coolest thing about having that CSCE in your pocket is that you can walk out of the exam session and immediately transmit on General license frequencies. No waiting around for the ULS to catch up to your new status. **As a Technician Class operator having a CSCE for General Class privi-**

leges, **you may operate on any General or Technician Class band segment,** but you have to make it known on the air with a special call sign identifier. The proper way to identify on General Class frequencies if you have a CSCE for General but your upgrade from Technician has not yet appeared in the FCC database is to give your call sign followed by "slant AG." (Or "stroke AG." or "slash AG.") Just think "*Approved General,*" and remember that **you must add the special identifier "AG" after your call sign when you operate using General Class frequency privileges,** but not when you remain within the Technician Class privileges. When your upgraded license appears on the FCC ULS database you may stop using the AG self-assigned indicator. But while you do use it, you'll likely receive many hardy congratulations on your upgrade from fellow hams on the air, and that's nice to hear!

What if you held a ham license before, but now it is expired? Do you get any credit for that in examination? Yes! **Any person who can demonstrate that they once held an FCC issued General, Advanced, or Amateur Extra class license that was not revoked by the FCC may receive partial credit for the elements represented by that expired license.** Thus, **to obtain a new General Class license after a previously held license has expired and the two year grace period has passed, the applicant must pass the current Element 2 exam** (Technician exam.)

With that tidbit dispensed, let's rule!

1.1 Rules and Regulations
Bands and Privileges

> **"** It's a privilege - I make the most of it.
> – David Bailey

The General Class license really adds to your operating privileges. Of course, you lose none of the Technician license band privileges that you've already earned, but you will:
- expand your 10 meter band phone privileges above 28.5 MHz
- get phone privileges on eight more HF bands
- increase your CW privileges by six HF bands
- increase your digital data privilege by nine HF bands

The step up to General Class from Technician Class license represents a substantial expansion of your privileges, and with those privileges come the

1.1 Bands and Privileges

expanded responsibilities of being a more knowledgeable and responsible station operator. Become very familiar with these new General Class license privileges and responsibilities so that you can make the most of them!

Band Privileges for General Class: Your General Class privileges are defined much like the Technician Class privileges, using bands, sub-bands, and mode-restricted sub-bands. Four of the HF bands on which your new General Class privileges apply will also have Extra Class and (grandfathered) Advanced Class exclusive frequency ranges. Be careful not to transmit in those exclusive sub-bands with only General Class privileges. However, in six of the 10 HF bands **a General Class license holder is granted all amateur frequency privileges: 160, 60, 30, 17, 12, and 10 meters.** There are no Advanced or Extra Class exclusive regions on these six bands to worry about. On the four bands **where General Class licensees are not permitted to use the entire voice portion of the band, the portion of the voice segment that is generally available to them is the upper frequency end.**

Figure 1.1: Boy Scouts work the HF bands with a summer camp portable station.

G1A01

G1A11

HF Band Definitions and Operating Provisions (reference Figure 1.2):

10 Meter Band: 28.0 – 29.7 MHz. **All frequencies in this range are available to a control operator holding a General Class license.**

G1A10

The phone sub-band ranges 28.3 – 29.7 MHz, and the digital sub-band extends 28.0 – 28.3 MHz. **The portion of the 10-meter band above 29.5 MHz is available for repeater use.** Note, however, that **a 10m repeater** (FM repeater) **may retransmit the 2m signal from a station having a Technician Class control operator, but only given that the 10m repeater control operator holds at least a General Class license.**

12 Meter Band: 24.890 – 24.990 MHz. All frequencies in this range are available to a control operator holding a General Class license. The phone sub-band ranges 24.930 – 24.990 MHz, with the digital sub-band below 24.930 MHz.

15 Meter Band: 21.0 – 21.450 MHz. **The General Class portion of the 15m phone band ranges 21.275 – 21.450 MHz (21275 - 21450 kHz).** The phone range 21.2 – 21.275 MHz is exclusive to Advanced and/or Extra Class licenses only. The General Class license digital mode sub-band is 21.025 – 21.2 MHz, with frequencies in this band below 21.025 MHz exclusively reserved for Extra Class.

17 Meter Band: 18.068 – 18.168 MHz. All frequencies in this range are available to a control operator holding a General Class license. The phone sub-band ranges 18.110 – 18.168 MHz, and the digital sub-band extends 18.068 – 18.110 MHz.

20 Meter Band: 14.0 – 14.350 MHz. **The General Class portion of the 20m phone band ranges 14.225 – 14.350 MHz (14225 - 14350 kHz).** The phone range 14.150 – 14.225 MHz is exclusive to Advanced and/or Extra Class licenses only. The General Class license digital mode sub-band is 14.025 – 14.150 MHz, with frequencies in this band below 14.025 MHz exclusively reserved for Extra Class operators.

30 Meter Band: 10.1 – 10.150 MHz. **Amateur operators are secondary users of this band and by FCC rules are allowed to use the band only if they do not cause harmful interference to primary users. The appropriate action if, when operating on the 30m band, a station in the primary service interferes with your contact, is to move to a clear frequency or stop transmitting. The 30m band is a digital mode band only; phone operation and image transmission is prohibited. The maximum transmitting power an amateur station may use** (on the 30-meter band) **is 200 watts PEP output.** (PEP is Peak Envelope Power, the measurement specified by the FCC rules that regulate maximum

1.1 Bands and Privileges

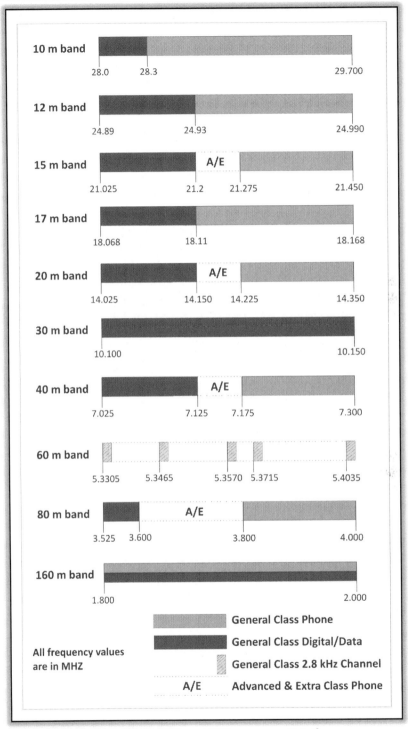

Figure 1.2: General Class HF Frequency Privileges.

power output. *See Section 6.1 Power and Principles.)*

40 Meter Band: 7.0 – 7.3 MHz (in ITU Region 2). The General Class portion of the 40m phone band ranges 7.175 – 7.3 MHz. The phone range 7.125 – 7.175 MHz is exclusive to Advanced and Extra Class licenses only. The General Class license digital mode sub-band is 7.025 – 7.125 MHz, with frequencies in this band below 7.025 MHz exclusively reserved for Extra Class. Note that in ITU Region 2 (includes North America) this band extends up to 7.3 MHz for amateur operators. **Outside of ITU Region 2, frequency allocations may differ even for areas under FCC jurisdiction.**

60 Meter Band: The 60m band is really different from any other band. **Instead of a range of frequencies, 60 meters allows only specific channels** – 5330.5, 5346.5, 5357.0, 5371.5, and 5403.5 kHz. Only one signal at a time is permitted on any channel. **USB on these 60m channels is limited in bandwidth to a maximum of 2.8 kHz** and **power is limited to effective radiated power (ERP) of 100 watts PEP with respect to a dipole** for all modes. **(Note: FCC rules require that you keep a record of the gain of your antenna when operating on 60m band if using an antenna other than a dipole.)** Amateur operators are secondary users of this band and by FCC rules are allowed to use the band only if they do not cause harmful interference to primary users. **The appropriate action if, when operating on the 60m band, a station in the primary service interferes with your contact, is to move to a clear frequency or stop transmitting.**

75 / 80 Meter Band: 3.5 – 4.0 MHz [3500 – 4000 kHz]. **The General Class portion of the 75/80m phone band ranges 3.8 – 4.0 MHz [3800 – 4000 kHz].** The phone range 3.6 – 3.8 MHz is exclusive to Advanced and/or Extra Class licenses. **The General Class license** digital mode sub-band **is 3.525 – 3.6 MHz,** with frequencies in this band below 3.525 MHz reserved exclusively for Extra Class operators. This band may be referred to as either 75m band or 80m band, as the wavelengths extend from 75 – 85 meters across this band. Since CW ops are in the lower frequency end of the band, that segment is usually called "80 meter band" while the higher frequency phone segment is the "75m band."

160 Meter Band: 1.8 – 2.0 MHz [1800 – 2000 kHz]. All frequencies in this Medium Frequency (MF) band are available to a control operator holding a General Class license. No sub-bands are imposed on 160m band. The entire band is available for phone or digital modes.]

1.1 Bands and Privileges

Transmitting Power Limits: The general FCC rules regarding transmitting power limits apply to all of the General Class bands, but two bands are more restrictive (30m and 60m). **Only the minimum power necessary to carry out the desired communications should be used on any band.** Further, **the maximum transmitting power an amateur station may use on any HF band is limited to 1500 watts PEP output.** The 30m and 60m bands only have lower restrictions on maximum power output, as noted in the description of each: The 30m band is restricted to 200 watts PEP output, and the 60m band is restricted to 100 watts PEP output.

G1C04 G1C02 G1C06 G1C05

Examination Strategies: Wow, that's a lot of band limits, sub-band limits, and special rules to remember, huh? In practice you will likely have a copy of a band chart next to your rig and you can practically check that you're within your General Class privileges. But for the exam you'll need to use some different strategies, even including just some rote memorization (ugh!), since you cannot reference a band plan chart or notes. Let's see if we can minimize that memorizing just a bit…

Identifying Band Frequencies & Limits: Use the frequency and wavelength calculation to help determine which band a given frequency resides within. This will usually help narrow the response options to just two items. Remember from Technician material that:

Frequency in MHz = 300 ÷ wavelength in meters.

The band name given in each question is an approximate wavelength in meters. 1) Use the band name value to calculate a frequency for the band. 2) Identify the two closest question responses to that frequency. 3) Select the lower of the two closest frequencies. This approach works for all of these band questions in the current question pool (G1A05 - G1A09) except one, G1A09. For that one exception, the *higher* of the two narrowed responses is correct.

Here's an example of this procedure using question **G1A08: Which of the following frequencies is within the General class portion of the 80-meter band?**
  A. 1855 kHz   **C. 3560 kHz**
  B. 2560 kHz   D. 3650 kHz

G1A08

1) 300 ÷ 80m = 3.75 MHz, or 3750 kHz.
2) The two closest values to 3750 kHz are C and D.
3) The lower of C and D is C, 3560 kHz.

The correct response is C. Try this for the other applicable questions, G1A05 through G1A08, and remember the exception is the question asking about the 15-meter band -- select the higher of the two narrowed responses in that case.

Here is one more specific example of this rule of thumb, G1A07: **Which of the following frequencies is within the General class portion of the 20-meter band?**

G1A07

A. 14005 kHz
B. 14105 kHz
C. 14305 kHz
D. 14405 kHz

Once again, perform the calculation:

300 ÷ 20m = 15 MHz (or 15000 kHz)

The closest two responses to 15000 kHz are C and D. **Option C, 14305 kHz** is the lower frequency of the two narrowed responses, and it is the correct one.

Practice the calculations, learn the exam rules, and you'll be privileged to ace the questions on the General Class bands. Test yourself online with the quiz for Section 1.1, the come back to see what special services you can contribute to the ham community!

HamRadioSchool.com/general_media

1.2 Special Services

> **"** *The little waiter's eyebrows wandered about his forehead in confusion.*
> — Douglas Adams, The Restaurant at the End of the Universe

As is often lamented, good service is sometimes hard to come by. Fortunately, the amateur radio community is one with a strong commitment to service and we all benefit from the efforts of others who choose to step up and take on the myriad chores and challenges that keep ham radio going. You can do the same, joining many of your fellow hams in serving the amateur radio family with your new and expanded General Class knowledge and skills. This section highlights just a few of the ways you can give something back, all the while keeping your eyebrows firmly attached to a singular location on your forehead.

Volunteer Examiner (VE): As a General Class license holder you can serve as a Volunteer Examiner, administering VE exams for Technician licensing. Volunteer examiners are licensed radio amateurs who give their time to administer FCC licensing examinations. You've likely already interacted with a VE team when you completed your Technician exam, and you'll see another when you test for General.

To become a VE you must complete training required by **a Volunteer Examiner Coordinator (VEC), the accrediting organization for VEs.** Multiple VECs are sanctioned by the FCC, and each has slightly different policies, but here are a few big picture rules about VEing that every ham should know:

- **The minimum age to qualify as an accredited VE is 18 years.**

- **An FCC General Class or higher license and VEC accreditation are sufficient to be an administering VE for a Technician Class operator license examination.**

- **As an accredited VE holding a General Class license, you may administer only Technician Class license examinations.**

Figure 1.3: Volunteer Examiner (VE) Exam Session. Serving as a Volunteer Examiner helps new hams get licensed. Consider becoming a VE for one of the several Volunteer Examiner Coordinator (VEC) organizations.

G1D04
- **A requirement for administering a Technician Class examination is that at least three General Class or higher VEs must observe the examination.**

G1D08
- **Any non-US citizen wishing to become an accredited Volunteer Examiner must hold an FCC granted Amateur Radio license of General Class or above.**

The bottom line on administering examinations as an accredited VE is that you may administer exams only for the license classes below your own license class. So, you must be at least a General Class VE to administer Technician Class exams. You must be an Advanced Class or an Extra Class VE to administer General Class license exams. Extra Class VEs must administer Extra Class exams. At least three accredited VEs of the proper license class must be present for any VE exam.

Consider becoming a VE and help expand the amateur radio community with new licensed operators!

G2D01
G2D02
Volunteer Monitors (VM): The ARRL **Volunteer Monitoring Program is amateur volunteers who are formally enlisted to monitor the airwaves for rules violations.** Hundreds of volunteer-appointees serve as Volunteer Monitors. **The objective of the Volunteer Monitoring Program is to encourage amateur radio operators to self regulate and comply with the rules.**

1.2 Special Services

The Volunteer Monitors help and advise amateur operators; they are not *band cops*. They are intended to provide unbiased operational advice and assistance to amateurs, helping to correct errors, but not to find fault or to place blame. They promote good amateur operating and engineering practice.

However, the VMs are trained and certified to collect and provide evidence to the FCC in enforcement actions related to any serious rule violations. For instance, in the case of malicious, repeated interference, a VM may record on-air transmissions and use **direction finding techniques to locate stations violating FCC rules.** So, **skills learned during hidden transmitter hunts are of help to the Volunteer Monitoring Program.** But the VMs are not allowed to enforce the rules in any way. That is a function exclusively of the FCC.

[G2D03]

A VM might have the ARRL dispatch to you a card called an Advisory Notice. Don't panic! It is not a citation. Rather, VM Advisory Notice is a friendly note to highlight to you possible operating practices or equipment issues that you may need to modify. You do not need to reply to any notice, but you should consider what caused the problem described in the notice and take action to get in line with the regulations and good amateur practice.

And don't worry about nit-picky things. The VMs are trained to avoid minor, easy-to-slip discrepancies such as untimely station identification. They're more concerned with patterns of clear, unambiguous rule violations. Still, take pride in your on-air procedures and endeavor to keep closely to the rules and to the guidelines of good amateur practice. After all, you're going to be a General Class operator now. Set a good example! You might get a *Good Operator Report* via a VM for operating practices of the highest standards; a model for others to follow.

If you are interested in becoming a VM, and if you believe you can be a friendly guide and assistant to other amateur operators (and not a *band cop*!), you may apply online at the ARRL web site or by contacting your ARRL Section Manager.

Emergency Communications Services and Procedures: Amateur radio tends to be a low-visibility hobby (except for those massive aluminum antenna farms, of course). Unless you're really looking for it, you won't hear too much about ham radio. There will almost never be features about ham radio operations in the news or the church bulletin, and the local pub chat will usually steer clear of the topic altogether. But, if there is any time when amateur radio gets a little publicity it's when operators come to aid in an emergency or disaster. This is when ham radio really shines!

A few special rules apply in emergency situations, and response organizations such as Radio Amateur Civil Emergency Service (RACES), Amateur Radio Emergency Service (ARES®), and Community Emergency Response Team (CERT), may use amateur radio to help manage communications traffic and to coordinate relief efforts.

G2B10 An amateur station is allowed to use any means at its disposal to assist another station in distress at any time during an actual emergency. When it comes to emergencies in which communications are directly related to the immediate safety of human life or protection of property, almost anything goes regarding the amateur rules if no other means of communication is reasonably available. For instance, in such emergency conditions you may ignore the broadcasting restriction and provide communications to broadcasters for dissemination to the public, if that is required to save life or property. Note, simply describing the scene of an accident or emergency for the convenience of broadcasters is not the same as advising an evacuating public on travel routes to take to avoid a wildfire that has suddenly exploded in a nearby forest community. Regardless of your license class or the radio

Figure 1.4: Radio Amateur Civil Emergency Service (RACES) volunteers typically receive special training to serve as communications specialists for civil authorities during emergencies or disasters. You can serve too!

1.2 Special Services

service at your disposal, **whichever frequency has the best chance of communicating the distress message should be used when sending a distress call** in an emergency scenario where life or property is at risk, and when other means of communication (cell phone, emergency responder on site, etc.) are not available to you.

RACES organizations consist of volunteers trained to assist civil authorities during times of emergency or disaster. RACES is provided for by FCC Part 97.407, and a RACES organization is certified by a local, county, or state civil defense agency in the area it serves, or by a related organization within civil defense such as law enforcement or fire response agencies. A RACES organization may be activated to utilize amateur radio resources to provide communications support to the civil agencies. **Only a person holding an FCC-issued amateur operator license may be the control operator of an amateur station transmitting in RACES to assist relief operations during a disaster.**

Consider volunteering for your local RACES organization. You will learn more about emergency communications and you can serve your community when it really counts!

Beacon Operations: A beacon transmits a repeating signal, usually a CW identifier and sometimes additional tones, **for the purpose of observing radio frequency propagation and reception, as identified in the FCC rules.** Many HF beacons operate on the 10m band and can be good indicators of sporadic E propagation and other ionospheric conditions.

Any amateur radio license holder may establish a beacon station, but some Part 97.203 regulations apply. **The power limit for beacon stations is 100 watts PEP output.** Further, you cannot establish a whole family of beacons on the same band from your station location. **There must be no more than one beacon signal in the same band from the same station location.** Most beacons use automatic control, but the FCC regulations allow this only in certain sub-bands of the 10m, 6m, 2m, 1.25m, and 70cm bands, or on the 33cm and shorter wavelength bands (microwave bands). For instance, **automatically controlled beacons on HF frequencies are permitted only in the range 28.20 MHz to 28.30 MHz**, in the 10-meter band.

A beacon station must cease transmission if an FCC District Director notifies that it is causing undue interference to other operations. Conversely, **an amateur operator should normally avoid transmitting on 14.100, 18.110, 21.150, 24.930, and 28.200 MHz because a system of propagation beacon stations operates on those frequencies.** These beacons are part of a worldwide beacon network operated by the International Amateur Radio Union (IARU), an organization dedicated to bettering the mutual use of radio spectrum throughout the world.

Beacon operators provide a great service to the amateur radio community, particularly to operators who like to chase DX by ionospheric skip propagation. The beacons can help you identify when conditions are right for propagation to particular regions of the earth and when those coveted sporadic E openings are available! You may find an interest in establishing your own beacon, especially if you are in an area where few beacons are currently operating.

These are just a few special services in which you can become involved in amateur radio. You may also consider forming a new amateur radio club, organizing or becoming a member of a CERT, helping to teach an amateur radio course, becoming an ARES volunteer, helping out a local amateur radio school club, or any of the other ample opportunities offered by amateur radio to provide service to your fellow citizens and your fellow hams. Give one or more of these opportunities a try. I think you'll find one that suits you and that becomes very rewarding!

For now, check out the question pool items for this section and test your new knowledge!

HamRadioSchool.com/general_media

1.3 Rules and Regulations — DX and Details

> **Men who wish to know about the world must learn about it in its particular details.**
> – *Heraclitus*

You have already learned a lot about the FCC Part 97 rules and regulations as a Technician Class license holder, and you have probably been complying with them regularly without much thought to the matter, and perhaps without digging into *particular details*. But, if you need a refresher on some of the FCC's most fundamental rules and regulations that apply to almost all stations, check out the *HamRadioSchool.com Technician License Course*, Chapter 2.

In your Technician license preparation you no doubt learned about activities that are prohibited on the amateur frequencies such as the use of codes or ciphers, creating harmful interference to other stations, transmitting music or obscene/indecent language, and broadcasting for a general audience. You learned that transmitting for pecuniary interests (payment or compensation) is disallowed, and that you must make your station available for FCC inspection upon request. You probably also learned a little about communicating with the world, although you may not have accumulated a lot of experience with those "DX" (distant) contacts to date as a Technician.

As a General Class license holder you are expected to be more knowledgeable of the Part 97 rules and regulations, and since you will be granted access to a vastly larger slice of the HF frequency pie some emphasis should be placed on the rules related to DX communications provided largely by those HF frequencies. Let's discover more about the *DX and General Class world* by highlighting some *particular details* especially pertinent to General Class operations.

DX Communications: DX communications commonly use ionospheric skip propagation to transmit and receive weak signals outside of the US. (See Chapter 3, *Propagation*.) Of course, it is necessary and efficient to have some agreement among nations on how various frequencies will be used, otherwise some country's commercial broadcast services or military transmissions may severely interfere with another's amateur radio signals, and vice versa. Such international interference is rude, if not potentially incendiary. But fear not!

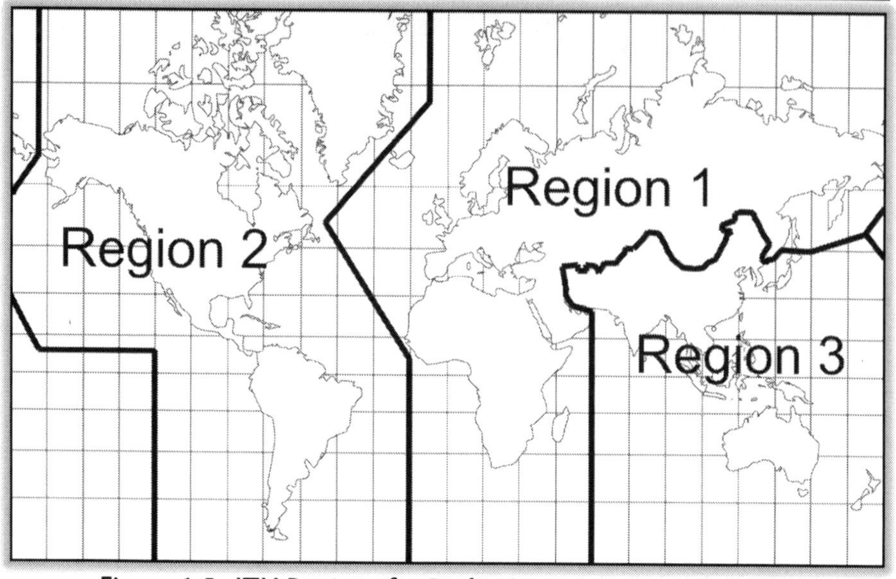

Figure 1.5: ITU Regions for Radio Spectrum Coordination.

We have international agreements regarding the use of the spectrum.

ITU: *The International Telecommunications Union* is a United Nations agency for information and communication technology issues. This agency, by international agreement, has partitioned the world into three geographic regions for managing and coordinating radio frequency use, as depicted in Figure 1.5. **The frequency allocations of ITU region 2 apply to radio amateurs operating in North and South America.**

International Waters: Within the international agreements made through the ITU, the FCC governs all spectrum use and radio stations inside the US, and FCC licensed amateur stations may transmit from any vessel or craft located in international waters that is documented or registered in the United States. So, as long as your yacht is out on the high seas and not within the international boundary of another nation, you can PTT with liberty and confidence under your FCC license and within the frequency use plans for the particular region.

Foreign Contacts and Communications may be limited by some nations and by agreements (or lack thereof) between nations. **It is permissible to communicate with amateur stations in countries outside the areas administered by the FCC when the contact is with amateurs in any country except those whose administrations have notified the ITU that they object to such communications.** Presently, practically no nations have ITU registered general restrictions on amateur radio communications, although North Korea and Yemen do not allow citizens to operate amateur stations at all.

1.3 DX and Details

Third Party International Communications: FCC Part 97.3 defines the term "third-party communication" as a message from the control operator (first party) of an amateur station to another amateur station control operator (second party) on behalf of another person (third party). Third party communication may also mean a non-licensed person transmitting on your radio under your licensed control operator supervision. Some countries get a little antsy about this sort of thing, and some additional rules apply to third party communications. Keep these in mind from FCC Part 97.3 and 97.115:

- Third party traffic is prohibited by every foreign country unless there is a third party agreement in effect with that country, with the exception of messages involving emergencies or disaster relief communications.

- **The types of messages for a third party in another country transmitted by an amateur station should only be messages relating to amateur radio or remarks of a personal character, or messages related to emergencies or disaster relief.** [G1E05]

- Revoked License: It is a very rare situation, but it can happen. If a person has ever had an amateur license revoked by the FCC, that person is not allowed to transmit on the amateur frequencies even as a third party operator. **A license revocation disqualifies a third party from participating in stating a message over an amateur station.** This applies internationally, or within FCC controlled territory. [G1E01]

Station Identification: What if you are practicing speaking your freshly learned Mandarin, French, or Spanish with a new DX contact friend? How do you identify your station? Even if you are using a language other than English in making contact using phone emissions, you must identify your station using English. Je suis désolé, c'est la règle!

Operating from Foreign Countries: Many hams enjoy the challenge and thrill of "DXpeditions," traveling to foreign nations and perhaps to quite rarely contacted geographical areas to operate a station. Be aware that you may operate an amateur station in a foreign nation only when authorized by that nation. Check the law carefully before traveling!

Reciprocal Agreements: The US has reciprocal operating agreements with many nations that allow FCC licensed stations to operate on foreign territory. Two notable international reciprocal agreements in which the US participates are the *European Conference of Postal and Telecommunications Administra-*

Buddipole's Chris, W6HFP, sets up a Mini-Buddipole on the east coast of 8P6/Barbados. Photo by Steve, WG0AT; Courtesy of Buddipole. www.buddipole.com

Figure 1.6: A DXpedition to a foreign nation can be both rewarding and challenging, and offer some once-in-a-lifetime operating scenarios!

tion (CEPT) and the *International Amateur Radio Permit* (IARP). CEPT includes most European nations and several others, but carefully research the reciprocity provisions by FCC license class and frequency privileges. The IARP is issued by the *Inter-American Telecommunications Commission* (CITEL) that includes many North American and South American nations. Again, check the reciprocity provisions of the IARP, as the operating privileges are not perfectly aligned to those of an FCC licensed station in the US.

Handling Interference: Interference happens. Stations bump into one another or occasionally stomp all over each other. Changing atmospheric conditions, less-than-careful operators, and improperly operating equipment are a few of the reasons for accidental interference between stations. In most cases interference can be handled by one station simply moving to a clear frequency, but a few situations are a bit more unambiguous and require specific action to be taken. Each of the following three circumstances apply to question **G1E04**:

1. *FCC Monitoring Stations* – The FCC operates monitoring stations to ensure compliance with regulations across the various radio services, including the amateur service. **If you are operating within one mile of an FCC Monitoring Station you may be required to take specific steps to avoid harmful interference.** According to the *Code*

1.3 DX and Details

of Federal Regulations, Title 47, FCC Protected Field Offices are located in or near the following US cities:

Kenai, AK	*Waipahu, HI*	*Canandaigua, NY*
Douglas, AZ	*Belfast, ME*	*Santa Isabel, Puerto Rico*
Livermore, CA	*Laurel, MD*	*Kingsville, TX*
Vero Beach, FL	*Allegan, MI*	*Ferndale, WA*
Powder Springs, GA	*Grand Island, NE*	

2. Secondary Privileges – As noted in the *Bands and Privileges* section of this chapter, some bands are available to the Amateur Service only on a secondary basis, and interference with the primary service users requires that you move to a clear frequency or cease transmissions. **Take these specific steps to avoid harmful interference when using a band where the Amateur Service is secondary.** [G1E04]

Spread Spectrum – Spread Spectrum (SS) is a transmitting method that spreads the power density of transmissions over a very broad band of frequencies. This is accomplished through *frequency hopping* or other methods where the transmitting station and the receiving station utilize a very broad band of frequencies. With frequency hopping stations skip rapidly from one frequency to another, transmitting only briefly on any given frequency. In amateur radio specific standards of frequency hopping and other spread spectrum implementations are imposed in order that transmissions may not be made covert through this operating mode's nature. **Stations transmitting spread spectrum emissions may be required to cease operations or take other steps to avoid harmful interference with other users or facilities. Additionally, the maximum PEP output allowed for spread spectrum transmissions is 10 watts.** [G1E04] [G1E08]

Antenna Height: I know you want to erect a giant antenna farm to get on all the new General Class bands that will be available to you, but the height of those antennas has some liming rules.

The maximum height above ground that an antenna structure may be erected without requiring notification to the Federal Aviation Administration (FAA) and registration with the FCC, provided it is not at or near a public use airport, is 200 feet. [G1B01] If your antenna is less than 200 feet high you do not need to register your antenna… unless…

If your antenna is at or near a public use airport, you must notify the FAA in some cases. Specific rules that relate the distance from the airport (or heliport) to antenna height by a slope calculation apply. If your antenna exceeds the height as determined by the slope calculation, you are required to notify the FAA. See the *Code of Federal Regulations, Title 14, Part 77.9* for the specifics of filing requirements if your station is within 20,000 feet (3.79 miles) of a public use or military airport. Also, see the HamRadioSchool.com online article, *"(G1B01) Maximum Antenna Structure Height."*

There are limits on how much control state and local authorities (like home owners associations) can impose on Amateur Radio Service stations and antennas. Federal statute requires that **state and local governments must reasonably accommodate Amateur Service communications, and regulations must constitute the minimum practical to accommodate a legitimate purpose of the state or local entity.** The details of interpretation of this relatively new statute are yet to be tested thoroughly in the courts, but your HOA must allow reasonable accommodation for your antennas, within the provisions of HOA covenants. That is, the HOA cannot just automatically or whole-sale deny all external antennas. For instance, if you can erect a low-profile HF wire, you must be allowed to petition the HOA that it meets any related pre-existing architectural covenants.

Exceptions to Rules: You're probably very familiar with most of the commonplace rules and regulations governing the Amateur Service, but let's review a few exceptions to the rules that you need to keep in mind also.

Codes and Ciphers: You recall from your Technician studies that secret codes or ciphers are not allowed on the amateur bands. However, **procedural signals in the Amateur Service may be used if they do not obscure the meaning of a message.** This means that procedural signals commonly used with Morse Code are fine, such as the very commonly used CQ, or SK for *end of contact*. This also applies to *Q signals*, such as the QSY reference to changing frequency, or the QRN reference to static noise. And one additional exception is that an amateur station is permitted to transmit secret codes to control a space station, such as an amateur radio satellite.

Weather & Propagation Transmissions: Many Amateur stations, especially repeaters, will make automatic transmissions from the National Weather Service regarding hazardous weather conditions in the area, or simply regular weather updates. Other automated transmissions of this type may be government-issued statements regarding radio propaga-

1.3 DX and Details

tion forecasts or atmospheric conditions. **Occasional retransmission of weather and propagation forecast information from U.S. government stations is permitted.**

Learning Morse Code: **One-way transmissions are permitted for transmissions necessary to assist learning the International Morse code.** Normally, "broadcasting" or transmitting messages one-way for a general audience is not permitted by FCC regulations. However, an exception is made for the transmission of Morse code for training and education purposes. The ARRL and other organizations transmit code practice text on specific bands and frequencies on scheduled days and times to help operators become proficient at CW operations. You can find the transmission schedule online at the ARRL web site under the W1AW Operating Schedule page.

You have now expanded your knowledge of the particular details of DX and other General Class amateur radio operations! You have also completed the first chapter material in your drive to General Class. Congratulations! Next we will examine some of the cool operating methods you can implement as a General Class licensee, but first be sure to check your recall online with the question pool items from this section.

HamRadioSchool.com/general_media

Stu and Barry KD0RQU set up a portable digital station for Field Day operations. Barry adjusts the transmitter and sound card interface to ensure proper modulation of the digital signal to keep within the boundaries of good amateur practice. You'll learn more about the meaning of "good engineering and good amateur practice" in this chapter, Operating Your Radio.

Photo courtesy Dan Oldfield Photography

2.0 Operating Your Radio

> **There's a fine line between fishing and just standing on the shore like an idiot.**
> – Steven Wright

If you want to hook lots of contacts as a General Class operator, how you operate can determine which side of Mr. Wright's line you fall upon in the ham radio fishing derby. This chapter will help you understand how to really *RF fish*.

In Section 2.1 we will define the concept of *Good Amateur Practice* and examine some specific examples of what it is, and of what it is not. In Section 2.2 you'll study some common operating tips and techniques for the HF bands that will open up to you as a General licensee. We'll particularly focus on single sideband operating techniques. The topic of Section 2.3 is *Continuous Wave* (CW). Even if you do not immediately become proficient sending Morse Code, you should be familiar with CW mode and its unique operating characteristics, and just maybe you'll catch the bug and try your hand at it! We will dig into digital operations in Sections 2.4 and 2.5, with particular coverage of digital modes commonly used on the HF bands.

Ready to toss your line into the General Class waters?

2.1 Good Amateur Practice

> **Good Amateur Practice is not operating so that whoever hears you becomes sorry they ever got into Amateur Radio in the first place."**
> – Riley Hollingsworth

The FCC requires an amateur station to be operated in conformance with good engineering and good amateur practice in all respects not specifically covered by the Part 97 rules. What does that mean, "good amateur practice," and who gets to decide whether an amateur practice is good or not? Seems rather vague, I know. However, it is **the FCC that determines "good engineering and good amateur practice" as it applies to the operation of an amateur station in all respects not covered by the Part 97 rules.**

Former FCC Special Counsel for the Spectrum Enforcement Division, Riley Hollingsworth, had some excellent words about good amateur practice in 2002. He said that while hard to define, it is "…operating with the realization that frequencies are shared, that there's going to be occasional interference and that's no reason to become hateful and paranoid." Other *Riley-isms* regarding the definition of good amateur practice include:

> Giving a little ground – even if you have a right not to – in order to help preserve Amateur Radio and not cause it to get a bad name…
>
> Not acting like an idiot just because you were stepped on.
>
> Operating so that if a neighbor, niece or nephew or news reporter hears you, that person will be impressed with Amateur Radio.
>
> *Source: ARRL*

So, with thanks to Mr. Hollingsworth for his wisdom and wit in framing this issue, let's cover a little ground on good amateur practice.

Log Keeping: Memory is tenuous. Very often I simply tilt my head and items of recall roll right out my ear and bounce off my shoulder, never to be found again. When it comes to radio station operation, contacts, call signs and the like, there is a virtual avalanche spewing from my auricles. To help with this exact problem, **many amateurs keep a station log,** even though the FCC does not require it. **A log may help with a reply if the FCC requests information** regarding your transmissions, station control operator, or other items that have long since exited your ear and disappeared into the couch. A log is also handy in keeping track of contacts for which you may seek a QSL card, particularly if you are chasing an award like Worked All States (WAS) or DXCC (for working 100 different countries).

At a minimum, the information traditionally contained in a station log includes:
- Date and time of contact, usually using Coordinated Universal Time (UTC, or "Zulu" or GMT time)
- Band and/or frequency of the contact
- Call sign of the station contacted and the signal report given

Signal reports are typically provided and recorded in RST format, as summarized in the box below.

You may wish to keep additional information about your contacts in your log, such as the contacted operator's name, geographic location or grid locator, and notes regarding the exchange or QSO content. This way, if you are ever called upon to provide information for an FCC investigation or if there is any question about your own station's operation, you have the records necessary to provide the requested input.

> RST Signal Report
>
> **R**eadability 1 to 5 (5 is best)
>
> **S**ignal Strength 1 to 9 (from S-meter)
>
> **T**one 1 to 9 (for quality of CW note)
>
> Phone reports are usually RS only.
>
> **"C" added to a CW report means "chirpy" or unstable signal tone.**
>
> G2C07

Logs may be hand written or electronic. There are numerous electronic log book programs available as free downloads online or as commercial products, or you may prefer a simple formatted spreadsheet. The advantage of an electronic log book is that it usually includes a search capability, making it easy to zero-in on previous contacts, dates, call signs, or other recorded information. Particularly with your HF and DX contacts you will want to keep a log of all the different places to which you have reached out on the air and of all the new friends made there!

Avoiding Interference: Mr. Hollingsworth's statements about good amateur practice focus on interference between stations and how to behave properly as an operator in handling it. The best behavior is to avoid the interference in the first place – head-off interference before it happens!

Contact Log

Rec #	Call Sign	Date	Band	Mode	Power	Sig Sent	Sig Rec	Time on	Time off	Country	State	City or County	Name	Freq	
1	KE7NCO	26-Oct-09	20	USB	100	5/9	5/9+	10:10	10:25	USA	NV	Sparks, NV	Scotty	14.251.00	Logged eQSL
2	W0KEN	26-Oct-09	20	USB	100	5/5 - 5/9	5/1 - 5/7	10:25	10:32	USA	WI	Hayward WI	Ken	14.251.00	Logged eQSL
3	AE4QK	27-Oct-09	40	LSB	100	5/7	7-May	13:25	13:36	USA	KY	Owensboro	Ron	7.237.00	Logged eQSL
4	K5LMI	28-Oct-09	80	LSB	100	5/9++	5/9++	10:05	10:10	USA	NM	Clayton	Herb	3.868.00	
5	W0DGG	28-Oct-09	80	LSB	100	5?9++	5/9++	10:05	10:10	USA	CO	Littleton	Dale	3.868.00	
6	KA1RBJ	28-Oct-09	20	USB	100	5/9	5/9	17:35	17:43	USA	CA	Martinez	Phil	14.310.00	
7	K7IT	29-Oct-09	40	LSB	100	5/7	6/5.	15:10	15:17	USA	MT	Townsend	Gary	7.195.00	Logged eQSL
8	W7EJB	29-Oct-09	40	LSB	100	5/7	5/7	15:10	15:17	USA	MT	Roundup	Cort	7.195.00	Logged eQSL
9	W8MWV/m	29-Oct-09	40	LSB	100	5/7	6/3.	15:10	15:17	USA	NV	Hwy 93	Jim	7.195.00	
10	KL7LF	30-Oct-09	20	LSB	100	5/5.	5/8	16:43	16:46	USA	AK	Fairbanks	Joe	14.244.00	Logged eQSL
11	KH7DX	1-Nov-09	20	LSB	100	5/9	5/8	17:45	17:55	USA	HI	Kailua, Kona	Stuart	14.245.00	
12	W1SW	5-Nov-09	20	LSB	100	5/9	5/9	9:36	9:36	USA	CT	Newington	Pete	14.266.00	Logged eQSL
13	4U1WB	5-Nov-09	20	LSB	100	5/9	6/9+	16:20	16:22	USA	DC	Washington	Fasa	14.236.70	
14	K4MDX	5-Nov-09	40	LSB	100	5/9	5/7	17:45	17:49	USA	VA	Charlottesville	Mario	7.195.00	
15	KI4KSY	8-Nov-09	20	LSB	100	5/7	5/5.	17:12	17:17	USA	FL	Pierson	Tim	14.247.60	Logged eQSL
16	YW5F	8-Nov-09	20	LSB	100	5/9	5/7	17:25	17:25	Venezuala	n/a	Caracas	?	14.237.00	
17	K8V	11-Nov-09	20	LSB	100	5/7	5/7	7:45	7:46	USA	MI	Iron Mountain	Scott	14.234.00	Special Event Veterans Day Station
18	N4TAT	11-Nov-09	20	LSB	100	5/9	5/9	8:30	9:05	USA	GA	WarnerRobbins	Don	14.313.00	Logged eQSL
19	K8MGA	11-Nov-09	20	LSB	100	5/9	5/7	10:00	10:05	USA	OH	Chillicothe	Jerry	14.249.60	Logged eQSL
20	K5KID	11-Nov-09	20	LSB	100	5/9	5/7	13:19	13:20	USA	LA	Baton Rouge	Mike	14.253.00	Special Event on USS Kidd Navy vessel, MS river

Figure 2.1: A simple spreadsheet logbook extract. A log book should record the contact call sign, date, time, frequency, and signal report, as minimum information. Most logs will include additional notes, such as locations and names of contacts.

Except during emergencies, no amateur station has priority access to any frequency, and common courtesy should be a guide. So, while no operator has a lock on the use of a frequency, things tend to work on a first-come, first-serve basis with common courtesy. It would be rude to muscle in on an ongoing QSO between two operators, or to do the same to a single operator calling CQ on a given frequency unless you are responding to the CQ, of course. How can you head-off accidental interference like this?

First, **choose your transmitting frequency with good amateur practice:**

- **Ensure that the frequency and mode selected are within your license class privileges.**
- **Be sure you are following the generally accepted band plans agreed to by the Amateur Radio community.**
- **And then monitor the frequency before transmitting** to avoid interfering with ongoing communications. It is usually good to listen for at least several tens of seconds, as you may be able to receive only one half of a QSO between two operators, and the one operator you can receive may be listening to his contact.

Second, **send "QRL?" on CW, followed by your call sign; or, if using phone, ask if the frequency is in use, followed by your call sign. This is a practical way to avoid harmful interference on an apparently clear frequency when calling CQ on CW or phone.** If you are answered with a CW "C," YES, or QRL, or if the phone response is "Yes, the frequency is in use," then graciously move on to another frequency and give it another shot. Sometimes the bands are crowded and finding an open frequency can be a challenge. Keep your courtesy and maintain your diligence, or possibly move to another, less crowded band.

Choosing a Frequency: Let's consider this frequency choosing step above in a bit more detail. What factors besides your license privileges are important when selecting a frequency on which to transmit?

Mode: Follow the voluntary band plan for the operating mode you intend to use. Remember, sub-bands are designated in many amateur bands for CW, digital, and phone transmission modes. Choose a frequency in the mode sub-band that complies with band plan guidelines.

DX Window: Depending upon your selected band and mode, you may need to consider whether or not you are in a *DX Window*. A DX Window in a voluntary band plan is a portion of the band that should not be used

2.1 Good Amateur Practice

for contacts between stations within the 48 contiguous United States, but rather used for making DX contacts outside of this region. For instance, **for U.S. stations transmitting within the 48 contiguous states in the 50.1 to 50.125 MHz band segment, a voluntary band plan restriction applies for only contacts with stations not within the 48 contiguous states.** The ARRL recommends DX windows on some bands and modes, as defined in the *ARRL Considerate Operator's Frequency Guide* that may be found at the ARRL web site. **Only stations outside the lower 48 states should generally respond to a station in the contiguous 48 states who calls "CQ DX."**

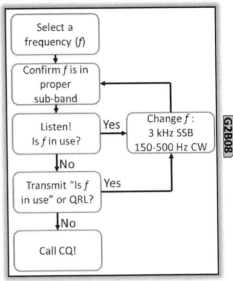

Figure 2.2: Flow chart of steps in selecting a frequency to call CQ.

Frequency Separation: A CW or Single Sideband (SSB) transmission uses a small band of frequencies adjacent to the carrier frequency value to which your station is tuned. The bandwidth of CW is typically quite narrow, perhaps 150 Hz, while SSB is usually around 3 kHz wide. Further, the bandwidth consumed by SSB will all be piled on one side of the carrier frequency, as depicted in Figure 2.3 – all above the carrier for upper sideband (USB) mode or all below the carrier for lower sideband (LSB) mode. Be sure there is adequate separation between your chosen frequency and nearby frequencies in use for the bandwidth of the mode you are using. The customary minimums are as follows:

For CW mode, the minimum frequency separation you should allow in order to minimize interference to stations on adjacent frequencies is 150 to 500 Hz. Notice that this separation allows for the bandwidth of a CW signal.

When selecting an SSB transmitting frequency, the minimum separation to minimize interference to stations on adjacent frequencies should be approximately 3 kHz. Again, notice that this conforms to the bandwidth of the typical SSB signal.

Example: Reference Figure 2.3. Suppose you want to call CQ on the 20m band with USB phone mode per the normal conventions for the band. You have checked that you are between 14.225 and 14.350 MHz, the General Class phone sub-band. You dial around the sub-band and note it is crowded, but there seems to be a clear frequency, 14.250 MHz. After listening a bit you hear one side of a QSO right on that frequency. To make sure you do not interfere with this ongoing QSO you move up at least 3 kHz to 14.253 MHz – a USB signal

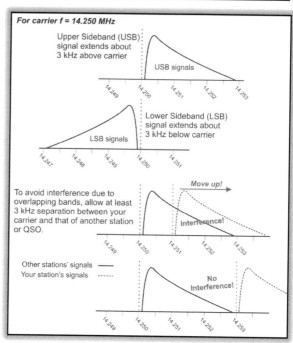

Figure 2.3: Minimum frequency separation of SSB carriers is customarily 3 kHz.

will extend 3 kHz above the carrier frequency shown on your transceiver display. You should also make sure your receive bandwidth is set to be *at least 3 kHz* so that you will hear any signals within your intended transmit band. If you hear no obvious signals after a few seconds be sure you are tuned on frequency and then make the call "Is the frequency in use? Is the frequency in use?" Follow with your call sign so that in the case you get a response you do not have to interrupt further with identification. If you do get a response indicating the frequency is in use, politely move on. If you hear no response, start your CQ calls.

G2D05

On a clear frequency in the HF phone bands, a good way to indicate that you are looking for a contact with any station is to repeat "CQ" a few times, followed by "this is," then your call sign a few times, then pause to listen, repeat as necessary.

Changing Propagation: Due to changing conditions in the ionosphere, HF propagation will ebb and flow through the day, sometimes changing suddenly. The direction and effectiveness of propagation may shift such that a station you heard at RS 5-9 a moment ago suddenly dips into the background noise, and a different station that you could not hear previously becomes prominent. In a matter of seconds you have lost your contact and you are interfering with

2.1 Good Amateur Practice

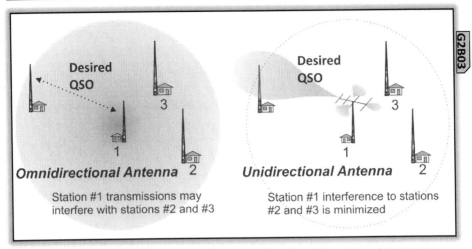

Figure 2.4: Comparison of omnidirectional and unidirectional (AKA *Directional* or *Beam*) antenna patterns.

another QSO of which you were completely unaware! It's all part of the magic, so don't let it rattle you. **If propagation changes during your contact and you notice increasing interference from other stations on the frequency, attempt to resolve the interference problem with the other stations in a mutually acceptable manner.**

Directional Antennas: The type of antenna used can have a significant impact regarding interference between stations. Although we'll cover more about antennas in a later section, you probably already understand that *omnidirectional* antennas radiate equally in all horizontal directions, while a *unidirectional*, or simply a *directional*, or *beam* antenna points most of the RF energy in a particular direction. A quarter-wave vertical is an example of an omnidirectional antenna, and a Yagi is an example of a directional antenna.

A directional antenna would be the best to use for minimizing interference, since you can point the beam in the direction of your contact, thereby reducing the RF signal strength radiating in other directions. The potential of interference from your station in those other directions is minimized. With the omnidirectional antenna you have no control over the directionality of your signal, so the potential for interference is generally greater. However, erecting directional antennas for the HF bands is no small or inexpensive chore, and your first HF station will likely employ a more omnidirectional antenna like a quarter-wave vertical or a horizontal dipole. Don't fret, many thousands of hams use these antennas successfully every day without imposing undue interference!

Additional Considerations: Just a couple more good amateur practices to be knowledgable of... What if you are dialing through the bands and encounter a truly spellbinding QSO in which you would just love to take part? Or, what if you hear a friend or familiar contact in a QSO to whom you wish to say howdy? There is a courteous practice to use: **The recommended way to break into a phone contact is to say your call sign once,** usually during a break between transmissions by the other stations. Simple as that. Just throw your call sign in there and await a courteous response inviting you to transmit.

Of course, **if you are communicating with another amateur station and hear a station in distress break in, the first thing you should do is acknowledge the station in distress and determine what assistance may be needed.** Then do everything you can to provide the assistance. A station in distress will usually break in using the term *emergency, mayday,* or *priority.* But it could also be a simple "Help!"

Phonetics: On the noisy HF bands the use of phonetics is good amateur practice helping ensure accurate on-air exchanges. The ITU standard phonetic alphabet is identical to **the NATO phonetic alphabet, starting with Alpha, Bravo, Charlie, Delta, and so on,** just as you learned in Technician studies.

Contests: Sometimes in the heat of a contest on a busy HF band it is easy for operators to forget even the basics of good amateur practice. **When participating in a contest on HF frequencies, identify your station per normal FCC regulations,** every ten minutes and at the end of a communication. And keep your cool when it comes to interference.

Now, the next time someone asks you what is meant by "good amateur practice," you are armed with superb, sage advice from Mr. Hollingsworth as well as numerous examples of it! You should be able to paint a clear, unambiguous picture of good practice, and you should be able to conduct your own station operations in conformance with it. Please do try your best, and take pride in your success. Your fellow hams are counting on you to help uphold our legacy of self-policed, on-air courtesy.

Go tackle the online quiz associated with this section, then come back for a little insight into common HF operating conventions.

HamRadioSchool.com/general_media

Operating Your Radio
2.2 Operating Techniques

> ❝ *In extreme situations, the entire universe becomes our foe; at such critical times, unity of mind and technique is essential – do not let your heart waver!*   – Morihei Ueshiba

There you are: It's the busiest point of the contest! You're working a giant SSB pile up, your VOX headset tweaked to perfection, your azimuthal projection map keenly guiding your commands to your directional's rotator, a thousand yearning contacts screaming call signs in your ear, and you can distinguish none of them in the jumble! You quickly decide to go split mode and wonder if you can sneak away under cover of the adjustment for that long-needed comfort break with the plumbing. You don't want to lose the pile up or the frequency – you'll have to shift to the split fast! Is your mind and your technique unified? Can you do it? *Or will your heart waver?*

Marshall arts Ōsensei Ueshiba would have made a fine ham operator, and while his advice may be just a smidgen over the top for most ham ops, the point is well taken. Technique matters.

With a General Class ticket your operations will likely focus much more on modes commonly used on the HF bands, including single sideband (SSB) phone, and on some of the associated operating techniques that will enhance your ability to make HF contacts. In this section we will explore commonly accepted HF conventions and describe some of the more advanced operating techniques that come in handy on the HF bands. Ready, *kōhai*?

Single Sideband: We will cover more detail on single sideband (SSB) mode a bit later in the *How Radio Works* chapter, but let's review some of the basic characteristics and then discuss SSB use on the amateur bands. (You may want to review the HamRadioSchool.com Technician License Course section 6.3, *Bandwidth and Sidebands*, for a refresher on the nature of SSB.)

Single Sideband phone (voice) mode is a special form of amplitude modulation, or AM. Its primary advantage for voice transmissions over AM or FM is its narrower bandwidth. As depicted in Figure 2.5 a modulated true AM signal has two bands of signals either side of the carrier frequency to which the

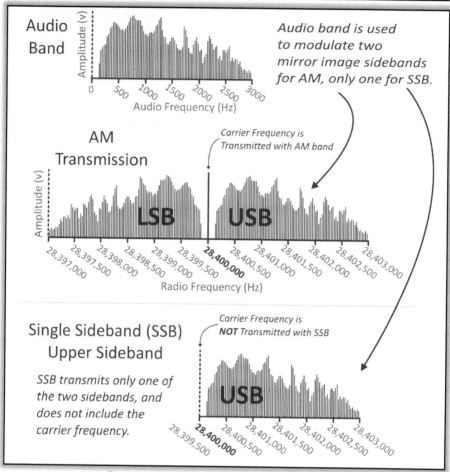

Figure 2.5: Comparison of AM and SSB.

transmitter is tuned – one band above the carrier frequency (*upper sideband*, or USB) and one band below the carrier frequency (*lower sideband*, or LSB). The USB and LSB are redundant mirror images of one another, each representing the phone modulation in approximately 3 kHz of signal bandwidth. Thus, the entire AM signal consumes about 6 kHz of bandwidth in total, and it offers a robust and good fidelity signal.

However, since the USB and LSB each contain a complete phone modulated signal, only one of these sidebands is necessary to affect voice communication. Single sideband mode is exactly that – the use of only a single sideband of approximately 3 kHz for phone transmissions. Either the USB or the LSB may be used in a SSB transmission at the discretion of the control operator. The carrier frequency signal, also transmitted in a true AM signal, is omitted from SSB transmissions as well. Using less than half the bandwidth of AM and much less bandwidth than typical FM signals, SSB is a very efficient voice mode, and

2.2 Operating Techniques

single sideband is the most commonly used voice communication mode on the HF amateur bands. As you may surmise, some fidelity of signal is sacrificed for this efficiency as compared to AM.

SSB Conventions: While either of the sidebands may be selected for use by a SSB operator, random selection of USB or LSB within a band would cause some hassles. For instance, a pair of operators using opposite sidebands will not be able to understand one another's demodulated audio. In such a case, signals intended for high audio frequency reproduction will be demodulated as low frequency audio and vice versa. The result is usually a garbled *"wah wah, grrr flump wah wah"* kind of audio reproduction that almost sounds like speech but is indecipherable. Such random selection would also complicate transceiver operations on a given band and muddle the matter of avoiding interference described in the previous section on *Good Amateur Practice*.

So, standard operating conventions for USB and LSB use have been established and accepted by the amateur community. **It is good amateur practice to follow these conventions:**

> **Upper Sideband (USB):** The sideband most commonly used for voice communications on frequencies of 14 MHz (20m band) or higher (17m, 15m, 12m, 10m), including VHF and UHF bands.
>
> **Lower Sideband (LSB):** The sideband most commonly used for voice communications on frequencies of 7 MHz (40m band) or lower (75/80m, 160m). [Note exception: The five 60m channels are restricted to USB only.]

Variable Frequency Oscillator (VFO): The VFO is the name used for the *big knob* on the radio, the one that is used to make incremental or continuous adjustments to the tuned frequency. Recall from the *Before We Begin* chapter, pre-designated or assigned channels are not typically utilized with HF operations as with VHF/UHF repeaters or simplex band plans. Rather, the VFO tunes the carrier frequency for both transmitter and receiver across the contiguous range of frequencies available in a HF band. Typically a transceiver's VFO will allow a minimum frequency change step size of 100 Hz or smaller.

Figure 2.6: The BIG KNOB, A.K.A. the VFO.

Split Mode: Many modern HF transceivers offer **dual VFOs that permit the monitoring of two different frequencies.** In HF operations, **operating the transceiver in "split" mode is a technique in which the transceiver is set to different transmit and receive frequencies,** thereby utilizing the dual VFO feature. A very common reason for doing this is to help reduce interference from many calling stations during a pile up.

Pile Up: A situation in which many stations are attempting to contact a single operator, such as a very rare or desirable DX station, is called a *pile up*. If numerous stations are calling a single DX station, many of those calling stations cannot hear the DX station respond due to the stronger and multiple signals of more local operators striving to make themselves heard over several seconds following the DX station's "QRZ?" (who is calling me?) transmission. So, even if the DX station replied to your call sign, you may not hear it due to the cacophony, resulting in delay, confusion, and finally a repeated cacophony of station calls. Rinse and repeat until frustrated.

One way to resolve this problem is for the DX station to operate in split mode, transmitting on one frequency and listening on another. The calling stations should be in the opposite, complementary frequency arrangement, listening on the DX transmit frequency but transmitting on the DX listen frequency. That way, the DX station's calls are clear to everyone, making for more efficient and effective contacts.

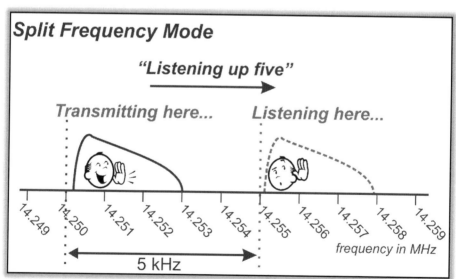

Figure 2.7: Operating in Split Mode sets the transceiver to different transmit and receive frequencies. This technique is often used during busy "pile ups."

2.2 Operating Techniques

However, the station *running the pile up* (the single highly desired station) needs to be sure to announce his transmit and receive configuration for this to work. Usually the station will announce something like "listening up five," meaning that the station will receive your transmissions 5 kHz higher than it is transmitting. You should put your station into split mode, listening to the DX station's frequency but transmitting 5 kHz higher. If you are fortunate enough to be running a pile up (*It can happen to you!*), it is a good practice to provide listening up/down instructions frequently so that late arrivals to your pile up understand the convention being used and will not re-create the problem you sought to solve by operating in split mode at the start of your pile up! Refer to your transceiver operator's manual for specific instruction on establishing a split frequency arrangement, or split mode.

SSB VOX: Voice operated transmit, or VOX, may be used with SSB. This is not different from any other VOX operation on VHF/UHF FM – **VOX operation simply allows "hands free" operation** by activating the push-to-talk function automatically when the relatively strong audio signal of the operator's voice is detected. Many HF operators prefer VOX for the convenience of hands-free operation, especially for extended time on the air such as a contest. Implementing VOX operation requires a special VOX circuit that most modern HF transceivers will support. The VOX circuit usually will provide a control to adjust the microphone sensitivity (gain) for actuating the PTT function and a delay control for adjusting the time that PTT will be held on after your voice is silent, thereby avoiding rapid and persistent on-off-on PTT actuations with brief verbal pauses. Use VOX with caution, and adjust it meticulously, as ambient sound can inadvertently key your transmitter.

QRP: QRP operation is low power transmit operation. This is the mode for operators who care to send the very least. The Q signal QRP refers to the CW shortcut "Reduce power" or "Shall I reduce power?" QRP operations typically imply 5 watts of power or less in transmissions, and often much less than that. Due to battery power necessity, low power operation is very popular for operators who enjoy operating portable from remote locations such as mountaintops or back country camps, and many operators simply enjoy the thrill of making long distance and DX contacts on just a few watts of power. Some digital modes in common use work particularly well for QRP, such as FT8, JT65, JT9, and others, but QRP using CW, PSK31, and even phone mode is also very popular. Try it! You may get a big kick out of very little.

Running Barefoot: Most modern transceivers include output power of about 100 watts PEP for HF operations. When using such a transceiver without any additional RF power amplification a station is said to be *running barefoot*.

In good conditions 100 watts is more than enough power to talk around the world on the HF bands with SSB and a simple dipole wire antenna. In poor propagation conditions a power amplifier may be used to boost power well above "barefoot" level to complete contacts, and we will examine amplifiers in greater detail in Chapter 6.

Azimuthal Projection Map: A handy tool, especially for the DX chaser, is an azimuthal projection map. **The azimuthal projection map is a world map projection that shows true bearings and distances from a particular location,** such as your station location. With such a map you can readily determine where in the world your signals are pointing when using a directional antenna, ensuring that you are pointing in the shortest path to your targeted geographical area. This determination might seem trivial at first consideration, but it is not!

The desired pointing direction of your RF signals to any given receiving station is depicted as a straight line from your station to the other. However, combining straight lines with a spherical planet is sometimes a tricky feat of mental gymnastics. The azimuthal projection keeps the mental gymnastics to a kindergarten-level playground exercise.

For example, suppose you are operating from the central US, perhaps near Kansas City. If you point your awesome 20m Yagi directional antenna due west, where will your signals go? You may be surprised to know that you will be pointing directly into Australia in the southern hemisphere! Japan and South Korea will be nearly 45 degrees north of your directional projection. To point to central Europe you'd turn your antenna northeast to roughly 030 degrees.

Long Path Contacts: Armed with azimuthal projection knowledge and excellent propagation conditions you can also try **long-path contacts with another station, in which your antenna is pointed 180 degrees from its short-path heading.** So, in our example above, to take the long-path to Europe you'd point your directional antenna 030 + 180 degrees, or to a southwest heading of 210 degrees. Such contacts are usually more difficult, and success will depend on atmospheric conditions. Either way, long path or short, it's all for fun and for the reward of achieving it!

2.2 Operating Techniques

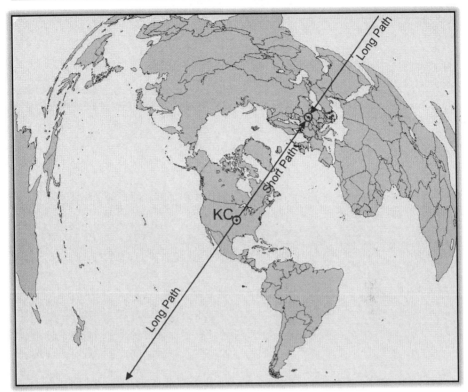

Figure 2.8: Example azimuthal projection map centered on Kansas City, MO, indicating both short path and long path propagation to a European contact.

Is your heart wavering yet? Maybe just thumping a little faster, anticipating getting on the air and trying out some of this newly acquired technique? You will learn much more about HF operational techniques and conventions when you're on the bands. Don't be afraid to ask your fellow hams questions, and listen to other QSOs to glean additional insight. Before long no one will be able to tell the operational difference between you with your sparkling new General ticket and an ancient, grey beard Ham Ōsensei!

Next we'll get find out how to achieve zero beat and hone our prosigns with an examination of CW operations. But first, be sure to review the questions for this section!

HamRadioSchool.com/general_media

Eric, WØRLY, works 20-meter band CW contacts with a straight key. Eric recently learned CW using various Koch Method online resources and apps. The Koch Method is a training approach focusing on learning to recognize the sound pattern of Morse Code characters at approximately 20 words-per-minute speed. Initially, only two different characters are presented, and additional characters are added to practice sets one at a time as proficiency with characters builds. Eric quickly became proficient with 20 wpm CW. He is a member of the *Straight Key Century Club* (SKCC) and enjoys earning SKCC awards and competing in sponsored CW contests. He also works CW using paddle keys of various design. You can learn CW like Eric and work the lower portions of the HF bands with dits and dahs! Let's learn more about the world of Continuous Wave ops...

2.3 Operating Your Radio — CW

> *Wave after wave*
> *Will flow with the tide*
> *And bury the world as it does*
> — Neil Peart (Rush), Natural Science

The joy of CW! Although proficiency with Morse Code is no longer required for any of the FCC Amateur Service licenses, continuous wave (CW) mode operations are far from buried in ham radio! Indeed, continuous wave continues!

Many operators prefer CW to any other mode, as it offers a pleasure and pride of skill development like nothing else in the hobby, and its power efficiency remains unmatched by most other modes. The prevalence of CW on the HF bands is greater today than ever, and you should try your fist at it! After all, popular theory is that the moniker of our hobby, "ham" radio, derived from the pejorative comparison of professionally competent wireless telegraphers whose code was beautifully consistent and readable with those "ham fisted" amateurs whose code exhibited numerous auditory warts. So, let's continue with some fine points about continuous wave.

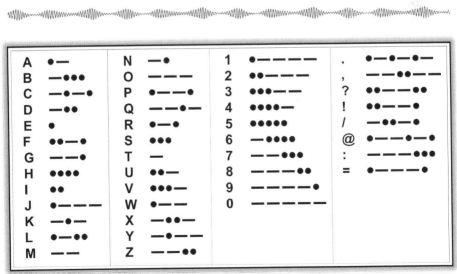

Figure 2.9 International Morse Code Characters.

CW Band Use: Recall from the *Bands and Privileges* section that most HF bands have digital and data sub-bands in the lower portion of the bands where phone transmissions are prohibited. This is where most of the CW action will be found, down where it doesn't have to contend with the broader band emissions and associated interference of the phone modes. However, a little-noticed line in the key of the ARRL US Amateur Band Plan chart states, "CW operation is permitted throughout all amateur bands." So, you may occasionally hear CW code in the phone and digital portions of the bands, and that's OK, but good amateur practice avoids using CW in the phone bands. Most operators prefer CW using the lowest frequencies for which they have privileges.

Keys and Keyers: You are probably familiar with the look and action of a conventional *straight key* for CW, as depicted in Figure 2.10– press the key down and a contact is made that activates the CW transmitter. Morse Code tones of *dits* and *dahs* are created by the duration of the key press by the operator. It requires quite some skill development to send consistently timed characters, words, and intervening spaces. Also depicted in Figure 2.10 is a paddle key and a touch key, each of which may be connected to an *electronic keyer*. **The purpose of an electronic keyer is to automatically generate strings of dots and dashes for CW operation.** A keyer is a digital circuit or

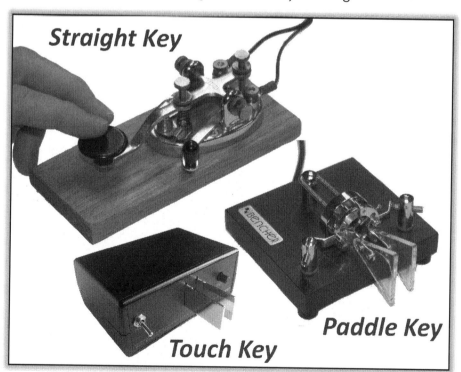

Figure 2.10: Example Keys and Paddles.

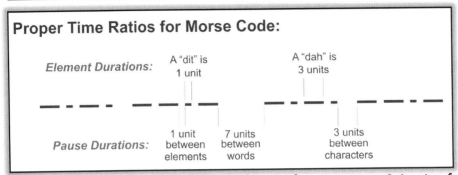

Figure 2.11: No matter your send speed, strive for a consistent 3:1 ratio of elements, in which the 'dahs' are three times the duration of the 'dits.'

microprocessor that detects activations of a paddle and generates the associated Morse Code element. For instance, pushing or touching one paddle will cause the keyer to generate a consistent duration *dit*, while the other paddle's activation will generate a consistently timed *dah*. While this helps make an operator's code more consistent, most operators find that electronic keyers promote faster sending speed as well, but the timing of character and word spacing remains with the operator's technique and skill. Some well-practiced operators are able to achieve speeds upwards of 50 words per minute (WPM). That's screaming!

Break-In: Suppose that you are sending a lengthy message with CW, at beginner's slow speed of perhaps 5 words per minute (WPM). If interference occurs during your send, or if the receiving station needs to interrupt you for an urgently required break, or if a station in distress desperately needs to break-in with an emergency message, how will you know of these problems if you're steadily transmitting? The answer is break-in telegraphy, or QSK. **Full break-in telegraphy means that transmitting stations can receive between code characters and elements.** In other words, when you are transmitting code characters your transmitter is rapidly switching on for the sending of each dit and dah element and just as quickly switching back to receive in between those elements – millisecond durations – while your relatively slow brain is coordinating your fingers. So, there is no solid, uninterrupted block of transmit time with full break-in operation, and it is possible to hear other stations transmitting or requesting to break-in even while you're frantically trying to pour out your CW heart to them.

Semi-break-in telegraphy is similar, only there is a somewhat longer delay after each dit or dah transmit time during which the transmitter continues, or 'hangs on.' The time for another operator to break-in is reduced, but still available, and you will hear the other's keying effort between your own transmissions. You may be able to adjust your transmitter's delay time to affect varying degrees of break-in capability. That is, you can adjust the duration that your transmitter will remain in transmit mode following the completion of a code element. Additionally, **transmitter keying circuits sometimes include a time delay to allow time for the transmit-receive changeover operations to complete properly before RF output is allowed.** This is a protection mechanism for the circuits, but most modern transceivers will have incredibly short time delays, usually on the order of a few milliseconds, and even the speediest operators will not usually notice interrupted code elements due to this feature.

CW Operating Conventions: Here are a couple of basic operating tips and tricks of the CW trade that may help you get started on the air once you have mastered basic code production and decoding.

The best speed to use answering a CQ in Morse Code is the fastest speed at which you are comfortable copying, but no slower than the CQ. As a beginner it may not be feasible for you to answer a rapidly coded CW transmission at equivalent speed, but there are many beginners and beginner's nets on the air that will allow you to exchange code at comfortable speeds before jumping into the fray of faster code. Further, most speedy CW operators will slow down if you reply to them slowly, and you should never send faster than you can receive for the same reason – the more practiced operators will match your speed.

Zero Beat: In CW operations "zero beat" means matching the transmit frequency to the frequency of a received signal. That is, you want the received signal tone to sound the same as your transmitted tone, aligning your CW transmitted band center precisely with the other operator's band center. (You will hear your *sidetone* for comparison when you transmit CW.) Achieving zero beat makes the received signal tone sound the same as your sidetone, helping to distinguish your contact from any interfering signals on a busy band. Zero beat also helps minimize the bandwidth that your QSO consumes, leaving more spectrum for others to enjoy. Most transceivers will

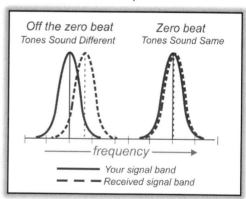

Figure 2.12: Zero Beat is achieved when the center of your transmitted band matches the frequency of the received signal's band, and the two tones sound identical.

provide a capability for checking the tone of your transmitted signal, so dig into that operator's manual and become more familiar with your rig. Usually this will involve the generation of a sidetone without transmitting it, while simultaneously listening to the received CW signal to be matched. The VFO is adjusted until the received signal tone and the comparison sidetone sound identical and have no *beat frequency* warbling sound. The tones should remain identical when you *reverse your sideband*, as well.

Reverse Sideband: On a busy band you will experience CW interference. Even though CW signals may be as narrow as 150 Hz, your receive filters will usually allow a significantly wider band of signals to be detected and demodulated. So, you're going to hear the guy next door on the band sometimes and, depending on where that other signal is located relative to your own frequency, its tone may be higher or lower than the one you are decoding and perhaps significantly annoying. A technique that most receivers will allow is reversing the sideband and, thereby, reversing the orientation of audio tone demodulation. Doing this, perhaps with a "CW-R" control on your transceiver, can turn that annoyingly high-pitched tone into a mellow low-pitched tone that is easier to ignore, thus allowing you to concentrate on your decoding. The reverse effect is feasible as well. So, if like me you have lost much of that high frequency perception the interference may seem to disappear altogether with sideband reversal! Thus, **an advantage of selecting the opposite or "reverse" sideband when receiving CW signals is the possibility of reducing or eliminating interference from other signals.** G4A02

Prosigns and Q Signals: Procedural signals, or *prosigns*, and *Q signals* are abbreviations for commonly used terms and were developed by telegraphers to reduce the burden of spelling out things all the time. Prosigns are two letters (three in the case of "SOS") that are transmitted together without pause, as if a single letter, and that have specific meanings in code exchanges. Q signals are three letter shortcuts beginning with the letter Q that are used extensively in CW and that have crept into phone mode usage as well. On the following page is a short list of prosigns and Q signals followed by an example CW exchange that uses many of them. A more exhaustive list of prosigns, Q signals, and other popular CW abbreviations may be found online at *HamRadioSchool.com*.

Pro sign	Meaning	Q Signal	Meaning
AR	Indicates end of a formal message	QSL	I acknowledge receipt. Do you acknowledge receipt?
K	"Over" or "Go ahead"	QRN	Static; natural noise. I am troubled by static.
KN	Similar to K, except listening for a specific station or stations.	QRV	I am ready to receive messages. Are you ready to receive messages?
CL	At the end of a transmission to mean "Closing station"	QRS	Send slower. Shall I send slower?
DE	"From" or "This is"	QRL	Are you busy? Is the frequency in use?
SK	Similar to AR, but used only at the end of last transmission of QSO	QRP	Reduce power. Shall I reduce power?

Example brief CW QSO:

Station 1: QRL
Station 1: CQ CQ CQ DE WØSTU WØSTU WØSTU K
Station 2: WØSTU DE KØNR KØNR KØNR K
Station 1: KØNR DE WØSTU UR 599 IN MONUMENT CO NAME IS STU STU AR KØNR DE WØSTU KN
Station 2: WØSTU DE KØNR UR 579 IN RICHMOND IN NAME IS BOB BOB AR WØSTU DE KØNR KN
Station 1: KØNR DE WØSTU QSL QSL TNX QSO MUCH QRN 73 SK KØNR DE WØSTU
Station 2: WØSTU DE KØNR QSL TNX 73 SK WØSTU DE KØNR CL

Now you're ready to go study code and practice it, getting up to speed! While CW is not for everyone, it adds a completely new dimension to your amateur radio fun, and I hope you will endeavor to pick up code. But first, let's get this General Class ticket under your belt. Check out the question pool quiz on CW, and then we'll get digital!

HamRadioSchool.com/general_media

2.4 Digital Mode Basics

> **I am not the only person who uses his computer mainly for the purpose of diddling with his computer.**
> – Dave Barry

> **The Universal Purpose of Amateur Radio is to have fun messing around with radios.**
> – Bob Witte, KØNR

A singular conclusion is reached by combining these two incontestable tenets of technological brilliance: *Delight in technological diddling increases as the multiple of radio-computer linkages.* This conclusion is the fundamental theorem of the ham digital modes. Let's see just how this diddling proceeds.

The Basics: As you probably learned in your Technician studies, digital modes utilize discrete signals or *bits* to encode characters and transmit them by radio frequency signals. Each character, whether a letter of the alphabet, a number, or other symbol is represented by a pattern of bits. In binary digital codes this is usually represented as a sequence of the digits 1 and 0, such as *10010110*.

A digital mode must have a defined protocol. A protocol is a set of established rules for encoding, sending, and decoding the digital patterns. The protocol will usually define a set of allowable characters, the structure of the transmitted patterns, and other characteristics of the data exchanges between stations.

Of course, a digital mode must also have some RF modulation technique such as FM or SSB. The digital codes are often translated into sequential sets of shifting audio frequencies that may be RF modulated for transmission over the air, and then demodulated back into audio tones by a receiver, and decoded back into readable characters. A computer will be interfaced to the transceiver to affect both the translation of characters into audio signals for the transmitter and the decoding of characters from audio signals via the receiver. In other cases the RF frequency is directly shifted by the transmitter via computer commands, avoiding the audio modulation step. Let's first examine where digital signals are found in the HF bands, consider some of the digital protocols that are used for digital communications, and then dig into some common digital modes used in ham radio.

HF Band Frequency Use: Recall from the *Bands and Privileges* section that digital mode sub-bands reside in the lower portion of many of the HF amateur bands. The very lowest portion of these sub-bands tends to be used for CW operations, while portions of the sub-band above the typical CW regions are commonly used for data transmissions.

The HF segments most commonly used for digital transmissions are:

 10m band   28.070 – 28.150 MHz
 12m band   24.920 – 24.930 MHz
 15m band   21.070 – 21.110 MHz
 17m band   18.100 – 18.110 MHz
 20m band   **14.070 – 14.112 MHz (avoiding DX beacons)**
 30m band   10.130 – 10.150 MHz
 40m band   7.080 – 7.125 MHz
 80m band   **3.570 – 3.60 MHz [3570 – 3600 kHz]**
 160m band   1.800 – 1.810 MHz [1800- 1810 kHz]

We will explore digital modes commonly used on the HF bands in Section 2.5, including PACTOR, PSK 31, and FT8. Be aware that many others exist and that new digital modes seem to spring up frequently, but we'll introduce some digital concepts next in this section using packet and RTTY examples.

Packet Delivery: A packet is a formatted package of data that includes additional information necessary for accurate transmission and reception. Some digital modes such as packet radio (using *ASCII code and protocol*) and *Automatic Packet Reporting System* (APRS) are used to deliver messages to specifically addressed receiving stations. Email by packet radio and text messages by APRS are two examples, and the PACTOR mode also utilizes packet delivery. A digital message or file may be delivered in multiple packets of data.

ASCII: American Standard Code for Information Interchange represents characters with a seven-bit code. It defines 128 characters, 33 of which are control characters for text spacing, appearance, and other functions. Many variations of ASCII have been developed using greater bits and greater variety of characters.

Each transmitted digital packet must have routing or destination information. Further, such packet structures require the receiving station to synchronize with the protocol structure and in some cases to facilitate retransmission of

2.4 Digital Modes

packets received with detected errors. This type of **routing and handling information is contained in the header part of a packet radio frame,** and that is followed by the data or body of the message. A trailer segment of information usually concludes a packet's data sequence. If the digital mode is an ***Automatic Repeat Query* (ARQ) data mode and the receiving station detects a packet containing errors, the receiving station will request the packet be retransmitted.**

Figure 2.15: A generic packet communications frame of information. Many protocol variations of this general frame format are used by different systems.

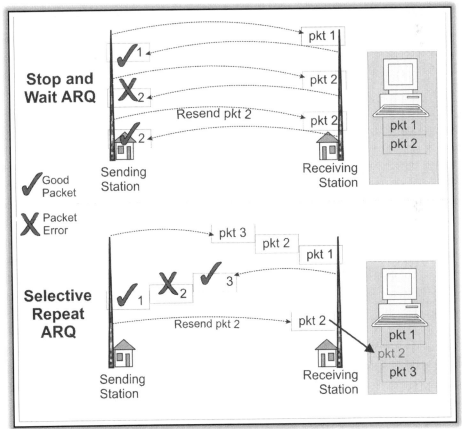

Figure 2.16: Different protocols may implement Automatic Repeat Queries (ARQ) in different ways, but each requires the receiving station to transmit a repeat request and/or an acknowledgement of valid packets received.

Various protocols are used for ARQ, including simple stop and wait ARQ in which an acknowledgement of valid packet receipt must be received by the packet sender within a limited time, and additional packets are not transmitted until acknowledgement is received. *Selective repeat* ARQ protocols provide more continuous sending of packets and packet resends when errors are acknowledged by the receiver, but the receiver must re-sequence packets into proper order based upon packet header control data.

G8C10 A different packet error correction method, **forward error correction (FEC), allows the receiver to correct errors in received data packets by transmitting redundant information with the data.** The redundant information is often efficiently encoded into the packets using mathematical algorithms that allow error detection and self-correction without the need for an ARQ or other retransmit request. However, the quantity of transmitted data is necessarily increased by this method, so it represents a trade-off with the ARQ method of error correction.

Baudot Code: Pronounced "*baw-doh*," Baudot Code was a precursor to modern ASCII code and it is used by the radio teletype (RTTY) mode. With
G8C04 **Baudot Code** each character is represented by **a 5-bit code sequence with additional bits used for start and stop.** With five binary digits Baudot code may represent $2^5 = 32$ different characters. However, two Baudot characters (called *FIGS* and *LTRS*) are used to implement something like the shift function of a keyboard by which a second set of characters is referenced. All characters that follow the FIGS character will be interpreted as the alternate set characters that include items like numerals, punctuations, and other special characters. The code interpretation is reset to the normal text character set by transmitting the LTRS characters. Thus, the total number of characters including FIGS and LTRS is 64.

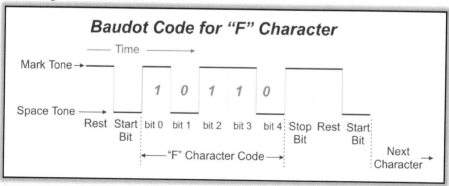

Figure 2.14: RTTY uses 5-bit Baudot Code for each character, with each bit value represented by either the "mark" or "space" frequency/tone. Start-stop bits maintain timing and sequence synchronization between sending and receiving systems.

2.4 Digital Modes

With a little protocol knowledge in our heads, let's now poke into the nature of RTTY mode to illustrate more digital concepts.

RTTY Mode: Radioteletype, or "ritty," is an older technology that was originally used to transmit text that was immediately printed upon reception by a mechanical printing device. Computers have replaced the teletype machines now in order to encode and decode RTTY data for computer screen display. A computer interface may directly manipulate transmitter frequencies, or a *sound card interface* (SCI) may be used to easily link computer and transceiver, with software to provide tone sequences for modulated transmissions and to decode received tones. RTTY mode employs Baudot Code.

RTTY is a *frequency shift keying* (FSK) method. **The FSK signal is generated by changing the transmitter oscillator's frequency directly with a digital control signal. The two separate frequencies of a Frequency Shift Keyed (FSK) signal are identified as *Mark* (binary 1) and *Space* (binary 0).** The frequency shifting may also be implemented by *audio frequency shift keying* (AFSK) using two audio tones of different frequencies that modulate mark and space RF shifts for transmissions.

In both frequency shift methods, the frequency shifts back and forth between the mark and space to encode a Baudot sequence of five 1s and 0s that represent each character. **The most common frequency shift for RTTY emissions in the amateur HF bands is 170 Hz,** with the standard AFSK tones being 2125 Hz (mark) and 2295 Hz (space). These tones are transmitted by SSB mode on the HF bands, and **normally the lower sideband (LSB) is used when sending AFSK RTTY signals with a SSB transmitter.**

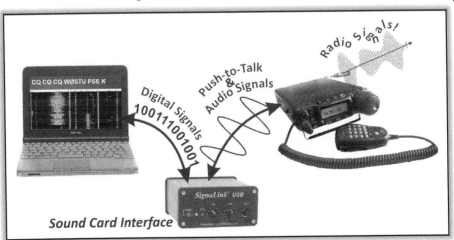

Figure 2.13: Many digital modes use a Sound Card Interface (SCI) between transceiver and computer, using tones to modulate digital signals.

Digital symbol rates are measured in *baud*. Derived from the use of Baudot Code, baud is a measure of the number of symbols that a digital mode transmits each second. With a simple code like Baudot each symbol transmitted represents one bit of data (a single 1 or 0 digit). So, with Baudot the baud is equivalent to *bits per second* (bps). With more complex digital communication codes this simple relationship equating baud and bps does not hold true, as multiple bits may be simultaneously transmitted with other codes in other digital modes, and structural, synchronization, or formatting bits for a data exchange protocol further complicate the baud calculation.

Principles of information science tell us that as the rate of information or data transmission increases the bandwidth used by the transmission must also increase to preserve the accuracy and reliability of the information. For instance, the rate of information exchange with CW is rather low, one character at a time tapped out by human hand relatively slowly, and the bandwidth required is narrow (~150 Hz). But with SSB phone mode you may transmit an entire word or two in the same time required to send just a dit or dah in CW, so the information transfer rate is much greater. Commensurately, SSB consumes much greater bandwidth (~3 kHz). With RTTY (or other digital modes) **the same relationship holds between transmitted symbol rate and bandwidth: Higher symbol rates require wider bandwidth.**

In order to maintain reliable RTTY information transfer with efficient bandwidth values, each of the amateur bands has a maximum permitted RTTY symbol rate in baud. Generally, the maximum permitted symbol rate decreases with lower band frequency. (Notice that total available bandwidth narrows generally with lower frequency of the amateur bands.) **The maximum symbol rates permitted for RTTY or data emissions transmitted on the amateur bands are as follows:**

1.25m and 70cm bands	56 kilobaud	
2m band	19.6 kilobaud	
10m band	1200 baud	
Below 28 MHz (10m)	300 baud	(includes 20m band)

Common Errors: Some caution is necessary to ensure that a RTTY or other FSK system is properly set up. **Some things that could be wrong if you cannot decode a RTTY or FSK signal even though it is tuned in properly include: The mark and space frequencies may be reversed, the wrong baud rate may be selected, or you may be listening on the wrong sideband.** Check your station settings carefully.

Some digital modes, including RTTY, have a 100% duty cycle that may cause trouble for some transmitters. The *duty cycle* is the ratio of on-air transmission time to total operating time of a transmitted signal. That is, the portion of time your transmitter is actually on and transmitting during a QSO, and with RTTY the transmitter gets no breaks during a message send (100% duty cycle). Each mode has a characteristic duty cycle, and with digital operations **some modes can have high duty cycles, possibly exceeding the transmitter's average power rating. So, be sure you know the duty cycle of the data mode you are using when transmitting,** as well as your transmitter's limits. A digital mode's duty cycle can usually be found in the mode creator's documentation or in online user group forums.

Digital Rules and Regs: Let's wrap up this initial section of digital diddling with a few special provisions from the FCC Part 97 rules and regulations about digital modes, and some practical comments about digital QSOs.

New Digital Modes: If you get into the habit of developing new digital modes, be aware that **the technical characteristics of the protocol must be publicly documented before a new digital protocol may be used on the air.** This is probably not a concern for the vast majority of hams, but for you handful of digital tinkerers, read and heed. An undocumented digital mode would be considered an encryption, an that violates Part 97.

Automatically Controlled Digital Stations: Some special rules exist regarding digital stations that operate under automatic control. *Automatically controlled digital station* is the FCC term referring to unattended digital stations, including those that transfer messages to and from the Internet, such as messaging gateways. Automatically controlled digital stations are authorized only in special automatic control band segments. **Automatically controlled stations transmitting RTTY or data emissions may communicate with other automatically controlled digital stations anywhere in the 6-meter or shorter wavelength bands, and limited segments of some of the HF bands. Communications with a digital station operating under automatic control outside the automatic control band segments requires that the station initiating the contact be under local or remote control** (an active human control operator in the communication). Additionally, Part 97 limits automatically controlled digital stations to a maximum bandwidth of 500 Hz. Check FCC Parts 97.221 and 97.305 rules if you plan to operate an automatically controlled digital station.

Third Party Digital Communications: Because of the ease by which email, texts, and other digital messages may be forwarded to others, and because

G1E09 of the linkages between amateur radio stations and the Internet, it is prudent to make special note of regulations about third party communications. **Under no circumstances are messages sent via digital modes exempt from Part 97 third party rules that apply to other modes of communication!** Remember, third party messages may be transmitted to other countries only if that other country has a third party agreement with the US. The control operator must be present at the control point when third party traffic is transmitted, supervising and monitoring the third party's participation. Except for RTTY and data emissions, automatically controlled stations may not transmit third party traffic. (See FCC Part 97.115.)

Linking computers and radios to communicate via the digital modes can be a lot of fun and they add yet another intriguing facet to the ham radio hobby – greater techno-diddling opportunities! You can use digital modes to transmit electronic files, still images, text, telemetry, email, digital control commands, digital voice, and more. It's easy to get started with Winmore, PSK 31, or RTTY with free software and a sound card interface. Don't miss out on the fun. Diddle digitally!

Go examine the online quiz questions on digital mode basics, then come back to learn more about several very popular digital modes that you can use on the air.

HamRadioSchool.com/general_media

2.5 Operating Your Radio — More Digital Modes

> *No one ever said on their deathbed, "Gee, I wish I had spent more time alone with my computer."*
> — Danielle Berry

Do not fret! With your computer connected to your ham radio you are never alone. Especially with some of the incredibly power-efficient digital modes, you will never have trouble making contact with another friendly ham operator somewhere in the world. And I am 100% certain that no ham radio operator has ever used final comments to bemoan too much time on the air.

We'll continue our examination of digital modes in this section with variable treatment of four very popular digital modes: PACTOR, PSK31, FT8, and WSPR. These are by no means an exhaustive list of the digital modes available to you, but these will provide you more understanding of digital operations and get you prepared for the exam.

Let's start with a look at a great digital mode for the noisy HF bands, PACTOR.

PACTOR Protocol: *Packet Teletype Over Radio* blends packet radio efficiency with the robust FSK modulation of RTTY. It sends packetized teletype over radio that allows error correction methods to be used. PACTOR offers very good performance on the noisy HF bands, and improvements have been made with PACTOR II, III, and IV variations. **The approximate bandwidth of a PACTOR-III signal at maximum data rate is 2300 Hz,** slightly narrower than a typical SSB signal. (An AFSK-based mode very similar to PACTOR is known as WINMOR, providing slightly reduced performance as compared to PACTOR, but using a sound card interface in lieu of a more expensive PACTOR modem. WINMOR maximum bandwidth is approximately 1600 Hz.) [G8B05]

The PACTOR protocols utilize two-way transmissions that are limited to just two stations, so joining an existing contact between the two stations is not possible. PACTOR implements ARQ in which an *Acknowledgement* (ACK) transmission of error-free receipt is returned to the sending station after each block of data. Conversely, **a *Not Acknowledged* (NAK) response is sent by the receiver to request the packet be re-** [G2E09] [G8C05] transmitted. PACTOR can achieve high data rates and is useful for transmitting large blocks of data on HF bands, including use with the Winlink amateur radio email system (see Winlink Email, below).

A PACTOR modem or controller may be placed in a monitoring mode without a connection to determine if the channel is in use by other PACTOR stations and thereby avoid accidental interference. **Other signals interfering with a PACTOR or WINMOR transmission may result in failure to establish a connection between stations, long pauses in message transmissions, and frequent connection retries or timeouts. (The PACTOR or WINMOR connection is dropped from a failure to exchange information due to excessive transmission attempts.)**

Winlink Email: As noted above, PACTOR and WINMOR represent two of the more popular methods of accessing the Winlink amateur radio email system. **The Winlink communication system sometimes uses the Internet to transfer messages** via internet gateway stations. Winlink requires users to register to be recognized by the system, but once you are part of the system you can access your messages from any worldwide Winlink station. Winlink is also accessible with VHF and UHF FM signals using a terminal node controller and connecting to a local Winlink Radio Mail Server (RMS) station. **To establish contact with a** Winlink **digital messaging system gateway station,** simply **transmit a connect message on the station's published frequency.**

PSK31 Protocol: *Phase Shift Keying 31* is a popular keyboard-to-keyboard text chatting mode that utilizes only a single transmission tone and uses very narrow bandwidth. It encodes characters as binary sequences by reversing the tone's waveform phase in timed intervals. An interval exhibiting a shift in waveform phase represents a 0, and the absence of a phase shift represents a 1 for the interval. **PSK31 sends characters using Varicode,** in which the number of bits sent in a single PSK31 character varies. In a manner similar to Morse Code, the PSK31 Varicode uses shorter symbols for the most commonly used characters, thereby enhancing the efficiency of communication. **Upper case letters use longer Varicode bit sequences and thus slow down transmission.** During any given station transmission a continuous tone is transmitted, with strings of 0 bits sent when no data is included in the transmission. This is necessary to keep the receiving station's decoding protocol synchronized with the transmission's phase shifting interval sequence.

The 31 in PSK31 represents the approximate transmitted symbol rate (baud rate), 31 baud. Although this symbol rate is slow relative to many

2.5 More Digital Modes

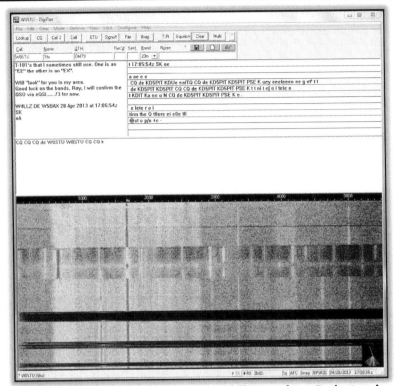

Figure 2.18: A typical PSK 31 "waterfall" interface. Each signal is displayed as a vertical pattern in the audio receive band that may be selected by mouse pointer for decoding and QSO.

other digital modes, it is quite adequate for most keyboard-to-keyboard communications. PSK31 provides very good performance on HF bands even in noisy conditions, and the narrow bandwidth of the mode provides a lot of punch with just a little power. It is a terrific QRP mode, with propagation performance similar to CW.

PSK31 tone sound is a unique, ghostly sounding whine, and easily distinguishable within the digital sub-bands. **On the 20 meter band most PSK31 operations are found below the RTTY segment, near 14.070 MHz.** Other bands have recommended calling frequencies and typical segments of the digital sub-bands where PSK31 is found, and just dialing through the sub-band will usually suffice for finding the group of ethereal PSK31 sounds.

A PSK31 waterfall display is depicted in Figure 2.18. Signals are depicted as streams flowing down the screen, with **a signal's frequency indicated on the horizontal. Signal strength is depicted by intensity** of the stream, **and time is vertical** with the flowing signal stream. **One or more vertical lines on either side of a waterfall display digital signal**

indicates overmodulation, a condition that may be corrected by adjusting the gain of the transmitting station's sound card interface.

Two different forms of PSK31 exist, Binary PSK31 (BPSK31) and Quadrature PSK31 (QPSK31). Binary PSK31 encodes the data using shifting waveform phases of two different values. Quadrature PSK31 encodes data using four different phase shifts. This allows QPSK31 to transmit two bits per transmitted symbol, whereas BPSK31 transmits only one bit per symbol. **QPSK31 is sideband sensitive, provides error correction in its encoding, and has approximately the same bandwidth as BPSK31.**

FT8 Protocol: FT8 is one of the WSJT-X family of digital operating modes. FT8 was developed by Steven Franke, K9AN and Joe Taylor, K1JT, and **FT8 uses 8-tone frequency shift keying (FSK). This narrow-band digital mode can receive signals with very low signal-to-noise ratios.** It is an excellent mode to use for meteor scatter propagation, earth-moon-earth bounce communications, or other weak signal and QRP communications. FT8 software can be downloaded free, and signal displays use a waterfall display configuration similar to PSK31.

Because coordinated transmissions are made on 15-second intervals, **FT8 digital mode requires computer time accurate within approximately 1 second.** This means you must synchronize your computer clock with accurate worldwide timing sources. You can find these resources and instructions for how to synchronize your computer at various web sites dedicated to FT8 operations. Additionally, with this timing constraint, **typical FT8 exchanges are limited to call signs, grid locators, and signal reports.** And, like its sister WSJT family modes **JT65 and JT9, FT8 digital AFSK signals in any amateur band use a standard upper sideband (USB).**

WSPR Protocol: Also created by Joe Taylor, K1JT, is the Weak Signal Propagation Reporter (WSPR). It is another USB FSK mode using four tones and a fixed format, compressed data transmission of call sign, grid locator, and signal power. **WSPR is used as a low-power beacon for assessing HF propagation.**

Digital QSOs: Beyond the typical emails or text messages that are really not different from Internet messages when delivered by radio, some digital modes have unique QSO characteristics. For instance, with the PSK31 mode many operators are fond of using pre-programmed stores of texts, called *macros*. With the click of a button a PSK31 macro will transmit your stored text data, such as a description of your transceiver, antennas, computer and software, or just about anything else. CQ calls and standard procedural signal strings are other

2.5 More Digital Modes

common macro transmissions. However, in between the macros and CQs and KNs there is often room for genuine *rag chewing* with a new friend, albeit in text form.

AREDN: A relatively recent development, an Amateur Radio Emergency Data Network (AREDN) is a high-speed *ad hoc* mesh network that links computers using modified commercial Wi-Fi equipment. **Amateurs share channels with the unlicensed Wi-Fi service on 2.4 GHz,** so commercial hardware may be legally modified and adapted for use by amateurs in establishing very wide area computer networks. Typically, this involves modified firmware loads on commercial Wi-Fi routers, and frequently employs modified antennas with directional gain and amplified power. When using modified commercial Wi-Fi equipment to construct an Amateur Radio Emergency Data Network, the maximum allowed PEP transmitter output power is 10 watts. This is substantially greater than the nominal 100 mW of a typical commercial router. However, **in no part of the 13-centimeter band** (2.4 GHz) **may an amateur station communicate with non-licensed Wi-Fi stations.** The custom firmware and unique protocols used with AREDN help ensure this type of violation does not occur.

AREDN states that its goal is, "to empower licensed amateur radio operators to quickly and easily deploy high-speed data networks when and where they might be needed, as a service both to the hobby and the community." The networks nodes are self-discovering, and routing of data from one station address to another is seamlessly routed via mesh-networked stations. Setting up the gear takes a little effort, but having an autonomous wide area data network available can solve myriad digital communications problems.

Look for more detailed information on specific digital modes online. Most have friendly user groups and wikis that can help you get a quick start with the mode, usually with a free software utility download, too.

With all these digital protocols, how could any ham ever be lonely? The ham radio world really is exploding in the digital domain, but solid, reliable analog phone will never lie upon its deathbed! Enjoy the plethora of options!

Hit the question pool items, digital ham, then return for some cosmic discussion of RF propagation. 1000011   0100000   1111001   1100001   0100001

HamRadioSchool.com/general_media

Summary of all Question Pool Topics Sections 2.4 & 2.5: Digital Modes

Digital Sub-bands:

20m band: 14.070-14.112 MHz
80m band: 3570-3600 kHz

RTTY – Radio Teletype FSK Protocol
- FSK directly changes oscillator frequency
- RTTY frequencies commonly shifted 170 Hz
- Two frequencies, "Mark & Space"
- Baudot Code – 5 bit code + start/stop bits
- Higher symbol rates require wider bandwidth
- Max RTTY symbol rates on bands
    - 1.25m & 70cm: 56 kBaud
    - 2m: 19.6 kBaud
    - 10m: 1200 Baud
    - 20m (below 28 MHz): 300 baud
- Common problems with decoding
- Mark & Space frequencies reversed
- Wrong Baud rate selected
- Wrong sideband (LSB used for AFSK RTTY)
- High duty cycles can exceed avg. power rating

Packet and ARQ Methods:
- Packet Radio Frame: Header contains routing and handling information.
- Automatic Repeat Request (ARQ): Receiving station responds to errors with requests that packet be retransmitted.
- NAK: Not Acknowledged response sent by receiver to request retransmission (PACTOR).
- Forward Error Correction (FEC): Redundant info sent with data for receiver correction of errors.

PACTOR & WINMOR Protocols
- PACTOR III has ~2300 Hz bandwidth at max rate
- Limited to two-station links only, no break-in join
- 'Monitoring mode' of PACTOR modem to check if frequency in use by other PACTOR stations
- Interference to PACTOR or WINMOR may cause:
- Failure to establish connection
- Frequent connection retries or timeouts
- Long pauses in message transmissions
- Excessive trx attempts = dropped connection
- Used with Winlink email system that transfers messages using Internet
- Transmit 'connect message' to connect with digital messaging systems.

New Digital Protocols:
characteristics must be publicly documented before on-air use.

Auto-Controlled Digital Station Rules:
- Maximum bandwidth by Part 97 is 500 Hz.
- Outside auto-control bands comm must be only with local controlled or remote controlled stations.
- No exemption from Part 97 3rd party rules.

PSK31 – Phase Shift Keying 31 Protocol
- Uses Varicode, number of bits varies
- Upper case letters use longer Varicode, results in slower transmissions
- 31 is approximate transmitted symbol rate
- 20m band ops near 14.070 MHz, below RTTY
- Waterfall display: Freq = Horizontal, signal strength = intensity, time is vertical, overmodulation = vertical lines on signal sides
- QPSK31 bandwidth slightly higher than BPSK31

FT8 Protocol
- 8-tone frequency shift keying
- USB is standard (same with JT65 and JT9)
- Receives with very low signal-to-noise ratios
- Requires computer timing within 1 sec accuracy
- Limited exchange: call sign, grid, signal report

AREDN Mesh Networks:
- 2.4 GHz shared channels with Wi-Fi
- 10W PEP max power
- No comm with non-licensed Wi-Fi on any part of 13 cm band

WSPR Protocol: Used as low-power beacon to assess HF propagation

3.0 Propagation

> **"** You must live in the present,
> launch yourself on every wave.
> – Henry David Thoreau

That's just what hams do. On every wave we propagate ourselves on an invisible journey to parts unknown and often to peoples unknown. That's half the fun of it! But we can know quite a lot about the paths of that invisible journey, even if we can't see our waves propagating. With a little insight about the nature of radio waves, the atmosphere, and even the sun, we can make some reasoned estimates of where we launch ourselves on every wave.

This chapter is all about RF propagation. We will start in Section 3.1 with a brief journey to the surface of the sun – sunspots, solar eruptions, and lots of thermonuclear violence! In Section 3.2 we'll soar through the atmosphere to study the ionosphere, magnetosphere, and some of their effects with frequencies. We will wrap up Chapter 3 with consideration of the practical impact on our radio operations resulting from all of that solar violence and related atmospheric reactions.

Ready yourself for launch into our local neighborhood's solar inferno!

3.1 Solar Activity

> **"** A day without thermonuclear fusion is
> like a day without sunshine. – Anonymous

Let's start our exploration of HF propagation with a journey to the surface of the sun! An incredible place born of thermonuclear fusion where complex solar dynamics rule and superheated tendrils of plasma erupt larger than thousands of earths and surge along invisible magnetic loops in spectacular displays of the star's power!

And where relatively dark sunspots dot the star's face like an adolescent's acne.

Sunspots: Those solar blemishes are really important to ham radio operators. Sunspots are correlated with solar energy output. That is, the more active and energetic the sun, the more sunspots there will be. Sunspots are regions of high magnetic activity on the sun's surface that produce relatively cool interiors, hence the somewhat darker "spot" appearance. But the perimeter of a sunspot will radiate much more intensely than other parts of the solar surface, and the net result is an increase in solar energy output with sunspots. In particular, sunspot edges absolutely glow with ultraviolet (UV) radiation, and UV is critical to the creation and maintenance of the ionosphere around our earth.

Of course, the ionosphere is the giant mirror in the sky that bends HF and lower VHF frequencies back toward earth to provide that amazing *over-the-horizon* propagation we call skip. Sunspot activity is strongly correlated with the signal-bending effectiveness of the ionosphere, and high sunspot numbers result in enhancement of long-distance communications in the upper HF and lower VHF range due to the greater density of ions in the atmosphere created by the UV rays.

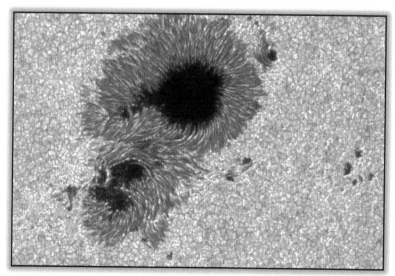

Figure 3.1: Sunspots increase solar ultraviolet radiation that helps create the earth's ionosphere.   Courtesy NASA/JPL-Caltech

3.1 Solar Activity

The sunspot number is a measure of the solar activity based on counting sunspots and sunspot groups. Scientists and many amateur radio operators keep close tabs on the sunspot number as a general indicator of radio propagation. The sunspot number and propagation conditions vary with two primary activities:

- **The sun's rotation on its axis causes HF propagation conditions to vary periodically in a roughly 28-day cycle,** as the sunspots rotate into and out of the sun's earth-facing hemisphere.

- The sunspot cycle (or solar cycle) in which sunspot activity varies over 11 year periods, with a high activity peak called *solar maximum* and a low activity lull called *solar minimum*.

During the solar maximum, when sunspots are most prominent in the 11 year solar cycle, HF propagation is typically best, and the higher frequency bands of 21 MHz (15m) and above *open* frequently for excellent long-distance skip ("*sky wave*") communications. During the solar minimum when sunspots are few, these higher bands may remain ineffective for skip for long periods. **The significance of sunspot numbers with regard to HF propagation is that higher sunspot numbers generally indicate a greater probability of good propagation at higher frequencies.**

Solar Flux Index: A basic indicator of the sun's activity and radiated output. The solar flux is measured in units of... wait for it... *Solar Flux Units* (SFU). **The Solar Flux Index is a measure of solar radiation at 10.7 centimeters wavelength** (~2.8 GHz), and it is essentially a measure of radio frequency noise. The index is a good indicator of the amount of ionization in the earth's atmosphere, so it usually provides a good hint of the skip propagation conditions. The index values tend to vary between about 50 and 300 SFU, with the solar max consistently generating 200+ values in average cycles.

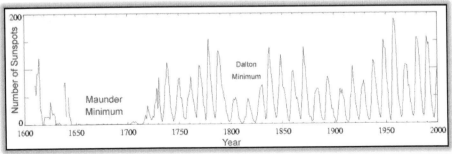

Figure 3.2: Historical observation of sunspots over 400 years shows variation in the 11-year solar cycle.   Courtesy NASA/JPL-Caltech

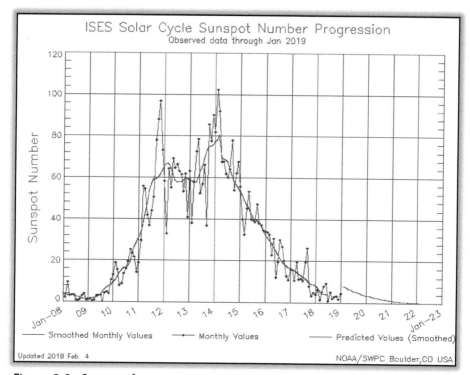

Figure 3.3: Sunspot history, 2008 to 2019. The current Solar Cycle 24 has been a low activity sunspot cycle by recent standards. Solar max peaked near a monthly average 80 sunspots, compared with several recent cycles peaking over 150.   Courtesy NOAA / SWPC Boulder, CO USA

Solar Flares: Occasionally the sun hiccups and produces a very intense projection of radiation called a solar flare. Solar flare emissions are electromagnetic radiation traveling at the speed of light. **The increased ultraviolet and X-ray radiation of a solar flare takes about 8 minutes to reach the earth and affect radio propagation.** When a solar flare is directed toward the earth, the very intense ionizing radiation can reach deeply into the atmosphere, disturbing the ionosphere and disrupting HF communications.

Coronal Holes: The sun's corona is an enveloping layer of plasma gas that extends millions of miles into space around the sun. Occasionally the sun's magnetic field lines loop and "bubble" above the surface and into the corona, creating spectacular visual images of enormous glowing loops and coronal prominences. When these magnetic field lines sever and fail to close back upon themselves, an open channel is created called a *coronal hole*. The stream of proton and electron particles that the sun continually emits is called the solar wind, and a coronal hole allows these solar wind particles to really gust out in a torrent! **HF communications are disturbed by the charged**

3.1 Solar Activity

particles that reach the earth from solar coronal holes due to the effects on the ionosphere.

Coronal Mass Ejections (CME): Other, more violent eruptions in the sun's corona may eject massive amounts of matter into space. A CME will be largely comprised of protons and electrons like the normal solar wind, but heavier element particles may also be included such as helium, oxygen, and iron. These particles are ejected at high speeds, as much as 2000 miles per second. **Charged particles from a coronal mass ejection will reach earth and affect radio propagation in 20 to 40 hours** after solar ejection.

G3A11

Wow! The sun is rather violent, huh? Thermonuclear fusion spewing out charged particles and hurling mass in our general direction, even irradiating us constantly with deadly rays of high energy. Fortunately, the earth protects us from most of this viciousness with the blankets of the ionosphere and the *magnetosphere.*

Each of these violent behaviors of the sun, from sunspot UV rays to solar flares to coronal holes and ejections, has an impact on the earth's protecting blankets. When those blankets become disturbed by absorbing and

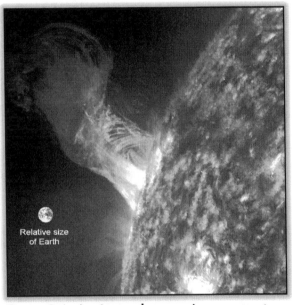

Figure 3.4: A minor solar prominence erupts from the sun. Earth added for comparison.
Courtesy NASA/JPL-Caltech

redirecting the sun's impolite and dangerous belches, our HF radio propagation is disrupted. In the next section we'll consider the features of our ionosphere and magnetosphere in relation to radio propagation in order to better understand these solar impacts on operations.

But before we move on, why not click through the questions on solar activity!

HamRadioSchool.com/general_media

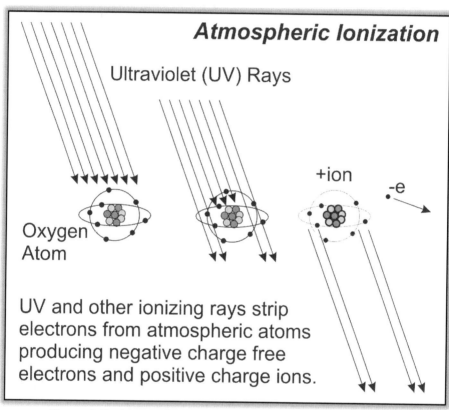

Figure 3.5: Atmospheric ionization creates the ionosphere.

3.2 Ionosphere & Magnetosphere

> **"** *Ogres have layers. Onions have layers. You get it? We both have layers.* — Shrek

We've returned from the dangerous and violent environs of the sun's surface to the good earth. However, let's soar over land and sea for a while at great altitudes and investigate the ionosphere and the magnetosphere. They're both rather interesting and critical features of our planet for both life support and good HF propagation! Like an onion – or an ogre – they have layers.

Overview of Ionosphere and Magnetosphere: Let's make sure we have a good general understanding of what these two earthly planetary features are all about, and then we'll fly into some details.

The *ionosphere* is the name we give to four prominent layers of the atmosphere in which many electrically charged atomic particles exist – ions, we call them. Ions include negatively charged *free electrons* and positively charged ions. Usually, an atom will have an electron or two stripped from it to be set free, leaving a net positive charge on the remaining atom. High energy radiation from the sun, such as ultraviolet rays and X-rays, impact atoms in the atmosphere and kick out an electron with their energy, leaving the charged particles in their wake. This ability of high energy radiation to strip electrons from atoms is why it is referred to as *ionizing radiation* – it creates ions. These charged particles in the atmosphere can bend RF signals back to earth, providing over-the-horizon radio communications, especially on the HF bands.

The *magnetosphere* is a region around the earth where the earth's magnetic field is dominant, as compared to the magnetic field lines associated with the solar wind emanating from the sun. The charged particles of the solar wind – those protons and electrons constantly flying out of the sun – interact with the earth's magnetic field lines and help shape the magnetosphere. The solar wind effectively pushes on the earth's magnetic field lines, compressing and bending them on the sun-side and leaving a trailing magnetic tail on the leeward side. The magnetosphere ebbs, flows, and wavers with variations in the solar wind, but its magnetic lines tend to direct much of the solar wind's particles around the earth. Some of the particles flowing along the magnetosphere's lines of magnetic force are directed down into the earth's atmosphere near the magnetic polar regions, highly energizing atmospheric atoms and producing aurora. Measured variations in the magnetosphere can provide good clues about the solar wind intensity and, therefore, provide indications of the state of the ionosphere and RF propagation conditions.

Now let's cruise through the layers of the ionosphere, illuminate their characteristics, and define some related radio terms with which every General Class ham should be intimately familiar. Afterwards, we'll revisit the magnetosphere to examine its metrics and related radio effects.

Ionospheric Layers: The ionosphere is comprised of four prominent layers that result from several interacting factors. The increasing density of the atmosphere from space to the earth's surface affects the rates at which free electrons will recombine with positively charged ions to reform neutral atoms. This reduces the quantity and density of ions. The depth to which ionizing radiation will penetrate the atmosphere also comes into play, affecting the rates at which new ions are created. The net result is the set of ionospheric layers D, E, F1, and F2, each with unique ion densities and characteristics.

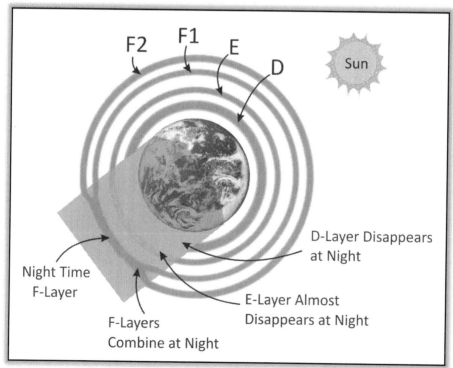

Figure 3.6: Layers of the Ionosphere.

3.2 Ionosphere & Magnetosphere

The ionospheric layers exist from about 40 to 250+ miles above the earth's surface, and they **reach their maximum height where the sun is overhead.**

D Layer: **The D Layer is closest to the surface of the earth,** roughly 40 to 55 miles in altitude. Because of relatively high atmospheric density, the rate of recombination of ions into neutral atoms is high, resulting in the D Layer effectively dissipating at night. Unique electron effects in this band produce **daytime conditions in which lower frequency HF signals (below 10 MHz) are absorbed by the D Layer.** The amateur bands below 30m will be absorbed, significantly reducing or eliminating skip propagation with these bands during daylight hours. However, once the D Layer disappears at night, these lower HF band signals are able to reach the higher ionospheric layers to be bent back to earth for effective over-the-horizon propagation. As a result, the lower frequency bands from 30m to 160m tend to be considered "night time bands" since their propagation is best after sundown.

During highly energetic solar events such as intense flares and CMEs, the D Layer may become ionized sufficiently to persist overnight and to absorb higher frequency signals, such as the 20m to 10m bands. This disruption of the normal D Layer condition degrades skip propagation and can even produce HF propagation blackout, in which HF skip communications are not possible.

E Layer: Roughly 55 to 75 miles in altitude, the E Layer is responsible for some of the most curious radio propagation behavior, sporadic E. Patchy clouds of ionization in the E Layer come and go sporadically, providing temporary over-the-horizon propagation that is effective for 10m, 6m, and (rarely) 2m bands. The dynamic E Layer may provide skip in only one particular direction from your station and into a limited geographical area. That's part of the magic of sporadic E propagation – you never know exactly when it's going to happen or where it's going to take your signals! Although unpredictable and possible almost anytime, sporadic E does have some seasonal peaks of occurrence. In North America, the peak sporadic E occurs in mid- to late-June, and may persist through July or August. A less significant peak occurs from mid-December into January.

F1 and F2 Layers: The F1 Layer exists roughly 90 to 150 miles in altitude, while the F2 Layer is sky high at more than 200 miles up. **The F2 region is mainly responsible for the longest distance radio wave propagation because it is the highest ionospheric region.** Geometry dictates that the skip distance of a signal increases with the height of the reflecting layer (given equivalent earthly takeoff angles of the signal). The F1 and F2 Layers combine at night into a single F Layer approximately 180 miles altitude. However, the height of the F Layers varies significantly with solar activity, time of day, time of year, and even latitude.

Critical Angle: The ionosphere is not a perfect mirror for RF signals. It is not really a mirror at all. Rather than being a reflecting surface it is a refracting medium, meaning that it bends or curves the RF signal as the signal passes through it, much like a lens bends light. With strong enough bending action, thanks to lots of ions, an RF signal may be curved back toward earth. If the bending action is not strong enough, the signal is instead directed off into space and is not receivable by earthly hams. The scenario is depicted in Figure 3.7.

As the figure depicts, low takeoff angle signals require the least severe bend angle to return to earth and travel the greatest distance, while higher takeoff angle signals travel shorter distances and must be bent at greater angles. As the takeoff angle increases an angle will be reached for which the ionosphere bending effect is insufficient to turn the signals back to earth, and they will fly off into space. The RF signal bending power of the ionosphere will change with atmospheric and solar conditions, as well as with the frequency being used. However, **under any specific ionospheric conditions the highest takeoff angle that will return a radio wave to the earth is the "critical angle."**

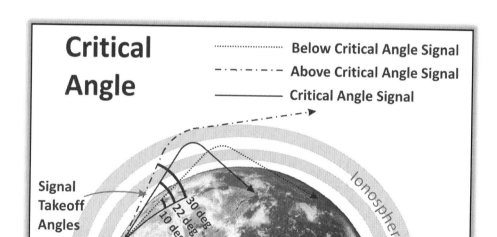

Figure 3.7: The Critical Angle – Signal takeoff angles above the critical angle will radiate into space, while takeoff angles at or below the critical angle will be returned to the earth's surface.

In the example of Figure 3.7 the critical angle is 22 degrees above the horizon – any greater takeoff angle (such as the 30 degree example), sends the signal into space. Takeoff angles lower than 22 degrees (such as the 10 degree example) are bent back to earth.

Maximum Usable Frequency (MUF): Consider that between your station and any other station over-the-horizon there is a takeoff angle that will result in a skip from the ionosphere such that the other station may receive your signal – the geometry is good. A higher skip angle will land your signals short of the other station, and a lower skip angle will land your signals beyond the other station. But that Goldie Locks takeoff angle is just right for the geometry to that specific station location.

Now consider that the ionosphere's bending effect weakens as frequency gets higher, as in Figure 3.8. Your 10m (28 MHz) signals will be bent less than your 15m, 20m, or lower band signals. What if the frequency you are using is a high one, perhaps in the 10m band, and it is not bent enough to achieve that Goldie Locks angle to the other station? You could choose a lower frequency for which the ionosphere will act more strongly and bend your signal at a greater angle, thereby achieving Goldie Locks and making your contact. You can imagine that there is a frequency that is just barely low enough for the ionosphere to provide enough bending to achieve that Goldie Locks angle to the other station. That is **the MUF, or the maximum usable frequency for communications between two points, and it is affected by factors of path distance and location, time of day and season, and solar radiation and ionospheric disturbances** that impact the ionosphere's bending performance.

Lowest Usable Frequency (LUF): **Similarly, the LUF is the lowest usable frequency for communications between two points.** The conditions of ionospheric absorption for a given time of day or solar condition determine the lowest frequency that will skip to another specific station location. **Radio waves with frequencies below the LUF are usually completely absorbed by the ionosphere.**

MUF & LUF Scenarios: In some circumstances **the lowest usable frequency (LUF) will exceed the maximum usable frequency (MUF) and no HF radio frequency will support ordinary skywave** (skip) **communications over the path** between stations. That is, for a given path the lowest frequency that will not be absorbed under the ionospheric conditions is a higher frequency than the ionosphere can bend down to the other station at the required Goldie Locks takeoff angle. This may occur during geomagnetic

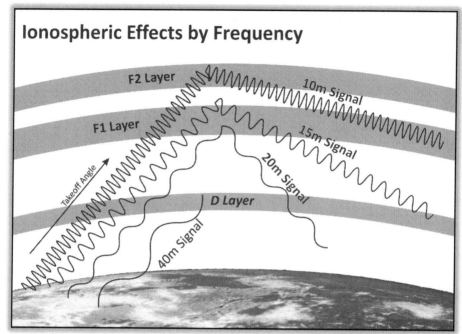

Figure 3.8: The ionosphere's bending effect decreases with increased frequency, helping determine the MUF between two stations. Primarily D Layer absorption of lower frequencies helps determine the LUF. In this simplified example all takeoff angles are equivalent. The 40m band and lower signals are absorbed, while higher frequencies are variably refracted depending on frequency.

disturbances during which RF absorption effects are intensified. You're just out of luck for HF skip communications in this situation.

However, **radio waves with frequencies below the MUF and above the LUF will be bent back to the earth when they are sent into the ionosphere.** That is, if your frequency is in between the two frequency limits of MUF and LUF, you can make your contact.

The Magnetosphere: Given all the effects of the ionosphere, why do we even care about the magnetosphere? It is because the magnetosphere and the ionosphere are intimately linked, with the magnetosphere somewhat regulating how much of the sun's energy reaches the atmosphere to charge up the layers with ions. Further, measurement of some magnetosphere characteristics can provide indications of the ionosphere's conditions.

3.2 Ionosphere & Magnetosphere

K-index: Magnetic observatories on earth use magnetometers to measure geomagnetic activity. Relative to an agreed reference condition, **the K-index indicates the short term stability of the earth's magnetic field.** The magnetometers detect fluctuations in the magnetosphere that may indicate changes in the solar wind impacting the earth's atmosphere. The K-index is collected every three hours for short term indications.

Figure 3.9: The earth's magnetosphere is shaped by the solar wind.

Courtesy NASA/JPL-Caltech

A-index: A daily average of the K-index is computed as the A-index. **The A-index indicates the long term stability of the earth's geomagnetic field.** By compiling the measured A-indices from around the world and over time, a long term picture of the magnetosphere's stability may be constructed, and impacts to the ionosphere inferred. The A-index reflects 24 hours of geomagnetic stability.

Geomagnetic Storms: **A temporary disturbance in the earth's magnetosphere is a geomagnetic storm.** When charged particles from a strong solar event reach the earth they may be trapped in the magnetosphere. This can cause some regions of the ionosphere to become highly charged with ions. For instance, such activation of the E Layer in the polar regions results in **degraded high-latitude HF propagation from a geomagnetic storm**, as well as aurora due to secondary photon emissions from energized atoms of nitrogen and oxygen. This phenomenon may also disrupt other layers of the ionosphere and cause poor propagation on the HF bands. The upper layers of the ionosphere tend to be most susceptible, resulting in higher HF frequency disruption first.

One possible benefit to radio communications that results from periods of high geomagnetic activity is aurora that can reflect VHF signals, particularly the 6m band signals. Aurora propagation tends to have a fluttery sound due to the rapidly fluctuating action of the particles bending the waves back to earth.

That's all pretty cosmic! Lots of dynamic interaction between the sun and the earth, and it all has an impact on the ionospheric layers and our radio signal propagation. A general summary of the effects discussed in this section is provided in the table below, so that you may easily peel back the layers of the propagation onion.

In the next section we'll focus more on the operational impacts of these atmospheric characteristics. But for now, check your knowledge online with the quiz for this section.

HamRadioSchool.com/general_media

Summary Table of General Propagation Factors:

Factor	Ionospheric Impact	HF Propagation	VHF Propagation
Daylight	Dense F layers. D layer absorbs low frequencies.	Best above 30m band. Poor below 30m band.	Possible Sporadic E.
Night time	Combined F layer. D layer dissipates.	Good below 30m band. Higher bands may close.	Little / no Sporadic E.
Plentiful Sunspots	Denser ionospheric layers generally.	Good; higher bands 15m, 12m, and 10m may open.	6m band may have F-layer skip
Sparse Sunspots	Weaker ionospheric layers generally.	Degraded propagation with higher HF bands.	
High A-index	Potential ionosphere disruption & D layer persistence	Degraded / Poor.	Possible aurora propagation.
High K-index	Potential ionosphere disruption & D layer persistence	Degraded / Poor.	Possible aurora propagation.
Geomagnetic Storm	Potential ionosphere disruption & D layer persistence	Degraded / Poor.	Possible aurora propagation.

3.3 Propagation Operational Impacts

> *The sun does not shine for a few trees and flowers, but for the wide world's joy.*
> *– Henry Ward Beecher*

Indeed, the sun shines even for the joy of hams the world over! Without its ionizing rays our HF signals would simply race out into space and DX would cease to exist. The sun, its rays, and our ionosphere have enormous radio operational impacts.

So, let's now float back down to earth and crawl into the shack to consider how some of the factors of the sun and atmosphere affect our radio operations. How can we estimate the kind of propagation we'll get? Why are some signals weaker than others? How long of a skip distance can my signals achieve? When will the various bands work best, and what frequency should I use?

Sky-Wave Skip Paths & Distances: From what we've covered about ionospheric skip propagation, the critical angle, and MUF and LUF considerations, and ionosphere-magnetosphere disruptions, you're probably wondering just how far a typical skip will allow your signals to travel. It is a good question! But there is no single correct answer beyond, "It depends."

F2 Layer Skip: The F2 Layer is the highest ionosphere layer. As noted already, a higher signal reflection altitude will result in longer potential skip distances. The longest single skip from your station may be achieved by the lowest takeoff angle possible from your station – perhaps that signal ray skimming uninterrupted just along the earth right down at horizon level. Assuming that signal is of one of the higher HF frequencies that is best reflected by the F Layers, **the approximate maximum distance along the earth's surface that it will normally cover in one hop using the F2 region is 2,500 miles.** Depending on specific ion density conditions, frequency used, and the impact of other ionosphere layers, your station's performance may vary, but a 2,500 mile hop with the 10m band during periods of high solar activity is not unusual.

Figure 3.10: VHF contesters love to see the E Layer highly activated to rack up points with over-the-horizon distant contacts on VHF frequencies!

E Layer Skip: The E Layer, being significantly lower than the F Layers, will provide reduced skip distances when it is active. **The approximate maximum distance along the earth's surface that is normally covered in one hop using the E region is 1,200 miles.** And, of course, the E Layer skip opportunities are sporadic but commonly very effective up to the 6m VHF band. A good indicator of the possibility of sky-wave propagation on the 6m band is short skip sky-wave propagation on the 10m band. Since 10m signals are normally reflected from the F2 Layer with very long skip distances (roughly 2,000 miles or more), if you hear 10m signals from stations within 1,200 miles on the 10m band those signals are potentially from lower E-Layer reflections, or sporadic E. If the E Layer is sufficiently energized you may achieve skip on 6m too! And if the 6m skywave propagation is short, check for sporadic E propagation on the 2m band. It's rare, but it happens occasionally.

3.3 Operational Impacts

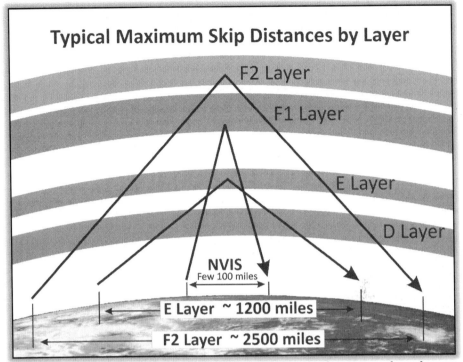

Figure 3.11: Longer skip distances occur with the higher ionosphere layers. NVIS is effective with 40m and lower bands for shorter distance HF communications of a few hundred miles.

Multiple Skips: Notice that the distances related above are for single skips. In good conditions it is common to achieve multiple hops between earth and sky with HF signals, each of an approximate maximum distance as stated above. In fact, under very good conditions it is even possible to skip a signal all the way around the planet! (Approximately 10 hops of 2,500 miles would be required, resulting in dramatically weakened signals, but feasible!) More common is the long path propagation as described in the *Operating Techniques* section of Chapter 2. Sometimes you may hear another **station's sky-wave signals arriving at your location by both short-path and long-path propagation, producing a slightly delayed echo** due to slightly different signal path propagation time. (An RF signal requires approximately 0.15 second to circumnavigate the earth, so echo delays on the order of 1/10 second are possible.)

G3B01

NVIS: Near Vertical Incidence Sky-wave propagation is short distance MF (medium frequency) **or HF propagation using high elevation angles.** Consider the RF signals from an antenna that radiate not toward the horizon but rather more nearly vertical, almost straight up. If the

G3C10

ionospheric conditions and the selected frequency allow severe refraction of the signals back to earth, the propagation distance will be much less than the maximum values discussed here for F2 and E Layer skip. The angle of incidence up to any layer of the ionosphere is steep and so is the reflection angle back down to the ground. The result is HF propagation usually effective for a few hundred miles around your station. We will discuss how to generate effective NVIS signals with antenna techniques in Chapter 5.

Scatter: With HF skip propagation your signals can travel great distances, but unless NVIS is effective for the frequency you are using you will not be able to reach nearer stations *under the skip path*. This region that is outside of your station's ground wave (local) distance but closer than the nearest skip arrival is called the *skip zone*. However, HF signals may be randomly scattered into the skip zone due to occasional reflection of signals from particulate matter high in the atmosphere, such as dust or moisture. So, **propagation that allows signals to be heard in the transmitting station's skip zone is scatter.** When these signals are reflected back toward the sending station they are known as *backscatter*.

HF scatter signals in the skip zone are usually weak because only a small part of the signal energy is scattered into the skip zone. Although very weak, scatter propagation can be very useful when sky-wave skip propagation is not available, or when getting signals into the skip zone is desired. An indication that signals heard on the HF bands are being received via scatter propagation is the signal being on a frequency above the Maximum Usable Frequency (MUF). Remember, skip is not possible on frequencies greater than the MUF because the ionosphere's bending effect is too weak for the frequency. Thus, hearing signals above the MUF is likely due to scatter.

A characteristic of HF scatter is that signals have a fluttering sound. This HF scatter signal distorted sound is due to the energy

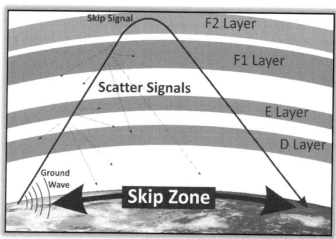

Figure 3.12: Scatter is weak signals reflected from atmospheric particles into the skip zone.

3.3 Operational Impacts

being scattered into the skip zone through several different radio wave paths, thereby producing multipath interference at your receiver.

Band and Frequency Considerations: Your selection of a band and even a frequency may be affected by many factors including the solar cycle and events, current ionospheric conditions, time of day, and desired propagation distance. Let's examine some of these factors in more detail

Solar Cycle: The 11-year solar cycle significantly changes ionospheric skip propagation. Near solar maximum when sunspot are plenty and the ionosphere is highly energized the higher HF bands will be open more frequently: the 10m through 15m bands will be busy with skip communications. During the solar minimum these bands may rarely open for skip beyond the occasional sporadic E occurrence – **15m, 12m, and 10m are least reliable for long distance communication during periods of low solar activity.** Fortunately, **the 20m band usually supports worldwide propagation during daylight hours at any point in the solar cycle.** And the lower bands (40m – 160m) are usually effective throughout the cycle during nighttime hours.

Solar Eruptions: As noted in the *Solar Activity* section, the violence of our star directly impacts HF radio propagation here on earth. Solar eruptions can shut down HF communications. Geomagnetic disturbances from a harsh solar wind first diminish the higher bands (10m – 20m) that tend to be reflected from the outer F Layers, while **Sudden Ionospheric Disturbances** (solar flares) quickly increase the level of ionization in the low D Layer with UV and X-ray radiation, causing greater attenuating absorption of HF signals and **disrupting the lower frequencies** (40m – 160m) **more than the higher frequencies**.

Time of Day: During daylight hours the higher HF bands (10m – 30m) will be more effective for skip. However, **long distance communication on the 40, 60, 80, and 160 meter bands is more difficult during the day because the D Layer absorbs signals at these frequencies during daylight hours.** At night the D Layer rapidly dissipates and these lower bands will open up for skip, being very effectively refracted by the higher E and combined F layers.

MUF: Keep in mind that D Layer absorption attenuates (weakens) HF signals, and the attenuation is more severe as frequency lowers. Remember also that above the MUF the ionosphere cannot bend your signals sufficiently to return them to earth. Therefore, **when selecting a frequency for lowest attenuation when transmitting on HF, select a fre-**

quency just below the MUF. This will help ensure skip propagation with the strongest possible signal for the attenuating conditions.

So, you ask, **what is a reliable way to determine if the MUF is high enough to support skip propagation between your station and a distant location? On frequencies between 14 MHz and 30 MHz (20m – 10m bands) you can listen for signals from international beacons in the frequency range you plan to use.** If you identify a beacon you can determine its location and frequency. By evaluating beacons that you can and cannot receive across the bands you may gauge whether the MUF is supporting skip into a distant area.

You can use other stations' reports and QSO success to gauge conditions as well. Further, online aids exist that evaluate propagation reports of operators and beacon reception around the world and conveniently summarize the MUF, LUF, and occurrences of sporadic E in various geographic regions.

Summer Static: One last common atmospheric condition that will often impact your operations is lightning. Not only should you shut down your station when lightning is in your local area, but even very distant storms will cause interference due to lightning's production of RF energy. Lightning is accelerated electrical charges and, like those charges surging up and down your antenna, it generates a wide spectrum RF signal when it strikes. **Typical of the lower HF frequencies during the summer, high levels of atmospheric noise or "static"** will be heard.

So, how do you take stock of all the impacts of the sun and atmosphere on the operation you're about to try out? Most operators prefer to just get on the air and see what happens. The main way you'll realize the impact of the current conditions is simply by trying to initiate contacts and seeing what you get.

But you should be familiar with the solar and atmospheric science affecting your emissions, their paths, and propagation effectiveness so that you can intelligently operate your station and make well-informed decisions to keep your station going when the sun and the sky conspire against you.

Wrap up Chapter 3 with a review of this section's questions online, and when you come back we'll get into the inner workings of your transceiver!

HamRadioSchool.com/general_media

4.0 How Radio Works

> *Anyone who has had actual contact with the making of the inventions that built the radio art knows that these inventions have been the product of experiment and work based on physical reasoning, rather than on the mathematicians' calculations and formulae.*
> — Edwin Armstrong, inventor of FM radio

I really like this perspective from Mr. Armstrong, and we will endeavor to adhere to its principle in this chapter. Let's undertake our contact with the inventions of the radio art with a little physical reasoning and leave most of the mathematics to the mathematicians.

Remember from your Technician studies that *modulation* is the process of encoding information into an RF signal by changing some characteristic of the signal. A modulating signal may be an audio signal from a microphone or other source. In brief review, the different types of modulation include:

Amplitude modulation (AM) encodes information by changing the power of the RF signal over time. Power is represented by the waveform amplitude, or height, of the wave. Section 4.1 discusses AM and its popular close cousin, *single sideband* (SSB) phone mode, along with some of the radio devices that are used to transmit and receive in these modes.

Frequency modulation (FM) encodes information by changing the frequency of the RF signal over time relative to a stable reference frequency, the *carrier frequency*. The change in frequency is called deviation, and Section 4.2 explores some details of FM and its inventions. We'll also touch on *phase modulation* here, encoding information with changes to the phase of the RF signal waveform.

Section 4.3 gets at methods of processing signals for enhanced operations. *Digital Signal Processing* is defined along with considerations for speech processors, signal filtering, and signal strength measurement.

Let's get on with the physical reasoning!

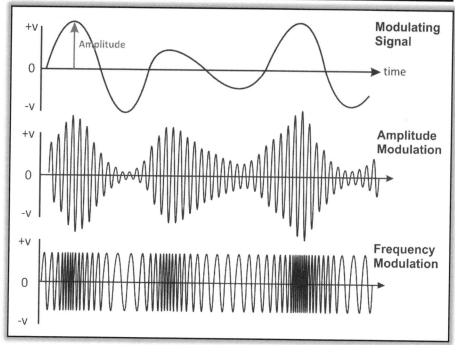

Figure 4.1: AM and FM radio signals relative to a modulating signal.

4.1 How Radio Works
AM and SSB

> **❝ The brain is like a muscle. When it is in use we feel very good. Understanding is joyous.**
> **– Carl Sagan**

If Carl was right, understanding a bit about how radio generates signals to carry our voice or our codes across hundreds or thousands of miles should make for some mighty jolly hams. As an author there is no greater satisfaction than knowing that I have helped bring such joy into your life. Let's get happy with amplitude modulation.

By far the most popular voice mode on the HF bands is single sideband, a special form of amplitude modulation. **Single sideband has these advantages over other analog voice modes on the HF bands: Less bandwidth used and greater power efficiency.** You'll probably use SSB quite a lot with your General Class privileges so let's take a close look at it. We'll start with a review of amplitude modulation and then slide into the particulars of SSB.

4.1 AM and SSB

Amplitude modulation (AM) varies the instantaneous power level of the RF signal to encode information. In simple depictions of radio waves the amplitude, or height of the wave, is an indication of the signal power. The modulating signal, such as a voice signal from a microphone, determines the amplitude of the RF waves from instant to instant. This concept may be visualized as the relatively long audio wavelengths of the modulating signal forming mirror image upper and lower boundaries for the relatively very short RF wavelengths to oscillate within, as depicted in Figure 4.1.

These upper and lower boundaries, envisioned as **the waveform connecting the peak values of the modulated signal, form the *modulation envelope* of an AM signal.** The process of changing the envelope of an RF wave to carry information is amplitude modulation. Any position along the axis of propagation (left-to-right in Figure 4.1) is the instantaneous amplitude, or power level, of the signal at the moment in time represented by that specific position in time along the axis.

Sidebands: You may recall that true AM signals contain two sidebands, the upper sideband (USB) of frequencies greater than the *carrier frequency* (the tuned or displayed frequency value), and the lower sideband (LSB) of frequencies below the carrier frequency. Each AM sideband consumes approximately 3000 Hz of bandwidth. With AM phone transmissions each of these sidebands encodes information from approximately 3000 Hz of audio signals captured by the microphone. As a slightly simplified mental model you may consider each AM RF sideband as a collection of 3000 modulation envelopes, each 1 Hz wide. Each of those 3000 envelopes is formed by RF modulation with one of the 3000 audio frequencies of your voice, as captured by the microphone. Figure 4.2 depicts the scenario with a frequency domain view.

Notice that the two AM sidebands are mirror images of one another, with the carrier frequency to which you tune your transceiver serving as the mirror. The distance away from the carrier, as measured in hertz, of any sideband RF frequency is equal to the audio frequency by which it is being modulated. For example, the RF frequency modulated by the 542 Hz audio waveform is both 542 Hz above the carrier and 542 hertz below the carrier frequency. The RF frequency encoding the 1263 Hz audio frequency is 1263 Hz above and below the carrier. So, if f is frequency, the AM sidebands extend as $(f_{Carrier} + f_{Audio})$ and as $(f_{Carrier} - f_{Audio})$ for the approximately 3000 Hz of audio frequencies modulating the RF signal.

SSB: The sideband above the carrier is called the *Upper Sideband*, or USB. The sideband below the carrier is called the *Lower Sideband*, or LSB. Each sideband consumes about 3 kHz of bandwidth. In a true AM signal both

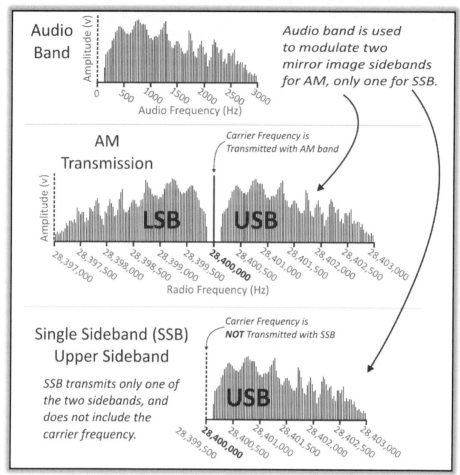

Figure 4.2: Frequency domain comparison of AM and SSB (USB) signals.

sidebands and the carrier frequency are transmitted, for approximately 6 kHz of total bandwidth. However, the AM signal is redundant, with each sideband carrying a complete set of audio information. **With the single sideband (SSB) voice mode only one sideband is transmitted; the other sideband and carrier are suppressed.** This leads to two primary benefits of SSB phone transmissions:

- **Single sideband phone emissions use the narrowest bandwidth** of any phone mode: About 3 kHz.

- Carrier suppression (and opposite sideband suppression) in single sideband phone transmissions allow the available power to be used more efficiently.

4.1 AM and SSB

With narrower transmission bandwidth the applied power is distributed over a smaller band of frequencies, thereby giving the narrower band greater average amplitude. That is, the signal has more punch than when the same power is distributed across a wider band. With SSB, all the power is poured into just the one sideband that's a little less than half the bandwidth of AM. Thus, SSB uses the available power more efficiently. (Keep in mind that the typical CW transmission is only about 150 Hz wide, and some digital modes approach this same narrow bandwidth, so the power is squeezed into a very narrow band of frequencies making for great efficiency as compared to phone modes like AM or SSB! With narrow bandwidth a little power goes a long way… literally.)

Bandwidth Considerations: Let's consider some practical implications of the SSB bandwidth. First, there are two possible sidebands to use, the USB or the LSB. Which shall we select? The agreed convention by the amateur community is that the USB is used on the higher frequency bands of 20m (14 MHz) and above, while the LSB is used on the lower bands, 40m (7 MHz) to 160m (1.8 MHz). There is one exception to this on the five 60m band channels on which USB is always used.

So, given these conventions and your knowledge that a SSB signal is 3 kHz wide, consider the following practical scenarios, referring to Figure 4.3 on the next page:

- **When the displayed carrier frequency is set to 7.178 MHz, what frequency range is occupied by a 3 kHz LSB signal?** Remember, the LSB is below the carrier, so the frequency range will go from the carrier value to the carrier − 3 kHz. In this 40m band case the range occupied will be **7.175 to 7.178 MHz.** [G4D08]

- **When the displayed carrier frequency is set to 14.347 MHz, what frequency range is occupied by a 3 kHz USB signal?** The USB used for the 20m band transmission extends from the carrier up 3 kHz, so the range occupied will be **14.347 to 14.350 MHz.** [G4D09]

- **How close to the lower edge of the phone segment should your displayed carrier frequency be when using 3 kHz wide LSB?** Since the LSB will occupy 3 kHz below the carrier, and since you may not transmit any signal below the lower edge phone frequency, your displayed carrier should be at least **at least 3 kHz above the edge of the segment.** (Exactly as in the first case above.) [G4D10]

- **How close to the upper edge of the phone segment should your displayed carrier frequency be when using 3 kHz wide USB?** Since the USB will occupy 3 kHz above the carrier, and since you may not transmit any signal above the General Class band edge, your displayed carrier should be at least **3 kHz below the edge of the band**. (Exactly as in the second case above.)

G4D11

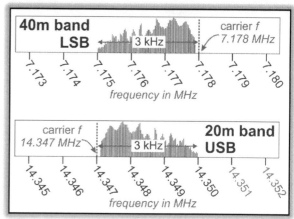

Figure 4.3: LSB and USB bandwidth examples.

Regarding operations close to the edge of the bands as in these exam question scenarios, it is prudent to give your transmitter a little buffer zone beyond the 3 kHz SSB width. Transmitters may have inherent error in the displayed carrier frequency, they may not be calibrated perfectly, and transmitter frequency can drift over time. Another 500 Hz buffer is a good practical rule of thumb to add when near band edges. For instance, in the 20m band case immediately above you would keep your VFO tuned another 500 Hz lower in frequency to provide the additional margin from the band edge – you would not tune above 14.3465 MHz.

Transmitters: With the structure of a SSB signal now in mind, let's see how it is generated. We will take a functional approach to transmitters in this chapter, defining the components as blocks that perform tasks or functions with the waveforms or signals. We will put the blocks together in diagram form to illustrate the integrated functions of transmitters. (We will consider the electronic innards of some transceiver circuits later in Chapter 6.) Let's start with the simplest transmitter form, a single frequency CW transmitter, and then we will add component blocks to it in order to vary the frequency and finally to modulate a SSB voice transmission.

Simple CW Transmitter: Figure 4.4 shows a block diagram of a very simple CW transmitter. The signal flow direction in block diagrams is usually left-to-right, so we begin with the *oscillator*. An oscillator is an electronic circuit that produces a regular and unvarying sine wave signal – an alternating current

4.1 AM and SSB

(AC) swinging back and forth in the circuit with smoothly varying positive (+) and negative (-) voltage values. For this simple CW transmitter we will establish that the oscillator produces only a single frequency of the RF value to be transmitted. Let's just pick this fixed frequency oscillator's value to be 14.050 MHz, square in the 20m CW band.

The output signal of the oscillator is routed to amplifiers that boosts the amplitude (power) of the sine wave signal. A power amplifier boosts the signal to full power for transmission via the antenna.

The CW key (or electronic keyer) interrupts or completes the transmitter circuit as a switch so that the continuous wave transmission may be affected in the *dit* and *dah* patterns of Morse Code. Beyond these "ON/OFF" patterns, no additional modification to the stable RF waveform is made – no other form of modulation is imposed.

With this transmitter you could happily make RF beeps to communicate with the world, if only on a single lonely frequency. But it is nice to be able to shift frequency, especially when a band is busy!

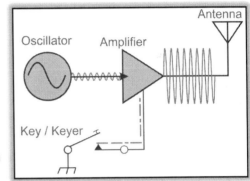

Figure 4.4: Simple CW Transmitter.

Variable Frequency Transmitter: The single frequency CW transmitter of Figure 4.4 can be made to emit other frequencies by simply varying the initial frequency created by the oscillator circuit. Assuming that the amplifier stages that follow are designed to accept and boost signals across a range of frequencies, a *variable frequency oscillator* (VFO) may be substituted for the fixed frequency oscillator with no other changes to the rest of the transmitter.

A VFO is an oscillator circuit containing electronic components that allow controlled variation in their values of electric *inductance* or *capacitance*. By changing these component values the oscillator's sine wave output frequency may be adjusted, and the amplified and transmitted frequency follows right along. The result is a CW transmitter that may be tuned across a limited range of frequencies, usually within a single RF band. Thus, our transmitter may now be adjusted across a range of frequencies in the 20m band, perhaps from 14.000 to 14.150 MHz.

Now you can move to another frequency to avoid interference from nearby stations or chase others' signals across a range of the spectrum! But gee, wouldn't it be nice to select a whole other band when the ionospheric conditions make the current band unusable for skip?

Multiband Transmitter: The variable frequency transmitter can be upgraded to transmit across a similar range of frequencies in more than one frequency band. That is, we can punch up the design such that it transmits on any selected frequency within a range of perhaps:

15m Band	21.000 – 21.150 MHz
20m Band	14.000 – 14.150 MHz
40m Band	7.000 – 7.150 MHz

But in order to achieve this flexibility of band selection we will need a method by which the oscillator's frequency can be altered wholesale! Twiddling a few inductor or capacitor values is not usually sufficient to shift frequency by such a huge amount. How can we make a grand change in the oscillator's sine wave signal? One common way is by frequency mixing.

Mixers: A mixer is a special circuit that does just what its name implies: It mixes together a pair of signals of different frequencies. The result is almost magic! Mixing frequencies is a common method used to shift an oscillator's frequency into entirely different frequency bands. Mixers are used in both transmitters and receivers to affect frequency selections. **Another term for the mixing of two RF signals is *heterodyning*.** You can learn more about how heterodyning works to shift frequencies in the *HamRadioSchool.com* online learning media for this section, but the bottom line concepts regarding frequency mixers and their heterodyning processes are as follows:

1. Two new signals result from mixing a pair of frequencies – a higher frequency signal that is the sum of the two mixed frequencies ($f1 + f2$) and a lower frequency signal that is the difference of the two mixed frequencies ($f1 - f2$). [Example: 14.000 MHz + 7.000 MHz = 21.000 MHz; and 14.000 MHz - 7.000 MHz = 7.000 MHz]

2. If one of the two mixed signals is amplitude modulated (varies in amplitude due to a modulating envelope), this signal modulation is preserved in the amplitude variations of the sum and difference output frequencies.

"Aha!" you should now exclaim, because you have suddenly had a giant light bulb illuminate overhead due to outcome #1 listed above. By mixing the VFO signal with a steady signal from a second oscillator, a much higher and a much

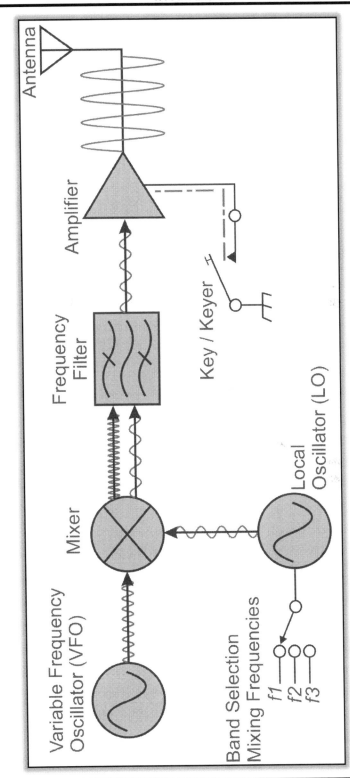

Figure 4.5: A multiband transmitter. VFO and LO frequencies are mixed to shift transmit frequencies into alternate RF bands. The LO frequency may be user-selected for band. The VFO affects a range of tuning within each selected band.

lower frequency can both be generated, shifting the frequency for transmission into entirely other amateur radio bands. The small frequency range across which the VFO may be tuned is effectively shifted to become a small frequency range for tuning in other radio bands, as noted in the previous multiband transmitter range examples. In the example of mixing outcome #1 the original unmixed 14.000 MHz signal may be transmitted (20m band), or when mixed with 7.000 MHz either a 21.000 MHz (15m band) signal or a 7.000 MHz (40m band) signal may be selected, and the VFO will affect its smaller tuning range within the selected band.

In a transmitter, the VFO signals are combined with signals from the *local oscillator* (LO) in the mixer. A *filter* allows only frequencies of the desired band to continue along the transmission path. You can imagine that frequency ranges in even more bands can be generated for transmission by providing different LO signal frequencies to the mixer. Keeping in mind mixing outcome #2 above, let's see what happens when the VFO signal is modulated by an audio signal envelope.

SSB Transmitter: Figure 4.6 depicts a typical SSB transmitter. Note that except for the deletion of the key the right half of the transmitter is identical to our multiband CW transmitter. However, we have inserted some additional components between the VFO and the mixer. Let's take a look at those.

> **Balanced Modulator:** No surprises here. The modulator does exactly what the name implies – it modulates the RF signal from the VFO. In this type of transmitter the VFO is also known as the *carrier oscillator*. The modulator accepts the carrier frequency from the VFO/Carrier Oscillator as well as the modulating signal from the microphone's speech amplifier. As described earlier, the modulator circuit combines the carrier frequency with each audio frequency to create the AM sidebands, enclosing the sidebands' RF waveforms within the modulating envelope of the audio frequencies' waveforms, varying the RF amplitude moment to moment.
>
> A balanced modulator is a special type of mixer producing sum and difference products of the 3 kHz wide audio band mixed with the carrier frequency. The output of a properly adjusted balanced modulator is a *double sideband* (DSB) signal – both the upper and lower sidebands – but *without* the carrier. This DSB signal with the carrier frequency added back in its unmodulated form is a true AM signal: Carrier, USB, and LSB altogether at 6 kHz of bandwidth. (A special technique allows the carrier to be generated in the modulator output, and this is referred to as an *unbalanced modulator*.)

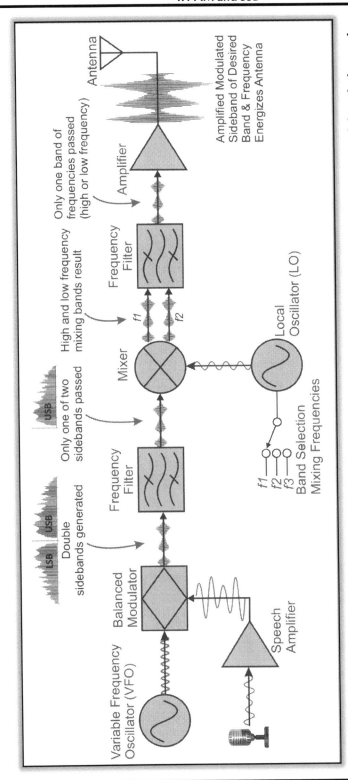

Figure 4.6: A SSB transmitter and signal processing stream. The balanced modulator creates dual AM sidebands, but only one is passed by the filter onto the mixer. The mixer also receives the LO signal that has been adjusted for a specific band-selecting frequency. The sum and difference mixer products are filtered to select the desired mixer product for amplification and transmission.

SSB Signal Generation: Starting with a DSB signal from a balanced modulator, an undesired sideband can be filtered out of the signal leaving only a single sideband, either USB or LSB. (Other methods of generating SSB signals are more complex, but this filter method is commonly used in SSB transmitters.) The filter depicted in Figure 4.6 between the balanced modulator and the mixer is used to remove one of the sidebands, leaving a single sideband modulated signal to be mixed with the LO signal and ultimately amplified and transmitted. **The balanced modulator is the circuit used to combine signals from the carrier oscillator** (the VFO) **and speech amplifier and to send the results to the filter in some single sideband phone transmitters. The filter is used to process signals from the balanced modulator and send them to the mixer in some SSB phone transmitters.**

AM Overmodulation: Sometimes you may get a little excited on the air and talk too loud. It's a natural reaction when we're struggling to communicate with someone in a noisy environment like a crowded room or on a noisy RF band, or when we really feel passionately about the point we're making! Occasionally these characteristics of human nature will slip into our radio operations and cause a little overmodulation. Having the microphone gain set too high for your voice can cause the same issue.

Overmodulation of AM or SSB signals means that our driving signals (the audio signal of the microphone) is varying the RF amplitude too much for a proper signal. Those envelope mirror image waveforms will meet and distort the envelope shape as depicted in Figure 4.7. Additionally, if your audio drive level results in your speech amplifier exceeding its maximum output power level, the tops (and bottoms) of your modulating audio waveforms may get *clipped* into a flattened shape, as in Figure 4.8.

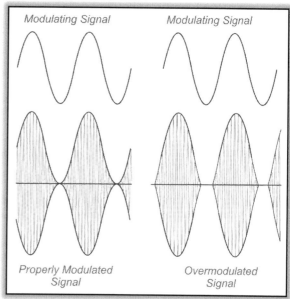

Figure 4.7: Comparison of the envelopes of a properly modulated and an overmodulated AM signal.

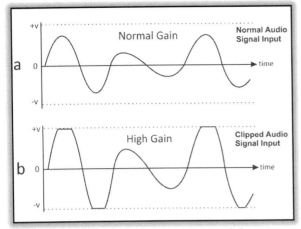

Figure 4.8: Clipping (flat-topping) of the modulating audio signal is caused by excessive drive or mic gain.

This SSB signal distortion caused by excessive drive is also called "flat-topping" due to the characteristic shape of the resulting waveform.

When overmodulation happens, additional frequency components are created in the frequency domain view of your transmission, spreading out the signal well beyond the normal 3 kHz wide SSB signal. That means you may create *splatter*, or RF frequencies beyond the desired bandwidth for good amateur practice with SSB transmissions. Fortunately most transmitters have a technological solution to this problem.

ALC: *Automatic Level Control* is a special type of circuit in a transmitter that reduces the drive power when it becomes too great for a properly modulated signal. The ALC will usually kick in during natural peaks in voice loudness. Most transceivers will require adjustments for proper ALC adaptation to your voice characteristics. In particular, **the transmit audio or microphone gain is a control that is typically adjusted for proper ALC setting on an amateur SSB transceiver.** While monitoring the ALC, adjust these settings so that ALC is activated only during your natural voice peaks. Additionally, **if the ALC is not set properly when transmitting AFSK digital signals using SSB mode, improper action of ALC distorts signals and may cause spurious emissions.** (See Section 6.9 *Avoiding Interference* regarding spurious emissions.)

Superheterodyne Receivers: With all those SSB signals flying around, bouncing from the ionosphere, and getting all jumbled up in your receiving antenna, your receiver faces a daunting task: Select only a small band of frequencies of interest, rejecting all the rest of the RF jumble, and demodulate those RF signals to reconstruct the audio waveforms that ride on them as the envelope in order to recreate the sound of the transmitting operator's voice. That's a tall order, but the superheterodyne receiver is up to the chore! The superheterodyne receiver is a widely used type of receiver for demodulating AM and SSB signals. As you may have surmised from the name containing that "heterodyne" term, this receiver uses the principle of mixing to shift received frequencies while retaining modulated information. Let's take a look at a block diagram of a superheterodyne receiver and consider the general signal processing steps that it undertakes. Then we will elaborate on a couple of the steps in greater detail. Again, the signal flow is left-to-right in the diagram of Figure 4.9 on the adjacent page.

1. Modulated RF weak signals create alternating currents on the receiving antenna. These signals are routed to an RF amplifier that boosts the weak signals' strength (increased amplitude or power).

2. **The amplified RF signals are routed to a mixer where they are mixed with a local oscillator (LO) signal. The mixer output is the sum and difference of the LO frequency mixed with received RF input frequencies.**

    a. The LO in the receiver is a variable frequency oscillator (VFO) that may be adjusted by an operating control on the receiver.
    b. The LO frequency is selected to produce a specific, desired mixing product frequency (the difference product) of a lower frequency value called the *intermediate frequency* (IF). **The local oscillator is the mixer input that is varied or tuned to convert signals of different frequencies to an intermediate frequency (IF).**
    c. The IF is a much lower RF frequency than the received signals, and the audio modulation is preserved in the IF. But the IF is not yet at the much lower audio frequencies necessary for sound reproduction.

3. **The mixer's output products** (sum and difference) **are routed to the IF filter.** The IF filter eliminates the sum frequency product (and other undesired signals) and passes only the specified (difference product) intermediate frequency.

4. The IF amplifier boosts the isolated IF signal strength and then routes it to the product detector. **The product detector** is another specialized mixer circuit that **combines signals from the IF amplifier and the beat frequency oscillator (BFO), and sends the result to the audio frequency (AF) amplifier.**

    a. The IF is a static, unchanging reference value, and the BFO frequency is engineered to mix with the IF and generate a difference product (a lower frequency than the IF) that recovers the audio frequency modulating signal from the IF. The originally transmitted modulating

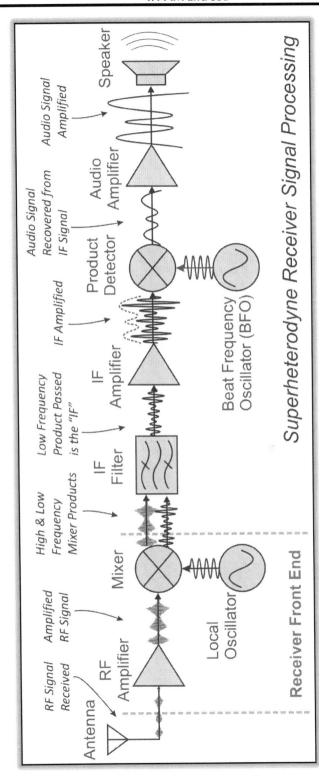

Figure 4.9: Basic signal processing of the superheterodyne receiver. The receiver front end shifts received signals to the intermediate frequency (IF) by mixing. The product detector shifts the IF lower, recovering the original modulating audio waveform.

audio signals have finally been liberated from their RF hosts!

5. The audio frequency output signal of the product detector is amplified further by an audio frequency (AF) amplifier in order to drive a speaker that reproduces the voice sound of the transmitting operator.

Note: Although the received RF and the IF are referred to as lone frequencies, realize that the entire 3 kHz band of SSB signal frequencies is being dragged through these steps simultaneously. The audio-value offsets from the RF carrier frequency are preserved as offsets from the IF value, and ultimately as a range of audio frequency values representing the original modulating signals.

These steps represent a single conversion superheterodyne. It is referred to as single conversion because only a single mixing step is used to convert from the received RF to the IF. Most modern heterodyne receivers having multiple broad frequency band demodulation requirements or high signal selectivity capability will use multiple mixing stages to achieve such high performance.

G7C07 **The absolute simplest combination of stages that implement a superheterodyne receiver would be an HF oscillator** (the local oscillator) **linked to a mixer** (that is also receiving antenna signals) **and the mixer products routed to a detector circuit.**

Intermediate Frequency: In step 2 of the superheterodyne signal processing a specific IF is a product of the mixing process of received RF signals with the LO. Further, as noted in step 4a, the IF is a single, unchanging frequency value that the IF filter passes on for additional processing into audio by the product detector. What exactly is going on here?

As noted, the LO in this case is a VFO with operator-selectable frequency values. This is the VFO control by which you tune your transceiver to a desired frequency. When you alter the LO frequency you select an oscillator frequency to be mixed with every RF signal received by the antenna – lots and lots of different frequency signals pulled from the air. Every one of those myriad mixes between a received RF signal and the selected LO signal results in a sum and difference product out of the mixer. So, in reality, there are myriad x 2 mixer products! Of course, only one received RF signal frequency value mixed with the LO signal will result in a difference product that is exactly the designated and unchanging IF value. And if you change the LO frequency you change the received RF signal frequency that mixes to the IF value. Perhaps a numerical example will help drive home the point.

IF Example: Suppose we are operating in the 20m band with a superheterodyne receiver. The receiver uses one of the standard IF values of 455 kHz. That

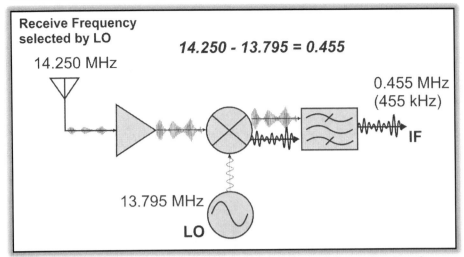

Figure 4.10: The received signal frequency is selected from all other frequencies by changes to the LO mixing frequency since the IF is unchanging at 455 kHz.

IF value never changes, and that is the only frequency value that the IF filter will pass for further processing into audio signals. That value of 455 kHz, or 0.455 MHz, is the desired difference product of the mixer circuit.

Let's say that the LO is providing a mixing signal of 13.795 MHz. In order for the IF of 455 kHz (0.455 MHz) to be the difference product of the mixer, the mixer must combine the 13.795 MHz local oscillator signal with a received input signal of 14.250 MHz. This is true because

14.250 MHz − 13.795 MHz = 0.455 MHz (or 455 kHz)

If the LO is altered to generate a signal of 13.820 MHz, it can produce a difference product of 0.455 MHz only by mixing with a received signal of 14.275 MHz:

14.275 MHz − 13.820 MHz = 0.455 MHz (or 455 kHz)

Thus, by adjusting the LO frequency to the mixer a received RF frequency is selected for continued processing into the IF. Even though there are uncountable other mixing products resulting from the mixing process, the only product that is passed along by the IF filter is the singular difference product resulting from the LO signal mixing with a received signal that produces that exact 455 kHz IF. This is how the VFO control tunes your transceiver to the desired frequency.

Image Response: You may have considered already that another RF frequency besides the desired receive frequency may result in the 455 kHz intermediate frequency. For example, **if a receiver mixes a 13.800 MHz VFO (LO) signal with a 14.255 MHz received signal to produce a 455 kHz intermediate frequency signal, a 13.345 MHz received signal will produce the same IF due to its difference from the 13.800 MHz VFO signal:**

> 14.255 MHz − 13.800 MHz = 0.455 MHz, and
>
> 13.800 MHz − 13.345 MHz = 0.455 MHz

So, if a signal exists on 13.345 MHz it will produce interference known as *image response*. In this example the IF of 455 kHz will contain signals derived from both 14.255 MHz and from 13.345 MHz received RF. If this occurs there is no convenient method of eliminating or filtering the undesired image signals.

However, most modern receivers will have *front end filters* or *image filters* that eliminate the signals that may cause undesired images like this. The *receiver front end* is considered the combination of RF amplifier, mixer, and local oscillator (LO or VFO) at the beginning of the receiver's signal processing stream, and filters added to these components would never allow the 13.345 MHz signals from our example into the mixer processing stream and IF.

IF Shift: In a case **when another station very close to the receive frequency is interfering, the IF shift control on a receiver may help to avoid the interference.** The IF shift control changes the IF passband higher or lower without changing the IF itself. In some cases this can help reduce interference from stations near the VFO-selected receive frequency by moving the passband of frequencies such that it no longer includes the interfering signal, but while maintaining proper audio demodulation of the IF passband.

There. Aren't you overjoyed? Isn't your brain muscle good and exercised, producing cognitive bliss? That is the exultant world of amplitude modulation and single sideband transmitting and receiving! Not so terribly complicated, huh? And boy, does it just radiate joy! Review the questions for this section and then we'll tackle a few concepts of Frequency Modulation.

HamRadioSchool.com/general_media

4.2 How Radio Works — FM

> *...atoms emit light waves of a specific length or oscillation frequency - their familiar characteristic spectra - and these can come in the form of electromagnetic waves only from accelerated electric quanta.*
> — Johannes Stark

Accelerated electric quanta – accelerated electric charge, such as electrons flowing back and forth in an antenna – is a fundamental concept in the production of radio frequencies. The frequency of alternation in the AC signal energizing an antenna will determine the frequency of emitted electromagnetic waves. Frequency modulation (FM) takes advantage of Stark's insight by encoding information in AC frequency variations that are mirrored in the antenna's EM radio frequency emissions.

Let's consider some of the characteristics of FM and contrast them with what we've learned about AM and SSB. Just because you earn your General Class ticket doesn't mean you will abandon the local VHF and UHF FM repeaters and simplex communications. In fact, you may be inspired to explore FM digital mode operations and other related facets of amateur radio. So, it pays to be knowledgeable of FM as a General Class operator.

Frequency modulation changes the instantaneous frequency of an RF wave to convey information. The audio signals generated by your transmitter's microphone and speech amplifier drive the modulation with FM just as with AM or SSB, but instead of an amplitude envelope encoding the audio signal a frequency shift encodes the audio signal. When a modulating audio signal is applied to an FM transmitter the RF carrier frequency changes proportionally to the instantaneous amplitude of the modulating signal.

[G8A03]

Figure 4.11 depicts the FM scenario. Note how the frequency is increased when the audio amplitude is positive and the frequency is decreased when the audio amplitude is negative. The greater the driving power (amplitude) of the audio signal, positive or negative voltage, the greater the deviation from the *carrier frequency* value. The carrier frequency is a stable or *resting* value that manifests when no modulating audio signal is present or when the audio

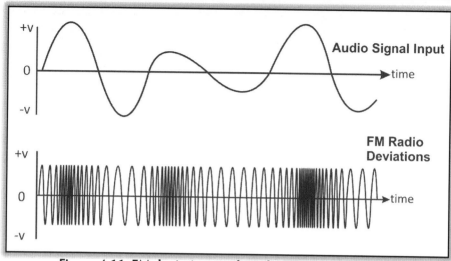

Figure 4.11: FM deviations with audio signal modulation.

signal is zero volts. All frequency deviations are relative to the carrier frequency, and the carrier frequency is what is depicted on your radio's tuning display (VFO display).

Spring Model: A simplified way to think of the FM scenario is to imagine the RF carrier waveform as a spring with a preferred extension (resting state frequency). Think of the spring coils as the RF waveforms. The spring may be compressed tighter than its preferred extension (higher frequency) or it may be stretched out greater than its preferred extension (lower frequency). When the modulating waveform is of relatively low power (weak audio signals from a soft voice), the spring oscillates back and forth at a frequency equivalent to the audio signal and to only a mild compression and a mild extension – a small *deviation* from its preferred extension, or resting state. When the driving audio amplitude is great (strong audio signals from a loud voice), the spring oscillates back and forth at the same audio frequency rate, but the deviations are much larger – very tight compressions and very stretched out extensions. In this way, the amplitude of an audio signal is encoded into the frequency deviations of the RF transmission.

As with AM and SSB, there is a band of audio frequencies that must be encoded this way in order to reproduce voice audio. Imagine a unique spring for each 1 Hz audio frequency in the band. You might imagine a set of a few thousand such "RF springs," each one compressing-and-extending at a rate equal to that of a single, unique audio frequency in the band, and each one representing the amplitude of its modulating audio frequency with the magnitude of its deviation from a standard resting state. In this way, the entire audio band of frequencies is represented by the commensurate band of spring deviation rates (the rate of frequency deviations), and the amplitude of each audio frequency is represented by the extent of the spring deviations (the magnitude of the frequency deviations from the carrier frequency reference). This multi-spring model is depicted in Figure 4.12. *However...*

Caution: This spring model image is an oversimplified view of real FM and it should not be taken as an accurate physical depiction, but it provides a good mental tool for describing the essence of FM. In a real FM transmission the full set of "spring oscillations" (frequency deviations) is an incredibly complex behavior of the RF carrier waveform that is adequately defined only by advanced statistical mathematics. It's sort of like having

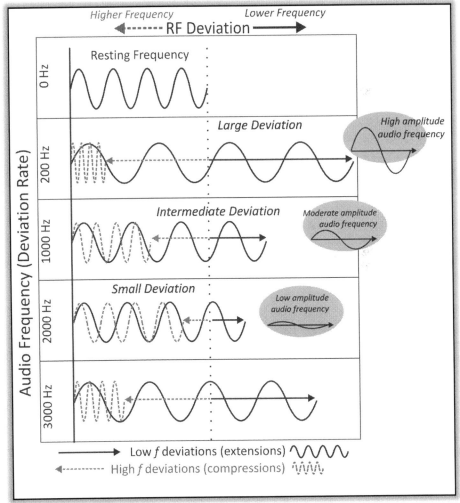

Figure 4.12: Simplified spring model of FM. Spring deviation rates represent audio band frequency encoding. Spring deviation magnitudes represent each audio band frequency's instantaneous amplitude.

all those jittering springs' dynamics crammed together in one really crazy dancing spring. Specifically, FM signals are characterized by *Bessel functions* that offer a solution to a differential equation describing the complex dynamics of frequency modulated waveforms. The exploration of this topic is left as an exercise for the advanced student. No exam questions test your knowledge of Bessel functions or differential equations. (Whew!)

FM Bandwidth: You may recall from your Technician Class studies that the bandwidth of FM phone signals depends upon the frequency deviation described above. As the frequency deviates to greater extents, a larger band of frequencies must be used by the FM signal. Since deviation is determined by the amplitude of the modulating audio signal, louder audio results in greater FM bandwidth. Thus, FM bandwidth changes constantly with the driving audio signal. The Technician Class question pool indicates 10 – 15 kHz as typical FM bandwidth, although in practice signals may be of somewhat wider bandwidth.

Most FM transmitters have limiting circuits that keep FM deviation within the bounds of good amateur practice. The limiter circuit's maximum allowed deviation (or a lower maximum driving signal amplitude) may determine the *peak carrier deviation* value for a transmission. The peak deviation, along with the highest modulating frequency, influences the bandwidth of the FM signal.

Carson's Rule: A good approximation of FM signal bandwidth may be calculated using Carson's Rule:

Bandwidth = 2 x (peak deviation + highest modulating frequency)

Let's consider an example from the question pool: **What is the total bandwidth of an FM phone transmission having a 5 kHz deviation and a 3 kHz modulating frequency?** Let's plug in the values for peak deviation and highest modulating frequency per the Carson's Rule formula:

Bandwidth = 2 x (5 kHz + 3 kHz) = 2 x 8 kHz = **16 kHz**

Notice this example provides an estimated bandwidth for FM about five times greater than the 3 kHz bandwidth of SSB. Many regions utilize 15 kHz to 25 kHz spacing of designated VHF and UHF FM channels. This spacing may not always be sufficient to avoid interference between adjacent FM channels, depending on operating practices and transmitter characteristics.

Note, you can over-modulate FM, too. Usually this is referred to as *over-deviation* with FM, where the limiter circuit will kick-in. But just as with amplitude modulation **an effect of over-modulation is excessive bandwidth** since the resultant deformed waveforms will generate frequency components beyond the desired bandwidth limits. However, if the transmitter's limiter circuit is functioning correctly, overdeviation of RF should never get transmitted – that's the whole point of having a limiter in an FM transmitter.

Frequency modulated (FM) phone is not used below 29.5 MHz (10m band) because the wide bandwidth is prohibited by the FCC rules. With the bandwidth of FM phone signals several times greater than SSB, a simple bandwidth analysis makes it clear why the FCC limits FM operations in the lower HF bands. The available spectrum in the amateur phone bands below 10m is relatively narrow: 400 kHz on 80m band to just 58 kHz on 17m band, and intermediate values on the other HF bands. Compare this to the 1.4 MHz of 10m band, the 3.9 MHz of 2m band, and 30 MHz of 70 cm band where FM is allowed. The 17m phone band would support only about four simultaneously detectable FM QSOs with an average bandwidth of 15 kHz. This really illustrates the squeeze that would result if wide bandwidth FM were permitted on the lower HF bands!

FM Transmitters: Two significant signal production techniques differentiate FM phone transmitters from SSB transmitters:

1. FM uses a *reactance modulator* instead of a balanced modulator. A reactance modulator uses a special circuit that varies capacitance values in electronic components in order to rapidly shift the frequency of a resonating circuit (oscillator). The FM oscillator initially produces a relatively low frequency signal, well below the desired operating frequency.

2. **FM transmitters shift the oscillator's frequency to the higher desired operating frequency using a *multiplier* stage that generates a harmonic of the lower frequency signal.** A *harmonic multiplier* is a circuit that produces signals that are integer frequency multiples of the input signal. Many multiples may be produced – 2x, 3x, ... 12x the input and higher – and a filter is used to select the particular frequency multiple needed for a transmitter design.

Figure 4.13 is a block diagram of a simple FM transmitter showing the left-to-right signal processing with the reactance modulator and harmonic multiplier components. The reactance modulator accepts the speech signals of the microphone and amplifier to affect frequency modulation with the oscillator. The output signal of the oscillator is a low RF frequency: For example, a 2m band transmitter oscillator will output about a 12.21 MHz frequency modulated signal. The filter eliminates undesired harmonics generated by the multiplier. For the 2m transmitter only the 12th harmonic is passed on to the amplifier:

   12 MHz x 12 = 144.00 MHz.

In order to generate the 2m calling frequency of 146.52 MHz the oscillator must generate a 12.21 MHz signal:

   12.21 MHz x 12 = 146.52 MHz.

The amplifier then boosts this signal for transmission by the antenna.

Transmitter Design Considerations: Interestingly, the harmonic multiplier not only multiplies the oscillator's frequency by 12 (or other desired values for other bands), but it multiplies the *frequency deviations* that are output by the oscillator as well. That is, the "spring oscillations" created by the reactance modulator and oscillator are magnified 12 times, too. The compressions are 12 times tighter and the expansions are 12 times longer!

Let's use our 2m band FM example above and the 5 kHz deviation from the Carson's Rule discussion for an example of the implications for transmitter design: **For a 146.52 MHz FM phone transmitter, a 12.21 MHz reactance modulated oscillator in a 5 kHz deviation will have a frequency deviation of 416.7 Hz.** That is, an initial oscillator deviation of 416.7 Hz is going to be multiplied by 12 in the harmonic multiplier for this 2m transmitter case:

   416.7 Hz x 12 = 5000 Hz (5 kHz) transmitted deviation.

Or, of course, the calculation may be inverted to:

   5000 Hz ÷ 12 = 416.7 Hz oscillator deviation.

You may wonder why harmonic multipliers are not implemented in AM and SSB transmitters instead of mixers to shift frequencies higher or lower. The multiplier is usually simpler and cheaper to use. However, a harmonic multiplier is not linear, meaning that it will distort the amplitude of the signal. In fact, it is a feature of this purposeful distortion that results in the generation of harmonic frequency multiples. An AM or SSB signal would not survive these distortions intact. However, since the FM information is encoded in the undistorted frequency deviations and not in an amplitude signal, the information is properly preserved, allowing FM use of the harmonic multiplier.

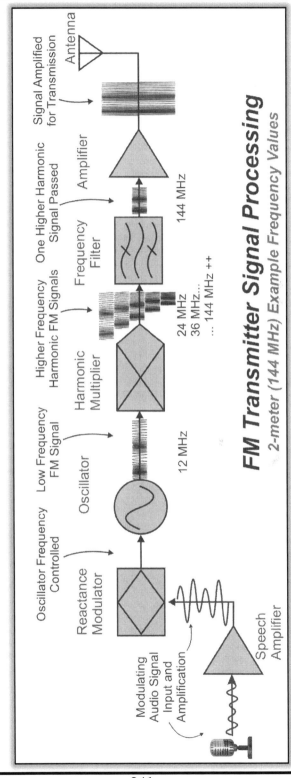

Figure 4.13: FM transmitter signal processing. The harmonic multiplier receives a relatively low frequency FM signal from the oscillator and outputs multiple higher frequency harmonic signals in which frequency deviations are preserved. The frequency filter allows only one of the harmonic frequencies to pass for transmission.

FM Receivers: The front end of the FM receiver is identical to the superheterodyne SSB receiver, but following the IF generation (by mixing and filtering) a different set of components is used to recover the audio information. As depicted in Figure 4.14, the FM receiver employs a *limiter*. The limiter removes any amplitude variation, and only the frequency deviations remain in a constant-amplitude square wave signal. Following the limiter is **a circuit called the discriminator, used to convert IF output signals to audio.** The discriminator circuit output is amplified for sound reproduction.

Phase Modulation (PM): Phase modulation is a process that changes the phase angle of an RF signal to convey information. Phase angle changes are illustrated in Figure 4.15. A continuous range of phase angle changes from 0 to 360 degrees can be used to encode a modulating signal with PM, just as a continuous range of amplitude changes or of frequency deviations are used in AM and FM.

A slight difference in the FM transmitter's reactance modulator connection will result instead in PM. FM results when the reactance modulator is connected to an oscillator tuned circuit, as shown previously in Figure 4.13; **Phase modulation results when the reactance modulator is connected to an RF transmitter amplifier stage** instead.

Phase modulation is less commonly used in amateur radio than either FM or SSB, but it is a viable modulating technique for voice transmissions. Recall that *phase shifting* is used with the popular

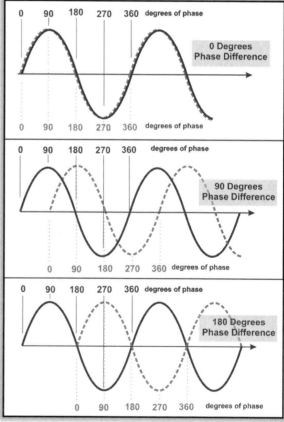

Figure 4.15: Example phase shifts of a waveform (dashed) relative to a reference waveform (solid).

4.2 FM

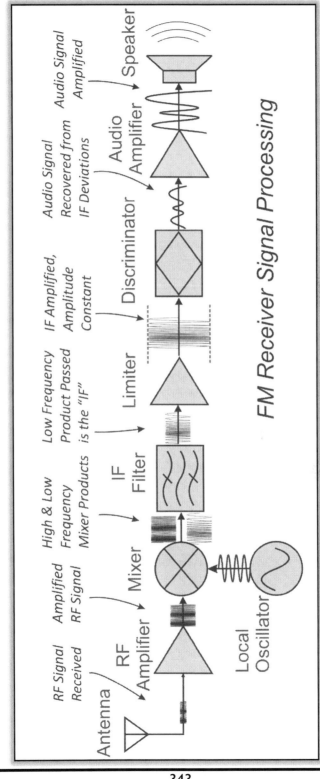

Figure 4.14: The FM receiver signal processing begins the same as the SSB superheterodyne, but a limiter circuit ensures a constant IF amplitude and a discriminator circuit recovers the audio signal from the IF deviations.

PSK31 digital mode described in Section 2.5 *More Digital Modes*. The PSK31 mode uses the presence or absence of a phase shift of a narrow bandwidth tone transmission within rigidly specified time intervals to convey 1s and 0s of digitally coded characters.

No matter how advanced you get in amateur radio license class, you will likely always enjoy the clear sound of FM and the convenience of FM repeaters for day-to-day local communications. There's just nothing like a good net on a repeater with a sizable group of hams participating from across the experience spectrum, and FM promotes that interaction like no other mode. Enjoy it, but understand it too!

Section questions wait for you at: *HamRadioSchool.com/general_media*

4.3 Signal Processing

> **All physical systems can be thought of as registering and processing information...**
> – Seth Lloyd

I'm certain that Professor Lloyd would agree that ham radio constitutes a physical system. We can generate and receive signals. We can make waveforms bolt across vast distances, bounce them from the ionosphere, modulating and demodulating information in electromagnetic dialog with our fellow hams – we can register a lot of information flying around as RF!

But what about the quality of those signals? Even if we are able to modulate, transmit, receive, and demodulate, we will not necessarily communicate if the quality of signals is poor due to weak signal strength, an improperly configured transceiver, or failure to take advantage of all the technological marvels available in modern transceivers.

Let's consider some of the ways that our RF signals can be analyzed and enhanced so that our RF communications capabilities are optimized. How can we gauge signal strengths? How can we enhance signals carrying our modulated voice and reduce signals carrying noise? How can digital technology improve our analog RF signals? The amazing capabilities of the modern amateur radio transceiver provide help with each of these questions. Let's see how our ham system can process the information it registers.

Signal Strength: No matter if you are operating QRP (low power) or blasting out a kilowatt, signal strength is a critical factor for communication success. Many different factors influence the strength of your signal at a receiving station including transmitter output power, atmospheric conditions, operating mode, and signal path. Signal strength is also one of the most commonly exchanged metrics of performance between operators during contacts. How is signal strength determined?

> **S Meter: Received signal strength is measured with an S meter** (S = signal). **An S meter will be found in virtually every receiver.**
> Figure 4.16 shows various styles of S meters on modern receivers. Notice

G4D04 G4D06

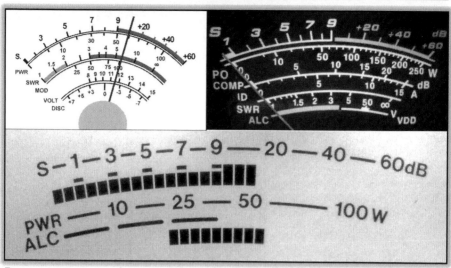

Figure 4.16: Example typical S meters. Top scale is the S meter scale in each example. Needle readouts and LCD segmented displays are common.

that they share some common features, and often will have multiple scales for various functions other than signal strength. The S meter scale is the top scale in each depicted example.

S Units: An S meter will usually depict *S units* on the left half of the scale, from S=0 to S=9. One S unit change in signal strength usually indicates a 6 dB change in received signal strength. As we reviewed in Chapter 0, *Before We Begin*, a 6 dB change is about a 4X change in power. **So, to change the S meter reading on a distant receiver by one S unit, say from S8 to S9, the transmitter power output must be raised approximately 4 times.** (Note: S meters scaling and accuracy may vary depending upon receiver manufacturer and quality, and automatic gain control [AGC] may also affect how the S meter responds to signal strength. Check your transceiver users manual.)

Strong Signal Comparisons: A reading of S9 is considered to be a strong signal, and most S meters will depict S9 centered on the scale. To the right, or *above* S9, the S meter scale will typically depict values of +20, +40, and +60 dB. You will hear very strong signals reported on the air such as "*20 over S9,*" or "*S9 + 20,*" or simply "*20 over,*" or other indicated levels above S9. **Assuming a properly calibrated S meter, a reading of 20 dB over S9 means the signal is 100 times stronger than an S9 signal** (20 dB = 100X change). A signal of S9 + 40 dB would be 10,000 times stronger than S9, and S9 + 60 dB means a 1,000,000 times increase!

4.3 Signal Processing

Attenuation: Signal strength varies over a very great range, hence the use of the logarithmic decibel unit for comparisons. When signals approach S9 + 60 dB strength and stronger your received signal may sound distorted. The amplifiers in the receiver produce linearly amplified signals in the normal signal strength range, but very strong signals can overdrive the circuit. That is, the amplifier cannot handle the extreme signal strength and it cannot accurately reproduce the amplitude modulated waveform or envelope signals being received. This effect may occur in the RF amplifier of the receiver front-end. This effect is called *overload*, or *front-end overload*. **To reduce signal overload due to strong incoming signals use the attenuator function present on many HF transceivers.** The attenuator circuit will reduce overall signal strength from the front end through the IF amplifier, improving the receiver's ability to handle very strong signals such as those from a strong, nearby station. But the attenuator will diminish your ability to receive weak signals, so usually you do not want to leave it on.

G4A13

Speech Processors: The purpose of a speech processor used in a modern transceiver is to increase the intelligibility of transmitted phone signals during poor conditions. This is accomplished by making changes across the frequency components of the transmitted AM or SSB signal, usually implemented by manipulation of the modulating audio band frequencies. Let's take a closer look at how a speech processor works in your transceiver, starting with just a smidgen of simple engineering speak wrapped in common experience.

G4D01

Signal detection is a common engineering task across many domains. Your receiver endeavors to detect RF signals among a chaotic sea of RF noise. A submariner strives to detect a whisper of the sound reflection from the sonar against the ocean's eerie background sound track. With my poorly functioning ears I endeavor to detect my wife's voice among the noise of screaming kids, loud music, barking dogs, and ringing tinnitus… OK, maybe sometimes I'm not endeavoring too hard, but let's use this example.

If the kids, their music, the dogs, and my tinnitus are all fussing and thumping and barking and ringing, generating a cacophony of noise, I will not hear the wife's stated orders even if she shouts them at the top of her lungs, per normal. Why not? Because I cannot detect her commanding verbal signals among all the noise in the environment. The ratio of signal to noise is too low for the signal to be detected by my faulty ears. (A low signal-to-noise ratio could also result if she tried to sweetly whisper through only my ringing tinnitus, hence low noise but also a very low signal, but that would be a very rare scenario in my home.)

In contrast, once the kids are at school, the electronics are turned off, and the dog is asleep, I am left in peace with only the persistent mild ringing in my ears to interfere with my darling's mellifluously squawked signals. With a large signal-to-noise ratio (SNR) like that, it is difficult to get out of honey-do chores no matter how bad the ears may be.

Back to radio now, before I get into trouble: In poor conditions a receiving operator has a similar problem – lots of noise and perhaps a weak signal imbedded in it. A voice signal may be heard but not clearly distinguished or understood. This is because some of the frequencies in typical voice audio are relatively weak while others are strong. For instance, lower frequency vowel sounds are usually bellowed with relatively strong sound pressure, while many higher frequency consonant sounds are much weaker in sound pressure, such as those of the letters c, f, n, s, v, or w. As a result, the audio band signals and their modulated RF sideband signals will have greatly varying signal strengths across the transmitted band's frequency range. It's like trying to hear a friend from across a crowded room at a party – you may hear the words but not understand them because too much of the detailed sound information is lost in the noise of many conversations.

A speech processor will usually implement *dynamic compression* of the audio band. Frequencies within the band that are relatively strong (high amplitude) are unaffected, but frequencies that are relatively weak (low amplitude) will be boosted in amplitude. This has the effect of "compressing" the range of amplitudes across the audio band or

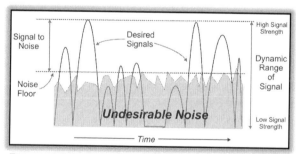

Figure 4.17: Signal-to-noise ratio. Noise (gray) can mask a desired signal if the signal-to-noise ratio is low, making detection of the desired signal difficult. Strong signals exceed the noise, producing a high signal-to-noise ratio, and are more easily detected by a receiver.

4.3 Signal Processing

reducing differences in amplitude across the frequencies. For those weaker frequencies, the SNR is increased. For a typical voice signal this means that the higher frequencies (those consonant sounds) are boosted and made louder when received, improving the intelligibility of the voice audio. In doing this, **the speech processor affects a transmitted single sideband phone signal by increasing the average power of the transmitted signal** (relative to the unprocessed signal and within the limits of the transmitter output).

G4D02

Speech processor compression is depicted in Figure 4.18: The range of power levels across the audio frequency band has been reduced or compressed, keeping all frequencies closer to a consistent peak power level and improving speech intelligibility – the weaker signals have been boosted out of the noise level with a greater SNR.

Your transceiver may also provide controls for *frequency shaping*, similar to what a graphic equalizer can affect. Figure 4.18 illustrates some minor frequency shaping as well with frequencies below about 800 Hz being slightly attenuated. However, be cautious about making manual adjustments to your transmitted audio. **An incorrectly adjusted speech processor can result in distorted speech, pickup of excessive background noise, and even splatter** caused by overmodulation or amplified frequencies outside the normal audio bandwidth. If you use a speech processor, start by trying the typical pre-programmed options. In most instances one of those configurations will improve your signal quality and keep you out of trouble. Follow the directions in your transceiver owner's manual, but also ask for on-air signal reports to check for audio quality.

G4D03

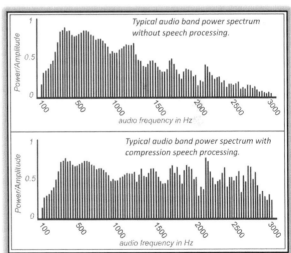

Figure 4.18: Example of compression of an audio band. The distribution of power across frequencies is adjusted for greater consistency, boosting weaker frequencies.

Digital Signal Processing (DSP): The transmitters and receivers described earlier in this chapter are analog devices, meaning they work with continuous electrical signals and waveforms. However, many modern transceivers now utilize *Digital Signal Processing* (DSP) to enhance received signals and to generate signals for transmission by digital methods. After a simple illustration of the nature of digital signals we will examine some typical applications of DSP.

Sampling: A smooth and continuous signal waveform may be approximately represented by *sampling* its values in regular intervals of time. Sampling means simply measuring a characteristic instantaneously with regularity and recording the measurements. For an AC signal in an electrical circuit we may measure the instantaneous voltage in equally timed intervals. We could represent our sampled waveform in a table that relates time to measured voltages, and we could plot the waveform according to the table as in Figure 4.19. (We will suppose the use of an oscilloscope to depict and measure the waveform voltages for illustration, and you will learn more about measurement with oscilloscopes in Chapter 6.)

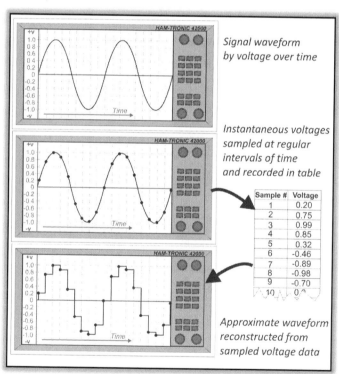

Notice that the reconstructed waveform is not a smoothed shape, but rather a squared distribution of points on a graph. If we sampled more frequently we would have more complete information to store, and if we sample less frequently we have to do more guesswork with less information. As long as the samples happen rapidly enough, the original signal can be accurately recreated from the digital data.

Figure 4.19: Digital sampling and storage of a signal's waveform voltages. The sampling interval trades accuracy with data quantity. Sampled data may be stored electronically and operated upon with mathematical functions to alter the reconstructed signal.

4.3 Signal Processing

According to the *Nyquist limit*, a signal must be sampled at a rate at least twice its frequency to be accurately reproduced from the sampled data. Modern DSP transceivers can readily sample at such speeds.

With Digital Signal Processing, RF signals are converted into digital representations through a sampling process. A digital microprocessor, programmed with appropriate software algorithms, may then be used to perform mathematical operations on the digitized signal data. These digital methods can affect many common functions such as signal filtering, audio equalizing, and noise reduction in received signals. We'll examine some of the functions more closely.

ADC and DAC: The sampling process described above is a method of *analog-to-digital conversion*, or ADC. Following the ADC process the signals may be manipulated by the digital processor. Following digital processing, the digital signal representations must go through a reverse *digital-to-analog conversion*, or DAC, so that audio waveforms can produce sound from a speaker. Any Digital Signal Processor function, such as an IF filter, requires an analog to digital converter, a digital processing chip, and a digital to analog converter, as depicted in Figure 4.20. All Digital Signal Processor filtering is accomplished this way, by converting the signal from analog to digital and using digital processing, and then converting back to analog waveforms.

Digital Filtering: A filter is a circuit that is designed to pass some frequencies

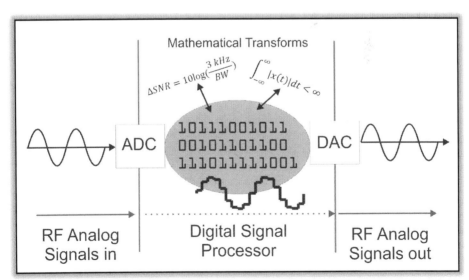

Figure 4.20: ADC produces digital data by sampling. DSP operates on the digital data to modify the signal representation. DAC converts the modified data into an altered analog signal.

applied to it and to attenuate, or reject, other frequencies applied to it. For example, the IF filter in a receiver is designed to pass only a small band of frequencies near the intermediate frequency value and attenuate all others. Filtering in modern transceivers is often accomplished with DSP. Let's first review some basics about RF filtering that apply to analog as well as digital methods, and then we'll return to characteristics of DSP.

Filter Basics: It is common for a filter circuit to be defined by the *passband* of frequencies it will pass, or alternatively by the *stop band* of frequencies it will attenuate or reject. A filter's *cut-off frequency* is a frequency value beyond which the filter will attenuate signals. For instance, a *high pass filter* will allow the passage of frequencies higher than the cutoff value, and it will attenuate frequencies below the cut-off value. Conversely, a low-pass filter passes frequencies lower than the cut-off value and rejects higher frequencies. A *band-pass filter* has two cut-off values, passing only the frequencies between the two cut-off values.

Most filters do not activate instantly at the cut-off frequency, but rather more gradually "roll off" in effect near the defined cut-off(s). The standard convention for defining effective cut-off frequency is where the filter attenuates the signal to one-half power. For instance, **the bandwidth of a**

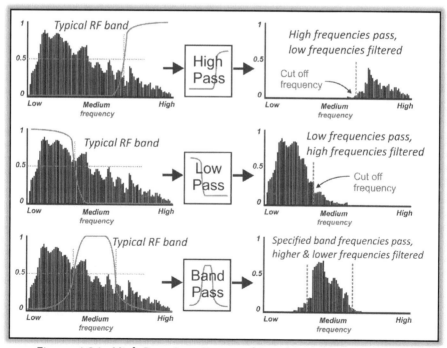

Figure 4.21: High Pass, Low Pass, and Band Pass filtering effects.

4.3 Signal Processing

band-pass filter is measured between the upper and lower half-power frequencies. **The cutoff frequency for a low-pass filter is the frequency above which output power is less than half the input power.**

Some filters may reduce signal power slightly even within its intended passband. **A filter's attenuation inside its passband is called *insertion loss*,** or loss of signal strength due to the insertion of the filter into the circuit. **Outside its passband, a filter's maximum ability to reject signals is termed the *ultimate rejection*.** This is the greatest signal attenuation capability of the filter.

A *notch filter* is a very narrow bandpass filter, and it will pass all frequencies except a narrow band either side of a defined *center frequency*. **The purpose of the notch filter found on many HF transceivers is to reduce interference from carriers in the receiver passband.** (See notch example described below and Figure 4.22 on the next page.)

Selectivity: Most of a superheterodyne receiver's frequency *selectivity* (the ability to reject undesired signals) is achieved with IF filtering in which the mixer products resulting from nearby receive frequencies are rejected and only the desired band of signals is passed to the product detector. **It is good to match receiver bandwidth to the bandwidth of the operating mode because it results in the best signal-to-noise ratio.** For instance, use a 3kHz wide filter (or narrower) with SSB and perhaps a 400 Hz wide filter for CW. A close matching of filter width to signal bandwidth enhances receiver selectivity by passing precisely the desired intermediate frequency band and rejecting all others, thereby eliminating noise from those rejected adjacent frequencies.

Noise Blanker: **A noise blanker** is a temporal filter that **reduces receiver gain during a noise pulse.** The noise blanker circuit in a receiver can react very quickly, blanking out repetitious noise such as pulsing power line interference or ignition system noise in a mobile station.

In a purely analog receiver, filtering must be affected with filter circuits that are designed with specific characteristics that are not readily changed or manipulated. Filter circuits may be physically swapped out when the available selections are inadequate for the desired operation or conditions, but this is not always a convenient or swift modification to make, as it usually requires opening the chassis of the transceiver and mucking about its innards. Digital filtering makes things much easier! Let's now return to considerations of digital signal processing.

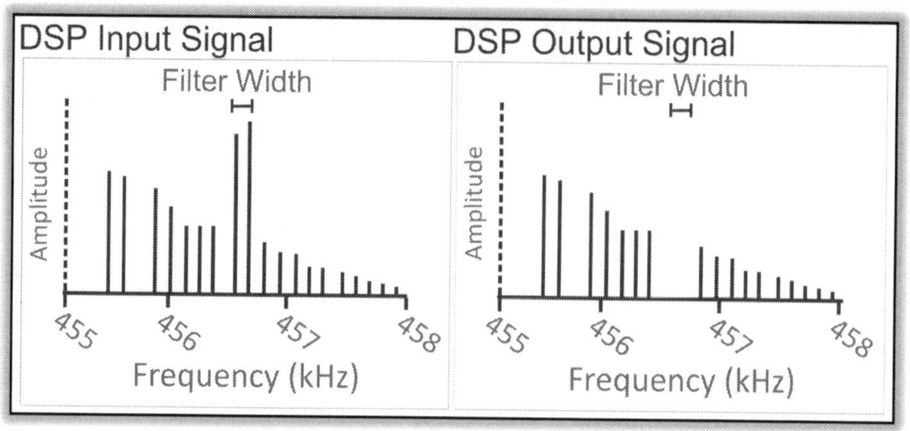

Figure 4.22: A DSP-designed notch filter effect, eliminating an offending narrow carrier signal from the IF pass band.

G4C12 **An advantage of a receiver Digital Signal Processor IF filter as compared to an analog filter is that a wide range of filter bandwidths and shapes can be created.** For example, the DSP can be programmed through simple receiver controls to implement an IF filter bandwidth of 2.4 kHz for a narrow SSB filter, or it can be configured for a comfortable 300 Hz CW filter. The DSP filters out the unwanted frequencies and passes the desired signal band, just like the band pass filtering illustrated in Figure 4.21. Other types of filtering can also be digitally accomplished, including notch filtering and *noise reduction*, all without the hassle of mechanically substituting filter modules!

> **Noise Reduction:** Noise reduction is one of the primary functions offered by DSP, and there are multiple noise reduction techniques that may be used singularly or in combination. Random noise reduction and mode-specific adaptive algorithms for notching or bandpass are common.
>
> However, DSP-implemented noise reduction is not perfect. Since some frequency components of a desired signal will overlap with frequencies of noise, the DSP algorithms necessarily effect components of the desired signal as well. Extreme filtering can negatively impact received signals. **As the** **G4A17** **noise reduction control level in a receiver is increased, received signals may become distorted.**

G7C11 Software Defined Radio (SDR): **SDR is a radio in which most major signal processing functions are performed by software.** Although various configurations are possible, an SDR receiver may use an analog heterodyning front end and subsequently digitize (sample) lower frequency mixing products for software processing of all signals via a high performance com-

4.3 Signal Processing

Figure 4.23: The ICOM IC-7300 is an example of the new generation of RF direct-sampling transceivers leveraging SDR technology. RF signals are converted directly to digital data and processed with software modules, providing a broad range of filtering, control, and display capabilities. Here, the spectrum scope exhibits several received signals in a waterfall display that can also tune the transceiver using touch-screen control.

puter. More modern SDRs now directly sample the RF signals, immediately converting them to digital data for all downstream processing. RF spectrum display, signal analysis, filtering, selectivity, and other signal processing capabilities of the SDR are impressive. The SDR leverages the power of a computer to perform a ton of DSP. Let's examine some additional SDRs characteristics.

I and Q Signals: Instead of a signal of a singular phase relationship like that modulated or demodulated by conventional analog transceivers, SDR uses two different versions of a signal to mathematically affect modulation and demodulation. One signal version is designated I for "in phase." The other is designated Q for "quadrature," meaning that the sinusoidal signal is 90 degrees different in phase from the I signal (one-quarter of the 360-degree sine wave). **The phase difference between the I and Q signals that SDR equipment uses for modulation and demodulation is 90 degrees.** In accordance with some very cool mathematical principles, a signal of any modulation can be created from, or decomposed into, the two amplitude-modulated I and Q signals. **The advantage of using I and Q signals in software defined radios is that all types of modulation can be created with appropriate processing.** While it isn't necessary to comprehend the complex vector math behind SDR processing to be a competent General Class ham, recognize that both the modulation and demodulation enacted by the SDR is a process of mathematical synthesis or decomposition using signals of differing phases. See Figure 4.24.

G7C09

G7C10

DDS: SDR and other types of transceivers may **apply a *Direct Digital Synthesizer* (DDS) to serve as a high-stability variable frequency oscillator in a transceiver.** The DDS stable digital clocking reference coupled with a numerically controlled oscillator and DAC can generate accurate and stable RF waveforms. The DDS provides great agility for variable frequency signal production under digital control. **An advantage of a DDS is variable frequency with the stability of a crystal oscillator** – the signals produced are typically rock solid and very clean, with almost no noise artifacts. This way, signals for modulation processing and subsequent transmission can be synthesized by the SDR.

Intermodulation: Something of a leftover topic in signal processing, intermodulation is an undesirable occurrence in radio. It results in the production of spurious signals or sidebands that increase signal bandwidth beyond normal ranges and may cause interference to adjacent communications signals.

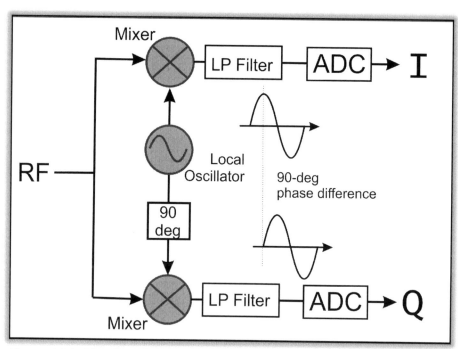

Figure 4.24: The digital sampling of In Phase (I) and Quadrature (Q) RF signals. The two signals are placed 90-degrees out of phase with one another by shifting the LO frequency to one received signal by 90 degrees. The low-pass filter in each path eliminates undesired mixing products, and DSP is affected using the I & Q sampled signal data obtained via ADC.

4.3 Signal Processing

Intermodulation combines two signals in a non-linear circuit or connection to produce unwanted spurious outputs. Just as with intentional signal mixing like that described in Section 4.1, intermodulation produces sum and difference products of combined signals that may include harmonic multiples of the frequencies involved. A non-linear response in an RF system, such as a receiver, results in harmonic signal products. The harmonic multiples and other signals combine in various ways to produce a slew of sum and difference products. Well-designed linear circuits and effective filters help to minimize the occurrence and effects of intermodulation in most modern transceivers.

Intermodulation may create apparent signals where none truly exist! For example, a NOAA weather transmitter on 162.425 MHz could intermodulate with a fire service signal on 154.60 MHz. The second harmonic of 154.60 MHz is 309.20 MHz which mixes with 162.425 MHz to create an intermodulation product of 146.775 MHz (difference product). This intermodulation occurs only in the front end circuitry of the receiver, and a signal is processed at 146.775 MHz through the rest of the receiver, even though no true signal was received on the antenna at that frequency.

A whole world's worth of signal processing methods, components, devices, and configuration choices exist on the market! It can be overwhelming and confusing. But most modern HF-capable transceivers are marketed with good features and ready-to-operate configurations, so you can get started without a lot of anxiety over the vastness of the signal processing universe.

Start with a basic rig, learn its inherent signal processing features, try them out, and then grow your shack as you learn more and as your needs and interests drive you. Given the explosion in Software Defined Radio in recent years, it is very likely that you'll eventually find an SDR HF rig that provides all of the signal processing capabilities you could ever want.

Go receive the passband of questions on signal processing, avoid any notch filtering of topics in the passband, and perform your own internal processing necessary to demodulate these signals into intelligible comprehension!

HamRadioSchool.com/general_media

Waterton Amateur Radio Society, NØLM

5.0 Antennas

> *I'm the antenna*
> *Catching vibration*
> *You're the transmitter*
> *Give information!*   - Kraftwerk, Antenna

I am convinced that almost one half of the people who get involved in ham radio were drawn to it by antennas. Really. Antennas gleam and radiate and fascinate, and they readily facilitate rewarding hands-on projects for even the beginner. Of course, a well-implemented antenna system that both *catches and dispatches RF vibration* is critical to the success of your station, too.

We will begin our climb into antennas with some review of basic concepts and definitions from Technician material. Section 5.1 will elaborate on the basics with some antenna theory and principles that have big operational impacts, especially for work on the HF bands. Section 5.2 is all about feedlines, connectors, and SWR, and getting them all to agree with one another in *giving information* to the antenna. Lastly, we'll take a look at a variety of directional antennas in Section 5.3 with particular focus on the popular Yagi design.

Gather up your copper wire and aluminum tubing, your coax and connectors, your analyzer and tuner... Let's catch some vibration!

Review Definitions and Concepts: Just in case your brain is a little rusty from your Technician License studies, let's refresh on a few key definitions and concepts about antennas, and perhaps a few new concepts. These will come in handy in the forward sections.

Impedance: The opposition to the flow of alternating current in an electric circuit. Impedance matching is very important in an antenna system to achieve high performance. Optimally, impedance should match from the transceiver to the feedline, connectors, and the antenna feed point. Impedance mismatches cause power reflections back toward the transmitter and drive up SWR... and usually that's undesirable.

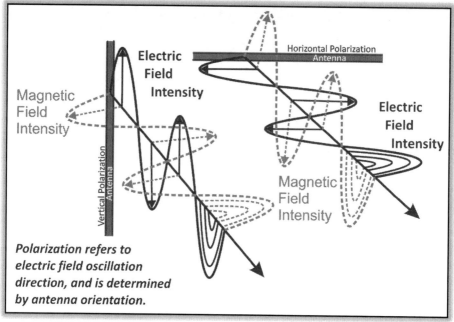

Figure 5.0a: Vertically and horizontally polarized RF signals.

Feed Point: The position at which the feedline connects to the antenna. Optimally, feed point impedance should be matched with the feedline, and feed point impedance is the ratio of RF voltage to current at the feed point.

Element: The components of an antenna that radiate and receive radio frequencies. The *driven element* is an element directly connected to the feedline. *Passive* or *parasitic* elements are not connected to the feedline, but they will interact with the driven element to help shape the antenna's radiating and receiving pattern.

Polarization: The orientation of the electric field oscillations radiated from an antenna, as determined by the orientation of the antenna elements. *Horizontal polarization* results from horizontally arranged elements, resulting in electric field oscillations that are parallel with the surface of the earth. *Vertical polarization* results from vertically arranged elements, resulting in electric field oscillations that are perpendicular to the surface of the earth.

Radiation Pattern: A graphical depiction of the relative strength of emitted signals from an antenna by direction. Two pattern graphs are typical: 1) *Elevation Pattern* – a side viewpoint of the antenna pattern, as if you are standing on earth some distance from the antenna. The elevation pattern shows the relative strengths of signals as radiated at angles above the horizon, or in the vertical.

2) *Azimuthal Pattern* – a viewpoint from directly above the antenna, looking down onto its horizontal signal pattern.

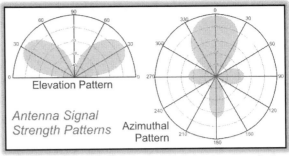

Figure 5.0b: Antenna elevation and azimuthal signal strength pattern examples.

Isotropic Antenna: An antenna that radiates equally in all directions. The radiation pattern would appear as a sphere around the antenna indicating equal vertical and horizontal signal strength in every direction. The isotropic antenna is a theoretical model for comparisons.

Omnidirectional Antenna: An antenna that radiates equally in horizontal radial directions. The azimuthal pattern will appear circular.

Directional Antenna: An antenna that radiates more strongly in one (or more) direction. The azimuthal pattern will usually contain *lobes* of signal strength to indicate stronger signals in the antenna's pointing direction.

Antenna Gain: The increase in signal strength for the antenna's pointing direction as compared to a reference antenna such as the isotropic model or an ideal dipole antenna. The unit of gain is the decibel (dB). **Antenna gain compared to the isotropic model is referred to as *dBi*, while the comparison with a dipole is referred to as *dbd*. Gain figures in dBi are 2.15 dB higher than dBd gain figures** since a dipole exhibits 2.15 dB of gain over the isotropic model.

Antenna Analyzer: A device connected to an antenna-feedline system to measure SWR or impedance across bands and frequencies. The analyzer generates its own signals and no connection to a transceiver is made.

SWR Meter / Directional Wattmeter: A device inserted in the feedline between the transmitter and antenna to measure the power in both directions for determination of standing wave ratio (SWR). The SWR meter typically displays SWR directly, while the directional wattmeter requires dual measurements (one in each direction of the feedline) and a manual computation of SWR. (See Figure 5.0c SWR meter, next page.)

Antenna Tuner / Transmatch: A device that presents a matching impedance (usually 50 ohms) to the transceiver for a feedline and antenna system that does not have a matching impedance. The impedance of the antenna system is not altered, but only that presented to the transceiver.

Field Strength Meter: A device that measures relative strength of received RF signals at a distance from the antenna. A field strength meter is useful for measuring the radiation pattern of an antenna.

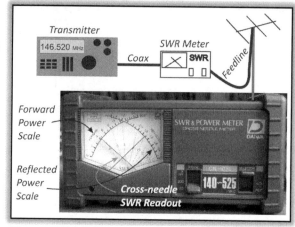

Figure 5.0c: SWR meter feedline insertion and cross-needle readout example meter.

Feedline Loss: Any feedline, such as coaxial cable or twin lead wire, will attenuate the signal directed through it, dissipating some of the energy as heat. Generally, feedline loss will increase with increasing operating frequency. Different types of feedlines and coaxial cable will exhibit different loss characteristics due to variations in materials and physical features.

Antenna Tradeoffs: There is no perfect antenna; every antenna represents tradeoffs among performance, design, convenience, environment, arrangement, materials, and other factors. A compelling reason to understand antenna theory and practice is to accurately judge your station situation and the related antenna tradeoffs for the creation of a well performing antenna system that fits your communications goals.

Radiating EM: Thanks to some basic laws of physics, an electromagnetic wave is emitted from any electric charge that is accelerated through space. An electron with a negative charge, or a positively charged ion, may be accelerated by applying a voltage. As electrons are accelerated back-and-forth in a conductor by an AC voltage, each radiates a tiny EM wave. The frequency of the EM wave is determined by the frequency of alternating current accelerations. Amass a gazillion charged particles all zipping back and forth at RF rates in perpetual acceleration along a wire and you have an antenna emitting an RF signal.

With that little review out of the way we can now consider some General Class antenna theory and principles!

5.1 Antennas: Theory & Principles

> **"** *In theory there is no difference between theory and practice. In practice there is.*
> *– Yogi Berra*

With your General Class license and much greater access to the HF bands, you will surely want to erect antennas for some of those bands. Of course, the HF band wavelengths are quite long compared to the VHF and UHF wavelengths you have been most accustomed to as a Technician Class operator, and so the HF antenna elements are necessarily much longer, too. This section will help you scheme on some simple antennas with which you can readily begin making some of those long wavelength signals. You really do not need a giant, complex antenna farm to get started on the HF bands.

First, we will consider a couple of basic antenna types in discussing some fundamental theory and principles of antennas: The half-wave dipole and the ¼ wave vertical antenna. Then we will briefly explore some more specialized antennas and their unique characteristics. At no point in this section will we challenge the *theory of practice*, but we will certainly engage in the *practice of theory*.

Half-Wave Dipole: Perhaps the most popularly used HF antenna, the half-wave dipole, is also one of the simplest. For HF communications the dipole is usually constructed from wire, so it is inexpensive, but it offers quite good performance when properly configured. The half-wave dipole is also the foundation for many more complex antenna designs, so it pays to understand the workings of this basic radiator.

Radiation Pattern: The dipole's basic electrical configuration and radiating pattern are depicted in Figure 5.1. The feed point is at the center of two wires of equal length extending in opposite directions. The dipole's two halves are each approximately ¼ wavelength long for the frequency of operation. **The radiation pattern of a dipole antenna in free space** (far away from the ground or any conductors) **in the plane of the conductor is a figure-eight at right angles to the antenna.** The strongest signals radiate broadside to the antenna wire axis and the weakest signals radiate out the ends of the wire axis. When installed about ½ wavelength high and parallel to

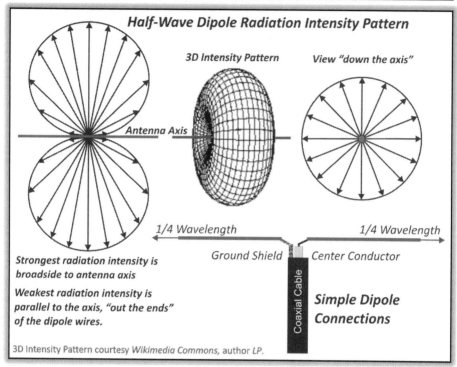

Figure 5.1: Radiation pattern of a dipole antenna in free space.

the earth (horizontally polarized), the elevation pattern of a half-wave dipole tends to direct strong signals low to the horizon, promoting long distance ionospheric skip. We will examine this phenomenon more in a moment.

Length Calculation: Although covered in your Technician Class studies, computing the length of a half-wave dipole is even more important for HF operations since this type of antenna is so often deployed by amateurs to operate on those lower frequency bands. The approximate length in feet of a wire half-wave dipole may be computed as:

Length (ft) = 468 ÷ frequency (MHz)

G9B10 For example, suppose you wish to construct a 1/2 wave dipole antenna for 14.250 MHz. What is the approximate total length?

Length (ft) = 468 ÷ 14.250 MHz = 33 feet

G9B11 Just to thrash the deceased equine: **What is the approximate length for a 1/2 wave dipole antenna cut for 3.550 MHz?**

Length (ft) = 468 ÷ 3.550 MHz = 132 feet

This formula will result in an *approximate* total dipole length, keeping in mind that each half segment of the antenna will be one-half of this length. You might notice that this estimated total length is a little shorter than the half-wavelength of the frequencies denoted. For instance, calculating the total wavelength for 14.250 MHz yields 21.05 meters [300 ÷ 14.250 = 21.05], or about 69 feet. One half of 69 feet (for one half wavelength) is 34.5 feet, so the half-wavelength dipole total length of 32 feet indicated by our construction formula is a little shy of the actual RF half wavelength values. A practical half-wave wire antenna will usually be roughly 5% shorter than the length of the actual half RF wave. Why?

The ends of the antenna wire (along with insulators and/or wire loops used to anchor them) add a little capacitance to the antenna circuit. As we will explore a bit later, adding capacitance to an antenna (or any circuit) has the effect of lowering its resonant frequency. This is called *end effect*. So, the wavelength for the frequency of resonance of the antenna will be longer (lower frequency) than the physical antenna length. The added capacitance increases with thicker antenna wire or radiating elements, so antennas with thicker elements will (within extreme limits) require shorter elements for a given target resonant frequency. In almost all cases the antenna will require trimming of the length to obtain the best matched feed point impedance for the desired operating frequency. [*See this HamRadioSchool.com web site article for a review of trimming and SWR curves: Trimming a Dipole Antenna.*]

Feed Point Impedance: Consistent with Ohm's Law, electrical impedance may be computed as the ratio of voltage (E) to current (I) in a circuit, including an antenna circuit. For a half-wave dipole cut to length for its driving frequency, the voltage and current along the antenna wire will ideally look like Figure 5.2 on the next page.

Notice that the voltage is of greatest magnitude (either positive or negative in value) at the ends of the antenna's length, and a minimum (but not zero) at the center feed point position. The current, however, is greatest in the center and drops to zero at the ends. Let's consider a few things about this voltage/current scenario:

- The impedance will be lowest at the center (E/I is the smallest value here).
- Typical feed point impedance of a center fed half-wave dipole is about 72 Ω (ohms).
- With each AC cycle the voltage values and the current direction reverses, at the RF frequency.
- As the current of charges surge back and forth across the antenna's

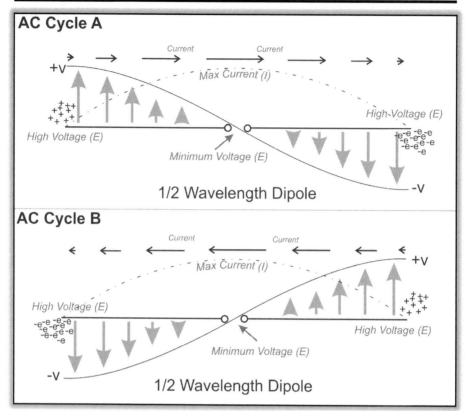

Figure 5.2: Half-wave Dipole Voltage and Current Relationship.

length, there is no place for them to go at the end points, so a charge of high voltage piles up on alternating ends each AC cycle.
- With a high voltage and low current near the antenna ends, the impedance (E/I) increases to become very large as compared to the center position impedance.

- **If the feed point location were moved from the center toward an end, the feed point impedance would steadily increase** with distance away from the center.

Height Above Ground Impedance Effects: Many half-wave dipole antennas will be fed with coaxial cable of 50 Ω or 75 Ω impedance. The center feed point impedance of the free space dipole is about 72 Ω, which results in a 1.44 SWR with a 50 Ω feedline, so not a bad match. However, dipoles in free space don't really exist and the antenna's impedance will be affected by objects in the environment and especially by that giant conductor called *the earth*.

5.1 Theory & Principles

The ground affects the antenna's characteristic impedance because it is a conductor, although sometimes a very poor one. The ground's conductance creates an inverse electrical image of the antenna. If the antenna and the image are close enough to one another they will interact. Since the image is like a mirror reversal of the real antenna, the interaction affect is a canceling or *shorting* one. The net result is that the center feed point impedance will vary with height above the ground.

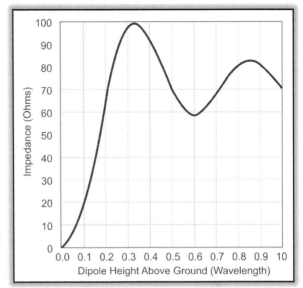

Figure 5.3: Horizontal dipole approximate feed point impedance for height above ground.

As a half-wavelength dipole is lowered from ¼ wave above the ground the feed-point impedance steadily decreases and will reach zero at ground level. At greater heights the impedance increases and decreases in an oscillatory manner above and below its free space value, ultimately becoming stable at several wavelengths above ground level, as in Figure 5.3. The feed point impedance tends to be approximately the free space value at ½ wave and at one wave above ground level. Many wire dipoles are erected to be about ½ wavelength or slightly higher above the ground in order to achieve a good feed point impedance match, but also to achieve low elevation pattern angles of radiation.

Height Above Ground Radiation Pattern Effects: The nice *fat donut* pattern of the free space dipole changes significantly when the dipole is within a few wavelengths of the ground. The antenna's radiation is reflected by the ground, so the pattern of signal strength at a distance from the antenna is a combination of the radiating element's emissions and those emissions reflected from the ground. But the path distance of a directly radiated signal and that of a ground-reflected signal are somewhat different, so the propagation time to any given location will also vary somewhat for the different waves. As a result the waves may add together *in phase* with one another (wave crests and troughs lined up to make a stronger signal), or they may cancel one another *out of phase* (wave crests and troughs exactly opposite one another, nulling the signal strength), or they may interact with some intermediate phase alignment and various intermediate signal strengths.

The upshot of this wave combining effect is that a half-wave dipole's elevation pattern exhibits *lobes* and *nulls* – strong signals at some angles of elevation and weak or non-existent signals at other elevation angles – that vary with the antenna's height above ground. Some typical elevation patterns for a dipole are shown in Figure 5.4.

Notice that when the antenna is ½ and 1 wavelength above the ground that most of the lobes of high signal strength are directed at relatively low angles. This will be most effective for long distance skip propagation, helping to keep take-off angles below the critical angle and affecting the longest distance for a single ionospheric skip. (See Chapter 3, *Propagation*.) One-half wavelength high dipoles are popular for long distance contacts.

When the dipole is less than ½ wavelength above the ground its azimuthal pattern is almost omnidirectional and a great amount of energy is also directed vertically rather than horizontally, as indicated by the elevation pattern. If the desire is for long distance skip this vertically directed energy is essentially wasted since these high take-off angle may be above the critical angle for the frequency used, and even if they are returned to earth the skip distance will be short. If the ionosphere will reflect a dipole's near-vertically radiated signals (usually 40m band or lower), such a low-to-the-ground antenna can be used for shorter range communications as an *NVIS antenna*.

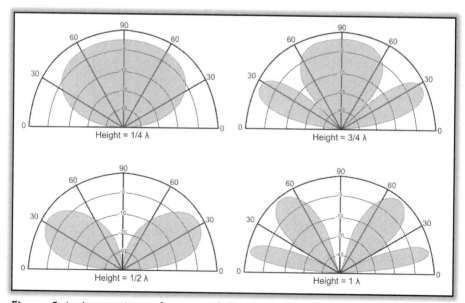

Figure 5.4: Approximate horizontal dipole radiation elevation patterns (gray) for various heights above ground.

5.1 Theory & Principles

NVIS: Near Vertical Incidence Sky wave. **A horizontal dipole for 40-meters placed between 1/10 and 1/4 wavelength above the ground will be most effective as an NVIS antenna for short-skip communications during the day.** Intentionally placing a dipole low to the ground to generate high vertical angle radiation can be advantageous for short distance HF communications of up to a few hundred kilometers. (Because the high incidence angle path through the ionosphere's D layer is relatively short and direct, D layer absorption during daylight hours is less severe than for the low angle paths, and daytime NVIS skip is feasible, particularly during winter months with weakened sunlight and D layer.) NVIS propagation can be very effective during daylight with 40-, 60-, and 80-meters bands.

Dipole Configuration: The simple dipole is usually configured in one of three ways: 1) Flattop, 2) Inverted V, or 3) Sloper. Figure 5.5 illustrates these three typical arrangements. **The inverted V** configuration is perhaps the most common since it **requires only a single central support** and less horizontal space to erect. The peak gain of the flattop is generally slightly more than the inverted V, but the downward sloping elements of the inverted V will provide greater radiation strength in the two directions off the ends of the flattop's axis, thereby improving the omnidirectional characteristics. The sloper configuration provides a similar omnidirectional advantage. More compromises!

In any configuration the best results will be obtained with the feedline running away at a right angle to the flattop or sloper, and directly down between the sloping elements of the inverted V. Feedpoint impedance can be affected by having the feedline running close to, or parallel with, the radiating elements.

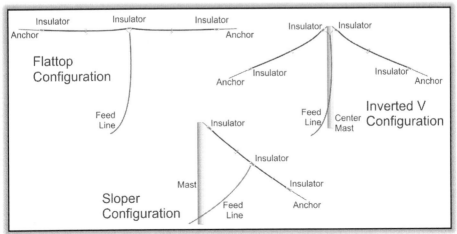

Figure 5.5: Three common dipole configurations.

The dipole is a terrific option for those seeking an inexpensive and simple way to get started on the HF bands. Many hams string them up in trees, using a high tree center support for an inverted V configuration, or pulling just one end high into a sloper. A flattop may be configured using two trees, pulling both ends up and allowing the feedline to dangle in the middle or run down a third, centered bark-covered mast. Of course, if you have the luxury of erecting dead masts such as fiberglass or aluminum poles, that works too!

Variations on the simple, single-band dipole are common for multi-band operations. We will come back to the beloved dipole shortly to examine these modifications on its basic theme, but for now let's chop that dipole in half and hold a mirror up to one end.

¼-Wave Vertical Antenna (Ground Plane Antenna): Another very popular HF antenna arrangement is the ¼-wave vertical antenna, usually coupled with a *ground plane*. This antenna may be considered to be one half of a dipole in which the other half is represented by a mirror electric image resulting from the ground plane, as in Figure 5.6. The real portion of the element is ¼ wavelength long, typically mounted above a ground plane conductive material. The feed point is where the real element meets the ground plane. The voltage-current dynamics for the ¼-wave ground plane antenna are similar to that of the dipole, with the ¼-wave voltage signal being minimum at the feed point and maximum at the element end. Of course, the orientation of the element is usually vertical rather than horizontal, so this antenna is often referred to simply as a "vertical."

Ground Plane: The ground plane is simply a conductor arranged at an angle to the vertical element. The ground plane may be a solid metal surface, a screen, or an array of *radials*. Ground planes are commonly comprised of radial elements extending from

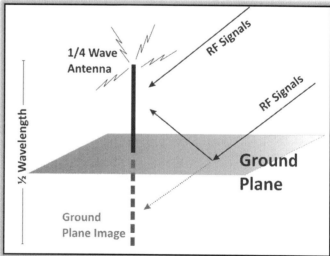

Figure 5.6: ¼-Wave Vertical Antenna with ground plane.

the base of the vertical element, and they may be perpendicular to the vertical or sloped downward from the vertical. **Verticals** designed for the low frequencies of the HF bands **are often ground-mounted with radial wires distributed along the surface or buried a few inches below the ground.**

Ground planes for HF verticals may be comprised of copper wire radials numbering from only a few to many dozens to over 200! Generally, the ground plane image is enhanced with greater numbers of radials, essentially allowing more ground current to flow in the antenna. However, the performance enhancement of more radials is coupled with their length: Greater numbers of radials may be made longer for greater current flow and enhanced antenna performance, while fewer radials do not benefit from great lengths. A rough guideline is to make ground radials about the same length as the height of the ¼-wave antenna, but be aware that actual performance will vary somewhat depending upon the earth's conductivity in your area and other factors, including the frequency band used. For multi-band verticals it is prudent to install ¼-wave radial lengths for the lowest band on which you wish to operate.

Figure 5.7: Laying ground radials just under the surface for a flag pole ¼-wave HF multi-band.

Feed Point Impedance: The feed point impedance of the ¼-wavelength vertical with a horizontal ground plane is about one-half that of the dipole, near 35 Ω. However, the orientation of the ground plane affects the feed point impedance. As the ground plane radials are changed from horizontal to downward sloping the feed point impedance increases. Since the most commonly used feedlines have impedance of 50Ω, **sloping the radial downward is a common way of adjusting the feed point impedance of a quarter wave ground-plane vertical antenna to be approximately 50 ohms.** If you were to continue to lower the ground plane radials' angles the impedance would continue to increase until the radials merged and physically formed the other half of a dipole configuration! At that point the impedance should, in theory, reach about 72 Ω. (See Figure 5.8.) In practice it may not be feasible to slope an HF antenna's radials at all, but the mild impedance mismatch of a perpendicular ground plane usually does not have a significant performance impact.

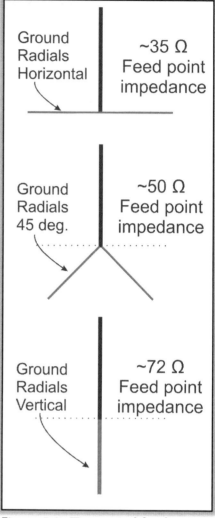

Figure 5.8: Theoretical feed point impedance changes with ground radial angles to the vertical. Most large verticals will have horizontal radials.

Length Calculation: If you can remember the calculation for the length of a half-wave dipole, you can simply divide by 2 to get the approximate length of the ¼-wave vertical. Of course, another way of viewing the calculation is to halve the 468 value used for dipole length calculations in units of feet to 234 and proceed identically to the dipole computation, as follows:

Length (ft) = 234 ÷ frequency (MHz)

For example, what is the approximate length for a ¼-wave vertical antenna cut for 28.5 MHz?

Length (ft) = 234 ÷ 28.5 MHz = 8 feet

5.1 Theory & Principles

As with the half-wave dipole, expect that some trimming will be required to get the lowest SWR.

Radiation Pattern: The vertical antenna radiates strongest broadside to its element, much like the dipole. **The radiation pattern of a quarter-wave, ground-plane vertical antenna is best described as omnidirectional in azimuth.** Thus, no worries about weak signals along the axis of the antenna and missing out on contacts in those directions. The vertical is often preferred for long distance skip contacts due to the low takeoff angles it can generate. However, like the horizontal dipole, the vertical antenna does suffer from ground reflection losses and generally these are somewhat greater than the horizontal antenna. As such, **an advantage of the horizontally polarized dipole as compared to the vertically polarized HF antenna is lower ground reflection losses.**

The vertical antenna can be a good option for getting started on the HF bands for many hams. They are simple and relatively easy to install. Particularly for the higher HF bands from 10m to 20m, portable or temporary verticals are feasible that can be erected and taken down in a matter of minutes for good HF operations in a covenant restricted area or for the camp site. See *HamRadioSchool.com* features and learning media for more ideas and details.

Multiband and Wide Band Antennas: A simple antenna design tends to work well on a single RF band. You can trim a half-wave dipole or a ¼ wave vertical to length for a frequency and in most cases the feed point impedance will be matched well enough and the related SWR will remain sufficiently low across a range of frequencies on the band. A common metric is the bandwidth for which the antenna system provides a 2:1 SWR or lower. (See SWR in Section 5.3 and in the *HamRadioSchool.com Technician License Course*, Section 7.2.) However, many simple dipoles or verticals may not be well matched across all of a single wide band such as 10m, much less across multiple bands without an antenna tuner to provide matching impedance at the transceiver.

Some antennas are designed to be *wide band* antennas, usable across a very wide bandwidth of spectrum including more than one band. Other antennas are designed to use more complex designs or electrical techniques to achieve good impedance matches on multiple bands. As you may already suspect there are tradeoffs with wideband and multiband antennas, but the convenience of operating on multiple bands via a single feedline and a single antenna is a most desirable characteristic for which to trade!

Random Wire: One of the simplest multiband antennas is the *random wire*, and it's just what the name implies: A random length of wire erected or configured in any way feasible and compatible with the environmental constraints. For example, I have seen a random wire run all around the interior perimeter of an apartment near the ceiling, in and out of bedrooms and living area, and even one end draped off the balcony. The random wire can typically be used on several bands and it does not pretend to be resonant on any particular one of them. So, what's the catch? What are the tradeoffs?

Tradeoffs: A random wire can be directly connected to the transmitter, but a significant impedance mismatch is likely. The random wire is not resonant and feedpoint impedance mismatch is almost guaranteed. So, a high quality antenna tuner is usually a *must*. Because of the unusual physical configuration that some random wire arrangements may assume, the lobes and nulls of the transmitting patterns are usually unpredictable and chaotic. **A major league disadvantage of the directly fed random wire antenna is that you may experience RF burns when touching metal objects in your station!** Unless you can affect a very good RF ground for the antenna it may induce significant RF currents in your shack that can give you a nasty bite. Still, if you just take what you get with lobes and nulls, if you can avoid the RF burn hazard, and if your antenna tuner can handle the impedance on a couple of bands or more, you can actually get some interesting and good performance with the random wire.

Trap Antennas: A multiband antenna may be created using traps placed in the antenna elements. A trap is a simple parallel circuit placed in-line with a radiating element, as depicted in Figure 5.9. **The primary purpose of antenna traps is to permit multiband operation.** Notice that the trap antenna has radiating element segments between the two traps and additional segments outside of the two traps.

The parallel circuits added into the antenna element are LC circuits. We will discuss LC circuits more in Chapter 6 *Hamtronics*, but you should recall from your Technician Class studies that an LC circuit has both inductance (L), usually from an inductor component, and capacitance (C), usually from a capacitor element. An LC circuit will *resonate* with an AC frequency, and the specific frequency of resonance is determined by the values of inductance and capacitance selected for the circuit. When in resonance the electrical energy is very efficiently traded back and forth between the inductor and capacitor in alternating cycles, with the inductor temporarily storing energy in a magnetic field and the capacitor storing it in an electric field.

High Band Function: When the traps are resonant they present very high impedance and do not allow current flow beyond them into the outer segments of the radiating element. In essence the traps become insulators when at resonance, electrically terminating the radiating element. With proper selection of L and C values, the trap may be made to resonate at the frequencies of a relatively high RF band for which the inner segment of the antenna is trimmed. For instance, the dipole length between the traps may be about 16 feet for 10 meter band operation (28 MHz) and the LC components would be selected for the trap to resonate at about 28 MHz.

Low Band Function: However, when AC frequencies much lower than the trap's resonant frequency are fed to the antenna the trap behaves differently. The trap is not resonant and no longer acts as an insulator. The capacitors will not pass the lower frequencies, but the inductors will, allowing the full length of the radiating element to be energized by the lower frequency. Fortunately, a lower frequency signal needs a longer radiating element to remain a half-wave antenna. So, if our example antenna were fed with a 20 meter band (14 MHz) signal, the traps allow the outer segments of the radiating element to be added to the antenna length and the overall antenna length is properly trimmed for 20m band operation.

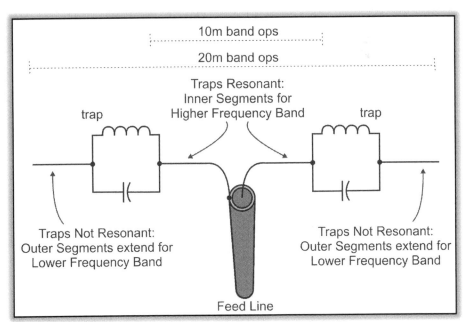

Figure 5.9: Trap dipole antenna configuration.

Voilà! Two bands with one trap antenna! By including two traps on each side of the dipole an effective tri-band antenna for 10m, 15m, and 20m bands may be created. Three bands with one antenna! This seems like a terrific technique to use, right? So, what are the tradeoffs?

Tradeoffs: You should understand that the inductor in the trap has the effect of electrically lengthening the antenna. With the inductor the antenna will trim to a shorter length for the desired operating band than an antenna without a trap or other inductive *loading coil*. A physically shortened antenna will have somewhat reduced efficiency – it will not transmit as well as a physically full length antenna, and some receive signal loss will be imposed by the traps. Further, since the antenna is designed to operate on multiple bands it may also strongly radiate any undesirable, out of band harmonic frequencies produced by your station. Harmonics are frequency multiples of the fundamental, or desired frequency. For instance, transmissions in the 40m band (7 MHz) may produce 3rd harmonics on the 15m band (21 MHz), as the two bands' frequencies are harmonically related. If your multiband antenna is designed for both 15m and 40m bands, you might radiate harmonics on the 15m band inadvertently when transmitting a 40m band signal. Similar harmonic relationships exist among other bands as well. While most modern transceivers will have good harmonic filters to avoid this as a significant issue, **the multiband antenna has the disadvantage of poor harmonic rejection.**

Fan Dipole: A popular multiband variation on the dipole is the *fan dipole* (also called multi-element or parallel wire dipole). A fan dipole has multiple half-wave dipoles of different lengths, each trimmed for operation on a different band and all fed from a single feedline as depicted in Figure 5.10. The various dipole wires are separated from one another using insulating spreaders or stand-offs. As compared to the trap dipole the fan dipole will usually

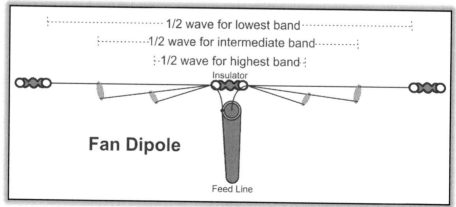

Figure 5.10: Typical fan dipole antenna configuration.

5.1 Theory & Principles

be slightly more efficient. Fan dipoles are generally more easily constructed than the trap antenna, but it is tedious and sometimes impossible to trim all elements for a low SWR value due to the electrical interactions among the multiple parallel dipole elements. As a result, some bands may necessarily be operated with an SWR higher than others, and an antenna tuner is usually necessary. The interaction among elements can be reduced by placing some at right angles to others and also by placing some in a flattop configuration with others in an inverted V configuration. Fan dipoles of three or four separate half-wave dipoles are common. The fan dipole is often a good choice for a beginning HF antenna, offering the advantages of a single feedline, good multi-band operation, and a low visual profile.

Loop Antennas: A loop antenna is one in which the conductive element is curved or bent such that the two ends are close to one another or connected into a true loop. Loop antennas are popular with hams who enjoy do-it-yourself projects, since they tend to be relatively easy to construct. Many different loop designs have been conceived: large and small, vertical and horizontal, circular, square (quad), triangular (delta), and more. Let's briefly examine two examples, the VHF/UHF "halo" and a large HF horizontal wire loop.

Halo Antenna: Take a half-wave dipole for 2-meter band and curve the element ends around in a circle until they nearly meet. Feed it off-center with a gamma match (see Section 5.2). You now have a simple halo antenna. **The VHF/UHF halo antenna's maximum radiation is omnidirectional in the plane of the halo.** A horizontally oriented halo will produce horizontally polarized signals with very little vertical polarization component, so it is not effective for most FM VHF/UHF simplex and repeater operations. However, the halo can be a good antenna solution for SSB operations on the VHF/UHF bands where horizontal polarization is desired. The compact footprint of the halo makes it an attractive option for mobile SSB communications on the VHF/UHF bands.

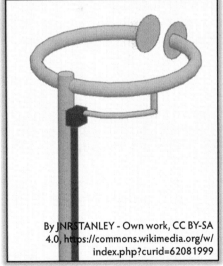

By JNRSTANLEY - Own work, CC BY-SA 4.0, https://commons.wikimedia.org/w/index.php?curid=62081999

Figure 5.11: The basic halo antenna configuration with gamma match. The end capacitive tuning plates are not included in many designs.

HF Horizontal Wire Loop: Easily constructed with bare wire, the large horizontal loop is a popular HF antenna solution, especially for low HF bands requiring a sizeable antenna conductor. Multi-band operation is feasible with horizontal loops using a wire that is one wavelength or more in length at the lowest desired operating frequency, and an antenna tuner for impedance matching. Such antennas should be fed with open wire, not coaxial cable.

As an example, a square HF horizontal loop for the 80-meter band is approximately 287 feet around, with each side at about 72 feet. This antenna could be operated on the 40-meter, 20-meter, or higher bands as a multi-wavelength antenna, given a sufficient impedance matching unit. At these higher frequencies the radiating pattern of the loop will produce lower angle radiation than for the 80-meter band operations. **The combined vertical and horizontal polarization pattern of a multi-wavelength, horizontal loop antenna is virtually omnidirectional with a lower peak vertical radiation angle than a dipole.** These lower angles of propagation achieved with multi-wavelength operation promote long-distance skywave communications with the horizontal loop.

Beverage Antenna: Used only for receiving signals. **The Beverage antenna** (named for its inventor, Harold Beverage) is a very long and low **directional receiving antenna for low HF bands** of 40m and below. The Beverage is a very inefficient radiator, having high losses compared to other types of antennas, and so is not used for transmitting.

Usually erected less than 20 feet above ground level, the Beverage is a long wire, usually between 1 and 4 wavelengths long, with a resistor terminating one end and the feedpoint on the opposite end. It receives directionally in the orientation of the terminated end and is excellent at noise rejection, hence its utility as a receiving antenna in spite of its poor efficiency or gain. This is a *traveling wave antenna,* meaning that it receives well only when the RF wave is aligned with the axis of the wire (the inverse of a dipole's broadside signal preference). Signals arriving from other directions do not create significant voltages on the wire and this reduces noise and reception in all but the direction of the wire's length. Because of its length and unique receiving dynamic it may be used across several low bands. Note that a one wavelength Beverage for the 160m band is over 500 feet long!

5.1 Theory & Principles

Mobile HF Antennas: In recent years amateur transceiver manufacturers have marketed very compact "all mode, all band" transceivers that make HF installation in vehicles relatively painless. One of the chief remaining challenges in taking the low frequencies on the road is the antenna. You can't readily mount a full length HF antenna on a vehicle. As such, techniques are used to electrically trick a shortened antenna into believing it is a full-sized radiator. **The** (relatively poor) **efficiency of the electrically short antenna most limits an HF mobile installation.**

G4E05

Again, antenna compromises are necessary. Shortened mobile antennas are very popular and use *loading techniques* to electrically lengthen the antenna in a manner similar to that described for trap antennas in this section. While loading works to achieve feed point impedance matching with very short antennas (relative to the operating wavelength), **one disadvantage of using a shortened mobile antenna as opposed to a full size antenna is that the operating bandwidth may be very limited.** That is, the range of frequencies for which acceptable impedance match is achieved can be extremely narrow. But there are ways of getting around that common problem, too!

G4E06

Loading Techniques: In order that a shortened antenna present an acceptable feedpoint impedance it must be made to resonate on the desired frequency using electrical methods. Inserting an inductive component in the antenna element is one method of making the antenna seem longer electrically than it is physically. Further, as with a simple tuned circuit, adding a capacitive element can further help achieve resonance of the antenna circuit.

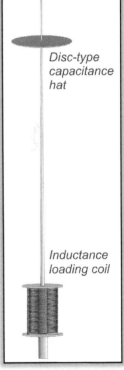

Loading Coil: You have probably seen loading coils on mobile antennas before. A loading coil is a coil of wire or conductor connected in the antenna circuit and commonly positioned at the base of a vertical whip antenna or near the center of the antenna. Again, this inductor makes the antenna seem electrically longer so that resonance can be achieved in a desired frequency range much lower than that provided by the physical length of the antenna alone. Some single band antennas may utilize a loading coil wrapped around all or part of the antenna element and typically sealed onto the vertical with a coating or wrap.

Figure 5.12: Physically shortened antenna with loading coil and capacitance hat.

Tapped Coil: A tapped coil is a loading coil that has a variable *tap point* along the coil that allows the inductance to be varied with operating frequency selected. This technique provides a method for the operator to change the resonant frequency of the antenna by adjusting the number of inductive turns or loops to be included in the antenna circuit. Even though any given adjustment provides a very narrow bandwidth with matching feed point impedance, the frequency of resonance may itself be readily varied by moving the tap point up or down along the coil to alter the inductance loading. In this way a broad band of frequencies may be used, bypassing the extremely narrow bandwidth limitation of the physically shortened antenna. The tapped coil is incorporated into many commercial HF mobile antenna designs, many of which use an SWR meter to help display and select the proper tap position for a chosen frequency of operation, and many implementing automatic tuning circuits to quickly achieve the proper tap position without manual adjustment. The popular "screwdriver" type of mobile antenna takes advantage of a slight variation on the tapped coil concept to tune across a broad bandwidth and operate on multiple bands. **The "screwdriver" mobile antenna varies the base loading inductance to adjust its feedpoint impedance.**

Photo: Paul, AAØK
Hi-Q-Antennas

Figure 5.13: A coil-loaded mobile antenna for the HF bands.

G9D08

G4E01

Capacitance Hat: Typically used in concert with a loading coil, a **capacitance hat** helps to achieve resonant frequency with a shortened antenna. It is another **device to electrically lengthen a physically short antenna.** As noted in the trap antenna discussion, the inductance coil imposes signal loss when it is used to electrically lengthen an antenna. The more turns in a loading coil the greater the loss. By adding a capacitive element to the antenna (the capacitance hat), resonance can be achieved

5.1 Theory & Principles

with fewer inductive turns and with less signal loss. A capacitance hat will usually take the form of a solid disc or a wheel with spokes placed about the vertical antenna element above the loading coil section. The larger the hat, the greater the capacitance, and the less number of inductive turns required to achieve resonance on a selected operating frequency.

Figure 5.14: Corona "balls" come in many forms, usually a simple broadened antenna tip.

Corona: As a mobile antenna moves through the airstream it develops static charge due to dust, moisture, and other statically charged particles in the air. Like the voltages that build up on the ends of the antenna due to RF energy, the static charge builds at the tip of a mobile vertical antenna. When the charge reaches severe voltage levels it can discharge to a ground level voltage like a little bolt of lightning! This *coronal discharge* can be dangerous and the build up of static will deteriorate your antenna's receive performance, inducing static noise on the audio. A common means of reducing these effects is to broaden the tip of the antenna so that the charge is spread out over a larger surface area, thereby alleviating a very high voltage pinpoint charge and reducing the chance of coronal discharge. **A corona ball on an HF antenna will reduce RF voltage discharge from the tip of the antenna while transmitting.** Most corona balls are simple teardrop or spherical add-ons to expand the antenna tip surface area.

[G4E02]

Zap! Mental corona! You now have covered the fundamentals of HF antenna theory, and I can see the little lightning bolts bouncing around inside your head ready to put theory into practice. But we're not done yet. There are more electrifying concepts coming up regarding *directional antennas* that will point most of your radiated signal in one direction. That has some operational advantages! First, trap the questions for this section inside your mind.

HamRadioSchool.com/general_media

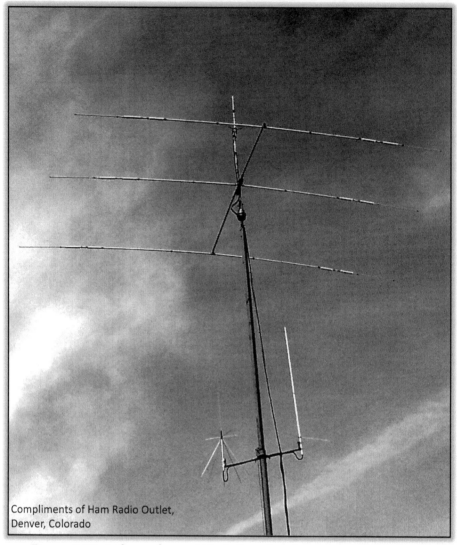

Figure 5.15: A three element Yagi directional antenna for HF bands.

5.2 Directional Antennas

> **" Beam me up Scotty!**
> *– James Tiberius Kirk*
> *(a.k.a. William Shatner)*

"Captain, we're receiving strong starboard interference! And now from port, too! And aft!"

"Shields up! Arm photon torpedoes! Phasers at the ready! Rotate the directional antenna and beam a concentrated RF signal to zero mark two seven zero. Transmit at will! Now! Push to talk!"

Yea, that'll show those pesky interfering Klingon stations. We'll just directionalize our signal.

There's no need to get up in arms over a little RF interference on a busy HF band, and if your station is equipped with a directional, or "beam," antenna, you can help minimize interference by aiming the bulk of your signal energy in a preferred direction. That way your signal will be strongest for only those stations in the preferred direction, and you'll receive signals most strongly from that direction, too. Those port, starboard, and aft interfering stations will fade into insignificance and you won't interfere with their communications either. It's almost like having a ham station cloaking device!

No question about it, Captain: Directional antennas can reduce tensions, avoid interference, improve your station's communications, and generally help promote peace and harmony across the Ham Galaxy. It's time to get your station beamed up.

In this section we will examine beam antennas with a laser focus on the very popular Yagi (Yagi-Uda) design. We'll also note two types of directionals based upon loop antennas, the quad and delta loops, and wrap up with a look at the log periodic wide band directional.

Yagi Antenna: Although originally designed by two Japanese inventors, Shintaro Uda and Hidetsugu Yagi, this antenna is popularly known as simply a *Yagi*.

The Yagi is simple to construct, it provides ample gain or directionality, and it is therefore the most popular directional antenna for hams.

Yagi Structure and Radiation: The Yagi is based on the half-wave dipole. The radiating element (*driven element*) is a dipole arrangement, but other parallel elements are added to it and all mounted along a boom to hold the elements in proper configuration. Figure 5.16 illustrates three typical arrangements of simple Yagi designs, but many others are feasible with different numbers and spacings of elements. As with the half-wave dipole, **the length of the driven element of a Yagi antenna will be approximately ½ wavelength.**

The additional elements that are not connected to the feedline are called *parasitic elements*. The two types of parasitic elements are *reflectors* and *directors*. **Compared to the driven element length, the Yagi reflector is longer and the director is shorter.** When the driven element radiates RF, a nearby parasitic element will receive part of the energy, inducing a current flow in the element. The current flow then produces RF re-radiation of the energy from the parasitic element. The re-radiated RF signal will interact with the signal from the driven element, with waveforms reinforcing or cancelling one another in a similar manner as the ground reflections discussed in Section 5.1 that produce lobes and nulls. With clever arrangement of the parasitic elements relative to the driven element, a radiating pattern can be generated that produces a single large lobe of great signal strength – a directional signal propagation pattern. **The direction of maximum radiated field strength from a directive antenna is called the *main lobe*.** Generally, the main lobe will be more directional and the antenna will exhibit more gain with additional elements on a longer boom, as depicted in Figure 5.16.

Reflector: A Yagi will usually have a single reflector parasitic element positioned on the boom in the direction opposite the main lobe. The simplest Yagi design consists of just two elements, the driven element and a reflector element, as in the left side of Figure 5.16. The reflector will be approximately 5% longer than the driven element and positioned about 0.15 to 0.20 wavelength aft of the driven element. When the reflector element re-radiates its RF energy the waveforms in the direction of the main lobe (forward) will be in phase and reinforce one another, while the waveforms in the opposite (rearward) direction will be out of phase and cancel one another. In this way a main lobe of signal strength is created in the forward direction. **A comparison of the power radiated in the major radiation lobe with that in the opposite direction is called the "front-to-back ratio" of the Yagi.** A simple two-element Yagi provides gain in the main lobe direction of about 5 dBi (comparison with isotropic pattern), or about 3 dBd (comparison with a dipole). Adding more reflectors does

5.2 Directional Antennas

not significantly improve the main lobe strength or front-to-back ratio.

Director: In a three element Yagi (center of Figure 5.16) the parasitic element on the boom forward of the driven element is called the director. The director will be approximately 5% shorter than the driven element, and this shortening helps to shift the re-radiated signal's phase slightly so that it further reinforces forward propagation and boosts main lobe strength. The inclusion of a director increases the front-to-back ratio and main lobe gain. The approximate theoretical forward gain of a three-element, single band Yagi antenna is 9.7 dBi. A Yagi may have multiple directors to increase the antenna's gain further, as illustrated in the right side of Figure 5.16.

Yagi Design Parameters: The basic **Yagi antenna** designs described above **can be adjusted to optimize forward gain, front-to-back ratio, or SWR bandwidth of the antenna,** including:

- **The physical length of the boom (a longer boom increases gain)**
- **The number of elements on the boom (Adding directors increases gain** and front-to-back ratio)
- **The spacing of elements along the boom** (spacing influences gain, front-to-back ratio, and SWR bandwidth.)
- **Diameter of elements (Larger diameter elements increase Yagi bandwidth)**

Additionally, stacked Yagis placed approximately ½ wavelength apart vertically reinforce signals in the horizontal (azimuthal) plane while canceling or nulling signals vertically. **The net advantage of vertically stacking**

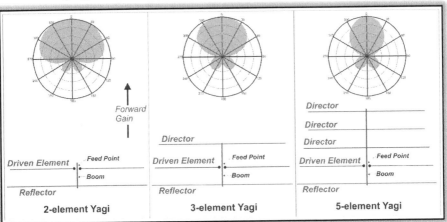

Figure 5.16: Three different Yagi antenna designs and approximate main lobe effects. *(Yagi dimensions not to scale.)*

horizontally polarized Yagi antennas is to narrow the main lobe in elevation pattern, as compared to a single Yagi, and thereby improve forward gain. **Two three-element horizontally polarized Yagi antennas spaced vertically ½ wavelength apart typically increase gain over a single 3-element Yagi by approximately 3 dB.**

Yagi Impedance Matching: The feedpoint impedance of a typical Yagi design is usually much lower than the 50 Ω value to match most common coaxial feedlines. The parasitic elements of the Yagi influence the voltage and current of the driven element dipole and alter the impedance value of the feedpoint. Yagi impedance values under 25 Ω are common and will result in undesirable SWR values of 2:1 or greater. Usually some type of impedance matching technique is required for the Yagi to get a matching impedance closer to 50 Ω.

While multiple techniques are feasible, the gamma match is very common on Yagis for the purpose of matching the relatively low feedpoint impedance to 50 Ω. As depicted in Figure 5.17, the gamma match extends a short, *unshielded* section of the feedline. The ground side or shield of the coaxial feedline extends to the driven element center point. The conductive center wire of the coaxial cable is routed parallel to the driven element. Electrical interaction between the driven element and the unshielded parallel feedline, along with the off-center feedpoint position, increases feedpoint impedance nearer 50 Ω.

However, this arrangement also creates *inductive reactance (one component of impedance)*, causing an undesirable shift in the phase relationship of voltage and current, as compared to the simple dipole case described in Section 5.1. To offset this phase shift a capacitor is inserted into the conductive parallel feedline to create *capacitive reactance (another component of impedance)*. As we will discuss more in Chapter 6, these two types of reactance counter one another, shifting the phases of current and voltage with opposite effect. The capacitor effectively nulls out the phase shifting of the inductive feedline element, but the antenna's off-center feedpoint impedance remains elevated at the matching value near 50 Ω.

The capacitive element may be implemented either by inserting a capacitor into the unshielded parallel feedline section or by insulating the feedline conductor from direct contact and inserting it into a metal tube that is a portion of the parallel feedline section (Figure 5.17). The metal tube is supported by a conductive *shorting strap* attached to the driven element. This arrangement effectively creates a linearly oriented capacitor (capacitance between center conductor wire and metal tube) that may be adjusted in capacitance value by adjusting the length of center wire and tube overlap. In practice the shorting strap position and capacitor value are adjusted until the lowest SWR is

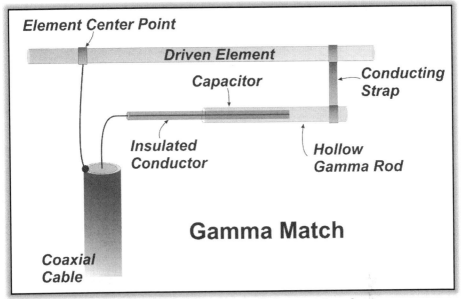

Figure 5.17: The gamma match uses a parallel capacitive element to achieve a near-50 Ω impedance match.

achieved, indicating closely matching feedpoint impedance. These two adjustments will interact, and getting things just right can be a delicate trial and error operation that requires some patience!

A further **advantage of using a gamma match with a Yagi antenna is that it does not require that the driven element be insulated from the boom,** assuming the boom is itself conductive. Non-conductive boom material is used with some Yagi designs, but aluminum or other conductive metal is more common. The gamma match allows the antenna elements to be mounted without concern of insulating the driven element from the boom. This can simplify the Yagi design and fabrication substantially!

Some Yagi designs may instead use a *beta* or *hairpin match*. **The beta or hairpin match is a shorted transmission line stub placed at the feed point of a Yagi antenna to provide impedance matching.** Typically, this match will connect to each side of the driven element, extending across the boom as a short curved wire.

Yagi Design Considerations: The design of Yagi antennas blends science and art. The spacing, number, and sizing of elements for desired performance, combined with impedance matching techniques and intended implementation can make design and execution challenging. Software packages are commercially available to aid with custom designing, but even with computer-aided design the implementation of impedance matching with a gamma match or other popular techniques can be tedious. Many proven Yagi designs are available from online and printed sources, and these are probably the best way for the beginner Yagi home-brewer to start.

And the payoff for a job well done is enormous! As alluded to in this section's spacey introduction, the Yagi is often used for radio communications on crowded bands like the 20 meter band because it helps reduce interference from other stations to the side or behind the antenna. Any directional can do the same, but the Yagi is simple elegance that many hams appreciate.

The Quad Antenna: A quad is a directional antenna constructed very similarly to a Yagi except that the elements are square loops of about one wavelength instead of linear ½-wavelength elements. Example quad antenna arrangements are depicted in Figure 5.18. The quad functions on the same principles as the Yagi, with driven element waveform reinforcement and cancellation by re-radiated emissions from the parasitic elements.

Since elements are approximately one wavelength long, **each side of the quad antenna driven element is approximately ¼ wavelength.** Like the Yagi, the reflector element is longer than the driven element, so each side of the quad antenna reflector element is slightly more than ¼ wavelength. **The configuration of the loops of a two-element quad antenna** (a driven element and a reflector) **operating as a beam antenna must have a reflector element approximately 5 percent longer than the driven element. The forward gain of a two-element quad antenna will be about the same as a three-element Yagi antenna.** So, although somewhat more difficult to construct than a typical Yagi, the quad offers improved gain with fewer elements.

The quad may be erected as a "square" or as a "diamond," as in Figure 5.18. Interestingly, the polarization is determined by the feedpoint selection. The polarization is summed up as follows:

	Square Config	Diamond Config
Horizontally Polarized	Bottom center feedpoint Top center feedpoint	Bottom corner feedpoint Top corner feedpoint
Vertically Polarized	Either side center feedpoint	Either side corner feedpoint

5.2 Directional Antennas

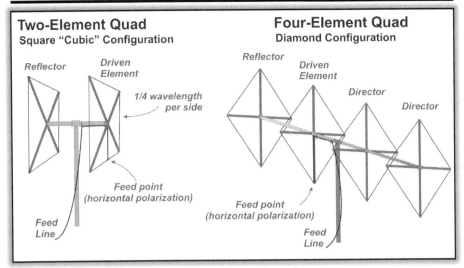

Figure 5.18: Example quad configurations.

Examples: For a square configuration, if the feedpoint of a quad antenna is changed from the midpoint of the top or bottom to the midpoint of either side, the polarization of the radiated signal changes from horizontal to vertical. For a diamond configuration, if the feedpoint is changed from a side corner to the bottom corner, the signal polarization changes from vertical to horizontal.

The Delta Loop Antenna: Another beam antenna based upon one wavelength loop elements is the multi-element delta loop. The concept is nearly identical to the quad antenna except that each element loop is formed as a triangle instead of as a square. Each leg of a symmetrical delta loop antenna will be approximately 1/3 wavelength. The gain of a two-element delta loop is about the same as a two-element quad.

A common configuration for the delta loop is to have one corner at the bottom and one side of the triangular element shape across the top horizontally. Feeding the loop at the bottom corner provides horizontal polarization. If instead the triangle element is oriented with a horizontal bottom side and an apex up, vertical polarization is affected with a bottom corner feedpoint. Other side feedpoints may also be used, and impedance matching techniques such as a gamma match may be required in some cases. As with the Yagi, a proven design and assistance for the new beam antenna home brewer is recommended!

Be aware also that one-wavelength loop antennas as single elements – just the driven element – may be used as a more omnidirectional radiator similar to the dipole. Quad loops or delta loops without parasitic elements are very effective and tend to offer somewhat better noise rejection than other single element designs.

Lastly on directional loop antennas, be aware that an **electrically small loop (less than 1/3 wavelength in circumference) will have directional nulls in its radiation pattern broadside to the loop.** Such loops can be loaded with capacitance for transmitting or used only as receiving antennas without loading. A small loop for the VHF or UHF range may be used as a compact and effective antenna for direction finding or foxhunting, taking advantage of the broadside receiving nulls in the pattern. A vertically mounted small loop may be rotated for directionality or to help avoid RF interference from specific directions.

Log Periodic Antenna: The log periodic antenna (Figure 5.19) has a general appearance much like a multi-element Yagi, but its characteristic design details and performance are significantly different. The log periodic's boom-mounted array of dipole elements will provide moderate directionality (signal gain), but not as much as the Yagi. Rather, **the primary advantage of the log periodic antenna is wide bandwidth.** It may operate over several bands while maintaining low SWR values on each band.

The log periodic will typically array multiple half-wave dipole elements together along a boom in a unique pattern. **The length and spacing of log periodic elements vary logarithmically along the boom,** as depicted in Figure 5.20. Elements on each side of the boom are fed alternatively by the electrically opposite

Figure 5.19: A log periodic antenna for HF bands.

sides of the feedline. The result of this unique arrangement is that different elements along the boom are *activated* to become the radiating elements as the feeding frequency changes. Lower frequencies are radiated by the longer elements and higher frequencies by the shorter elements. The log periodic is another good option for multi-band performance from a single antenna-feedline system, although its mechanical and mounting requirements are substantially more demanding than those associated with the horizontal wire multi-band antennas discussed in Section 5.1.

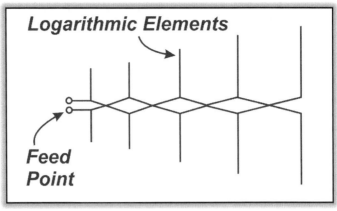

Figure 5.20: The log periodic design is an array of dipoles with alternating feed polarity.

You'll encounter even more varieties of directional antennas, but the Yagi, the quad, the multi-element delta loop, and the wide-band log periodic are four of the most common in amateur radio. Many hams enjoy the challenge and reward of fabricating their own antennas. Give it a try! You'll learn even more and perhaps open up an entirely new hobby *enterprise* to enjoy.

> Captain: "Status report, Technician?"
>
> Technician: "All hands beamed up, Captain. Ready for questions."
>
> Captain: "Very good, Technician. You're well on your way to a promotion to General!"

HamRadioSchool.com/general_media

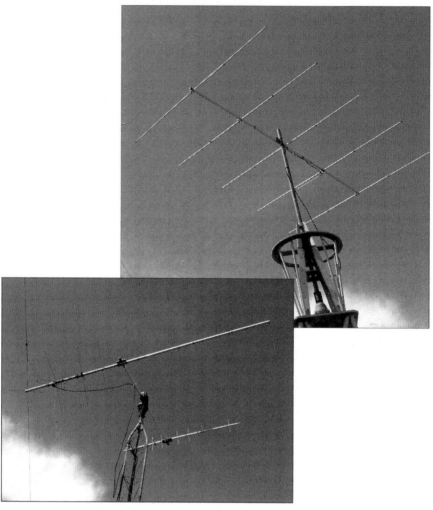

Waterton Amateur Radio Society, NØLM

5.3 SWR & Impedance Matching

> *… what we are concerned with here is the fundamental interconnectedness of all things.*
> – Dirk Gently

While he may have been just another offbeat character from the depths of Douglas Adams' warped sense of humor, Detective Gently's words apply equally well to ham radio antenna systems as to his uncommon investigations. Indeed, from the transceiver to coaxial feedline to cable connectors to characteristic impedances to reflected power to standing wave ratios… All these things are bound together, affecting one another. All fundamentally interconnected. Let's see how.

SWR: In an antenna system the *forward power* travels from the transmitter to the antenna. If the impedance of the feed line and the antenna are perfectly matched, say each at exactly 50 Ω, none of the power will reflect back toward the transmitter. This is the optimal situation, and essentially all the power is transferred to the antenna to help make RF waves. However, **a difference between feed-line impedance and antenna feed-point impedance will reflect some power at the point where the feed line connects to the antenna,** sending power back toward the transmitter.

G9A04

The signal waveforms of *reflected power* will superimpose with the waveforms of forward power in the feed line as the waveforms travel in opposite directions. The superimposition of the oppositely traveling waves of equal wavelength set up a *standing wave* in the feed line, as depicted in Figure 5.21. As the oppositely traveling waveforms' amplitudes combine, the resulting summation waveform seems to remain stationary, unmoving, but with amplitude rising and falling in place due to the cycle of variably reinforcing and nulling combining waves.

Typically, the power (amplitude) of the forward traveling wave is greater than the power of the reflected wave. The peaks of the standing wave will rise and fall between two extreme conditions: 1) the two traveling waves will constructively superimpose, adding together their momentarily in-phase waveforms to produce a high peak amplitude, and 2) the two traveling waves will be exactly

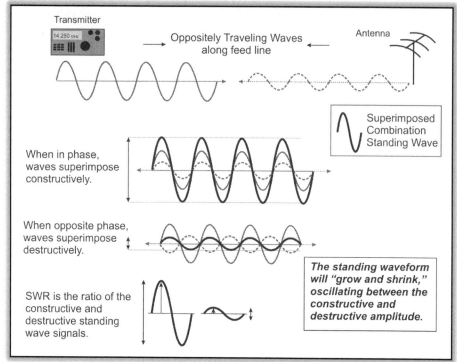

Figure 5.21: Standing waves result from the constructive and destructive superimposition of oppositely traveling waves of equal frequency, as in a feed line. SWR is the simple ratio of the maximum and minimum standing wave voltage amplitudes as the waves interact in passing.

out-of-phase, superimposing destructively to produce a momentary low peak amplitude.

SWR is the ratio of these two alternating standing wave voltage peaks, hence the name standing wave ratio. SWR can be computed from a measure of the power in each direction in the feed line, like this:

$$SWR = \frac{\sqrt{Fwd\ Pwr} + \sqrt{Refl\ Pwr}}{\sqrt{Fwd\ Pwr} - \sqrt{Refl\ Pwr}}$$

Measuring SWR: An *SWR meter* placed in the feed line will measure the signal in each direction simultaneously and display the computed SWR as a digital value or, more commonly, via a scale on which SWR values are read at the position where two indicator needles cross – one needle is driven by the forward power and the other by the reflected power, with crossing position indicating SWR. A cross-needle SWR meter is depicted in Figure 5.0c on page 132. These types of meters most often measure feed line *voltages* in each di-

5.3 SWR & Impedance Matching

rection and derive SWR from the comparative values. Alternatively, **standing wave ratio may be determined with a directional wattmeter,** measuring the forward and reflected power separately and then manually calculating with the preceding formula. With each of these instruments the antenna system must be connected to a transmitter to provide power for measurement.

An *antenna analyzer* provides its own signals for measurement, eliminating the need to connect the antenna system to a transmitter. Rather, **the antenna and feed line must be connected to the antenna analyzer when it is being used for SWR measurement.** An antenna analyzer will generate signal frequencies of known power, measure the reflected power, and then compute and display the SWR value. Most popular analyzers provide user controls for selecting the desired frequency band and for "dialing through frequencies." The SWR may be observed on a display as the bands and specific frequencies are changed. Some newer analyzers generate a rapid sequence of signals across a frequency band, storing a whole set of measures and displaying the graphical function of SWR by frequency ("SWR curve") on an LCD display.

Figure 5.22: Antenna analyzer examining 20m band SWR.

Strong signals from nearby transmitters can affect the accuracy of measurements made on an antenna system with an antenna analyzer, so some caution should be taken to avoid this problem. [Note: **Other than measuring the SWR of an antenna system, an antenna analyzer may also be used to determine the impedance of coaxial cable.**]

Impedance Ratios and SWR: The SWR of an antenna system will also be equivalent to the ratio of the impedance mismatch between feed line and antenna feed point. For example, **the connection of a 50 Ω feed line to a non-reactive load** (such as some antenna feed points) **having a 50 Ω**

impedance will result in an SWR of 1:1 (50 Ω ÷ 50 Ω = 1/1). The SWR resulting from feeding a vertical antenna with a 25 Ω feed point impedance with a 50 Ω coaxial cable will be 2:1 (50 Ω ÷ 25 Ω = 2/1). A 50 Ω coaxial cable feeding an antenna with a 300 Ω feed point impedance will result in an SWR of 6:1 (300 Ω ÷ 50 Ω = 6/1). Notice that regardless of the orientation of the impedance mismatch – high coax with low feed point, or low coax with high feed point – the SWR ratio is always expressed as a ratio greater than or equal to one (i.e. 3:1, never 1:3). Further, since SWR is always a ratio comparing with unity (1), many hams will drop the ratio terminology and simply state the SWR as the higher number in the ratio – "The SWR is 2.5."

Additional question pool items on this topic are:

50 Ω feed line and 200 Ω non-reactive load = 200/50 = 4/1 or **4:1 SWR**

50 Ω feedline and 10 Ω non-reactive load = 50/10 = 5/1 or **5:1 SWR**

Common Feedlines: **To prevent standing waves on an antenna feed line the antenna feed point impedance must be matched to the characteristic impedance of the feed line.** Let's take a look at two common feedline types and their characteristics to which we must match:

Coaxial Cable: "Coax" [kō' aks] is used more often than any other feed line for amateur radio antenna systems because it is easy to use and requires few special installation considerations. **The typical characteristic impedances of coaxial cables used for antenna feed lines at amateur stations are 50 and 75 ohms.** The characteristic impedance of coax is determined primarily by the diameters of the center conductor and the surrounding shield, as well as the type of insulating dielectric material that separates the two. Coaxial cable will impose some loss, or *attenuation*, of signal power over its length.

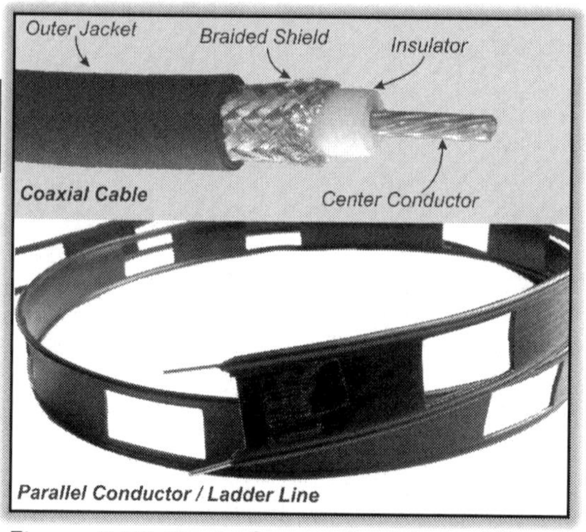

Figure 5.23: Typical coaxial cable and "window line" parallel conductor feed line.

5.3 SWR & Impedance Matching

Feed line losses are usually expressed in decibels per 100 feet. The attenuation of coaxial cable increases as the frequency of the signal it is carrying increases. Hence, coaxial feed line losses are generally low on the HF bands but may become quite significant into the UHF range, especially for long runs of 100 feet or more. Some typical loss values are summarized in the following table, depicting the greater loss with higher frequency in each type.

Cable Type	Frequency (MHz)	Loss (dB / 100 ft.)
RG-8/U	50	1.2
	100	1.7
	200	2.6
	400	3.9
RG-58/U	50	2.5
	100	3.8
	200	5.6
	400	8.4
RG-8/U Low Loss	50	0.9
	100	1.3
	200	1.8
	400	2.7
Twin Lead / Ladder	50	0.7
	100	1.1
	200	1.6
	400	2.5

SWR and Loss: Consider that a feedline imposes signal loss as the signal travels along a length of the feedline. With high SWR a significant portion of the signal will be reflected back-and-forth through the feedline, effectively increasing the length of feedline through which it travels. Thus, **if a transmission line is lossy, high SWR will increase the loss.** Additionally, **the higher the transmission line loss, the more SWR measured at the input to the line will read artificially low.** This is because signal reflections traveling back down the feedline from the antenna will be attenuated over the doubled length of the lossy feedline.

Parallel Conductor, TV Twinlead, and Ladder Line: These types of feed lines have the advantage of lower loss than coax, and they are used by amateurs in many situations where feed line shielding is unnecessary or undesirable for the characteristics of the antenna. **"Window line" parallel transmission line has a typical characteristic impedance of 450Ω.** These lines are also called *ladder line* or *open wire* feed lines. **The characteristic impedance of a parallel conductor antenna feed line is determined by the distance between the centers of the conductors and the radius of the conductors.** Parallel conductors often exhibit very low signal loss values, and they are excellent feedlines for some antenna types and scenarios, such as HF horizontal loop antennas.

Impedance Matching: As discussed in Sections 5.1 and 5.2, achieving an antenna feed point impedance matching the feed line as closely as possible will result in reduced power reflections and greater power transfer to the antenna. A close natural match is achieved with some systems such as a 50 Ω coaxial feed line coupled with a vertical antenna with downward sloping radials. The implementation of matching techniques like the gamma match described in Section 5.2 with Yagi antennas also help achieve antenna feed point match to the feed line impedance. Trimming antenna length can also impact the match.

Trimming: Dipoles and other antennas may be trimmed in length to obtain closely matching feedpoint impedance as indicated by the measured SWR curve. A common antenna metric is the bandwidth with SWR of 2:1 or less, as depicted in Figure 5.24. The SWR curve, and hence the 2:1 SWR band, may be moved to a higher frequency range by shortening the antenna or moved to a lower frequency range by lengthening the antenna.

Q Factor: Notice that the SWR curves of Figure 5.24 do not indicate 2:1 SWR or less across the entire 20m band from 14.000 to 14.350 MHz. This is a common scenario with many antennas, particularly physically shortened, loaded antennas as described in Section 5.1. This operating bandwidth of an antenna is called the *quality factor,* or "Q." High Q antennas have narrow SWR bandwidth, such as the physically shortened, loaded case. Wide SWR bandwidth antennas, such as a full sized dipole, are *low Q* antennas.

Antenna Coupler or Tuner: Most modern transceivers will begin to reduce transmit power when SWR exceeds 2:1. While trimming the antenna length can move the 2:1 band higher or lower as preferred, this is not an activity you'll want to undertake every time you wish to dial to another portion of the band! An *antenna tuner* or *coupler* can help with this scenario.

5.3 SWR & Impedance Matching

An antenna coupler or antenna tuner is a device often used to match transmitter output impedance to an impedance not equal to 50 Ω. Also known as a *transmatch*, antenna couplers use circuits or networks of adjustable value capacitors and inductors to present a 50 Ω impedance to the transmitter while maintaining the coupling to the antenna system, no matter its characteristic impedance (within extreme limits). The device is placed between the transceiver and feed line to affect this coupling. Higher quality couplers will be able to handle larger impedance mismatches, while others may match only up to a limited SWR value of perhaps 3:1 or 4:1.

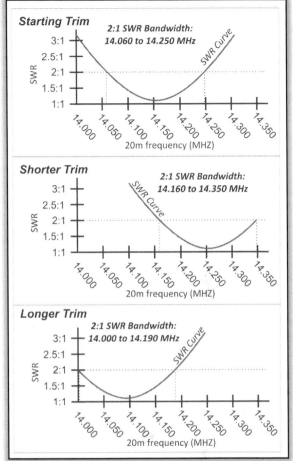

Figure 5.24: Example dipole 2:1 SWR bandwidth and trimming effects.

However, just because the transceiver "sees" 50 Ω from the antenna tuner does not mean that the antenna system characteristics have changed. Only the matching impedance at the transceiver has been altered – *an antenna tuner does not actually tune the antenna!* So, **if the SWR on an antenna feed line is 5:1 and a matching network at the transmitter end of the feed line is adjusted to 1:1 SWR, the feed line SWR will remain 5:1.** That means that you will still get reflections back toward the transmitter and the power transfer to the antenna will not be optimal. So, what's the point in doing it? A couple of fine points...

> *First, remember that most modern transmitters are designed to begin reducing transmit power at a detected SWR of 2:1.* As the SWR increases the transmitter power decreases. This is done to avoid any chance of harming transmitter circuits with high power reflections. So, with the poor imped-

ance match you get the reflections and the imposed loss in the feed line plus the double-whammy of your transmitter reducing output power! Rats!

But the antenna coupler and its nicely presented 50 Ω impedance comes to the rescue and avoids the power shutdown! The transmitter knows no difference, seeing only the desired matching 50 Ω impedance from the tuner, so it does not power down. Further, the coupler will handle those nasty power reflections and not allow them through to the transmitter.

Secondly, even when you have a mismatched impedance you can have a very usable antenna system. Even with a poor match, some of the power is going to be transferred to the antenna and get your signal out. Yes, there will be reflected power and it will essentially bounce to the antenna coupler and then back again to the antenna. But, the upshot is that even with a significant impedance mismatch you can radiate and communicate, even if not with optimal efficiency, and the antenna coupler keeps your power up and your transmitter happy!

End-Fed Antenna Matching: End-fed half-wave antennas are a popular option due to the convenience of the feed point location at one end of the antenna, reducing feed line length. However, as discussed in Section 5.1 impedance of a half-wave antenna increases as the feed point moves away from the center position. Thus, **the feed-point impedance of an end-fed half-wave antenna is very high!** These antennas must use a voltage transformer at the end feed point to match the feed point impedance to the feed line. We will address impedance matching concepts more in Section 6.4.

Feed Line Components: Transceivers and feed line cables and couplers and antenna feed points are not the end of the story! You should probably now realize that anything placed in the antenna system has the potential to cause power reflections and drive up SWR. That includes things like moisture (a common coaxial cable problem), a power amplifier, or an in-line filter. Any intentional component of a feed line should have matching impedance to avoid reflections. For instance, **as**

Figure 5.25: Common amateur radio connector types.

5.3 SWR & Impedance Matching

compared to the impedance of the transmission line into which it is inserted, the impedance of a low-pass filter should be about the same as the transmission line. That goes for any component in a feed line or antenna system through which the transmission signals must pass.

Coaxial Connectors: Connectors, too, have characteristics that can impose losses or reflections. While the loss values for most common connectors at HF frequencies is not significant, a poorly attached or faulty connector can create reflections and cause SWR values to go up or to be erratic.

- **N-Connector: Moisture resistant RF connector useful up to 10 GHz.**
- **PL-259** (and SO-239) **Connector: Commonly used for RF connections at frequencies up to 150 MHz.**
- **SMA Connector: Small, threaded connector suitable for signals up to several GHz.**

Most transceivers will use the PL-259/SO-239 connector. An HF station antenna system will typically use the PL-259/SO-239 connectors throughout the feed line, soldered solidly onto coaxial cable, or directly welded connections of parallel line to an antenna feed point component or line adapter. Many amateurs prefer to use N-Connectors throughout a coaxial feed line in lieu of the PL-259/SO-239. In either case, make certain that your connectors are protected from moisture if they are exposed to the elements, and make sure your solder welds are solid to avoid SWR problems.

Yep, make sure that *all your things are interconnected…* all bound together, as Dirk suggested, and do it in an effective way. Now you have some idea of how your antenna system's performance is measured and how many different characteristics and components must bind together in a harmonious, fundamental interconnectedness to effectively connect you with the amateur world…

Wow. It's the circle of antenna systems.

OK, don't get too deep. The questions….
Just hit the online questions. *HamRadioSchool.com/general_media*

6.0 Hamtronics

> *I am an expert of electricity. My father occupied the chair of applied electricity at the state prison.* — **W. C. Fields**

You don't have to be an expert in electricity to be an amateur radio operator. You also don't want to accidentally experience what it was like to hold the honorable position of Mr. Fields' father! So, let's acquire enough expertise in electrical principles and electronics to set up an advanced ham station and to do it very safely.

This chapter has nine sections, and that should provide an indication of how important electrical concepts are to ham radio. At least, that provides insight into how many exam pool questions are related to hamtronics.

- We'll start our electrifying discussion with fundamental principles of electricity and of electrical power in 6.1.
- In 6.2 we will examine many electronic components and their functions in electric circuits.
- Section 6.3 introduces combinations of multiple components in series and parallel circuit arrangements and how to compute equivalent single components.
- Impedance and reactance in electric circuits is covered in 6.4, with practical application to power transfer to loads like antennas.
- Sources of power are discussed in 6.5, and we will learn the details of how a basic power supply works.
- Section 6.6 is all about vacuum tube amplifiers and how to safely operate them.
- Integrated circuits and computers go well with ham radio, especially with digital operating modes, and we'll explore this connection in 6.7.
- Electrical measurements are critical to ensuring your station's proper operations, and this topic is covered in 6.8.
- Finally, Section 6.9 considers issues of radio interference and how to resolve them using simple electrical techniques.

It's a big chapter, so let's waste no more time… Have a chair and apply yourself to electricity.

6.1 Hamtronics Power and Principles

> **"** *The measure of a man is what he does with power.*
> — Plato

How will you measure up? What will you do with power? Most likely you'll radiate your message to the world, and maybe even include a few words from Plato. He would likely be rather amazed at what a ham radio operator can do with merely a few watts of power.

Since electrical power is fundamental to radio operations – in transceiver electrical circuits and RF emissions – it is prudent for the General Class license holder to have a more advanced understanding of the principles by which power is applied and controlled. You'll need your middle school math skills, so grab your calculator and let's see what we can do with power.

Ohm's Law Reprised: Unlike the Technician Class exam pool there is not a single question in the General Class pool directly derived from Ohm's Law. However, it will help us to relate to some newly introduced power principles, so let's review Mr. Ohm's insight. [You may want to review the Technician Class introduction to Ohm's Law and Power Law in the *HamRadioSchool.com Technician License Course*, Section 8.2.] First, the quantities represented within Ohm's Law:

- E: Electromotive Force (EMF) in units of volts
- I: Current in units of amperes, or amps
- R: Resistance in units of ohms

Ohm's Law: $E = I \times R$

Also: $I = E/R$ and $R = E/I$

The triangle representation of Ohm's Law helps to keep these relationships easily in mind. Cover the quantity you wish to find and the relationship of the other two defines the calculation to be made – the side-by-side remaining quantities are to be multiplied together, while top-over-bottom remaining quantities are to be divided. For example, to find E (cover E) you multiply I x R. Or, to find I (cover I), you divide: $E \div R$.

6.1 Power and Principles

Power Law: Power Law also embodies a simple relationship among quantities:

P: Power in units of watts
E: Electromotive Force (EMF) in units of volts
I: Current in units of amperes, or amps

Power Law: P = E x I

Also: E = P/I and I = P/E

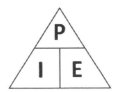

In an identical manner to the Ohm's Law triangle, the power law triangle can help you keep straight this simple relationship. Again, cover the quantity you seek to compute and the remaining two quantities will either multiply (side-by-side) or divide (top-over-bottom).

Example: **How many watts of electrical power are used by a 12 VDC light bulb that draws 0.2 amperes?**

P = E x I = 12 volts x 0.2 amps = **2.4 watts**

Power and Resistance: Now let's combine Ohm's Law and the Power Law to forge a new equation that broadens our computational repertoire. Since by Ohm's Law E = I x R, and also I = E/R, we can substitute the right side definition of both E and I from these equations into the Power Law equation, like this:

P = E x I
E = I x R
I = E/R

Thus,

P = (I x R) x (E/R), and substituting again for E
P = (I x R) x (I x R)/R, simplifying to
$P = I^2 \times R$

Example: A resister opposes the flow of current in a circuit, and it dissipates power as heat when a current flows through it. How much power? Let's use $P = I^2 \times R$ and find out:

7.0 milliamperes flowing through 1250 ohm resistance?

First let's convert to standard measures of amps and ohms:

0.007 amps flowing through 1250 ohms resistance...

Now we'll calculate with our derived equation:

$P = I^2 \times R = (0.007 \text{ amps})^2 \times 1250 \text{ ohms} = $ **0.06125 watts,** or about **61 milliwatts**

Power and EMF: With a little more algebraic wizardry we can derive another relationship for power that uses EMF, or voltage. Beginning with the basic Power Law once again:

$P = E \times I$; and $I = E/R$, thus
$P = E \times (E/R)$, or
$P = E^2 / R$

Example: An appliance, like a light bulb, a fan, or a radiating antenna is called a load on the circuit. Loads offer resistance in DC circuits, much like a resistor component. A load may convert electrical power into work. How much power does it convert? Let's use $P = E^2/R$ to find out:

400 VDC supplied to an 800 ohm load

We are already in the standard units of volts and ohms, with no pesky math prefixes attached this time. So…

$P = E^2/R = (400 \text{ volts})^2 \div 800 \text{ ohms} = $ **200 watts**

Pretty simple, huh? Just be sure to keep these three formulas in mind for the exam, or better yet be sure you can derive them as we've done here. And be sure to bring a calculator. OK, let's take it up a notch now.

Decibels (dB): The Technician Class materials provided a solid foundation on decibels, the logarithmic unit of measure used to compare two power values. Remember, the decibel is not a conventional unit of measure, but rather a tool for relative comparisons. Because power can vary over such a broad range, the logarithmic scale makes comparisons a little easier to handle than giant, multi-digit numbers that would be necessary otherwise. You should recall a couple of easy shortcuts when using decibels:

A factor of two increase or decrease in power represents a change of approximately 3 dB.

A factor of 10 increase or decrease in power represents a change of 10 dB.

6.1 Power and Principles

Those two Technician Class rules will get you through 90% of practical application of decibels and one of only two questions on this topic in the General Class pool. The remaining 10% of application and the other potential exam question require only a little more cognitive consideration, in lieu of a bunch of ugly equation manipulations.

A change in power may also be considered as a percentage relative to the initial power level that is always considered to be 100%. For instance, in the rules listed above, the "factor of two increase or decrease in power" could instead be characterized as "200% power" or "50% power," each referring to a factor of two change. So, we might ask the question, "What percentage of power results from a 3 dB decrease?" We can confidently answer that a 3 dB decrease equates to power about 50% of the starting value. Here is how decibels and relative percentages line up, with percentage values rounded:

Resulting Power
(Relative to 100% Starting Power)

dB change	% of starting power
-1 dB	-21%
-2 dB	-37%
-3 dB	-50%
-4 dB	-60%
-5 db	-68%
-6 dB	-75%
-7 dB	-80%
-8 dB	-84%
-9 dB	-87%
-10 dB	-90%

Resulting Power
(Relative to 100% Starting Power)

dB change	% of starting power
1 dB	125%
2 dB	160%
3 dB	200% (2X)
4 dB	251%
5 dB	316%
6 dB	398%
7 dB	500%
8 dB	630%
9 dB	794%
10 dB	1000% (10X)

Example 1: Suppose you wish to know what percentage of transmitter power is reaching your antenna given a coaxial feedline loss value in decibels: **What percentage of power loss would result from a transmission line loss of 1 dB?** Since we are interested in the percentage of loss, this is a decrease in power, specifically a decrease of 1 dB. A decrease of 1 dB (or -1 dB change) is equivalent to about a 20% decrease (-20%). Among the responses to this example exam pool item, **20.6%** is easily identified as the correct one.

Example 2: What percentage of power loss would result from a transmission line loss of 2.4 dB? This is not an exam pool item, and from our table of dB and percentages we can interpolate that the percentage of loss is roughly 43%. For those who have ample math skills, this may be precisely calculated with the following equation:

$$\%P = 100\% \, anti\log\frac{dB}{10} = 100\% \, anti\log\frac{-2.4}{10}$$
$$= 100\% \times 0.575 = 57.5\%$$

100% - 57.5% = 42.5% decrease

(Note: Antilog is computed as 10^x where x is the value following "antilog.")

Power and AC Waveforms: By now you've seen your share of the simple sine waveforms used to represent both the electric field oscillations of an RF electromagnetic wave and the back-and-forth oscillations of voltage in an AC circuit. When representing AC voltage the positive voltage (+v) part of the wave means the voltage is providing potential in one direction in the circuit, thereby pushing the electric current that way. The negative voltage (-v) means the voltage is pushing in the opposite direction in the circuit. The up and down undulation of the sine wave from +v to –v represents the voltage reversing back-and-forth in the circuit over time. The amplitude, or height of the wave relative to the zero voltage line is a representation of the magnitude of the voltage over time.

The AC voltage is not like DC voltage when it comes to measurements. DC voltage does not oscillate from one direction to the other, changing value constantly. Rather, DC remains steadily in a single direction in the circuit with a constant value for conditions. Our previously derived equations for power, such as $P = E^2/R$ work beautifully for DC because the EMF is a non-changing voltage value. But what voltage are you going to use in this formula with an AC circuit?

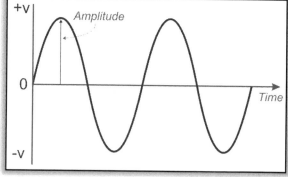

Figure 6.1: AC waveform time domain view.

- Will you use the peak amplitude voltage as determined above or below the zero line?
- Will you use the total voltage change from the +v peak to the –v peak?
- Will you use the average voltage? (That would equal zero, wouldn't it?)
- Will you use some other value of voltage?

You see the point. How do we define AC voltage? Do not fret. There is an answer!

6.1 Power and Principles

Root Mean Square Voltage: A rather convoluted computation may be made to determine a statistical average of a varying signal value such as an AC voltage signal. It is called the Root Mean Square, or RMS. The RMS may be determined for the +v portion of the waveform or for the –v portion. To compute the RMS of an AC signal across one-half wavelength (all above or all below the zero line) you would follow these steps:

1. Measure the amplitude of every voltage point along the wave.
2. Square each of the measured amplitude values.
3. Find the average (the mean) of all the squared values.
4. Take the square root of this average.

Wow, that's a pain, huh? Well, fortunately for a nice sine wave form with a peak amplitude normalized to 1, this calculation always yields the same value: 0.707. The E_{RMS} is different for differently shaped voltage waveforms, but it always equals 0.707 for our AC voltage sine waves of amplitude unity (1). Memorize that number!

Figure 6.2 depicts the E_{RMS} value on an AC sine waveform for both +v and –v, relative to peak voltages. **The RMS value of an AC signal produces the same power dissipation in a resistor as a DC voltage of the same value.** Thus, E_{RMS} may be used in the $P = E^2/R$ calculation for an AC circuit.

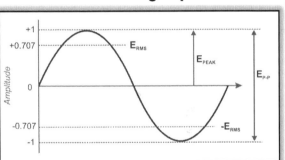

Figure 6.2: Root Mean Square voltage is 0.707 x peak voltage, and is the AC voltage used for power calculations.

Example: **What would be the RMS voltage across a 50 ohm dummy load** (resistor) **dissipating 1200 watts?**

$P = E_{RMS}^2 / R$, and rearranging this with a little algebra yields

$$E_{RMS} = \sqrt{P \times R}$$

$$E_{RMS} = \sqrt{P \times R} = \sqrt{1200 \times 50} = 245 \; volts$$

You can compute E_{RMS} if you know the peak voltage, and you can compute the peak voltage if you know E_{RMS}, like this:

$E_{RMS} = E_{Peak} \times 0.707$

And by computing the inverse $1 / 0.707 = 1.414$ you may compute:

$E_{Peak} = E_{RMS} \times 1.414$

Example: **What is the RMS voltage of a sine wave with a value of 17 volts peak?**

$E_{RMS} = E_{Peak} \times 0.707 = 17 \times 0.707 =$ **12 volts**

Example: What is the peak voltage of a sine wave with E_{RMS} of 50 volts?

$E_{Peak} = E_{RMS} \times 1.414 = 50 \times 1.414 = 70.7$ volts peak

Peak-to-Peak Voltage: It is sometimes important to work with the peak-to-peak voltages of a waveform, designated V_{p-p} or E_{p-p}. The peak-to-peak value is also indicated in Figure 6.2. For the sine waveform the peak-to-peak voltage will be twice the peak voltage. Thus, peak-to-peak voltage is also calculated using E_{RMS}, and E_{RMS} is calculated using E_{p-p}, as follows:

$E_{(P-P)} = 2 \times E_{RMS} \times 1.414$

$E_{RMS} = (E_{p-p} \times 0.707) / 2$

Example: **What is the peak-to-peak voltage of a sine wave with an RMS voltage of 120 volts?**

$E_{p-p} = 2 \times E_{RMS} \times 1.414 = 2 \times 120 \times 1.414 =$ **339.4 volts**

Example: What is the RMS voltage of a sine wave with measured peak-to-peak voltage of 339.4 volts?

$E_{RMS} = (E_{p-p} \times 0.707) / 2 = (339.4 \times 0.707) / 2 = 120$ volts

Peak Envelope Power (PEP): The formulas discussed so far are fine for a very simple signal, but that's not the typical practical case. Most commonly hams will be more concerned with a complex modulated signal. Given an amplitude modulated signal as described in Section 4.1, an envelope will shape the peaks of the carrier frequency sine waveform, resulting in continuous change of the peak voltages and associated power over time. For instance, with phone mode the modulation envelope will expand and contract with the ebb and flow of our voices, creating frequent *high power peaks* of modulation as our

6.1 Power and Principles

voice rises, interspersed with vocal pauses of almost no modulation at all, and many levels in between.

How can we characterize the power of a varying amplitude envelope of signals like this in a practical and useful manner?

Peak envelope power (PEP) is the average power (RMS) supplied to the antenna transmission line by a transmitter during one radio frequency cycle at the crest of the modulation envelope. As depicted in Figure 6.3, PEP is the average power of the signal calculated where the envelope peaks to its highest voltage (*Peak Envelope Voltage*). The PEP is an index of the highest power peaks to be expected for given conditions of the transmitter, load, and modulating signal – a *practical* measure!

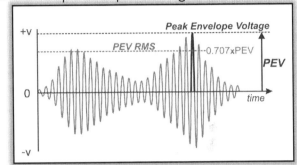

Figure 6.3: In amplitude modulated signals the RMS of the Peak Envelope Voltage is used to compute the Peak Envelope Power (PEP).

The FCC uses PEP to set maximum power standards for amateur radio transmitters. An averaging wattmeter will display a time averaged value for PEP (usually across many envelope peaks in its averaging time) for adjustments of transmitter or amplifier drive levels. A signal PEP may also be calculated using the previously derived equations for power, remembering that it is the *average power at the envelope peak*. So, the *RMS voltage* of the peak cycle must be used for calculation of PEP. And if the RMS voltage is not provided it may be calculated from the peak-to-peak voltage of the envelope peak measurement. Let's drive this home with a couple of examples:

Example 1: **What is the output PEP from a transmitter if an oscilloscope measures 200 volts peak-to-peak across a 50 ohm dummy load connect-**

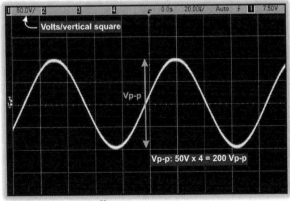

Figure 6.4: Oscilloscope screen measurement of 200 volts peak-to-peak, at 50V per vertical scale unit. *Compliments Agilent Technologies*

G5B06

ed to the transmitter output? (Don't let the oscilloscope or dummy load mentions confuse you… that's just a measurement technique scenario that is irrelevant to the numerical facts provided.) So, we're asked for PEP, and we are given $E_{p\text{-}p}$ and R.

$P_{PEP} = (E_{RMS})^2 / R$ at the envelope peak. This is the same $P = E^2 / R$ equation used earlier for the sine waveform power calculation, only changed to use the RMS voltage.

Recall: $E_{RMS} = 0.707 \times E_{p\text{-}p} / 2 = 0.707 \times (200\ v) / 2 = 70.7\ v$

Again, this is the same method of computing RMS voltage already introduced in which we must use only the peak voltage, or one-half of peak-to-peak voltage ($E_{p\text{-}p} \div 2$).

Plugging E_{RMS} into the P_{PEP} formula above then gives:

$P_{PEP} = (70.7\ v)^2 / (50\ \Omega) = (4998.5)/50 = \mathbf{100\ watts}$ (rounded)

Example 2: **What is the output PEP from a transmitter if an oscilloscope measures 500 volts peak-to-peak across a 50 ohm resistive load connected to the transmitter output?** Exactly the same equations apply since we are asked for PEP and given $E_{p\text{-}p}$ and R. Consolidating, we get:

$$P_{PEP} = \frac{(0.707 \times \frac{E_{P-P}}{2})^2}{R} = \frac{(0.707 \times \frac{500}{2})^2}{50} = 625\ watts\ \text{(rounded)}$$

Unmodulated Carrier PEP: One last PEP consideration: What if the carrier is unmodulated? That is, what if there are no peaks and valleys of amplitude on the envelope, but only a steady AC carrier frequency of some given power?

In such a case the PEP is equal to the steady carrier power. The peak voltage of the signal is unchanging so any calculated RMS voltage equals the steady RMS voltage value, as depicted in Figure 6.5. Further, the PEP will be equal to the average power of the steady carrier signal at any point in time since an "envelope" is non-existent without modulation. Put another way, **the ratio of PEP to average power for an unmodulated carrier is 1.00.**

Example: **What is the output PEP of an unmodulated carrier if an average reading wattmeter connected to the transmitter output indicates 1060 watts?**

Since the PEP to average power for an unmodulated carrier is 1:1, the output PEP is equal to the wattmeter's average power reading of **1060 watts.**

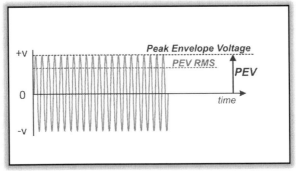

Figure 6.5: An unmodulated carrier's Peak Envelope Power will equal the carrier RMS power, since the PEV is equal to the carrier peak voltage (V_{PEAK}).

As you can see, there's a lot to be done with power! If you didn't quite measure up, check out the next page summary table of equations used in this section and review each of those areas representing question pool items. It may require a little practice, but you'll be powering up in no time!

Review questions: *HamRadioSchool.com/general_media*

Section 6.1 Study Review Summary:

Ohm's Law	$E = I \times R$	(E/I,R triangle)
Power Law	$P = I \times E$	(P/I,E triangle)
Power (P)	$P = I^2 \times R$	$P = E^2/R$
Decibels (dB)	3 dB = 2X change	-1 dB = -20.5%
Peak Voltage (E_{PEAK})	$E_{PEAK} = E_{P-P} / 2$	$E_{Peak} = E_{RMS} \times 1.414$
Root Mean Square Voltage (E_{RMS})	$E_{RMS} = E_{PEAK} \times 0.707$	$E_{RMS} = \sqrt{(P \times R)}$
Peak-to-Peak Voltage (E_{P-P})	$E_{P-P} = 2 \times E_{RMS} \times 1.414$	$E_{P-P} = E_{PEAK} \times 2$
Peak Envelope Power (P_{PEP})	$P_{PEP} = (E_{RMS})^2 / R$	Uses PEV in E_{RMS}

6.2 Hamtronics Components

> *We must break problems down into small, digestible bits. We must define the concepts that we use and explain what components they consist of. We must tackle small problems. – Abdolkarim Soroush*

When it comes to electronics Dr. Souroush couldn't be more correct. To begin to understand what's really going on inside a transceiver, an amplifier, or any other chunk of radio gear, a lot of insight can be gained from an examination of the individual components from which the equipment is constructed. Let's tackle these small problems, these electronic components, and later we'll put some of them together into bigger working pieces.

You may recall from your Technician studies an introduction to several types of electronic components. Here's a summary of some of those basic components, just to jog your brain into action:

Component	Symbol	Units	Description
Resistor	—/\/\/—	ohm [Ω]	Opposes the flow of current in a circuit; dissipates energy as heat
Capacitor	—|(—	farad	Stores energy in an electric field; passes higher frequency AC, opposes lower frequency AC and DC
Inductor	—UUU—	henry	Stores energy in a magnetic field; passes lower frequency AC and DC, opposes higher frequency AC
Diode	—▶|—	N/A	Allows current to flow in only one direction; leads are anode and cathode
Transistor	(symbols)	N/A	May act as an amplifier or as a switch; small controlling current or voltage regulates larger current flow

First we'll consider some common general characteristics of most electronic components, and then we'll tackle each component listed in the table in appropriate General Class detail.

Electronic Component Characteristics: Imagine you're trying to select a car to purchase. Each automobile type is unique, but they all share some common characteristics that you can use for comparison and that will help you judge how well the vehicle will perform for you. For instance, each car will have a gas mileage estimate, an engine size and horsepower, a maximum seating capacity, and so on. In some cases the characteristic will be an approximation, with some variance expected among individual vehicles of the same make and model – gas mileage, for example, will usually vary by individual car and driver, and even by the driving environmental factors, such as altitude.

Electronic components are much the same as cars in this regard. While each type is unique and may perform differently, some common characteristics may be defined for them all. These characteristics will tell you how you may expect the electronic component to perform.

- *Nominal Value* – The intended or designed unit quantity the component should provide. For instance, a resistor may have a nominal value of 1000 Ω resistance; a capacitor may provide 2000 microfarads of capacitance; an inductor may be rated at 0.004 henry of inductance. Consider a component's nominal value to be like an EPA gas mileage rating for the car – it is the target value, but with understanding that variations will occur.

- *Tolerance* – The amount of deviation from the nominal value that is considered to be normal for the quality of the component. Tolerance will typically be a percentage. For instance, the 1000 Ω resistor may have a tolerance of +/- 20%. That means the resistor is within normal operating performance if it provides a measured resistance of anywhere between 800 – 1200 Ω. Similarly, your vehicle's gas mileage may vary from the EPA rating and actually measure somewhat higher or lower than the rating. With electronic components, different tolerances may be specified for a circuit design to ensure the circuit performs within required ranges.

- *Voltage/Current/Power Rating* – The maximum value of voltage, current, or power that the component can handle without being toasted. A component is usually designed for a limited range of input values and if the limits are exceeded the component may not be able to shed the heat generated by the excessive current or power. In such a case the component may break down due to the accumulation of heat or voltage stress. Similarly, your car or truck may be designed with a maximum towing capacity weight. If you try to pull a trailer heavier than the towing capacity, your engine may overheat and fail.

- *Temperature Coefficient* – A description of the component's performance variation with temperature. The nominal value of many components will shift with temperature. For instance, if the temperature is increased the resistance of a resistor will change depending on its temperature coefficient – a resistor may be rated at 1000 Ω at 80 degrees Fahrenheit, but its resistance may decrease at temperatures above 80 degrees at a steady rate of 10 Ω per degree. Similarly, your car may accelerate and speed along very well in average temperatures, but on a scorching summer day with the air conditioner running you may find the acceleration to be lacking and the top speed more difficult to achieve due to an overheating engine.

Additional characteristics may apply to various component types, but these are the basics that will help you identify the performance parameters of most electronics. Now, let's consider the functioning of each of the component types listed in the preceding table.

Resistors: A resistor offers electrical resistance, opposing the flow of electric current in a circuit. Resistance is measured in units of ohms.

> **Resistor Water Model:** Recalling the water model of electricity from the *HamRadioSchool.com Technician License Course*, an electric circuit can be thought of like plumbing, as in Figure 6.6 on the next page. Water current flows in pipes as electric current flows in wires, and a water pump provides pressure to push the water current through the pipe just as a battery provides electromotive force to push electrical current though wires. If you constrict the pipe, perhaps narrowing its diameter or placing objects inside to interrupt the water flow, you are creating opposition to the flow of the current – resistance! A resistor is like a narrowing or a blockage in the electrical circuit that similarly opposes the flow of current in the circuit. (A load in the circuit, such as an appliance, also imposes resistance.)

Resistors of various types are made from different materials, each with unique characteristics and typical applications. For high power applications, such as power supply circuits, resistors may be wire-wound, using resistive wire wrapped about a non-conductive core such as ceramic. However, such a coil of wire with current flowing will store energy in a magnetic field that is cre-

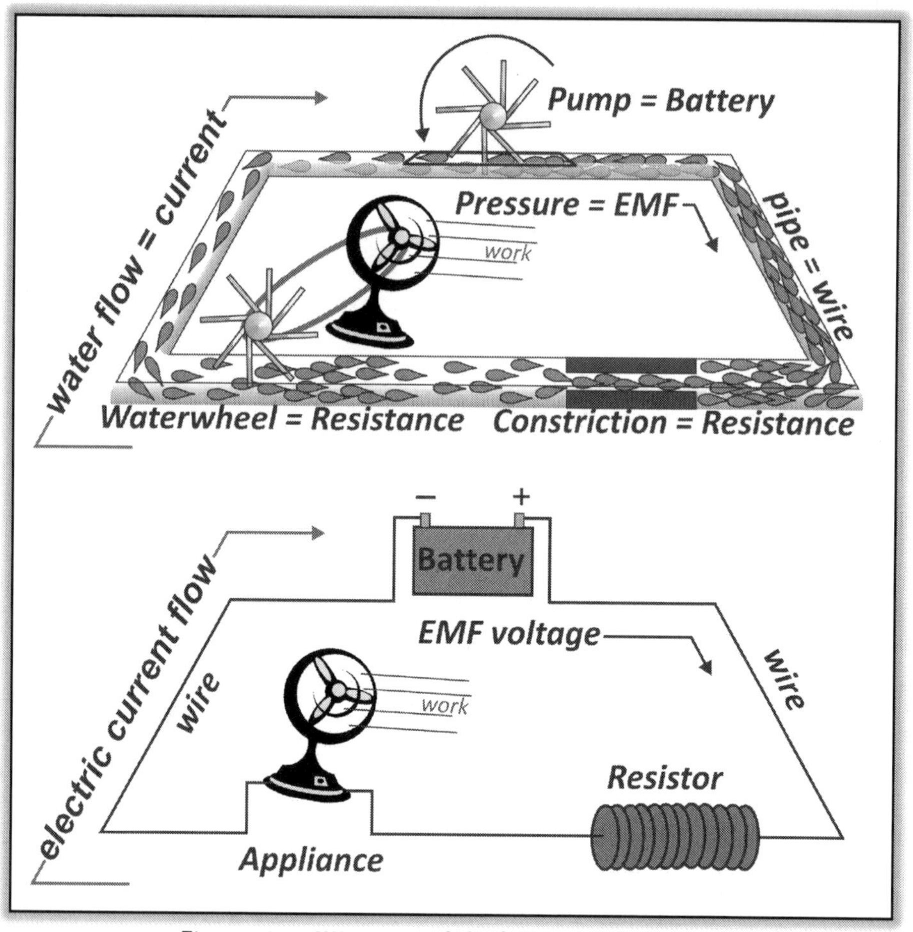

Figure 6.6: Water model of an electric circuit.

ated around the coiled windings. This is called *inductance*, as we will explore further with the *inductor* component. Care must be taken to ensure that a wire-wound resistor's inductance does not interfere with the function of other components in nearby circuits. So, **wire-wound resistors are not typically used in RF circuits because the resistor's inductance could make circuit performance unpredictable.** Rather, non-inductive resistors made from metal oxide or carbon are typically used for RF applications.

A resistor's nominal value will usually be either printed on the resistor or indicated with a series of colored bands around the resistor using a standardized color code. Various tolerances are available from less than 1% precision components to 10% or greater for less demanding applications. Power ratings vary vastly and depend on the construction, material type, and physical size of the resistor. Temperature coefficients also vary substantially, and the coefficient may be positive (increased resistance with increased temperature) or negative (decreased resistance with increased temperature).

Thermistor: A device having a specific change in resistance with temperature variation is a *thermistor*. Thermistors may be used to construct temperature sensing and control circuits, such as in a thermostat used to control temperature with a cooling fan, an air conditioner, or a furnace.

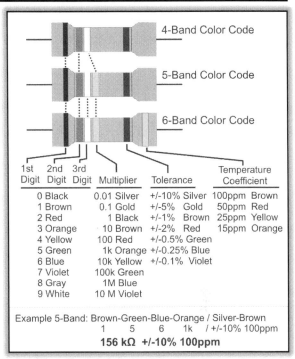

Figure 6.7: Resistor value color codes.

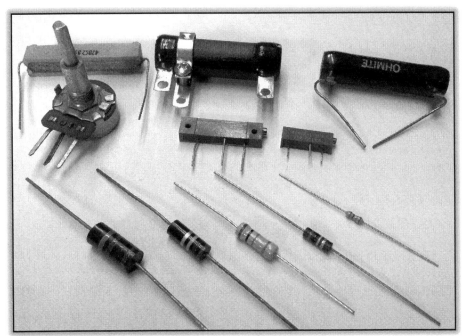

Figure 6.8: Resistors and potentiometers come in a variety of packages for different functions and ranges of power handling capacity.

Potentiometer: A resistor that can be varied in resistance value is called a potentiometer, or a *pot*. Variable resistors are commonly used to control voltage or current in a circuit by adjusting the potentiometer's resistance, such as in a volume control on a radio. Potentiometers included in some circuits for the purpose of making minor calibrations of the circuit and not regularly controlled by an operator are called *trimmers*, since they are used to tweak or *trim* the final circuit performance.

Capacitors: A capacitor stores electrical energy in an electric field. This component consists of two or more conductive surfaces separated by an insulator, or *dielectric*. Since the surfaces are separated, DC current is prevented from flowing through a capacitor, but AC current is not interrupted – the back-and-forth current flow allows electric charge to build across the capacitor's two surfaces, one surface becoming positively charged and the other negatively charged, until the voltage applied to the capacitor reverses. Upon reversal, the respective surfaces discharge and then recharge with opposite polarity. This repeats with each cycle of AC.

Generally, higher AC frequencies are less impeded by a capacitor since they are less likely to allow the capacitor's plates to reach maximum charge capacity, while lower AC frequencies may accumulate a maximum capacitance charge on the plates that begins to oppose further current flow. Capacitance is measured in units of farads, and greater capacitance (more energy storage capacity) is created with larger surface area and with narrower separation of the surfaces.

Capacitor Water Model: An admittedly over-simplified water model may be used to help comprehend the function of a capacitor. A capacitor may be thought of as a pliable, rubber diaphragm stretching across the interior of the pipe, as in Figure 6.9. The diaphragm will stretch in one direction with the current flow, storing energy elastically. Once the current direction reverses the stored energy is released, accelerating the current flow in the new direction with the force of the elastic contraction. As the current continues to flow, the diaphragm is stretched again, now in the opposite direction, again storing energy until the next cycle of alternating current flow releases it. The stretched diaphragm is loosely analogous to the potential difference that builds across the two plates of the capacitor.

Consistent with the description above about the capacitor's reaction to AC and DC current, you may envision that a high frequency alternating water current would stretch the capacitor diaphragm only mildly before the current direction is reversed, thereby not having a great impeding effect on the current's rapid back and forth flow. However, if the frequency

6.2 Components

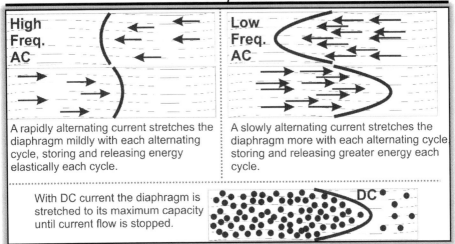

Figure 6.9: In the water model of electricity, a capacitor is like a stretching diaphragm in the water pipe, storing and releasing energy with each alternating cycle of current direction.

of current reversal is low, the diaphragm may be stretched to its maximum capacity before the reversal of flow direction, and the current flow is then significantly impeded. And of course, if the current is DC, never reversing, the capacitor will reach maximum capacity in the one DC direction and then stop further current flow.

Capacitor Packaging: A wide variety of capacitor types and constructions exist. A capacitor may be fabricated from a pair of metal plates separated by air. Sandwich a thin insulating material between two layers of thin metal foil, roll up the sandwich into a cylindrical package, and you have another capacitor form. Stack up multiple alternating layers of insulating and conducting surfaces like a Dagwood sandwich, keeping the layers flat and unrolled, and connect alternating conducting surfaces electrically at their edges, and yet another capacitor packaging is affected.

Plastic Film Capacitors are typically rolled sandwiches of plastic insulating film between metal foil layers. As noted with the wire-wound resistor, a rolled capacitor will impose some undesirable inductance due to its rolled or coiled form. As a result, plastic film capacitors are not typically used in RF circuits requiring higher frequency signal processing where this *parasitic inductance* can affect performance.

Ceramic Capacitors have many narrow plates of ceramic metallically coated on one side and stacked in the Dagwood sandwich configuration. **Compared to other types of capacitors they have the advantage of low cost.** Being a flat stack arrangement, ceramics do not generate parasitic inductance like the rolled capacitors, so they are used in VHF and UHF circuits. However, the wire connection leads do produce small but significant inductance for VHF and above, termed *lead inductance*, which reduces the effective capacitance. As we will see in Section 6.4 inductance and capacitance effects offset one another within a circuit, and even within a component.

Electrolytic Capacitors are typically a rolled form also, but the insulating dielectric is a moist chemical gel (the electrolyte) that coats the conducting layers. **Electrolytic capacitors are optimized for energy storage, offering the advantage of high capacitance for a given volume.** Because they are rolled, they produce parasitic inductance, but they are often used in power supply circuits to filter the rectified AC. (See rectifiers in Section 6.5.)

[G6A04]

Electrolytic capacitors are usually *polarized* capacitors, meaning that they are used in circuits where the two leads have a consistent applied potential relationship. That is, one lead (+) is always at a higher potential than the other lead (-). **If the applied voltage polarity is reversed the polarized capacitor could overheat and explode, it may short-circuit, or the voltages may destroy the dielectric layer.**

[G6A13]

Capacitance Values: Capacitors in RF circuits are often of fractional values of the unit *farad*. The standard mathematical prefixes are attached to the unit to indicate these fractional values of one farad, as follows:

picofarad (pF)	one trillionth	0.000000000001	10^{-12}
nanofarad (nF)	one billionth	0.000000001	10^{-9}
microfarad (µF)	one millionth	0.000001	10^{-6}
millifarad (mF)	one thousandth	0.001	10^{-3}

Converting among these fractional values involves moving the decimal point three places for each of the standard fractional steps. A thorough examination of this is provided in the *HamRadioSchool.com Technician License Course* book, Section 8.3. Let's examine two exam questions regarding conversions.

What is the value in nanofarads (nF) of a 22,000 pF capacitor? Converting from pF to nF is one prefix step, moving the decimal left by three positions. **22,000 pF = 22** nF.

[G5C17]

What is the value in microfarads of a 4700 nanofarad (nF) capacitor? Similarly, this is a one-step conversion moving the decimal left. **4700 nF = 4.7** µF.

[G5C18]

6.2 Components

Inductors: Inductors store energy in a magnetic field that is created around the inductor when electric current flows through it. An inductor is usually composed of a coil of wire, in many cases wound about an iron or ferrite core to increase the magnetic energy storage capacity. You may be familiar with the magnetic field generated by an electromagnet, essentially an inductor comprised of a coil of wire connected to a battery or other DC power source.

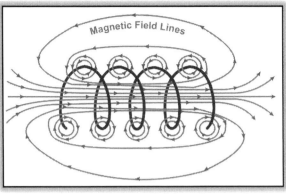

Figure 6.10: A magnetic field "inflates" about an inductor as current flows through the coil.

An inductor reacts to AC and DC in a manner opposite that of a capacitor. The inductor allows DC current to flow freely once the initial current's magnetic field is established around the inductor, with magnetic field lines stable in one orientation, or *polarization*. However, the constantly reversing AC requires that the magnetic field be created with one polarization, then eliminated and rebuilt with the opposite polarization each AC cycle. This persistent *inflation* and *deflation* of the magnetic field expends electrical energy and thereby opposes AC current. The inductor's opposition to AC increases with frequency. Let's drive home this concept with the water analogy for an inductor.

Inductor Water Model: Imagine the inductor is a very massive waterwheel extending into the water current. As the current begins to flow it will require some time and applied force to get the heavy wheel rotating with the speed of the current. The inertia of the heavy wheel opposes the current flow until it gets up to rotational speed with the flow. Once rotating, the water wheel has kinetic energy stored with its revolving mass, just as the inductor has stored energy in the magnetic field it created.

If the current suddenly stopped flowing the heavy waterwheel would continue to rotate for a while, expending its energy by pushing the water on until the rotation wound down to a stop. As the waterwheel slows to a stop its kinetic energy of rotation is converted back into water current, just as the inductor's magnetic field is converted into continued electrical current until the magnetic field is depleted. Once the wheel's stored energy is depleted and it stops turning, the current flow also stops.

Because energy is expended over time to inflate the magnetic field (to get the waterwheel turning), the inductor offers resistance initially to the current. Once the steady state magnetic field is achieved (waterwheel at current flow speed), the resistance is eliminated. This is the case with a DC current.

If the electrical current reverses direction the magnetic lines of force are induced in the opposite direction also. Thus, the magnetic field must collapse and rebuild with opposite polarity of the lines of force; i.e. the waterwheel would resist the reversed water current, but ultimately it will grind to a halt and gradually pick up rotational speed in the opposite direction with the current. During this process opposition to the flow would be offered until the new steady state is achieved with the waterwheel turning at speed in the opposite direction. This cycle repeats.

As the frequency of current alternation increases, the inductor's opposition also increases. You can imagine the water wheel trying to rapidly start and stop with higher frequencies of AC, never quite getting up to speed and constantly opposing current flow in either direction. You can also imagine the waterwheel just becoming a static blockage in the current if the water flow reversed direction too frequently, with insufficient time to start wheel rotation in either direction before the next reversal.

Inductance: The measure of the ability to store magnetic energy, *inductance*, is determined by the number of wire turns in the inductor, by the area that each turn circumscribes, by the density of turns (longitudinal spacing or length of inductor), and by the *magnetic permeability* of the core material. Permeability is the core's ability to store magnetic energy. Iron or ferrite cores enhance permeability, and permeability may be engineered to fit specific circuit needs. **The performance of a ferrite core at different frequencies is determined by the composition, or "mix" of materials used.**

Variable Inductors: Inductors that provide variable inductance values may be created by shifting the core into or out of the coil, changing the effective permeability. Another technique applied in higher power circuits is to *tap* the inductor with a contact that may be moved among the coil's turns, effectively changing the number of turns used in the circuit by moving the tap position, just as in the tapped coil antenna of Section 5.1.

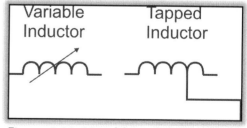

Figure 6.11: Variable and **tapped inductor** symbols.

Mutual Inductance: As noted in the capacitor discussion, an induced magnetic field can extend well beyond a component to affect the performance of other components. In the case of inductors the changing magnetic field of one inductor can induce current flow in another nearby inductor. This is called *mutual inductance*. We will see in Section 6.5 that mutual inductance is the principle by which transformers operate, but it is undesirable in virtually every other type of circuit. It is important to minimize mutual inductance between two inductors to reduce unwanted coupling between circuits. Methods of reducing mutual inductance depend upon inductor form factors.

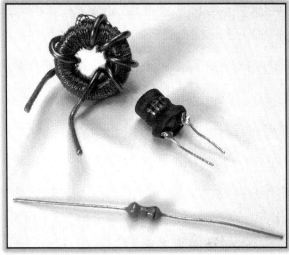

Figure 6.12: Inductors may be toroid coils, solenoid coils, or other forms.

Inductor Forms: Two common physical forms of inductors are 1) the *solenoid inductor*, having a straight axis or core, and 2) the *toroid inductor*, having a circular or "donut" core on which windings are wrapped. With a solenoid inductor the magnetic field lines loop through the coiled windings and back outside the coil, primarily pointing along the axis of the core. Placing the winding axes of solenoid inductors at right angles to one another minimizes their mutual inductance, since the field lines of one inductor are not in an orientation for inducing a current in the other inductor. **The ferrite core toroidal inductor contains most of the magnetic field in the core,** minimizing mutual inductance. **It also has the advantages of relatively large inductance values and optimization for specific frequency ranges by altering the magnetic properties of the core.**

Inter-turn capacitance in an inductor may cause the inductor to become self resonant at some frequencies. Just as the rolled form of some capacitors creates stray inductance, the gaps between wire coils of an inductor can produce stray capacitance, much like the capacitor's separated plates. This inter-turn capacitance can be significant if an inductor is comprised of many turns. As noted in Chapter 5, a circuit with both capacitance and inductance will resonate at specific frequencies, and these types of circuits are the basis for RF oscillators. However, even an individual component can become undesirably self resonant due to the effects of parasitic capacitance or inductance, altering the component's intended performance by the resonant reinforcement of select frequencies. **When an inductor is operated above its self-resonant frequency, it becomes capacitive,** due to parasitic capacitance offsetting and exceeding the inherent inductance of the inductor component.

Diodes: A diode is a *semiconductor* component that allows current flow in only one direction. It has two connection leads called the *anode* and the *cathode*. Current flows when a positive voltage is applied from the anode to the cathode, and in this condition the diode is said to be *forward biased*. When the diode is reverse biased the voltage is oppositely applied and the diode allows no current flow in the *reverse bias* direction.

> **Diode Water Model:** A diode is analogous to a one-way plumbing valve, such as a check valve or flap valve, that allows water to flow through a pipe in one direction by opening with the flow, but that stops the opposite direction flow by closing the pipe entirely.

A semiconductor is a material with electrical conductivity between that of an insulator such as glass and a conductor such as metal, and its electrical properties may be manipulated by additives or impurities distributed throughout its form. Silicon (Si) is one of the most common semiconductors, and others include germanium, gallium arsenide, and silicon carbide. The addition of impurities is called *doping* the semiconductor. By using two different types of *dopants* in semiconductors, a *junction diode* may be constructed.

Junction Diode: One type of dopant in semiconductor promotes an excess of electrons (negative charge) in the semiconductor. This is called an *N-type* material. Different dopants promote an excess of positively charged ions, usually called "holes." (Think this: A negatively charged electron fits into a positively charged hole as current flows, and holes flow in the opposite direction of electrons in a circuit.) This positive charge inducing material is a *P-type* material.

Place a P-type material and an N-type material together and you form a *junction* of the two types (a "PN junction"). Due to the behavior of the excessive electrons and holes near the junction, current will flow in one direction but not the other, and then it will flow only when a sufficient voltage is applied across the PN junction (forward bias voltage). This is like the minimum water pressure required to open the flap valve and allow water current to flow.

The voltage required to promote forward current flow is called the *junction threshold voltage*. **For a conventional silicon diode the approximate** junction threshold voltage is 0.7 volts. For a germanium diode the approximate junction threshold voltage is 0.3 volts. Note that the voltage *must* be in the forward bias direction to pull the electrons across the PN junction. Of course, given enough reverse bias voltage, the junction will break down and current will be forced to flow in the reverse direction. Diodes have a *peak reverse voltage* rating describing this limit, and a *forward bias current limit* describing the maximum forward current it can handle without being damaged.

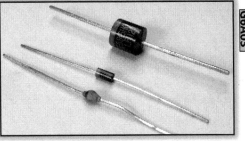

Figure 6.13: Diode packages for various current handling. The stripe indicates the cathode.

There are several different types of diodes that lend themselves to a variety of applications. These include:

- **Schottky Diode** – named for German physicist Walter H. Schottky, it requires a relatively small forward threshold voltage and has the advantage of lower capacitance compared to a standard silicon diode as a result. This allows for very fast switching times and use in RF switching circuits.

- **Zener Diode** – named for Clarence Zener who discovered the electrical properties of this unique device. When forward biased it acts as a normal diode, but when reverse biased above its reverse break down voltage it will maintain the reverse voltage at or near a stable value even with significant current variations.

- **Light Emitting Diode (LED)** – **When forward biased an LED emits light.** These diodes are commonly used as visual indicators in modern electronics.

Additional varieties of diodes are available for specialized applications.

Transistors: A transistor is a semiconductor component capable of using a small current or voltage to control a larger current flow. A transistor may be used as a signal amplifier or as a switch. A transistor has three leads for connections in a circuit. One of the leads is connected to the controlling current or voltage while the larger current flows through the other two leads.

Transistor Water Analogy: You may think of a transistor like the mechani-

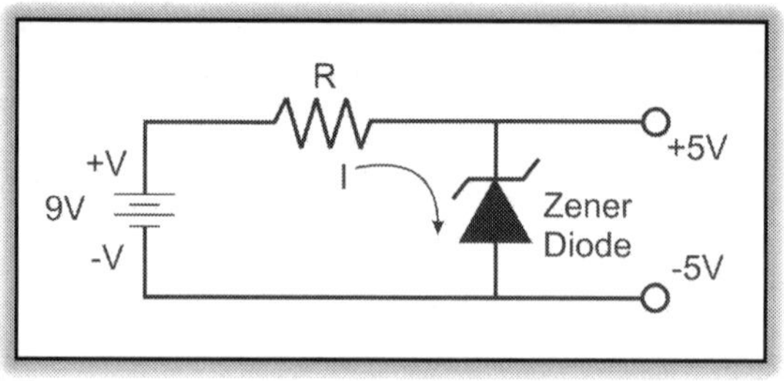

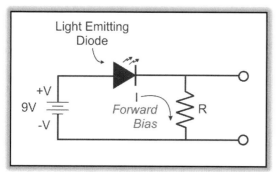

Figure 6.14: A **Zener diode** keeps the reverse bias voltage near a stable value. In this example the 9V reverse bias source is kept at 5V by the Zener diode.

Figure 6.15: The LED will illuminate when forward biased, as shown here. If the voltage is reversed the LED will not emit light.

Bipolar Junction Transistor (BJT): As the name implies the BJT is a pair of junctions, as described in the previous P-N junction diode discussion. The P-type and N-type materials may be arranged in a PNP sandwich or an NPN sandwich. The center material in the sandwich is connected to the *base* lead that provides the controlling current to the BJT. The outer two materials are connected to the *collector* and *emitter* leads through which the larger controlled current passes.

cal water gate shown in Figure 6.17. A controlling "signal" is provided by the relatively small flow of the water hose. With a high current water source available to the trough, the output "signal" will be a strong variable current that mirrors the small input signal of the hose flow. While the hose flow may be adjusted with a light crimping or nozzle adjustment, the output current flow can be a strong, varying surge of water. In this way the transistor acts to amplify the input signal, producing a much stronger signal of a pattern identical to the small input signal. If the input signal is taken only to the extreme conditions, turning off the hose flow entirely or opening it completely wide, the transistor may function as a switch.

Figure 6.16: Transistors for various power handling.

The BJT has three operating regimes:

1. Cut-off: As with the junction diode, a minimum base current (center material connection) is necessary to allow current flow. With no base current greater than the threshold current there is no current flow from collector to emitter electrode. This stable operating point is called the *cut-off region* for the bipolar transistor.

2. Amplification: As base current exceeds the cut-off value, the current flowing from collector to emitter will be proportional to (but usually greater than) the base current. Any base current variations (signals) are amplified as variations in the collector-to-emitter current.

3. Saturation: Some value of high base current will produce *saturation*, another stable operating point at which increased base current will no longer increase the collector-to-emitter current through the transistor.

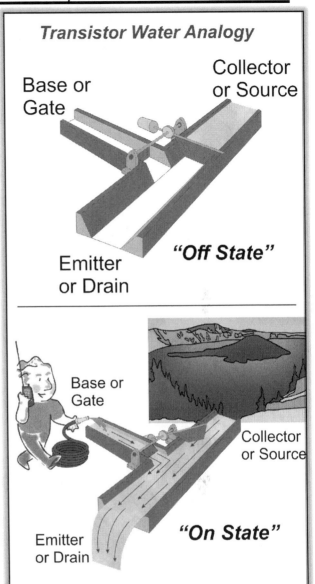

Figure 6.17: A water model for the transistor. A large current flow is controlled with a relatively small "signal" from the hose. The gate opens variable amounts commensurate with the small input signal, allowing a large flow of current that mirrors the changes of the small input signal flow.

The saturation and cut-off regions are the stable operating points for a bipolar transistor used as a switch in a logic circuit.

You may now be wondering what difference is made by the PNP versus NPN material sandwiching? The difference comes in the voltage bias that must be applied between the base and emitter to achieve current flow. With the PNP BJT the emitter voltage must exceed the base voltage. For the NPN BJT the base voltage must exceed that of the emitter. The symbol arrows for PNP and NPN BJTs point in opposite directions, with the PNP arrow "pointing in," and the NPN arrow "not pointing in" (NPN).

Field Effect Transistor (FET): The FET utilizes a P-type and N-type combination also, but in a different configuration from the BJT. A *channel* of one material is routed through the other to affect a sort of variably squeezing tunnel for charge passage. The three FET electrodes are referred to as the *gate* (the control signal input, analogous to the BJT base), the *source* (analogous to the BJT collector), and the *drain* (analogous to the BJT emitter).

Like the BJT, the FET amplifies signals input to the gate by controlling current flow from source to drain electrodes. However, instead of a *current signal* to the gate a *voltage signal* is applied. The variable voltage at the gate controls the width of the charge tunnel described above, opening wider or closing smaller to vary current. A variably pinched water hose analogy applies here!

MOSFET: Very similar to the FET is the MOSFET, or *metal-oxide-semiconductor field effect transistor*. A variation on the FET, **the MOSFET inserts a thin insulating layer to separate the gate from the channel.** This construction can offer some enhanced performance due to improved conductivity.

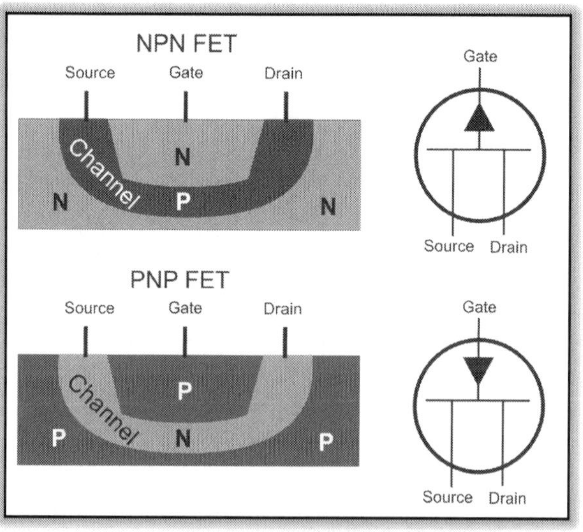

Transistor Packaging: Many different packages of transistors are available. Plastic insulated transistors are common for low-power applications. High power transistors will commonly have metal packaging through which heat may be dissipated.

Figure 6.18: Field Effect Transistors apply a voltage at the gate electrode to vary the width of a charge channel created by the P&N materials. Source-to-drain current varies with channel width, determined by the gate voltage.

6.2 Components

Now you have many of the small, digestible bits of electronics that make radio work! Of course there are other components in most circuits, such as switches, op amps, relays, and more complex combinations of the components we've discussed here. A General Class exam circuit diagram follows below that highlights the component symbols we have covered in this section, and those in the exam question pool are in boldface print. A summary table of electronic components also follows on the next page focusing on the exam question concepts.

Next we'll piece together some of these components to see what they do, and gain greater understanding in the process. But first, review the diagram below and the table on the next page, and then go hit the section 6.2 questions!

HamRadioSchool.com/general_media

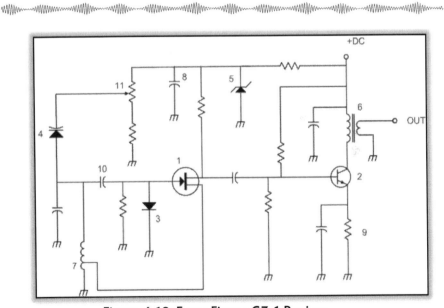

Figure 6.19: Exam Figure G7-1 Review

1. **Field Effect Transistor**
2. **NPN Junction Transistor**
3. Diode
4. Voltage Variable Capacitor
5. **Zener Diode**
6. **Solid Core Transformer** (See Section 6.5)
7. **Tapped Inductor**
8. Capacitor
9. Resistor
10. Capacitor
11. Variable resistor

431

Section 6.2 Components Exam Question Content Review

Component	Symbol	Unit	Exam Question Concept
Resistor	—/\/\/—	Ohm	Wire wound resistors produce inductance that affect circuit performance unpredictably, so not used in RF circuits.
Capacitor	—|(—	farad	Electrolytic type have high capacitance for volume. Ceramic capacitors advantage are low cost. Lead inductance reduces effective capacitance at VHF+ frequencies. Polarized capacitors must not have reversed polarity or explosion, damage dielectric, or short circuit may occur. Convert among pF, nF, µF by moving decimal 3 positions for each prefix step. (Each question item requires moving decimal 3 positions to the left.)
Inductor	(coil symbol)	henry	Inductor becomes capacitive when operated above its self-resonant frequency. Ferrite core toroids allow large inductance values, keep magnetic field mostly within core, and allow optimization for frequencies. Ferrite core performance is determined by the composition (mix) of materials used.
Diode	—▶|—	N/A	Threshold voltages: germanium = 0.3v, silicon = 0.7v.
Light Emitting Diode (LED)	—▶|—	N/A	Emits light when forward biased.
Bipolar Junction Transistor	(NPN symbol)	N/A	Stable operating points for switch function are saturation and cut-off regions.
MOSFET	(MOSFET symbol)	N/A	Construction has gate separated from channel with thin insulating layer.

6.3 Series & Parallel Components

> *You can't get more, or less, water out of an upturned bucket than you filled it with.*
> *– Kirchoff's Current Law, restated*

Even though water and electronics do not mix well in everyday applications, using wet analogies for thinking about electronics works remarkably well. Gustav Kirchoff was a German physicist of the mid-nineteenth century who expressed the brilliant concept above about the water in and out of the bucket in much more elegant and mathematical terms. Essentially his current law states that for a closed circuit, the current entering a junction must equal the current exiting the junction. Kirchoff was referring to electricity, of course, but the plumbing analogy to this rule also *holds water*. <Ahem.>

Current Law: Imagine, perhaps, a lawn watering system of pipes. Suppose the pipe from the water spigot (the current source) runs to a junction where three pipes connect, each routed to a different area of the yard where a sprinkler head awaits to scatter the water to parched blades of grass. Kirchoff's insight was that the quantity of current flowing into the junction of the pipes from the spigot must be equivalent to the sum of the current spritzing out of the three sprinklers and onto the grass. Makes perfect sense, right? Duh! Well, keep in mind he was in the early 1800s and working with the relatively new, cutting edge discovery, electricity. I wonder how many times he got shocked.

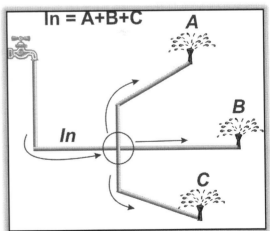

Figure 6.20: Kirchoff's Current Law water model. Current into the junction must equal the sum of sprinkler outputs.

Voltage Law: In spite of any painful jolts he may have received, Kirchoff didn't stop with the consideration of just current. He proved a somewhat more challenging rule about voltage (analogous to water pressure). Imagine that you operate a self-serve car wash that provides high pressure sprayers in each of four washing stalls, but all fed from one central water pump. Folks pull into the stalls, swipe a debit card, and blast the crud off their vehicles with the handheld spraying nozzle. If you measure the drop in water pressure that occurs between the high pressure line feeding the spray nozzle to the water released to lower pressure to fly free and splatter against the car, and if you sum up that pressure change across all four wash stalls in operation, it will be equal to the pressure provided by the central water pump. Kirchoff discovered that electricity in a closed circuit follows this same concept – the sum of voltage drops across components in a circuit (resistors, appliances, inductors, capacitors, etc.) equals the voltage applied by the battery.

The upshot of Kirchoff's current law and voltage law is that multiple electronic components arranged in series and parallel circuits may be "replaced," mathematically or in reality, by a single *equivalent component*. These neat math tricks are really handy for engineering and circuit design simplification or modification. Thus, from the fine work of Kirchoff we have today a nifty set of simple mathematical relationships for each of the basic component types that define the equivalent single component values of arrangements in either series or parallel. Let's check it out, especially since several question pool items are based upon these equations.

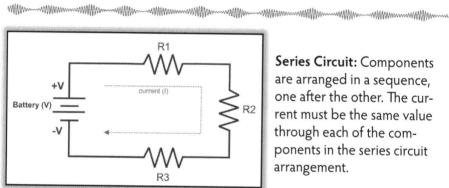

Figure 6.21: Components in series.

Series Circuit: Components are arranged in a sequence, one after the other. The current must be the same value through each of the components in the series circuit arrangement.

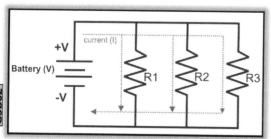

Figure 6.22: Components in parallel.

Parallel Circuit: Components are arranged in separate, unique paths that branch from a common path. **The total current must equal the sum of the individual currents through each branch (for a purely resistive parallel circuit).**

6.3 Series & Parallel Components

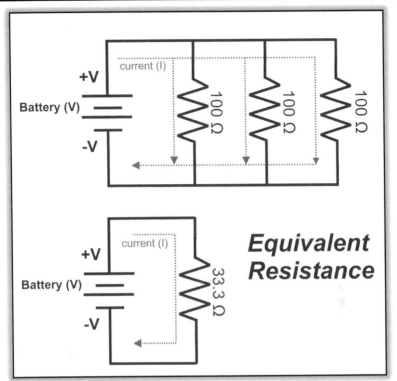

Figure 6.23: The three resistors in parallel may be replaced by a single resistor offering equivalent resistance as calculated from equation form #2 below. This concept applies to each type of component, but the proper equation form varies with component type and configuration.

Two Equation Forms: You need to remember two simple equation forms for six circuit scenarios: Each of three components (resistors, inductors, capacitors) may be configured in either of the two arrangements (series or parallel). One of these two general equation forms applies to each of the six cases:

1. *Sum of Components Equation* – If X is the component value, such as resistance in ohms, capacitance in farads, or inductance in henries, the equivalent component value Xeq is simply:

   $X_{eq} = X_1 + X_2 + X_3$ ... and so on for all of the components in the circuit.

2. *The Reciprocal of Reciprocals Equation* – If X is the component value, the equivalent component value Xeq is:

   $$X_{eq} = \frac{1}{\frac{1}{X_1} + \frac{1}{X_2} + \frac{1}{X_3}}$$

Resistors and inductors in a series configuration sum as components, using equation #1. **Resistors and inductors in parallel configuration** combine with the reciprocal equation, #2.

Capacitors are the reverse of resistors and inductors. **Capacitors in series** combine as the reciprocal of reciprocals, equation #2. **Capacitors in parallel** sum as components, using equation #1. See Figure 6.24 for a graphical depiction of these relationships.

Let's consider examples using each of these two equations:

Example 1: What is the inductance (L) of a 20 millihenry inductor in series with a 50 millihenry inductor? Inductors in series add simply, so we'll use the Sum of Components Equation form #1 to calculate:

$L_{eq} = 20$ mh $+ 50$ mh $= 70$ mh   The correct answer is **70 millihenry**.

Example 2: What is the total resistance of three 100-ohm resistors in parallel? Resistors in parallel use the Reciprocal of Reciprocals equation form, #2 thus:

$$R_{eq} = \cfrac{1}{\cfrac{1}{R_1} + \cfrac{1}{R_2} + \cfrac{1}{R_3}}$$

$$= \cfrac{1}{\cfrac{1}{100} + \cfrac{1}{100} + \cfrac{1}{100}}$$

$$= \cfrac{1}{\cfrac{3}{100}} = 33.3 \text{ ohms}$$

Notice from Figure 6.24 that resistors and inductors use the same equation forms for the same component configurations, while capacitors are the *odd component out* in each case, using the opposite form for each configuration. If we perform sample calculations we find the following effects on the equivalent values of components when we add a component:

Component	Adding a Series Component	Adding a Parallel Component
Resistor	**Increases total resistance**	Decreases resistance
Inductor	**Increases inductance**	Decreases inductance
Capacitor	Decreases capacitance	**Increases capacitance**

6.3 Series & Parallel Components

Given the water analogy and what you have learned in the previous section about these components, the preceding table should make sense. Consider the following observations about each component type that *increases the effective value*, keeping in mind the opposite arrangement will have the decreasing value impact:

- Stringing resistors along in a series line is like making one longer resistor, so resistance increases.

- Stringing inductors along in a series line is like lengthening a single inductor, increasing its number of windings, and thereby increasing its inductance.

- Arranging capacitors in parallel is like creating a single capacitor of much larger surface area, thereby increasing its capacitance.

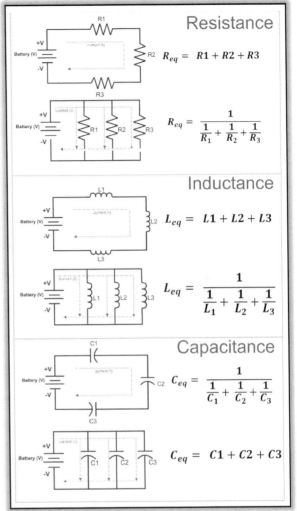

Figure 6.24: Series and parallel components with equations.

Let's work through a few more examples. Sharpen your pencil and grab your calculator, and let's get comfortable with series and parallel computation.

Example: What is the total resistance of a 10 ohm, a 20 ohm, and a 50 ohm resistor connected in parallel? Resistors in parallel use the Reciprocal of Reciprocals equation form #2, and by our table relationships we know that we should expect decreased resistance with the parallel configuration. Calculating, we obtain:

$$R_{eq} = \cfrac{1}{\cfrac{1}{R_1} + \cfrac{1}{R_2} + \cfrac{1}{R_3}} = \cfrac{1}{\cfrac{1}{10} + \cfrac{1}{20} + \cfrac{1}{50}} = \cfrac{1}{\cfrac{17}{100}} = 5.9 \text{ ohms}$$

Think back to middle school math on this one… when adding those three fractions in the denominator, the denominator of each fraction must be common. Convert each fraction so that it has a denominator of 100, and the numerator values convert to 10, 5, and 2, respectively.

$1/10 = 10/100; \quad 1/20 = 5/100; \quad 1/50 = 2/100$

These three fractions then sum to 17/100. Following this conversion and summation, use the "1/x" or "reciprocal" key on your calculator to easily compute the final solution.

G5C09

Example: What is the capacitance of three 100 microfarad capacitors connected in series? Capacitors in series use the Reciprocal of Reciprocals equation form, and result in decreased capacitance:

$$C_{eq} = \cfrac{1}{\cfrac{1}{C_1} + \cfrac{1}{C_2} + \cfrac{1}{C_3}}$$

$$= \cfrac{1}{\cfrac{1}{100} + \cfrac{1}{100} + \cfrac{1}{100}}$$

$$= \cfrac{1}{\cfrac{3}{100}} = 33.3 \text{ microfarads}$$

In contrast with the resistance example above, this problem already has common denominators since the capacitors are of equivalent value. Again, the "1/x" calculator key comes in handy for computing the final reciprocal.

G5C10

Example: What is the inductance of three 10 millihenry inductors connected in parallel? Inductors in parallel also use the Reciprocal of Reciprocals equation form, also decreasing inductance:

$$L_{eq} = \cfrac{1}{\cfrac{1}{L_1} + \cfrac{1}{L_2} + \cfrac{1}{L_3}} = \cfrac{1}{\cfrac{1}{10} + \cfrac{1}{10} + \cfrac{1}{10}} = \cfrac{1}{\cfrac{3}{10}} = 3.3 \text{ millihenry}$$

6.3 Series & Parallel Components

Example: What is the capacitance of a 20 microfarad capacitor connected in series with a 50 microfarad capacitor? Again, the Reciprocal of Reciprocals equation form, but only two capacitors:

$$C_{eq} = \frac{1}{\frac{1}{C_1} + \frac{1}{C_2}} = \frac{1}{\frac{1}{20} + \frac{1}{50}} = \frac{1}{\frac{7}{100}} = 14.3 \text{ microfarads}$$

Once again, obtaining a common denominator for the two fractions is necessary before adding them (100).

Example: What is the equivalent capacitance of two 5.0 nanofarad capacitors and one 750 picofarad capacitors connected in parallel? First, convert picofarads to nanofarads by moving the decimal left three places, making the units common as nF. Then, capacitors in parallel use the simple Sum of Components equation form:

750 pF = 0.750 nF

C_{eq} = 5.0 nf + 5.0 nf + 0.750 nf = **10.750 nanofarads**

Example: If three equal value resistors in series produce 450 ohms, what is the value of each resistor? Resistors in series add together simply by equation form #1, so the value of three equal value resistors summing to 450 ohms must each be **150 ohms.**

150 + 150 + 150 = **450 ohms**

Diodes in Parallel: Beyond the resistors, capacitors, and inductors, diodes are sometimes used in a parallel arrangement to increase current handling capacity. Although either diode alone may not have sufficient current rating to handle the circuit's peak current, the pair of them in combination can handle it with one-half

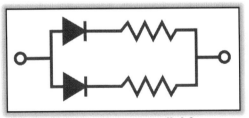

Figure 6.25: Diodes in parallel for increased current handling, with low-value resistors in series.

of the current flowing through each of the two diodes. The pair of diodes are equivalent to a single larger or higher rated diode.

However, it is necessary to ensure that the current is indeed shared equally between the two parallel diodes, or one of them could carry most of the current unintentionally. A resistor placed in series with each diode ensures that one diode doesn't carry most of the current, but that it is equally shared. Low value resistors are typically used as shown in Figure 6.25 to balance the current throughput between the diodes.

Hopefully your bucket is now filled sufficiently with series and parallel circuit concepts that you may pour forth equivalent knowledge on your VE exam and ace any of these questions you see. Make sure you have the pattern of equation form application in your bucket for the combinations of arrangement and component type, make sure the equation forms don't leak out, and be familiar with the functions of your calculator! Good luck!

Go snag the questions for this section online and practice again, and then come back to learn more about the reaction we get from these components – less math, more science.

HamRadioSchool.com/general_media

6.4 Impedance & Reactance

> **❝** *The impeded stream is the one that sings.*
> *— Wendell Berry*

Indeed, currents in the absence of impedance would be boring. In many ways it is impedance that allows our radios to modulate and to radiate – in essence, to *sing*. In this section we will examine impedance more closely, including the component reactions to alternating current that contribute to impedances. We will also discover how the manipulation of impedance with electronics is important to our control and transfer of power, from the wall socket to the antenna feedpoint.

Impedance (Z): The opposition to the flow of current in an AC circuit. The unit of measure for impedance is the ohm (Ω). Much like simple resistance to DC, impedance opposes the back-and-forth current flow of AC. However, impedance is resistance combined with another oppositional force called *reactance*.

Reactance (X): Opposition to the flow of alternating current caused by capacitance or inductance. The unit of measure for reactance is also the ohm. Capacitors and inductors *react* to AC in different, quite opposite, ways. The reactance imposed by capacitors and inductors depends upon the component value of capacitance or inductance and upon the frequency of AC.

Capacitive Reactance (X_c): Opposition to the flow of alternating current in a capacitor. The designation for capacitive reactance is X_c, and it is calculated as

$$X_C = \frac{1}{2\pi f C}$$

The frequency in hertz of the AC is designated by f and the capacitance in farads of the component by C. ($\pi \approx 3.14$.) Although there are no question pool items requiring this computation, it is useful to illustrate the reactance to capacitance and frequency. **As frequency of the applied**

AC increases, the reactance decreases. And, as capacitance increases, reactance decreases.

Recalling our water model of capacitors, this makes sense. The capacitor was imagined to be a stretchy diaphragm across the interior of the water pipe, stretching back and forth with the alternating current flow, storing energy in the elastic stretch, but having a maximum capacity that when reached stops further stretching and storage. For a given AC voltage, if the frequency of alternation is rapid enough (high frequency)

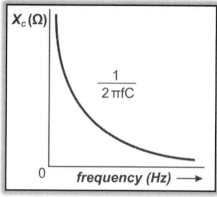

Figure 6.26: Capacitive reactance decreases as frequency increases. A capacitor passes high frequency signals and impedes low frequency signals.

the maximum charge capacity may never be reached in either direction of current, so little opposition to the AC flow results (low reactance). But with the same voltage and a low AC frequency, the diaphragm may stretch to maximum capacity (maximum charge) and reduce or stop further current flow (increased reactance) until the AC cycle reverses. The greater the capacitance the less opposition to current flow results from cycle to cycle (lower reactance).

Strictly in electrical terms, the capacitor is storing electric charge until the maximum feasible charge is accumulated on its plates, and opposition to current flow builds up gradually over that time of accumulation each AC cycle. At higher frequencies or with higher capacitance, the plates do not approach the maximum charge and reactance remains low. At lower frequencies or lower capacitance the plates approach or achieve maximum charge capacity and offer great opposition each AC cycle, or higher reactance. So, the capacitor readily passes high frequency AC and opposes low frequency AC and DC.

Inductive Reactance (X_L): Opposition to the flow of alternating current in an inductor. The designation for inductive reactance is X_L, and it is calculated as

$$X_L = 2\pi f L$$

Again, the frequency in hertz is designated f, and the inductance of the component is L. Note that **if either frequency** or inductance **increases,**

the inductive reactance will increase. Notice that these effects are opposite that of the capacitive reactance.

In the water model an inductor was likened to a massive water wheel extending into the current flow. It stores energy in the rotational inertia of the heavy wheel turning, analogous to the inductor *inflating* a magnetic field to store energy. Inflating the magnetic field requires time and work, as does accelerating the wheel rotation up to water current speed. During this initial inflation period (wheel acceleration) great opposition to the current flow is offered, but it diminishes gradually with time, and once fully inflated (spinning at speed) the opposition is eliminated. This effect is opposite that of the capacitor where initially little opposition is offered in the cycle but great opposition builds over time as the plates charge, or the diaphragm stretches toward its limit.

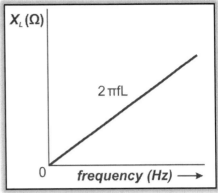

Figure 6.27: Inductive reactance increases as frequency increases. Inductors pass low frequency signals and impede high frequency signals.

The inductor readily passes DC or low frequency AC that allows the magnetic field time to inflate and stabilize during the AC cycle. A rapid reversal of current with high frequency AC requires constant work inflating the magnetic field in opposite polarizations each cycle, never achieving stability, and thus providing constant opposition to AC current flow.

Resonance: In the language of physics (*no, don't run!*), resonance occurs in a system when it is easily able to store and transfer energy between two (or more) storage modes. Think about a playground swing, for instance. At the bottom of a swing's cycle the energy is *kinetic*, stored as the high velocity of your body's mass moving along the swing's arc. As the swing rises and slows the energy is transferred into *gravitational potential*, your body suspended high above the ground, and the maximum transfer to potential energy has occurred at the moment of weightlessness when you get that little thrill in the pit of your stomach! That energy transfer was pretty easy, huh? Fun, too! (*See, physics can be fun!*)

Following that high suspended state of abdominal delight you will fall. Gravity will pull you down. Your potential energy is being transferred back to the kinetic energy of speed once again. Fortunately, the swing directs that speed

Figure 6.28: Resonance, like that of a swing, occurs in circuits having both capacitance and inductance.

onto the arc defined by the length of its chains or ropes, and the kinetic-potential-kinetic cycle is repeated again and again, much to your intestine's joy.

This is easy transfer of energy between two storage modes. But there is some opposition to this swinging cycle presented by air resistance as you zip along and by the rubbing friction at the chain attachment points. However, if only a tiny amount of energy is added each cycle, perhaps by someone giving just the slightest push regularly timed with your downward motion, the small amount of resistance to your swinging cycle is overcome and perhaps exceeded, sending you higher and higher! The natural frequency of the swing's oscillation, and the frequency with which reinforcing pushes are added to be most effective, is the *resonant frequency*.

The same condition can arise in AC circuits containing inductors and capacitors. This type of circuit is an *LC oscillator*, also known as a *tank circuit* because of its similarity to a sloshing tank of water transferring energy between kinetic and potential modes. *When the inductive reactance and capacitive reactance are equivalent, the circuit will achieve a state of resonance.*

The two energy storage modes in an LC oscillator are magnetic field storage (inductance L) and electric field storage (capacitance C). When a circuit's inductive reactance and capacitive reactance are equal the two components can easily transfer

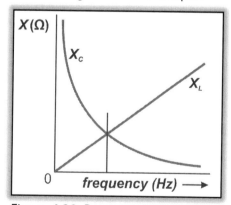

Figure 6.29: Resonance occurs for the frequency at which inductive and capacitive reactances are equivalent.

6.4 Impedance & Reactance

energy back and forth, just like the swing. In a series circuit arrangement the opposite effects of the inductive and capacitive reactances cancel one another out, leaving only the internal resistance of the inductor and capacitor to contribute to overall impedance, as shown in the left of Figure 6.30. In a parallel circuit these reactances reinforce one another, causing circuit impedance to peak to a maximum, as in the right of Figure 6.30. You may recognize this case from the antenna trap discussed in Section 5.1 (and Figure 5.9) where the resonant frequency causes high impedance and electrically terminates the inner antenna segments.

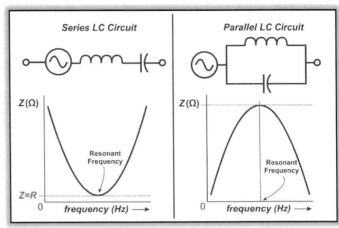

Figure 6.30: Impedance of a series LC circuit minimizes to simple resistance at the resonant frequency. Impedance of a parallel LC circuit maximizes at the resonant frequency and includes simple resistance and reactances.

Further like the swing, the transfer of energy back and forth between capacitor and inductor will have a characteristic frequency of oscillation, or resonant frequency. The swing's resonant frequency is determined by the length of the swing and by the strength of gravity's pull. (A longer swing has a lower resonant frequency, and a swing on the moon would have a lower resonant frequency than the same swing on earth.) Similarly, **the frequency of an LC oscillator is determined by the inductance and capacitance in the tank circuit.** By selecting appropriate values of inductance and capacitance, an LC oscillator can be created to resonate at a specific frequency for the purposes of filtering (as in the antenna trap) or in tuning circuits to respond strongly to selected frequencies (as in an RF oscillator). As noted in Section 6.2 *Components*, some inductors create inter-turn capacitance that causes them to be self-resonant at some frequencies where the parasitic capacitive reactance equals the inductive reactance. One final analog to our swing: In an LC oscillator circuit the applied AC frequency is the reinforcing push provided each cycle of energy transfer to overcome the remaining simple resistance.

Impedance Matching: Thanks to another 19th Century German physicist with the impressive name *Moritz Hermann von Jacobi*, we are able to take advantage of the *Maximum Power Transfer Theorem* in our radio circuits. With this theorem von Jacobi proved that **a power source can deliver maximum power to an electrical load when the impedance of the load is equal to the output impedance of the power source.** Let's untangle that mouthful just a bit.

In a radio station, an electrical load may be an antenna, a dummy load, a resistor, coaxial cable, or other circuit type – it is the thing to which we wish to transfer power with the source, or transmitter. A load will have characteristic impedance resulting from the combination of resistance, capacitive reactance, and inductive reactance. In some cases, such as antennas, coaxial cable, and engineered circuits, we can adjust the impedance of the load to a desired value by manipulating components or materials. Similarly, with signal sources like an RF transmitter, the output impedance (at the connector) may be engineered to a desired value. As an example noted in Chapter 5, *Antennas*, most amateur radio transmitters and commonly used coaxial cables are designed to have 50 ohm impedance.

The Maximum Power Transfer Theorem reveals that impedance matching is important so the source can deliver maximum power to the load. To deliver maximum power to our station antenna the impedance of the transmitter, feed line, and antenna feed point should be well matched. As discussed in Section 5.3, an impedance mismatch will result in power reflections, reducing power delivered to the antenna.

Impedance Matching Devices: Depending upon the application or situation, various practical circuits may be used to match the impedance of a load to that of the source. **At radio frequencies and to maximize the transfer of power, impedance matching may be achieved with an impedance matching transformer,** an LC circuit (**Pi-network** or T-circuit), or even a simple **length of transmission line** (a "stub"). Transformers will be described in the next section, but let's examine two popular LC circuit matches here.

LC Circuit: Inserting an LC network between two circuits is one method of impedance matching between AC circuits. The *Pi-network* and *T-circuit* are two common LC circuits used for this purpose. (Network is just a more formal term for a circuit, particularly when a general design concept is to be related.)

By selecting appropriate inductor and capacitor values these circuits will present the desired matching impedance on each side of the circuit to the source or load to which it is connected. Variable inductor and capaci-

6.4 Impedance & Reactance

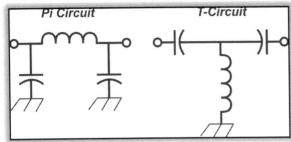

Figure 6.31: The Pi Circuit and T-Circuit used for impedance matching.

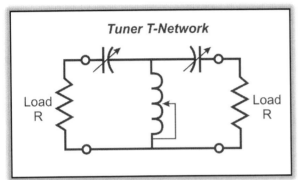

Figure 6.32: A T-Network using variable components for tuning the impedance match between two loads.

tor components may be used to create adjustable matching networks when load impedance is expected to vary, such as in an antenna tuner used to match impedance between a transmitter and an antenna across a broad band of RF frequencies. The T-circuit is commonly used in antenna tuning devices, and the Pi-network is often incorporated in higher power applications such as amplifiers.

Practical Application:
The most common application of impedance matching for most amateurs is in the realm of antenna tuning. The maximum power will be transferred to your antenna when the antenna system's impedance matches that of the transmitter. In the simplest and most common scenario this will mean a 50 Ω transmitter output with 50 Ω coaxial cable connected as a feedline. The feedline will attach to the antenna feed point. The impedance presented at the antenna feedpoint will be a function of the antenna design, antenna installation height, and the environment near the antenna.

Rarely will an antenna present a feed point impedance of precisely 50 Ω, especially across a wide range of frequencies in a typical amateur band. Thus, it is at the antenna feed point connection where an impedance mismatch will most commonly occur and thereby generate power reflections and elevate SWR.

Using an antenna tuner or an impedance matching network between the transmitter and feedline is a partial solution. Most modern transmitters will begin reducing power as SWR exceeds values of about 2:1. The matching network presents 50 Ω to the transmitter so it will not reduce power, but the impedance mismatch is still present at the feed point and causing a higher

SWR on the antenna system. The matching network or tuner does not improve power transfer to the antenna, but it helps avoid power reduction by the transmitter. The reflections are still bouncing back and forth along your feedline. *Your antenna system is not at resonance,* but that's OK.

Your antenna SWR will rarely, if ever, be 1:1 on the nose, and very rarely will your antenna be operating perfectly at resonance. This *might* happen at one frequency on one band when the humidity is just right, the moon is full, and you wear two different colored socks, one of wool and the other of cotton, while your spouse pulls the aluminum gutter away from the house at the precise angle required. But even without all that you can get it *good enough* for superb operation. The perfect antenna system impedance match is a very rare thing.

So you see, the impeded stream really is the one that sings. The impeded transceiver sings its RF melody, particularly when the impeded antenna system is singing in harmony. Next we'll examine power sources and learn about their inner workings. First, the questions on impedance and reactance!

HamRadioSchool.com/general_media

Note: If you would like to learn more about complex impedance and the relationship among resistance, capacitive reactance, and inductive reactance, see the *HamRadioSchool.com* three-part article on Complex Impedance online.

6.5 Power Sources

6.5 Power Sources

> **"** With great power often comes great confusion.
> – Dan Allen, Seam in Action

When it comes to supplying power to your station, great confusion should be avoided. In this section we will examine the workings of power sources. We'll cover several types of power sources, but we will focus on what's going on inside those DC power supplies that you plug into the 120 VAC wall socket and that provide about +13.8 VDC to power your ham radio. This should help to clear up, or at least reduce, any great confusion you may have about supplying power.

Power Supply Overview: You have probably used a DC power supply of one type or another a million times. Plug in a battery charger for an HT ham radio, a cell phone, a tablet computing device, an electric razor, an electronic toy, or nearly any other battery operated electronic device on the market today and you're using a power supply. Many small appliances will have them integrated internally, such as clocks, commercial radios, and computers. An amateur radio base station will often be operated with a supply capable of delivering the power necessary for transmitter RF output of 50 to 100 watts. A power supply will integrate three basic circuits to convert higher voltage AC into lower voltage DC:

1. *Transformer:* Shifts AC voltage from one value to another. For example, 120 VAC may be transformed into an AC voltage nearer the desired 13.8 volts output level.
2. *Rectifier:* Converts the AC waveform into a varying voltage DC. Even though the voltage is providing EMF in only one direction after being rectified, it still contains the sine wave-like variability in voltage value over time.
3. *Filter Circuit:* Smooths the varying DC voltage into a steady DC voltage that is usable by the radio electronics.

Let's consider each of these types of circuits and the tasks they accomplish for the power supply.

Transformer: Contrary to popular belief, a transformer is not a giant alien robot that can camouflage itself as a tractor trailer rig or spiffy hotrod car. In electronics, a transformer is two (or more) inductors whose wire windings are wrapped around the same core. The symbol for a transformer looks like a pair of parallel inductors with a bar between them, mimicking the physical reality. While not nearly as sensational as a giant alien robot destroying high rise buildings, real transformers are a lot more practically useful and a lot less trouble.

Recall from the 6.2 *Components* section that an inductor creates a magnetic field about itself to store energy when a current passes through its coiled form. Recall also that inductors near one another may have *mutual inductance* – that is, the changing magnetic field of one inductor can induce an electric current in the other inductor as its magnetic field inflates and deflates with AC cycles. While mutual inductance is to be avoided in most circuits, a transformer is designed specifically to take advantage of mutual inductance. This is why the windings share a common core.

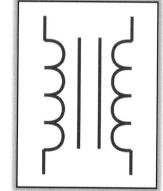

Figure 6.33: Symbol for a solid core transformer. See also Figure 6.19 (G7A12).

If AC is applied to one of the windings it will produce a magnetic field that inflates and deflates with the AC cycle with alternating polarity of the magnetic flux. This part of a transformer that is normally connected to the incoming source of energy is called the primary, or *primary winding*, and it is the primary that is often energized by household 120 VAC. The other winding on the core, called the secondary winding, is also within the alternating magnetic field of the primary. As the primary's magnetic field inflates and deflates, an alternating current is induced in the secondary winding. **An AC voltage across the secondary winding of a transformer is caused by mutual inductance when an AC voltage source is connected across its primary winding.**

Transforming Voltage: The AC voltage and current induced in the secondary winding depends upon the ratio of the number of turns between the two windings. Specifically, the ratio of the voltages of the two windings will equal the ratio of the number of windings. Letting E_p and E_s be the primary and secondary voltages (EMF), and letting N_p and N_s be the number of turns in the primary and secondary, the relationship is

$$\frac{E_S}{E_P} = \frac{N_S}{N_P}$$ or, solving for the secondary voltage $E_S = E_P \times \frac{N_S}{N_P}$

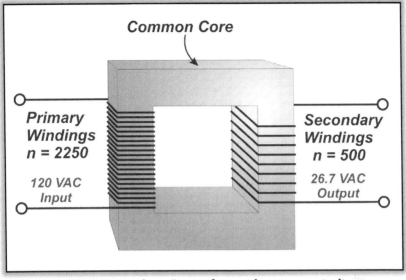

Figure 6.34: A "step down" transformer has more windings on the primary than on the secondary, and it reduces voltage by the ratio of windings.

The second form of the equation lets us compute the voltage induced in the secondary from the primary voltage and the windings ratio, as in the following example. We will work with RMS voltages as described in the 6.1 *Power and Principles* section.

Example: **What is the RMS voltage across a 500-turn secondary winding in a transformer if the 2250-turn primary is connected to 120 VAC?** (Figure 6.34)

$$E_S = E_P \times \frac{N_S}{N_P} = 120v \times \frac{500}{2250} = 120v \times 0.222 = \mathbf{26.7v}$$

This is an example of a *step-down* transformer, since the voltage is decreased from the primary to the secondary windings. The current of the secondary will be proportionally greater than the current of the primary, as the power (P=EI) transfer of the two sets of windings must be equivalent (in an ideal case). **In a step-up transformer** in which the primary conducts greater current so that the secondary may have a higher voltage, **the primary winding conductor** (wire) **may be larger in diameter than the conductor of the secondary to accommodate the higher current of the primary.**

A transformer will work in both directions -- the input and output sides may be reversed, reversing the step-up or step-down nature of the transformer.

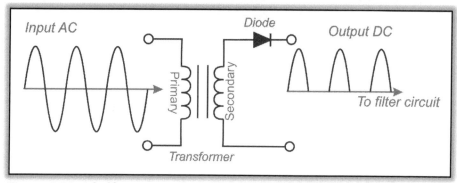

Figure 6.35: A half-wave rectifier allows only one-half of the transformed AC waveform to pass, resulting in a pulsing and varying DC output.

For example, **if a signal is applied to the secondary winding of a 4:1 voltage step-down transformer instead of the primary winding, the output voltage is multiplied by 4** (stepped up 4:1).

As noted in Section 6.4, transformers may also be used as impedance matching devices. This method is often used to match high impedances at the feed point of an end-fed antenna. The impedance ratio across the transformer is related to the square of the windings ratio.

Rectifier: After the AC voltage has been adjusted to a desired value by the transformer, the rectifier will convert the AC to DC. That is, the back-and-forth alternating direction cycle of current will be changed to flow in just one direction. Let's consider two basic types of rectifiers, the *half-wave* and the *full-wave* rectifier.

Half-Wave Rectifier: **A half-wave rectifier converts to DC** only one-half of the AC wave, or **180 degrees of the AC cycle**, as depicted in Figure 6.35. The complete 360 degree AC waveform is applied to the primary winding of the transformer, but the diode circuit on the secondary winding output allows only one-half of the transformed AC waveform to pass – the positive voltage portion in this figure. The sine wave-like variation of voltage remains, but all voltage is in a single direction. The voltage "pulses" and varies, however, since the negative voltage half of the waveform is deleted, leaving the positive voltage sine wave signal and a gap of zero volts during the negative voltage times of the AC source.

An advantage of the half-wave rectifier in a power supply is that only one diode is required, as shown in Figure 6.35. The diode selected for the half-wave rectifier must be rated to withstand the negative peak volt-

6.5 Power Sources

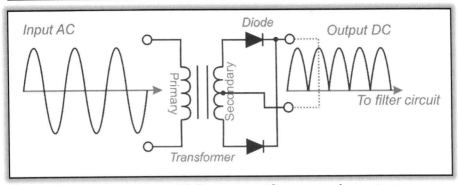

Figure 6.36: A center-tapped full-wave rectifier passes the entire transformed AC waveform, resulting in a varying DC output.

age of the transformer for which current will attempt to flow in the inverse (non-conducting) direction through the diode. This is referred to as the peak-inverse-voltage (PIV) rating of a rectifier, the maximum voltage it will handle in the non-conducting direction. For the half-wave power supply the PIV is typically two times the normal peak output voltage of the power supply for reasons we will explore under the filter circuit topic later in this section.

Full-Wave Rectifier: **A full-wave rectifier converts to DC the entire 360 degrees of the AC cycle,** as depicted in Figure 6.36. **This full-wave rectifier circuit type uses two diodes and a center-tapped transformer** to obtain DC output.

Each of the two diodes in the full-wave rectifier circuit passes one-half of the AC voltage waveform, either the positive or the negative half. And due to the circuit arrangement, each diode passes its current to a common directional path beyond the diodes and toward the filter circuit of the power supply. This is like having two one-half wave rectifiers working together, each converting to DC one-half of the AC waveform. As a result, **the output waveform of an unfiltered full-wave rectifier connected to a resistive load is a series of DC pulses at twice the frequency of the AC input.**

Full-Wave Bridge Rectifier: Another full-wave rectifier design is the bridge rectifier. As shown in Figure 6.37, this rectifier uses an arrangement of four diodes instead of two. The four diodes of the full-wave bridge rectifier allow two different current paths to the load (or to the filter circuit of the power supply), with each path arranged for identical output current direction as illustrated in Figure 6.37.

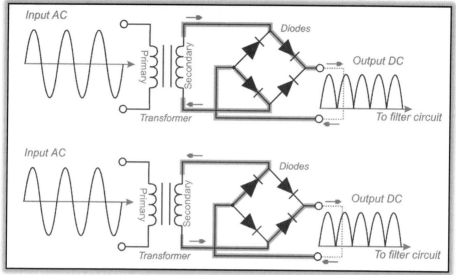

Figure 6.37: The full-wave bridge rectifier passes the entire transformed AC waveform using a diode bridge to ensure output current flows in only one direction. The current paths of each half of the AC cycle are highlighted in grey.

Filter Circuits: The output of a rectifier is DC, but a pulsed DC. Most electronics are designed to use a constant, stable DC voltage. It is the job of the power supply's filter circuit to smooth the variable DC pulses of a rectifier into a steady voltage for output. One of the simplest forms of a filter circuit is a *filter capacitor* following the rectifier circuit, as depicted for a half-wave rectifier power supply in Figure 6.38.

The filter capacitor connected across the output of the rectifier will reduce the variability in the voltage. The capacitor will be charged by the rectifier output when the rectifier voltage exceeds the capacitor's voltage, and the capacitor will discharge when the rectifier voltage is lower than its own. With the water analogy you may imagine the filter capacitor swelling and stretching during the higher voltage portion of the rectifier output, storing energy in its elasticity, and then supplementing the power supply output current by releasing its energy during the lower voltage portions of the rectifier cycle. The capacitor will constantly charge and discharge commensurately with the voltage of the rectifier, providing a steady output voltage. [Note, this is an idealized description, and some *ripple* will remain in the DC voltage, depending upon filter capacitor ratings and performance.]

Bleeder Resistor: Notice the bleeder resistor included in the bridge rectifier power supply diagram of Figure 6.39. A commonly implemented safety

6.5 Power Sources

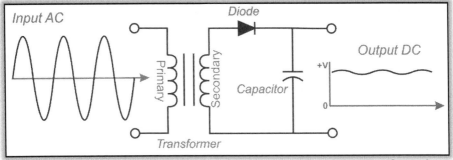

Figure 6.38: The filter capacitor smooths the variable DC output from the rectifier circuit, charging during high voltage periods and discharging during low voltage periods. Some ripple remains in the output voltage.

feature, **the bleeder resistor ensures that the filter capacitors are discharged when power is removed.** Any charge remaining on the capacitor will *bleed off* through the resistor over a short time, eliminating its stored energy as heat, and eliminating a potential shock hazard. Large power supply capacitors can hold substantial and potentially deadly electric charge.

Choke Input: More elaborate filter networks are commonly used that may provide greater smoothing than a lone filter capacitor. An *inductor input filter*, also called a *choke input filter*, **combines inductor components with capacitor components in a power supply filter network.** Since an

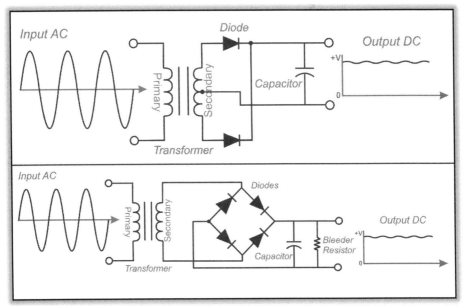

Figure 6.39: Full-wave rectifier power supply circuits including simple filters.

inductor opposes changes in current, the choke input filter helps to smooth current variations as well as voltage variations. The inductor as a choke was introduced in Section 6.2, *Components*.

Switch-Mode Power Supply: Also known as a *switching supply*, this unique and popular type of power supply **offers the advantage of high-frequency operation that allows the use of smaller components.** The switch-mode supply uses a power *switching transistor* to provide high frequency output that is rectified and smoothed by a filter network. The high frequency DC pulses allow the switching supply to rapidly respond to changes in current demands, such as when a transmitter is keyed on and off. And since the pulses are brief the transformer (and other components) may be of reduced performance capacity, smaller and lighter, relative to other types of power supplies.

Batteries: Many amateur operators prefer to use battery systems to power a station. Batteries are used with HTs regularly, and mobile stations are usually wired to the automobile battery. But batteries may also be used to power base stations in the shack, to serve as a backup supply in the event of power outage, or to operate a portable rig in the field. Batteries store energy chemically, and a variety of chemical types are available, each with unique characteristics and performance.

Storage Cells (Lead-Acid): Perhaps the most commonly used batteries for higher power rigs such as base stations are so-called *storage cells*. Storage cells include deep-cycle marine or recreational vehicle batteries that use lead-acid chemistry and are rechargeable. Lead-acid storage cells offer low internal resistance that provides excellent surge current capability for transmissions at higher power levels. Lead-acid batteries tend to hold charge well over time and require only occasional *maintenance charging*, or *topping off*. The lead-acid electrolyte may be a liquid (as in car batteries) or the very popular *gel cell* type in which the electrolyte remains in a semi-solid gel form greatly reducing the potential for spills or leaks. Most storage cells should be maintained at 13.8 V, even as they may be rated, and called, "12 V batteries." **The minimum allowable discharge voltage for maximum life of a standard 12 volt lead-acid battery is 10.5 volts.** Below this output voltage the battery's voltage will fall off sharply with time. Discharging below this level can reduce the effective life of the battery, so recharge at or before reaching the 10.5 volt level. However, deep-cycle batteries are just that – they are designed to be discharged to a very low percentage of their capacity, and a commensurately low voltage, with little long-term negative effects.

6.5 Power Sources

The table below summarizes the features of several additional battery types that are popular for amateur radio use. The energy storage rating in *milliamp-hours* is an indication of the capacity of the battery to provide current with a stable voltage for a period of time, and it may be used as an index to compare relative capacities of cells.

Internal Resistance: A battery will have *internal resistance* resulting from its own construction and materials, and this internal resistance will govern the rate of electric current that may flow from the source. For example, **an advantage of the low internal resistance of nickel-cadmium batteries is high discharge current,** and the same has been noted already for lead-acid cells. This comes in handy when a strong surge of current is required to power an HT radio transmission, for instance. Other batteries may impose high internal resistance to ensure current is limited to a low value for stable, long term operations, such as powering a wrist watch.

G6A02

Battery Type Summary

Chemistry	Typical Packaging	Voltage (V)	Energy (mAh)	Notes
Alkaline	AAA to D 9v 6v	1.5v 9v 6v	1100 to 12000 580 11000	Disposable; Recharge only if designated "rechargeable." Good for emergency backup of HT or other portable devices.
Nickel-Metal Hydride	AA 9v	1.2v 9v	1500 to 2200 200	Rechargeable; Often multiple AA cells in molded package for HT snap-on.
Nickel-Cadmium	AA 9v	1.2v 9v	700 120	Rechargeable; Older technology. AA cells combined in snap-on package.
Lithium-Ion	AA Coin Cell	1.7v ~3v	2100 to 2400 25 to 600	Rechargeable; New technology. AA cells combined in snap-on package. Now used in most HT products.
Carbon-Zinc	AA	1.5	600	Disposable. Not rechargeable. Older technology moving out of use.

Alternative Power Sources: Even with batteries, it is sometimes desirable to have longer term power available. Solar and wind power are becoming more prominent as personal power sources for the home or the field. Having a solar panel to recharge batteries when camping or backpacking can come in handy, and modest modern solar power systems can keep your home station storage cell batteries charged up and even power your rig directly while the sun shines.

Light weight, compact, foldable or roll-up panels are available on the market complete with the simple electronics needed to affect recharging of a battery or voltage conversion for powering a small device. Generally, the power available from a panel or panel array will be a function of the total area of the panels, the conversion efficiency, and the illumination available. Different types of solar cells are made from different materials, and each type has an efficiency rating that may be used to estimate the output of the system. Higher quality silicon cells have efficiency ratings greater than 20%, and advances in efficiency are being made rapidly. More than 100 watts of power may be generated by a large, modern solar panel in bright sunlight.

The name of the process by which sunlight is changed directly into electricity is photovoltaic conversion. Typical solar cells from which panels are constructed are special PN-junctions that generate small currents when sunlight is absorbed by the material. **If you measure the open-circuit voltage of a modern, fully illuminated silicon photovoltaic cell, it will be approximately 0.5 VDC.** By connecting cells in various series and parallel arrangements, panels of a variety of output voltages may be created. For instance, a 12 volt system for powering a radio station could be fabricated from a set of 24 cells of 0.5 volts all connected in series. Multiple 12 volt strings like this can be connected in parallel to provide increased current and available power. **Usually a diode will be connected in series between a solar panel and a storage battery that is being charged by the panel to prevent self-discharge of the battery through the panel during times of low or no illumination.** (Blocking diode.)

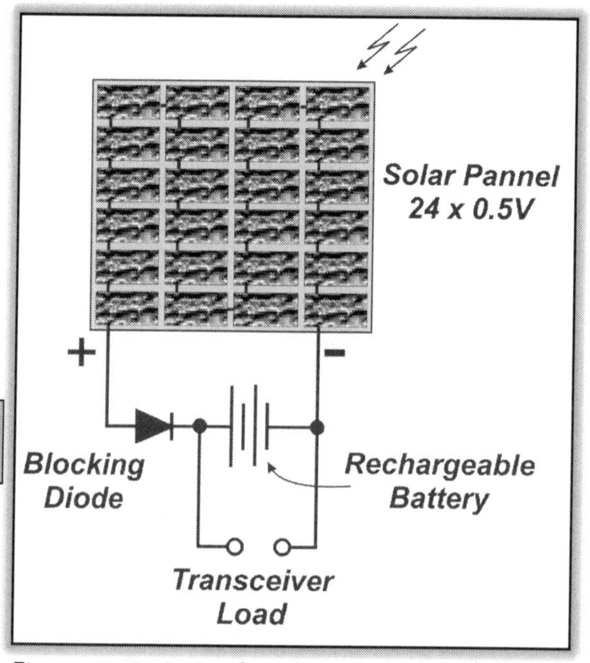

Figure 6.40: A simple solar panel circuit for powering a transceiver and charging a battery.

6.5 Power Sources

Check out solar power for your station or for your portable field operations. It's remarkably easy and much more convenient than lugging batteries around!

Wind generators may be effective in some locations, depending upon the typical atmospherics. Wind power generation requires heavier mechanical systems than solar – a generator and gearbox typically, and more complex electronics to ensure voltage regulation with variable speed generators. This increases costs associated with wind power. Further, **the disadvantage of using wind as a primary source of power, such as for an emergency station, is that a large energy storage system is needed to supply power when the wind is not blowing.** Nature can be unreliable in this way, and if your luck is like mine, the wind will die exactly when you need it most.

The bottom line is that wind generation may work well for some locations and with a solid battery storage system, but solar is usually more reliable and becoming less expensive. The combination of solar panels and modest storage capacity is usually a winning one.

Transforming Impedance: Let's return briefly to the topic of transformers to consider one other task they can accomplish. In addition to transforming voltage, a transformer may be used to match impedances, as noted earlier in this section and in Section 6.4. Transformers are sometimes used at antenna feed points to achieve a match. Here's how it works.

The power (P) into the transformer must equal the power out of the transformer by the power law P = EI. Thus, if the voltage (E) of the secondary winding differs from the voltage of the primary, the current (I) of the secondary must also change in order that input and output power equate. And for AC, impedance (Z) is the ratio of voltage to current, as noted in Section 5.1 *Antennas - Theory and Principles:* Z = E/I. Putting this together, since the voltage and current of the secondary differs from the voltage and current of the primary, the impedance (Z_s) of the secondary must also differ from the primary impedance (Z_p). A relationship of the turns ratio and impedances is

$$\frac{N_P}{N_S} = \sqrt{\frac{Z_P}{Z_S}}$$

Notice that since a transformer adjusts impedance it can be used as a method of impedance matching. Power circuits and antenna circuits may use a matching transformer, as will other components of a station and other electronic circuits, such as an audio amplifier driving a speaker.

Example: What is the turns ratio of a transformer used to match an audio amplifier having a 600 ohm output impedance to a speaker having a 4 ohm impedance?

$$\frac{N_P}{N_S} = \sqrt{\frac{Z_P}{Z_S}} = \sqrt{\frac{600\Omega}{4\Omega}} = \sqrt{150} = 12.2$$

The turns ratio is 12.2 to 1. Note that in this example the amplifier is serving as the primary winding source voltage, and the turn ratio is stated with the larger number (12.2) first, as 12.2 : 1.

How's the confusion with power? Some of it wiped away? If not, review this section and online materials, and particularly practice the questions on *Power Sources*. And if you've really got it all, no more confusion at all…. More power to you!

Next up, we'll consider various types of amplifier circuits, including some that utilize those ancient, glowing vacuum tubes! (Yes, they are still used.)

But first, the quiz questions…

HamRadioSchool.com/general_media

6.6 Hamtronics Amps & Tubes

> **Nigel Tufnel:** The numbers all go to eleven. Look, right across the board, eleven, eleven, eleven and...
>
> **Marty DiBergi:** Oh, I see. And most amps go up to ten?
>
> **Nigel Tufnel:** Exactly.
>
> **Marty DiBergi:** Does that mean it's louder? Is it any louder?
>
> **Nigel Tufnel:** Well, it's one louder, isn't it? It's not ten. These go to eleven.
>
> *- This is Spinal Tap,*
> *Rob Reiner, Director*

Let's be clear: Nigel was *not* a licensed amateur radio operator. Thankfully. However, many stations do use RF amplifiers to boost signal strength. Most of them probably go only to ten, but they can still be very effective when atmospheric propagation conditions are poor or when it is important to provide a solid, clear signal over a large area – perhaps to serve as net control for an HF band net, for instance. Let's consider two basic categories of amps: *Solid State and Vacuum Tube* amplifiers.

Solid State Amplifiers: Recall from Section 6.2 *Components* that transistors will behave as amplifiers in the region between high and low stable states. The controlling signal input to the base (BJT) or gate (FET) is represented in the stronger current flowing from collector to emitter (BJT) or source to drain (FET). Amplifiers for amateur radio may be *solid state*, meaning the construction is entirely of solid materials such as semiconductor electronics including amplifying transistors. That is, no glass vacuum tubes. With most solid state amps you may essentially plug them in and operate with little concern for meticulous adjustment or tuning. Most of that is handled automatically by cleverly designed circuits, although **permanent damage to a solid-state amplifier can be caused by a condition of excessive drive power** (the control input signal power from the transmitter). But, particularly for higher power HF, solid state amps tend to come at a premium price point.

G4A07

Vacuum Tube Amplifiers: Vacuum tubes are like *glass FETs* – they behave in a very similar manner to field effect transistors, amplifying a control input signal across other electrodes. In fact, you might say that vacuum tubes were transistors before there were transistors! Some of us recall a day when televisions emitted a warm glow through the ventilation holes in the TV's cabinet housing due to the vacuum tubes helping to amplify signals for display on a giant vacuum tube called a cathode ray tube (CRT).

Generally, the price point for RF power with vacuum tubes is a bit lower than with solid state RF amps. Vacuum tube RF amplifiers remain very popular in amateur radio for not only the price advantages but for the quality of performance and high power output provided. Tube type amplifiers require more careful adjustment during use, usually with manual impedance tuning and power control.

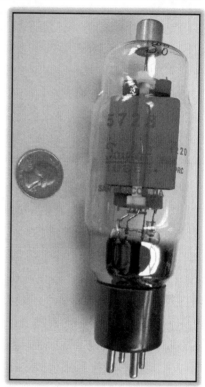

Figure 6.41: An RF amplifier vacuum tube.

So, crank it up to eleven and let's rock out to some tubular amplification of RF. Dude.

Amplifier Classes: Amplifiers are categorized by *class*, as determined by the characteristics of signal amplification and resulting performance. Different classes of amplifier are appropriate for different types of radio operations. Along with each description that follows is a figure depicting the portion of each AC cycle that the class of amplifier operates upon. That is, only the highlighted portion of each waveform will have its amplitude boosted to a greater value by the affiliated amplifier, and this has an impact on the accuracy with which the amplifier can recreate the input signal without distortion as well as the efficiency with which the amplifier class operates.

G7B08 Amplifier efficiency is determined as the RF output power divided by the DC input power – the ratio of output to input power.

Class A: A *linear amplifier* offering low distortion of the amplified signal. It amplifies the entire waveform of the input signal (full 360 degrees of each cycle), but it is the least efficient type of amplifier.

A linear amplifier is one in which the output preserves the input waveform. With amplitude modulated signals such as SSB phone this is critical to preserving the modulation envelope by which audio signals are encoded in the RF. (*See SSB and AM section.*) Unlike the other types of amps, the Class A amplifies the entire RF waveform cycle equivalently, boosting the signal amplitude while maintaining the amplitude-derived envelope shape.

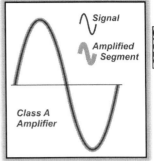

Figure 6.42: Class A amplifier signal.

Class B: Given high quality of design the Class B amplifier can also be highly linear. This amplifier uses two complementary signal amplifying components, one to boost only the negative half of the input waveform (180 degrees) and one to boost only the positive half (opposite 180 degrees). For this reason the Class B amp is also known as a *push-pull amplifier*. If both amplifiers perform identically with well-matched, duplicate input signals, good linearity of the output amplified signal can result. Power efficiency of a push-pull is significantly improved over the Class A.

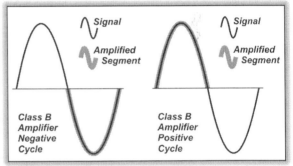

Figure 6.43: Two Class B amplifier signal halves

Class AB: A combination of Class A and Class B types. A push-pull configuration is used as in Type B, but each complementary amplifying device boosts slightly more than one-half of the input signal cycle, either positive or negative plus a bit of the other. Both devices operate around the crossover time from positive to negative, helping to eliminate distortion problems of the Class B push-pull design. The AB amplifier is sufficiently linear for SSB mode, but less power efficient than the Type B due to the longer cycle active periods.

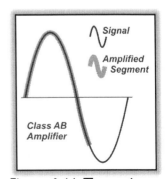

Figure 6.44: The positive cycle of a Class AB amplifier signal.

Class C: Less than one-half of the input signal is amplified, typically between 100 – 150 degrees of the cycle. **Class C is the highest efficiency class of amplifier,** but its linearity is very poor. This can be inferred by examining the amplified segment of the waveform – any modulating amplitude envelope would be severely distorted by this amplifier's small active period. So, Class C amplifiers should not be used with SSB or AM. However, CW mode requires only a narrow bandwidth tone and does not contain a modulating envelope, so the Class C amplifier is often used with CW. Further, since FM depends only upon frequency deviations, this amp's amplitude distortions do not degrade FM signal demodulation. **The Class C power stage is appropriate for amplifying FM mode signals.**

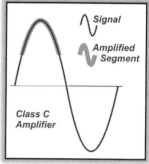

Figure 6.45: Class C amplifier signal.

Some RF amplifiers for amateur use may be operated as Class AB and also as Class C. A longer amplification period Class AB functioning supports SSB mode with low distortion while a brief period Class C functioning provides excellent efficiency in CW mode.

We will examine the operating adjustments and cautions required of RF tube amplifiers, but to better understand those adjustments we'll next consider the workings of the vacuum tubes used as amplifying components in many RF amplifiers. Let's go tubing.

Vacuum Tubes: The solid state Field Effect Transistor (see *Components* section) is most like a vacuum tube in its general operating characteristics, as a tube uses a controlling input signal to regulate a larger current flow much like the FET. Recall from Section 6.2 that the FET base electrode receives a controlling voltage that regulates the current passing between the source and gate electrodes. The vacuum tube has similarly functioning elements.

With some variation depending upon specific design, a tube will have the following basic elements:

- *Cathode* – a source of electrons, analogous to the FET *source* electrode.

- *Heater* – a resistive heating filament that heats the cathode to cause electron emission.

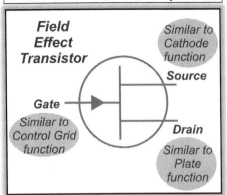

Figure 6.46: The FET is similar to the vacuum tube in its functions for amplification.

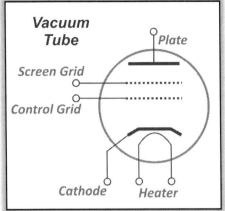

Figure 6.47 Tetrode (4-element) Vacuum Tube controls current with an input voltage, similar to a FET.

- *Control Grid* – the **control grid of a triode vacuum tube,** located between the cathode and plate, **is used to regulate the flow of electrons between the cathode and plate;** analogous to the FET *gate* electrode; the controlling signal (*drive power*) is applied here.

- *Screen Grid* – located between the control grid and plate, **the primary purpose of the vacuum tube screen grid is reducing the grid-to-plate capacitance** that degrades high frequency amplification performance.

- *Plate* – an electrode that collects electrons as the *plate current*; analogous to the FET *drain*.

The heater heats the cathode which begins to emit electrons into the vacuum within the tube. Relative to the cathode's voltage, the plate is placed at a positive voltage to attract the electrons. The electrons must pass through the open gaps of the control grid to reach the plate. The grid is mainly open gaps between fine interlaced wire or other conductive material, so few electrons are actually collected by the grid. The voltage of the control grid controls the passage of electrons. If the control grid voltage is negative with respect to the cathode, the electrons will be repelled, reducing the plate current or even terminating it completely (*cutoff state*). If the control grid voltage is positive relative to the cathode, the electrons will be accelerated to the plate, increasing plate current. An input voltage signal to the control grid varies the plate current, and since the plate current may be quite large, the input signal is amplified via the plate electrode.

A vacuum tube with three elements (excluding the screen grid) is a *triode*, and a four-element tube such as that depicted in Figure 6.47 is a *tetrode*. Additional grids may be included in design variations and other physical configurations are common.

Amplifier Adjustments: Radio frequency power amplifiers will receive a signal from the transmitter, amplify it, and output a signal to the antenna system. Since the amplifier is coupled to the antenna load, all of the previous discussions of impedance matching and power transfer apply. The amplifier must be tuned for the band and frequency of operation, and the input and output power must be adjusted for the desired safe operating levels. Typically three types of operator controls will be used to get the amp set up for operating:

- *Band Switch* – used to select the frequency band of operation. Impedance matching networks and filters for both input and output signals are configured. This is typically a set of discrete selections of amateur bands requiring no fine adjustment. The band may be automatically detected and selected on some amplifiers without user intervention.

- *Tune Control* – used to tune the amplifier output circuit for the selected operating frequency. Component values of an impedance matching circuit, such as a Pi-network (see *Impedance and Reactance* Section 6.4) are adjusted until a match is achieved as indicated by the plate current. This adjustment interacts with the *load adjustment*.

- *Load Control* – used to adjust the coupling of the amplifier to the antenna load. Component values of an impedance matching network are adjusted to achieve an output impedance match with the antenna as indicated by the output power reading. This adjustment interacts with the *tune adjustment*.

Read and heed your vacuum tube amplifier manufacturer's instructions for tuning and operating your amplifier, as specific tuning requirements may vary.

A tube RF amplifier tuning activity will generally proceed something like this:

1. Select the operating band with the band switch.

2. Apply a small amount of drive power from the transmitter.

6.6 Amps & Tubes

3. **Adjust the tune control to obtain a pronounced dip** (minimum value) **on the plate current meter, indicating correct adjustment** and that the matching network is resonant for the operating frequency.

4. **Adjust the load control (coupling control) to achieve maximum power output without exceeding maximum allowable plate current, indicating correct adjustment.**

5. Repeat adjustment to the tune control to achieve plate current dip and load control adjustment to obtain peak power iteratively until the desired operating output power or plate current is achieved. Drive power may also be adjusted during these iterations to achieve the manufacturer's recommended value or recommended control grid current.

Drive Power: Refer to your transmitter manufacturer's instructions on adjusting the drive power provided to an RF amplifier. If too much current is applied to a vacuum tube control grid, the grid may be damaged or destroyed, and excessive plate current can also result, causing overheating failure. Many manufacturers will provide special protection circuits in amplifiers to ensure that excessive grid drive cannot damage the tube. Next to an 11, these protection circuits are a great feature to look for when amp shopping.

Excessive drive may also cause distortion of your signal, particularly at modulating signal peaks, such as loud audio. As noted in Section 4.1 *SSB and AM*, the Automatic Level Control (ALC) can be used to reduce the transmitter drive when power becomes too great for proper modulation. **The purpose of using Automatic Level Control with RF power amplifiers is to reduce distortion due to excessive drive.** Refer to your transmitter user's manual for proper implementation of ALC with RF power amplifiers.

Neutralization: Due to the capacitance that arises between electrodes, some amplifiers (particularly triode tube amps) can become self-oscillating circuits at some frequencies. Such component resonance was discussed in the Section 6.2. This can cause erratic behavior or poor operation of the amplifier. To combat this problem that is very rare in most modern amplifiers, **the final amplifier stage of a transmitter may need to be neutralized to eliminate self-oscillations.** This process imposes negative feedback in the circuit at the frequency of oscillation, eliminating the oscillatory positive feedback. Usually this is accomplished by inserting a variable capacitor of manufacturer-recommended range between the output and input filtering circuits and adjusting the capacitor to neutralize the oscillation. Most modern amplifiers will not require this modification to be implemented by the user.

So, dude… Now you can safely operate your RF amplifier, cutting through the difficult conditions with the power of eleven!

Or maybe just ten. Or perhaps with the maximum rated plate current for your amp, properly tuned up for frequency and with correct grid drive. As always with the more complex operations of amateur radio it is a good idea to seek the initial sage advice of an experienced elmer. That policy certainly applies to RF amplifier ops. Besides, that old head-banging elmer may just be able to show you how to wheedle an eleven out of your system!

Rock on over to the web site and quiz yourself on the question pool items.

HamRadioSchool.com/general_media

6.7 ICs and Computers
Hamtronics

> *The number of transistors on a chip will double approximately every two years.*
> — Moore's Law, Gordon Moore

Mr. Moore, cofounder of Intel Corporation, posited his law in 1965 and claimed that it should apply for at least ten years into the future. More than 50 years later the trend he identified remains generally valid. The forming of multiple miniature transistors, resistors, capacitors, diodes, inductors, switches and more on a tiny slab of silicon all wired together into functional complex circuits has had an incalculable impact on our world and on amateur radio technology.

As a General Class operator, you should have a basic comprehension of integrated circuits (ICs) and digital logic, the combination of ICs as microprocessors and computers, the common language and names in this domain, and familiarity with IC interfaces and connectors that may be used with radios. Let's integrate and connect these topics.

Analog versus Digital ICs: The broadest categories of ICs are analog or digital logic. Analog ICs are also called linear circuits, operating over a range of voltage and current values and outputting continuous signals. Digital circuits use discrete voltage and current values rather than a range, usually activated in either of two stable states – "on" or "off," representing binary digits of 1 and 0, respectively.

Analog ICs: **Operational Amplifiers (op amp)** and linear voltage regulators are two common **analog integrated circuits.** The op amp schematic symbols and packaging are represented

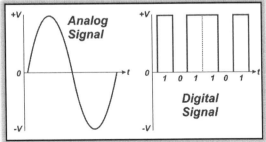

Figure 6.48: Analog vs. Digital Signal representations.

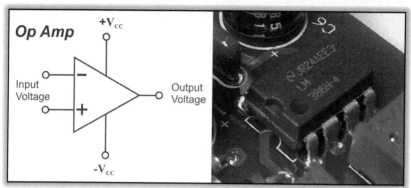

Figure 6.49: Operational Amplifier symbol and typical packaging on a circuit board.

in Figure 6.49. The op amp is used in audio and other circuit types to provide signal gain. Typically a voltage difference is applied between the + and − input terminals (differential input) and the output voltage (relative to the input voltage) is hundreds or thousands of times greater than the input differential value. The VCC inputs are the supply voltage source supporting amplification. Most **sine wave oscillators will use the basic components of a filter and an amplifier operating in a feedback loop** to produce a sine wave voltage signal, varying the op amp input voltage in a regular repeating cycle.

Linear voltage regulators supply a constant voltage output across a range of current for stable power supply to circuits. A voltage regulator will have *input, output,* and *ground* terminals.

Digital ICs: When processing digital signals ICs take advantage of the ease of representing binary "ones" and "zeros" with an "on" state or an "off" state, analogous to the two stable states of transistors described in *Components* Section 6.2 (saturation and cut-off regions). Combinations of digital ICs can be constructed to perform complex computational tasks using binary logic.

TTL and CMOS Logic Families: Although several different families of digital ICs have been created, two commonly used families are the *transistor-transistor logic* (TTL) family and the *complementary metal-oxide semiconductor* (CMOS) family. These names refer to the types of materials and component construction used in the logic circuits. **As compared to TTL, CMOS integrated circuits have the advantage of low power consumption.**

6.7 ICs and Computers

Logic Gates: Digital circuits of great complexity are built from basic logic building blocks called logic gates. Logic gates are created with combinations of transistors and other electronic components to provide specific binary outputs (on or off, 1 or 0) for given binary inputs. In the language of binary gate circuit logic, inputs and outputs are said to be "high" (high voltage) if the saturation voltage is applied (on, or 1), and "low" (low voltage, off or 0) if in the cut-off state. Gates are given names that reflect their input-output logical function. Consider a few salient examples:

Two-Input AND Gate: Output is high only when both inputs are high. In other words, if the two inputs are called A and B, this gate outputs a binary 1 (high) only in the case that Input A *AND* input B are provided binary 1s, or high voltage. If either or both of the two inputs are a binary 0 ("low") the output will be 0. The logic of the two input AND gate is summarized in Figure 6.50 along with other gate examples and associated schematic symbols.

Two Input NAND Gate: Meaning "Not AND" the NAND gate is the logical inverse of the AND gate. The output is low only when both inputs are high.

Two Input OR Gate: As the name implies, the output is high when either or both inputs are high. The output is low only when both inputs are low.

Two Input NOR Gate: This is the logical inverse of the OR gate. **Output is low when either or both inputs are high.**

Two Input XOR Gate: Meaning "Exclusive OR," the output is high when either, but not both, inputs are high. That is, for an output 1 to occur just one, and only one, input must be high.

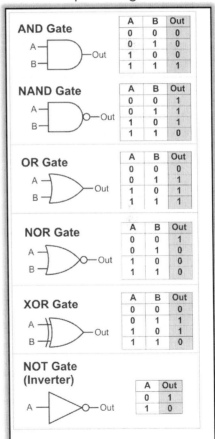

Figure 6.50: Common logic gates with symbol and input-output truth table.

NOT (Inverter): The NOT Gate has but a single input. The output state is always the opposite of the input state.

Sequential Logic Circuits: Another type of digital IC is the sequential logic circuit. The output state of these ICs depends upon time or upon sequential input states. The foundational building block of sequential logic is a storage element called the *flip-flop*. A flip-flop circuit has two stable states and it can be made to change state by applying the appropriate high or low states to its inputs. The flip flop will maintain its state (storing a value) until the inputs are properly cycled or changed. If several flip flops are sequenced together such that the output of one is fed to the input of the next, a *counter* or a *shift register* may be constructed.

Counters: A counter represents a binary number in the latched states of the linked flip flops. A clocked signal (input state change) affects state changes through the flip flops such that the collective 1 and 0 states increment sequentially with each clock signal or input state change. The binary representation counts up (or counts down) the input signal occurrences. One flip flop stores one bit of data with its latched state. For a set of flip flops in a counter circuit, the number of different binary states that can be represented is 2^n, where n is the quantity of flip flops. This determines the largest number that the counter can represent. For example, Figure

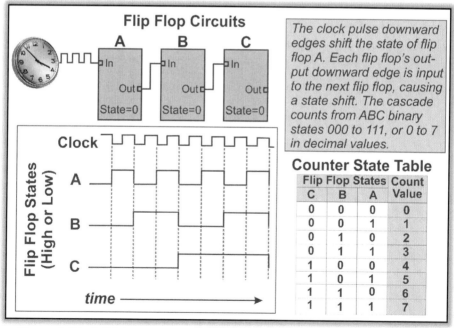

Figure 6.51: A 3-bit counter using flip flops counts from 0 to 7 decimal.

6.7 ICs and Computers

6.51 depicts three linked flip flops as **a 3-bit binary counter having 8 states: $2^3 = 8$.** `G7B05`

Shift Registers: Essentially a memory element, **a shift register is a clocked array of circuits that passes data in steps along the array.** A 3-bit shift register would operate similarly to the 3-bit counter except that the arrangement between flip flops (or other memory elements) is altered. In the simplest case the sequence of flip flops are linked such that a new input state fed into the first flip flop results in the former state of the first flip flop being *shifted* into the second flip flop in the sequence. Similarly, the former state of the second flip flop is shifted to the third. When the register runs out of flip flops the last data state is lost, as there is no flip flop element for it to be shifted into. You might imagine the states of each shift register flip flop getting shoved from one flip flop to the next in a left-to-right sequence through the flip flops, with the last one falling out of the far right flip flop to be lost! Other arrangements of shift registers are feasible to affect various input and output functions and memory storage or recall. `G7B06`

Microprocessor ICs: With millions or billions of tiny gates and logic arrays integrated onto a single chip, the microprocessor can perform millions or billions of logic operations each second. It implements a program of sequenced steps using binary computations in a *machine language* of logic programming. The ability to execute a stored *program* from *software* or *firmware* is what distinguishes a microprocessor from mere digital logic circuits. Microprocessors are used in personal computers and many other general purpose devices.

Microcontroller: An integrated circuit often replacing complex digital circuitry. A microcontroller may have a core microprocessor, memory, and input/output peripheral devices to serve an imbedded function in a device. Your transceiver may have one or more microcontrollers, as do most modern automobile engines, TV remote controls, electronic toys, military missiles, and lots of other commercial products. The microcontroller is essentially a small computer on a single chip, and thus more flexible than the simpler, custom-engineered digital logic circuits.

MMIC: *Monolithic Microwave Integrated Circuit.* The MMIC is a specially designed RF integrated circuit to affect functions up to microwave frequencies of operation such as modulation, demodulation, frequency mixing, and amplification. An MMIC may contain several transceiver block functions in a single chip, and they are used extensively in cellular telephone devices. `G6B02`

Digital Memory: Microprocessors and microcontrollers require digital memory capacity in order to store and recall input and output data or programming options. **Read Only Memory, or ROM,** means exactly that – the memory data cannot be changed or altered or replaced, but only accessed to read out. ROM will be **non-volatile memory, meaning that the stored information is maintained even if power is removed** from the circuit. A ROM memory bank may contain the start-up or core programming for a processing IC. *Random Access Memory* (RAM) is flexible and may be read, written, rewritten, or deleted altogether. RAM is used to hold temporary data for computation, display, or data output operations. The *flash memory* used in small solid state plug-in memory devices ("thumb" or "flash" drives) is a type of *non-volatile RAM*, providing random access to data but also retaining it following the termination of power.

Visual Displays for ICs: Several types of visual displays may be driven by ICs and used in amateur radio. The following summarizes two of the most common display types in modern use that are easily driven with ICs.

LED: The LED discussed in the *Components* section is commonly used to create visual displays that may be a simple on-off illuminated indicator or a multi-character digital readout. LEDs are self-illuminated requiring no separate light source. Segmented LEDs used to create numbers, letters, or other characters are turned on or off by the digital logic of ICs.

Figure 6.52: Self-illuminated segmented LED display (upper) and a backlit LCD display (lower).

Liquid Crystal Display (LCD): Very common on newer amateur radio transceivers and related components, the LCD uses a crystal material between two layers of glass. The crystal blocks, filters, or reflects light with crystal patterns driven by electronic circuits. **A characteristic of the liquid crystal display is that it utilizes ambient or back lighting** to be clearly visible.

Connectors: It takes a lot of cables and connections to make ham radio stuff happen. Hooking up computers to radios, audio devices and speakers, power

6.7 ICs and Computers

supplies and meters... It's just a lot of stuff passing all those signals back and forth for amateur radio bliss! The zoo of various connectors can get a little confusing, even frustrating, so let's review a few common connector types that you might need to use to connect computing devices with your radio.

Keyed Connectors: Many connectors will have multiple individual connectors, or *pins,* that must be aligned and connected with specific commensurate sockets to properly route signals. In order to assure that the proper connection alignment, or *mating,* is achieved by a user, the connector body housings, inserts, and pin configurations will often be designed so that only a single connection orientation is possible with complementary connectors. The main reason to use such keyed connectors instead of non-keyed types is to reduce the chance of incorrect mating. Incorrect mating in the ham shack is just trouble.

Numerous types of data and audio signal connectors are available, but the following are a few of the more common connectors you will encounter when linking together IC-based modules.

USB Interface: The *Universal Serial Bus* interface has become almost... well... *universal* as a connector for modern electronic devices. (USB – has absolutely nothing to do with the upper sideband!) It can transfer data and power between devices, and it has several different keyed physical forms, four

Figure 6.53: Common USB connector formats, left-to-right: Type B, Type A, Mini B, and Micro B.

of which are depicted in Figure 6.53. The more recent USB-C is a symmetrical variation of the USB that may be connected without concern for keying or mating orientation. Nearly every cell phone, tablet device, computer, digital camera, printer, and video game will have one or more USB ports. Newer transceivers will commonly use the USB for digital mode connections with a computer. Some sound card interfaces also use a USB cable to connect to the computer. Transceiver channel programming utilities often use a USB connection between computer and transceiver.

Figure 6.54: DE-9 Connector

DE-9: **A good choice for a serial data port would be the DE-9 connector,** very commonly misrepresented as "DB-9." The D refers to the shape of the keyed shell which resembles the letter D. The E refers to the size of the shell, and the 9 refers to the number of pins within the shell. Many other D type connectors exist, but the DE-9 is very common for many data interfaces, including amateur radio connections to computers or other devices.

DIN Connector: The DIN family is a round, slotted key form with multiple pins. DIN connectors are popular on many amateur radios for connecting external control devices. Older computers may use DIN connectors for keyboard and mouse connections, although the USB has replaced the DIN for those functions on most newer computers.

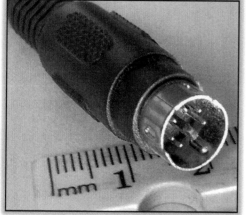

Figure 6.55: DIN connector

RCA Phono Connector: An older connector still **commonly used for audio signals in amateur radio stations** and other audio devices. This non-keyed connector has a single pin/socket and can be used for

6.7 ICs and Computers

numerous applications including video signals, control signals, and some RF signals.

Many other connector types may be used in amateur radio for power connections, RF feedline connections, network connections, even audio and data connections. *It is good to be connected,* so familiarize yourself with the range of options in your station and integrated circuit-based devices.

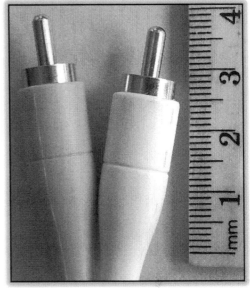

Figure 6.56: RCA phono connectors

Much like Moore's Law, perhaps your knowledge of integrated circuits has doubled in just the last few minutes! It's quite likely that you have encountered hundreds, even thousands of integrated circuits, microprocessors, electronic displays, connectors, and myriad other things that create, manipulate, and pass electronic signals. Now you have a little taste of what's going on inside all that electronic wizardry so you can intelligently integrate and connect your General Class station!

See the chart on the next page summarizing IC characteristics, and don't forget to review the question pool items for this section!

HamRadioSchool.com/general_media

A Summary Organization of Integrated Circuits

Integrated Circuits			
Analog	Digital [TTL & CMOS]		
Op Amp Linear Voltage Regulator MMIC Other devices	Logic Gates	Sequential Logic	Microprocessors Microcontrollers
	AND Gate NAND Gate OR Gate NOR Gate XOR Gate Not (inverter)	Flip Flops Counters Shift Registers	Memory Modules

6.8 Measurement
Hamtronics

> **"** Every line is the perfect length if you don't measure it.
>
> — Marty Rubin

And every circuit has the perfect voltage if you don't measure it.

And every transmitter creates the perfect signal if you don't measure it.
And every antenna radiates the perfect pattern if you don't measure it.

You get the point. In order to ensure that your radio station is operating properly you must, on occasion, measure things. Let's take a look at some basic test and measurement equipment and techniques for amateur radio so that the "perfect station" may be avoided.

Meters: Perhaps the most fundamental piece of test equipment for the ham is a meter for electrical measurements. While individually functioning voltmeters, ammeters, and ohmmeters are available, the *multimeter* is now the most common type of handheld meter. The multimeter combines several measurement functions into one device and provides user-selectable controls for measurement type and display scales. You can pick up one at the hardware store, but be careful of quality – generally you get what you pay for, and some low-end meters may not have the resolution or accuracy for RF electronics applications.

> **Analog versus Digital:** Analog meters typically use a needle indicator that moves against one or more static calibrated scales. Digital meters will usually present numerical digits by LCD or LED display. **An advantage of a digital meter (such as a voltmeter) as compared to an analog meter is better precision for most uses** – the digital readout can provide better resolution of values than the analog needle display. However, in a measurement task in which a null value or peak value is sought among a continuous range, such as **when adjusting tuned circuits, an analog readout may be preferred over an instrument with a numerical digital readout** – the analog meter movement and

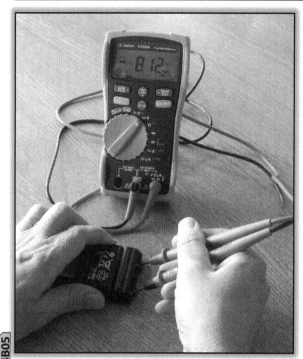

Figure 6.57: Measuring cell voltage with a multimeter. *Photo: Sara Ray, KCØAMO*

maximum or minimum position is usually easier to interpret than dancing digits! However, many digital meters now include analog-like bar graphs to aid visual perception.

Regardless of the type of meter, digital or analog, it is important that the measurement device itself not affect the circuit being measured. At least, the impact upon the circuit should be minimized to avoid grossly inaccurate measurements. For example, **high input impedance is desirable for a voltmeter to decrease the loading on circuits being measured.** If the meter's input impedance were relatively low, significant current would flow from the circuit being measured through the meter circuits, altering the normal voltage drop across the measured circuit positions. High impedance avoids significant current flow through the meter, keeping the voltage drops very near the non-measurement activity value.

Oscilloscopes: The most versatile electronic measurement instrument, the *oscilloscope,* displays a real-time image of voltage over time. The voltage is displayed for a window of time that may be adjusted by the user. Typically the window of time is depicted across the horizontal extent of the oscilloscope display with a time scale superimposed on the

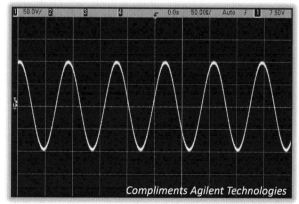

Figure 6.58: A sine wave signal voltage displayed on an oscilloscope. The vertical scale is voltage units, and the horizontal is time.

6.8 Measurement

image, left to right. The voltage signal is depicted in the vertical dimension, usually as a continuous function – an unbroken curve or line. A vertical scale is also provided to indicate specific voltage values. As an example, a well-formed AC voltage sine wave is depicted in Figure 6.58. The time window from left edge to right edge can be varied to "zoom in" or "zoom out," viewing less or more of the signal waveform over time.

Most modern oscilloscopes will provide horizontal as well as vertical signal inputs so that another signal can drive the horizontal dimension of the signal, in lieu of simply time. In this way very complex signals may be depicted on the scope. Further, **an oscilloscope will contain horizontal and vertical channel amplifiers** to boost weak signals for improved display.

The clear advantage of an oscilloscope versus a digital voltmeter is that complex waveforms can be measured. For example, the RF output of a transmitter may be displayed to examine the modulated waveforms generated. **To check the RF envelope pattern of a transmitted signal the attenuated RF output of the transmitter is connected as the signal source to the vertical input of the oscilloscope.** For a single modulated tone the display would look similar to Figure 6.59. In a similar manner **the keying waveform of a CW transmitter may be checked with an oscilloscope** to identify any undesired noise or anomalies in the keyed signals.

An oscilloscope can also be useful in analyzing your station audio processing, microphone gain, digital signal output from a circuit, a computer, or a sound card interface, and more! It takes a little practice to become adept at adjusting and interpreting an *O-scope*, but it is a measurement skill that will come in handy for ensuring your station is functioning properly. One typical use of a scope in an amateur station is for the *two-tone test*.

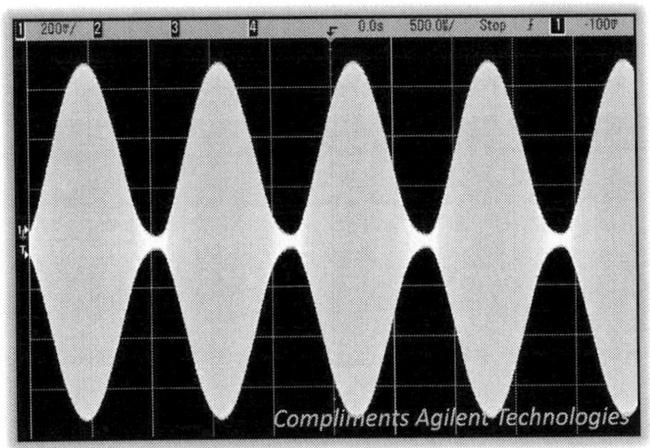

Two-Tone Test: **The two-tone test analyzes transmitter linearity.** If two different audio frequency signals have equivalent amplitude, a transmitter should modulate those two different signals with equivalent amplitude, or RF power. If the transmitter does

Figure 6.59: Complex waveforms, such as this 100% AM modulated RF signal, can be measured with an oscilloscope.

modulate with equivalent RF power it is exhibiting good linearity. If the two audio signals are modulated with different RF power output the transmitter is not linear. Of course, each of the pair of audio frequency signals is perceived as a different audio tone by our ears, hence the *two-tone test*. **To conduct a two-tone test, two non-harmonically related audio signals are used** (700 Hz and 1900 Hz are a common pair selection). The oscilloscope representation of each modulated tone is examined for any RF power output differences, or distortion. Transmitter adjustments may be made to alleviate the *distortion* while monitoring the signals in real-time via the oscilloscope.

Field Strength Meter: A field strength meter is used to measure the strength of a transmitted RF field. For instance, **a field strength meter may be used to monitor relative RF output when making antenna and transmitter adjustments.**

Signals are received with a conventional antenna (such as a dipole or ¼ wave monopole) and routed to circuits that detect the relative strength of the RF voltages. Unless the meter is carefully calibrated, all measurements are relative – no

Figure 6.60: A simple field strength meter for relative measures. A collapsible dipole antenna extends left and right from this meter.

specific signal strength measurements are made, only "stronger or weaker" measurements on a unitless scale. However, with such relative signal strength readings **the radiation pattern of an antenna may be determined with a field strength meter.**

Go forth and measure! Using the tools and techniques of this section you can now absolutely, positively, unquestionably ascertain that your station is imperfect. And just exactly how imperfect. And you can be proud of the imperfections and your ability to quantify them! But first, please perfectly answer the online quiz for the questions of this section. Good luck!

HamRadioSchool.com/general_media

6.9 Hamtronics: Avoiding Interference

> " *No matter which way they pointed the antenna, no matter how clean and precise the receiving apparatus, a persistent background hiss interfered with the measurements.*
> *— Regarding Penzius and Wilson's discovery of Cosmic Background Radiation*

What Penzius and Wilson accidentally discovered in 1965 is that radio frequency interference has been around since the beginning of the universe. Really. The annoying hiss detected by the giant horn-shaped microwave antenna they were using at Bell Telephone Laboratories in New Jersey in relation to a set of experiments on communication satellites was actually part of the radio echo left over from the cosmic Big Bang from which the universe originated. In spite of numerous tweaks and adjustments, including the scrubbing of all pigeon droppings accumulated in the horn and the purging of all pigeons seeking to roost within it, the interference persisted and they were awarded a Nobel Prize in physics for it.

So, while it has been around for about 14 billion years, give or take a few hundred millennia, radio frequency interference is a relatively recent bother to human kind. And while the Cosmic Background Radiation is unlikely to annoy most hams, the several billion new radio emitters that have sprung up on our planet in the last 100 years are sure to get in one another's way on occasion. Let's take a look at some of the things you can do to reduce the chances of RF interference between your station and other radiating or receiving devices, and even between your station and your body!

RF Interference: The undesired reception of RF signals produced properly or improperly by an electronic device is *interference*. Interference may be received by your radio station from other emitters, either intended emitters like other radio stations or unintended emitters such as poor or faulty electronic devices. Additionally, some devices may be unintentional

Figure 6.61: Other electronic devices may become inadvertent receivers of amateur signals.

or incorrectly operating RF receivers that will pick up signals from your station's transmitter by mistake. These may include telephones or audio equipment. Let's characterize some common types of RF interference and common solutions to avoid it.

Fundamental Overload: If your transceiver or another device is unable to reject very strong signals from a nearby transmitter, the electronics may be overloaded, and distorted or unintelligible audio may result. For example, your HT radio may experience fundamental overload when another nearby amateur station transmits strongly on the same band to which you are tuned, even if the two are not on the same frequency. This will usually override any weaker signals you may be intending to receive.

Solution: To alleviate fundamental overload you must reduce the signal level hitting the receiver. This may be accomplished in one or more ways: 1) By separating the offending transmitter and receiver by a greater distance, 2) By reducing the offending transmitter's power, 3) By using a directional antenna on one or both transmitting and receiving stations, or 4) By putting a filter on the receiver. The filtering option usually applies to non-amateur radio receiving devices that are inadvertent receivers, such as telephones, televisions, or other electronic devices.

Direct Detection or Unintentional Receivers: Strong RF signals can be picked up by nearly any kind of electronic device, particularly those with lengths of speaker leads, power cords, or cables. These wires can act as unintentional antennas directing signals into the electronic circuits to cause erratic behavior or noise. For instance, **Interference from a nearby single-sideband phone transmitter unintentionally received by a telephone or audio device will sound like distorted speech, while a nearby CW**

G4C03

6.9 Avoiding Interference

transmitter will produce on-and-off humming or clicking. Transmitted RF picked up by an audio cable carrying AFSK data signals between a computer and a transceiver may cause VOX circuit to not un-key the transmitter, distorted transmissions, and frequent connection timeouts.

Solution: **RF Interference of this kind caused by *common-mode currents* on an audio cable (or other types) can be reduced by placing a ferrite bead around the cable, as the ferrite bead or core creates an impedance in the current's path.** Also referred to as ferrite *chokes*, snap-on filters of various sizes are readily available at radio and electronics retail outlets. **Alternatively, RF signal interference to audio-frequency devices may be reduced with a bypass capacitor.** Also called a *decoupling capacitor*, a small capacitor from an audio connection to ground voltage (such as a chassis connection) will "bypass" the higher RF frequency signals, allowing them to go directly to ground without effecting the much lower frequency audio signals.

Figure 6.62: Ferrite chokes for common-mode filtering come in many packages including snap-on beads and rings.

Harmonics: Spurious emissions that are frequency multiples of the intended (fundamental) frequency of a transmitter are called *harmonics*. For instance, the 2nd harmonic will be twice the fundamental frequency, the 3rd harmonic three times the fundamental, and so on. Virtually all transmitters produce some harmonics of much lower power levels than the fundamental frequency. Harmonics generated by your station may lie outside of the amateur bands and cause interference in non-amateur receivers or devices.

Solution: Harmonics can be reduced or eliminated by proper implementation of RF filters in a feedline. A low-pass filter selected to allow the fundamental to pass while impeding the higher frequency harmonics can be inserted into the feedline, but take care that the filter is matched to the feedline impedance. (See Section 5.3 *Antennas, SWR and Impedance*

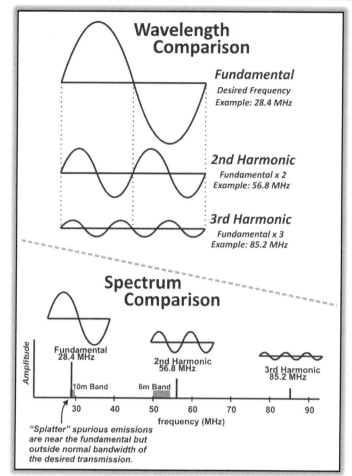

Figure 6.63: Example comparison of fundamental frequency with 2nd and 3rd harmonic frequencies.

Matching.) Harmonic filters are a common integrated feature in most modern transceivers.

Splatter: A spurious emission beyond the necessary and proper bandwidth for the mode and frequency band in use is referred to as splatter. Poor or faulty transmitters may generate excessively broad signals that interfere with communications on adjacent frequencies. For example, a SSB transmitter emitting a 20 kHz signal instead of the necessary and proper 3 kHz maximum bandwidth is splattering 17 kHz of spurious emissions. Correct your transmitter operation if you are splattering. A transmitter repair or simply an adjustment of microphone gain or ALC may be needed.

Arcing: **Arcing at a poor electrical connection could be the cause of interference covering a wide range of frequencies.** Electrical arcing may be generated by almost any electric device, sometimes intentionally such as an electric igniter on a furnace. High voltage utility power lines or transformers can have faults that produce regular arcing and generate a broad band crackle or buzzing on receiver audio. To eliminate local suspect arcing equipment, simply turn off equipment and see if the interference goes away.

6.9 Avoiding Interference

Solution: For malfunctioning equipment or appliances, electrical repair or replacement may be warranted. Power line noise will usually need to be isolated to an offending location or device, perhaps with the use of simple direction finding equipment. A request should be made to the power utility company to check and correct the offending source.

Mobile Station Interference Sources: Automobiles can produce arcing and sparking and all sorts of RF noise from electrical and electronic devices. Alternator whine is a common source of high-pitched whine that varies with engine speed. Popping or crackling that varies with speed is likely spark plug noise. Connect your transceiver's power leads directly to the battery with in-line fuses and avoid using any of the automobile wiring to reduce the effects of alternator whine – don't use the cigarette lighter or power connections provided in the cabin of your vehicle. Using the transceiver noise blanker can also help to filter this kind of regular pulsing interference.

Many automobile microcontrollers operate at frequencies in the HF range of 3 – 30 MHz. **A radio installed in a vehicle may receive interference from the battery charging system, the fuel delivery system, or the vehicle control computer.** Alleviating computer interference can be a challenge in some cases. Check with your automotive dealer for available upgrades or replacement controllers, or consider options for shielding the controller enclosure.

Grounding: Proper grounding of your station is necessary to alleviate *ground loops* and to reduce "*RF in the shack*". These problems can promote noise, erratic equipment behavior, and even offer a nasty RF burn or shock to the operator.

Ground Loops: If the various components of your station have differing ground level voltages, a ground loop may result – currents flowing among the components due to the ground level potential differences. **One symptom of a ground loop somewhere in your station is received reports of "hum" on your station's transmitted signal.** A ground loop may also cause erratic behavior of some equipment. **Avoid ground loops by connecting all ground conductors to a single point,** as depicted in Figure 6.64 on the next page. Typically this will involve using a broad conductive flat strap to connect individual station equipment chassis to a common single ground panel or ground bus. This common connection among station component grounds will maintain a common ground voltage level and alleviate ground loops.

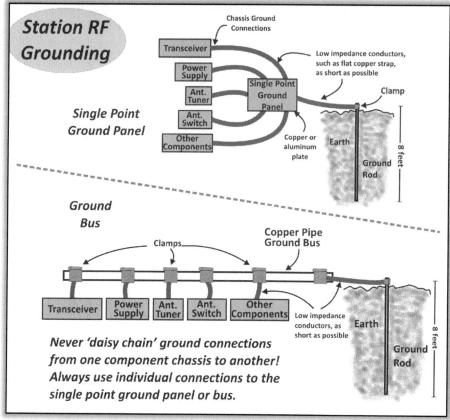

Figure 6.64: Station single point ground configurations.

RF in the Shack: The conductors in your station – ground connections, equipment chassis, cables and wires – all act as antennas. Some antennas are better than others, but radio frequencies can induce currents in your shack on any conductor, and particularly on longer ones. A low impedance connection to earth ground can help reduce this problem.

The single point ground panel or bus should be connected by a short, low impedance conductor to a ground rod imbedded in the earth. Any stray currents on your station equipment will have a direct path to earth ground level. Connecting all equipment grounds together will help to avoid unwanted effects of stray RF energy in an amateur station, and a solid earth ground will route them away from your equipment. (Be sure that you are following the National Electric Code [NEC] recommendations for grounding systems in your home or shack. If unsure, check with an electrician.)

Ground Conductors: Broad, flat conductive strap with only gentle bends or turns is best for station grounding. A broad conductor such as copper strap provides very low impedance at RF frequencies due to the large surface area of the conductor, helping to ensure that RF currents easily flow to ground. **If you receive an RF burn when touching your equipment while transmitting on an HF band** (*RF hot spot*), **the ground wire likely has high impedance on that frequency even if connected to a ground rod,** or your grounding system may be poorly implemented (or not at all implemented).

RF Hot Spots: The ground conductors should be made as short as physically possible for your station arrangement. Any conductor that approaches 1/8 wavelength or longer will serve as a nice antenna for receiving RF and inducing currents on the conductor. A ground conductor can become resonant with the RF resulting in "hot spots" of RF currents on its length. **A resonant ground connection can affect high RF voltages on the enclosures of station equipment,** representing a significant hazard for burn or shock. **Bonding all equipment enclosures together helps minimize RF hot spots.**

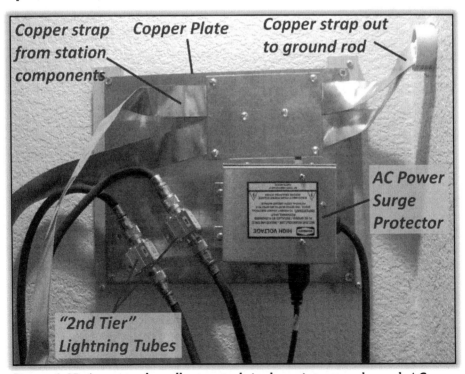

Figure 6.65: An example wall-mounted single-point ground panel. AC surge protector and second-tier coaxial lightning protection tubes are grounded to panel along with flat strap from station component chassis.

Note that on the 10 meter band a ¼ wavelength conductor is only about 2.5 meters long, or under 8 feet. Achieving this short of grounding conductor from the single point panel or bus to an external ground rod may be infeasible for many stations. In a difficult situation, careful planning with the use of multiple lengths of grounding conductor, avoiding the resonant multiples, may help to avoid potential resonance hot spots for your favorite HF operating bands.

Interference happens. It will happen to you eventually. It has been around a lot longer than any of us mere humans, and it'll exist long after we've departed. It's something we just live with as hams.

Don't panic, you can handle most interference that you will encounter. Sometimes you may need the patience and dogged determination of Penzius and Wilson to chase down the source of an annoying interference source, but hopefully you won't have to scrub up pigeon poop or trap the flying rats. Plan and implement your HF station RF grounding arrangement as best you can, and snag a nice set of ferrite snap-on chokes and telephone filters to distribute to your neighbors, should the occasion arise. Good luck, and be sure to cover the online questions from this section.

HamRadioSchool.com/general_media

7.0 Safety

> **❝** *Better dead sure than sure dead.*
> *– Anonymous*

Hams take safety seriously. It's good to do so when you're handling equipment that can produce many deadly amps of electrical current, or when you're climbing a tower many dozens of feet high, or when you're erecting an antenna and power lines are near, or even if you're just soldering together a connector and coaxial cable. There are a million ways to get hurt or killed, but only one dead sure way to avoid it. Practice safety.

In Section 7.1 we will review basic precautions for handling electricity and for erecting towers and antennas. Section 7.2 is all about RF exposure safety and how to ensure your station is not overexposing you, your family or your neighbors to RF radiation. Read on to help ensure you're dead sure.

7.1 Electrical & Antenna Precautions

> **❝** *Electricity can be dangerous. My nephew tried to stick a penny into a plug. Whoever said a penny doesn't go far didn't see him shoot across that floor. I told him he was grounded.* – *Tim Allen*

The chances of getting seriously injured with amateur radio are probably less than the chances of getting injured playing with Tim's nephew. Still, it is prudent to be very familiar with common hazards affiliated with ham radio and, most importantly, to understand how to take precautions and avoid those hazards. Let's consider a few hazards and precautions regarding electrical safety in the shack and some related safety factors with antennas and towers.

Electric Shock: The commonly accepted value for the lowest voltage that can cause a dangerous amount of current to flow through the human body is about 30 volts. However, it is the current flow and not the voltage that is dangerous. Currents flowing through the body cause health hazards by heating tissue (burning), by disrupting the electrical functions of cells (nervous system dysfunction or loss of consciousness), and by causing involuntary muscle contraction (inability to control movement and interruption of heart rhythm).

How much current is dangerous? Just 10 mA or so can cause involuntary muscle contractions, 30 mA begins to feel painful, and at 50 mA you may not be able to "let go" of the conductor before losing consciousness! Your heart rhythm can be disrupted by 100 mA, possibly leading to death if the current continues for some time. Of course, greater amperage can lead to more rapid serious injury, and very high currents can burn tissues.

Typical household AC of 120 volts RMS is more than enough to be deadly. Take great precaution to avoid injury by powering down equipment before working on it unless it is absolutely necessary to work with a powered circuit. Disconnect power sources or transmitters altogether before working. Remember that large capacitors can hold a dangerous charge for long periods, so carefully discharge them with a bleeder resistor before working.

Codes and Wiring Conventions: The National Electric Code (NEC) covers electrical safety inside the ham shack and your home. It describes the requirements for safe electrical wiring and handling conventions. Local codes may also apply and be more restrictive than the NEC, so check with your local authorities if you are modifying your shack electrical wiring. If you are not comfortable doing your own work in this regard, be sure to consult a licensed electrician. The following are some commonly applied conventions and guidelines from the NEC.

120 V and 240 V Household Circuits: Most US households receive AC power in a 240 volt circuit with two wires each at 120 volts relative to a third "neutral" wire. The neutral wire is insulated white while the two "hot" wires will usually be insulated red or black. (Variations do occur, so use your meter to check!) Most household circuits are 120 volts provided by one of the hot wires and the neutral wire. Some household circuits for large appliances (or for high power amplifiers) will utilize both hot wires and the neutral wire to provide 240 volts. A separate *safety ground* wire, either green insulated or bare, is also included for the typical modern 120 V "three-prong outlet" circuits and for the four-conductor 240 volt source receptacle. Standards in other countries may vary from this description.

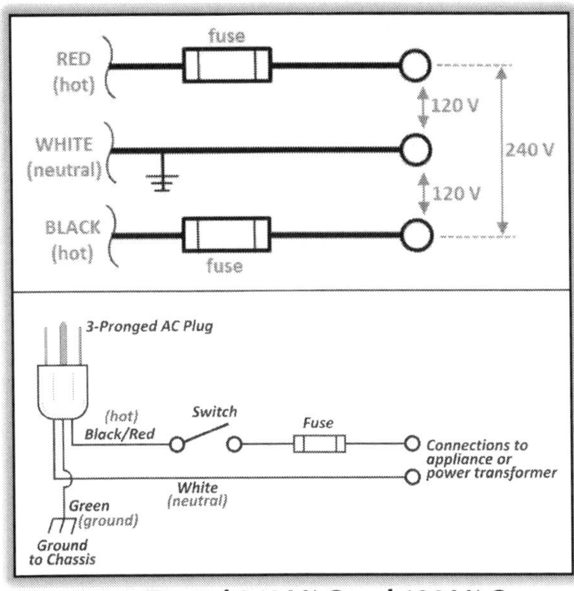

7.1 Electrical & Antenna Safety

Figure 7.1: Typical 240 VAC and 120 VAC household circuit configurations.

Fuses and Circuit Breakers: Any 120V hot wire should use a fuse or circuit breaker in the hot wire connection. **In a device operated from a 240 VAC single phase source, only the two wires carrying voltage in the four-conductor connection should be attached to fuses or circuit breakers.** A fuse has a wire that will melt from heat when too much current is drawn through it, thereby opening the circuit and avoiding a dangerous over-current condition. A circuit breaker will "trip" to open the circuit in overload conditions, but it may be reset after the cause of the overload has been resolved.

Wire Current Ratings: *Ampacity* is the maximum safe current carrying capacity of a wire. Generally, larger diameter wire can handle greater current. *American Wire Gauge* (AWG) defines wire diameter, with smaller AWG values being larger wire diameters. Exceeding the current rating of a wire may cause the wire to overheat, possibly causing a fire.

Two of the most commonly used AWG wire sizes are number 12 and number 14, depicted in the **NEC-derived ampacity table** on the following page. **For a circuit with a 20 amperes circuit breaker, the AWG number 12 is the minimum wire size that may safely be used** – that is, the NEC table indicates that drawing more than 25 amps through AWG #12 wire is unsafe, so a margin of safety is provided with a 20 amp circuit breaker. Similarly, by NEC

Figure 7.2: One form of common 240 VAC electrical outlet.

restrictions, **a 15 ampere fuse or circuit breaker would be appropriate to use with a circuit that uses AWG number 14 wiring** that has an ampacity of 20 amperes. (This NEC-extracted table is for insulated copper wire, and separate values for aluminum conductors are specified by NEC.)

Copper Wire AWG	Allowable Safe Ampacity (A)	Maximum Fuse or Circuit Breaker Allowed (A)
8	40	40
10	30	30
12	25	20
14	20	15

Preventing Electric Shock: Special types of devices and circuits can be used to help prevent electric shock. These include Ground Fault Circuit Interrupter (GFCI) circuits, equipment cabinet safety interlocks, and equipment chassis grounding.

Ground Fault Circuit Interrupter (GFCI): This special circuit and associated electrical outlet contains a circuit breaker that will trip when an imbalance is detected in the hot wire to neutral wire current. The current drawn through the GFCI circuit should equal the current returning to the GFCI, else a problem exists. A short circuit or current flow on an unintended path will cause the trip. Thus, if current flows into a person an imbalance will cause the trip, quickly terminating the shock. **Current flowing from one or more hot wires directly to ground will cause a GFCI to disconnect the 120 volt or 240 volt AC line power to the device.**

Safety Interlock: Many pieces of equipment using high power, such as a transmitter **power supply,** will incorporate a cabinet safety interlock. **The purpose of a safety interlock is to ensure that dangerous voltages are removed if the cabinet is opened.** The interlock is a switch,

Figure 7.3: A GFCI 120 VAC electrical outlet.

often integrated with the chassis housing, that will disconnect the powering circuit if the enclosing cabinet chassis is unlocked or opened. With the interlock switch in the open position dangerous or unprotected electrical contacts inside the enclosure cannot offer electrical shock if they are touched.

Chassis Grounding: Equipment with a metal chassis should always have the chassis connected to the green safety ground wire of the powering circuit. **Grounding the metal enclosure of every item of the station equipment ensures that hazardous voltages cannot appear on the chassis.** Most modern amateur radio equipment will use a power cord that includes a safety ground wire that is already connected to the chassis of the device, and the ground connection is made automatically when you "plug in." In the case that an improper short or contact occurs with the enclosure, the safety ground wire provides a path to ground for the currents, reducing the chance of someone receiving an electric shock from touching the metal chassis.

[G4C13]

Mobile Station Electrical Precautions: Although most often operated from the 12 volt battery of an automobile, electrical precautions must also be taken even with this lower voltage level. Caution must be exercised as significant current can be drawn from the car battery. **If you are operating a 100-watt HF transceiver in an automobile, it is best NOT to draw the DC power from an automobile's auxiliary power socket** (lighter socket) **because the socket's wiring may be inadequate for the current being drawn.** The wires feeding the socket could overheat quickly and start a fire. Rather, **a fused power connection direct to the battery using heavy gauge wire would be best for the 100-watt HF**

[G4E04]

[G4E03]

Figure 7.4: For mobile station power connections use dedicated heavy gauge wire with in-line fuses routed directly to the battery.

mobile installation, and this is a good precaution to use with any portable or mobile station. The heavy gauge wire ensures the current can be safely handled, the direct connection avoids any possibility of using lighter gauge automobile wiring, and the in-line fuse is the safety switch in the case of a short or other fault that draws an excessive amount of current through the power wire.

Backup Power Safety: In an emergency or portable operating scenario such as a power outage or a field operation, hams may use power from liquid-fueled portable generators or from storage cells such as lead-acid based batteries. Each of these backup power sources introduces safety concerns.

Electrical Generators: Portable electric generators using gasoline or diesel fuel are popular emergency preparedness and portable power supply equipment items. Because they burn petroleum-based fuels, care must be taken to properly ventilate the area in which they are used. Carbon monoxide in exhaust fumes can accumulate quickly in a poorly ventilated enclosure, and CO is a deadly gas. **The danger of carbon monoxide poisoning is a primary reason for not placing gasoline-fueled generators inside an occupied area.** Don't take chances. Follow these guidelines:

- **For emergency generator installation, the generator should be located in a well-ventilated area.**
- Ensure that the generator is positioned so that fumes cannot be drawn into windows, air intakes, or any other breach into occupied areas.
- Install a carbon monoxide detector in any enclosed occupied area near the generator installation.

Additionally, take proper precautions in the handling of liquid fuels for a generator. Keep a fire extinguisher nearby and avoid spark, flame, or exhaust system heat when refueling the generator. Use the generator's ground terminal and connect it to an earth ground to avoid potential arcing, and store fuels well away from the generator.

If you are using an emergency generator to power your home or other structure that receives commercial utility power, **you must disconnect the incoming utility power feed.** Typically, the disconnection is accomplished by tripping the large "Main" circuit breakers. If the utility service power is not completely disconnected, the generator may *back-feed* onto the utility power lines creating a potential hazard of unusually high voltage on the lines.

Restored utility power may also damage the generator if it is still connected. Once utility service power is completely disconnected, it is safe to power the structure with an emergency generator. Most local electrical codes require a *transfer switch* that may be installed by a licensed electrician that safely disconnects utility power and connects your generator, disallowing both to be connected simultaneously.

CAUTION! If you are not completely confident of the procedures necessary to safely connect and disconnect an emergency generator to your home or shack, consult a licensed electrician.

Storage Cells: As described in the Chapter 6 *Power Sources* section, storage cells can be a good emergency or portable power source for amateur radio operations. They require proper care in recharging to avoid hazardous conditions. Most newer types of storage cells require a smart charger to ensure a proper voltage profile is maintained over the duration of the charging process. Check the battery manufacturer's recommendation for charging, and stick to it, to avoid overheating that can occur from recharging too rapidly. Lead-acid storage batteries can give off explosive hydrogen gas when being charged, so they should be maintained in a well-ventilated area outside the shack to avoid hydrogen build-up in an enclosed area and potential resultant explosion or fire.

Soldering Safety: Plenty of hams enjoy *home brewing* electronics, building up coaxial cables, and making their own equipment repairs. Soldering is a very common activity for those involved in amateur radio. And, of course, soldering requires a couple of safety precautions.

Solder is a blend of metals that melts at temperatures of about 190° F and higher, with specific melting tem-

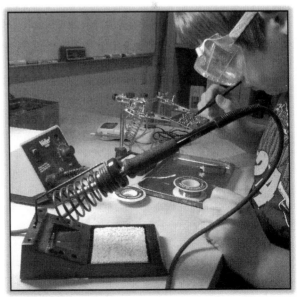

Figure 7.5: A stable iron holder, safety glasses, and good ventilation keep soldering safe.

peratures depending upon the metal blend. Solder is melted around electrical contacts using a hot iron and allowed to cool and solidify to provide a jointing or connection with excellent electrical conductivity. Of course, with a hot iron up to several hundred degrees Fahrenheit, you should take great care to avoid burns. Use a stable soldering iron holder and place the iron within it any time you are not heating the solder connection.

A common blend of solder combines tin with lead, and often a small amount of silver to enhance electrical conductivity. Lead is a toxic metal and you should avoid ingesting it. **A danger from lead-tin solder is that lead can contaminate food if hands are not washed carefully after handling it.** When lead-tin solder is melted, it will release fumes with visible smoke. While solder smoke can contain isocyanates, aldehydes, and other unhealthy particulates that should be avoided, the lead metal is not typically heated sufficiently to vaporize it and cause lead particles to be included in the smoke. A solder fume absorber or other ventilation method is recommended, especially if you frequently engage in soldering work. And finally, safety glasses can help to avoid getting a hot splatter of solder or an ill-aimed soldering iron in the eye! Ouch!

Antenna Safety: Whether your antenna work requires climbing a high tower or simply raising or lowering a wire from a tree, always take proper precautions before starting your work. Especially if you are erecting a new antenna in a new or unfamiliar location, go slowly, attend to the local environment, think through every step, and double check all precautions.

As you learned in your Technician Class studies, keep all antennas well clear of utility lines and service feed lines to your home or shack! If the antenna should fall, it should have absolutely no possibility of contacting electrical lines, and vice versa – a fallen utility line should not be able to contact your antenna. Keep the two well separated, with plenty of extra clearance. The following additional precautions are prudent for safe antenna work.

Electrical Clearance: It pays to reiterate this point – make sure your antenna absolutely cannot contact electrical lines. This may be the #1 greatest hazard for most ham radio operators!

Power Down: Any time you make adjustments or repairs to an antenna, turn off the transmitter and disconnect the feed line. This removes any possibility of the antenna being energized while you are handling it, potentially avoiding painful RF burns or excessive RF exposure. Similarly, **if any person is preparing to climb a tower that supports electrically powered devices, make sure all circuits that supply power to the tower are locked out and tagged,** whenever possible. This means physically securing the circuits with locks so they cannot accidentally be powered until all personnel are safely clear of the tower.

Figure 7.6: Tower climbing safety gear includes goggles, hardhat, and properly configured harness.

Climbing Gear: All members of a tower work team should wear safety goggles and hard hats to protect the head and eyes from falling tools or other objects. Members climbing a tower should use a proper climbing harness to protect against that sudden stop at the end of a long fall. **When using a safety belt or harness on a tower climb, confirm the belt is rated for the weight of the climber and that it is within its allowable service life.**

Safe Clearance: **Any antenna, and particularly ground-mounted antennas, should be installed so that it is protected against unauthorized access.** (See Section 7.2, *RF Safety*.) A ground mounted antenna, such as the ¼-wave vertical, may need to be located where it cannot be readily accessed by people, perhaps within a fenced enclosure. Avoid areas easily entered by the public or near property lines. If possible, raise the antenna out of reach.

Lightning Safety: It is good practice to protect against lightning strikes and the potential of lightning energy being routed into your radio shack. Grounding towers and antennas properly is one primary precaution to take against lightning. Grounding requirements for amateur radio towers or antennas are established by local electrical codes, so ensure that you comply with them.

Grounding arrangements for towers should use a minimum of a separate eight-foot long ground rod for each tower leg, bonded to the tower and also to each other, as depicted in Figure 7.7. Tower ground connections should be short and direct. A broad conductor such as copper strap is best for grounding connections since it provides large surface area and low impedance for

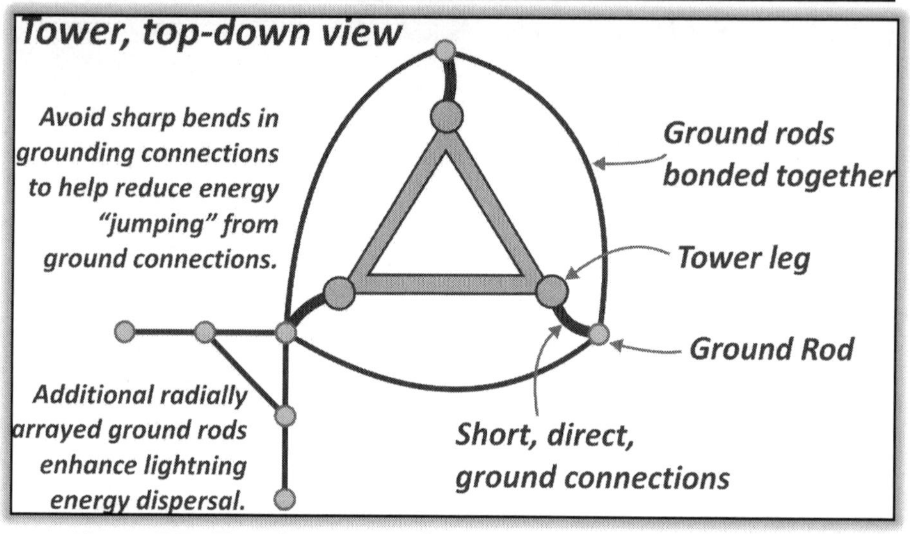

> **Tower, top-down view**
>
> Avoid sharp bends in grounding connections to help reduce energy "jumping" from ground connections.
>
> Ground rods bonded together
>
> Tower leg
>
> Ground Rod
>
> Additional radially arrayed ground rods enhance lightning energy dispersal.
>
> Short, direct, ground connections

Figure 7.7: Top-down view of a tower grounding configuration.

current flow to ground. Sharp bends or creases in the grounding strap should be avoided, as these increase impedance and encourage lightning energy to depart from the conductor and jump to nearby structures or objects.

For enhanced lightning mitigation more ground rods are better! They help to dissipate the lightning energy into the earth when a strike occurs. To avoid saturating the local earth with charge, rods should be separated 16 to 20 feet. If saturation occurs the energy will seek other paths to ground level voltage, such as through your shack or equipment. Again, **good engineering practice for lightning protection grounds calls for them to be bonded together with all other grounds,** thereby distributing the energy most effectively for dissipation. **However, soldered joints should not be used with the wires** (or strap) **that connect the base of a tower to a system of ground rods because a soldered joint will likely be destroyed by the heat of a lightning strike.**

Feed Line Lightning Protectors: Lightning protectors or "tubes" use common coaxial connector interfaces such as the N-connector or the SO-239/PL-259 so they may be easily inserted into a coaxial feed line. If a strong electrical surge from lightning strike energy flows down the coaxial cable, the lightning tube will break like a fuse very rapidly to minimize the surge currents that continue down the feed line toward the shack, and instead route the lightning energy directly to earth ground. Lightning protectors should be mounted to a grounded conductor plate on an external wall of your radio shack or home structure. This entry panel should be well grounded to earth rods in a manner similar to that described for a tower so that lightning energy has a direct, low-impedance path to earth ground.

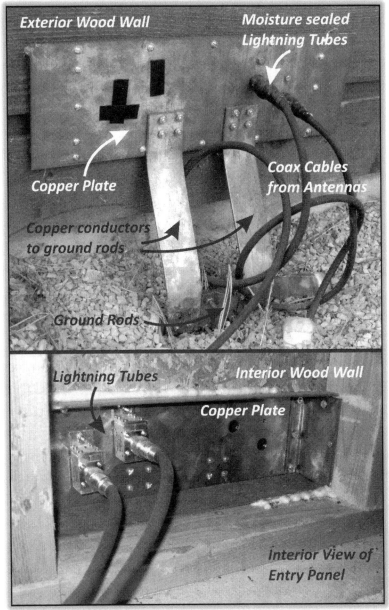

Figure 7.8: A well-grounded copper entry panel with lightning protection tubes.

Many hams prefer to insert a secondary set of lightning protectors in the feed line inside the shack grounded to the single-point ground panel or bus, as described in Section 6.9. These secondary tubes will help to stop any residual surge current on the feed line that was not stopped by the primary protectors and shunt it to ground.

Indeed, electricity can be dangerous, especially when it comes to lightning! And fumes from generators, batteries, or solder can also be hazardous, especially when combined with ignorance. And antennas and towers can be dangerous, especially when combined with live transmitters or utility power lines. So, what are the lessons learned?

- Protect against electric shock by ensuring your antenna cannot contact electrical lines even if it falls.

- Protect against lightning with a robust grounding system and protection tubes.

- Protect against electrical shock by powering down gear for any work, by sticking to codes, and by using proper fuses, proper wiring, good grounding procedures, and safety devices.

- Protect against battery explosions and battery damage by investing in that smart charger and using an appropriate charging profile for the battery type.

- Protect against fumes with good ventilation and careful positioning of sources.

- Protect against antenna and tower mishaps by avoiding power lines, powering down equipment before work, using all the proper climbing gear, and positioning to avoid human contact.

In spite of our humorous start to this section, compliments of Mr. Allen, safety is no joke. Most ham radio operations will present little if any hazards, but some circumstances can be quite dangerous. Here we have presented only a surface scratch of the most common safety considerations for the ham. Be careful and be smart, and become more educated about safety, perhaps with the help of a wise and experienced elmer. Good luck, stay safe!

But it is always safe to examine the question pool items for the section!

HamRadioSchool.com/general_media

7.2 Safety — RF Exposure

> **❝** *I have this complex. I don't like too much exposure. I don't know why it is.*
> — *Mark Viduka*

When it comes to radio frequencies, too much exposure can indeed be a bad thing, but it's really not very *complex*. We know why it is that we don't like it. Let's wrap up our General Class studies with a simple explanation of RF exposure hazards and mitigation practices. Here we *glow*…

RF Exposure Safety involves understanding the FCC RF exposure limits and how to apply them with your station, ensuring that your station does not expose any person to levels of RF energy that exceed recommended levels. In most amateur stations, RF exposure is not a great concern, but as a General Class amateur operator you should be very familiar with limits and requirements to evaluate exposure to assure safe operations for yourself, your family, and your neighbors. You should also understand how to mitigate excessive exposure when the potential for it arises. First, a little clarity about RF radiation.

Non-Ionizing Radiation: UHF, VHF, and HF emissions are non-ionizing radiation. This means that the RF emissions do not strip electrons from atoms in the way that ionizing radiation does. (Examples of ionizing radiation are ultraviolet rays and X-rays, the EM waves of much higher frequency than RF.) Non-ionizing radiation does not directly cause biological molecular changes or adverse effects on DNA genetic material.

RF Heating of Tissues: **RF energy is absorbed by tissues in our body causing heating of those tissues.** With excessive RF exposure, tissue damage can occur due to the body's inability to dissipate the heat delivered. Think of the way a microwave oven works – a great amount of microwave RF energy is delivered inside the oven, rapidly cooking the items placed there that have no way of shedding the absorbed energy and resultant heat. This type of damage is referred to as *radiation burn*, and radiation exposure is the primary topic of this section. The term *RF burn* has a somewhat different connotation referring to damage due to RF electric shock, as follows.

[G0A01]

RF Burns: Electric currents at RF frequencies flowing through your body's tissues can cause an RF burn. RF burns are painful and may happen if a person accidentally touches your antenna while you are transmitting. Unlike conventional heat burns, RF burns may extend deep below the skin surface and may require long healing times. RF burns are not a significant hazard with HT radios emitting 5W or less, but take care to ensure that no person touches your mobile or fixed station transmitting at higher power levels.

Maximum Permissible Exposure (MPE): The FCC recommends radiation exposure limits for each amateur frequency range that are referred to as the *Maximum Permissible Exposure* (MPE). You may need to evaluate your station to determine whether anyone is exposed to RF radiation beyond the MPE. Several different factors of your station operations affect RF exposure.

G0A02 Factors Affecting RF Radiation Exposure: **Each of the following properties is important in estimating whether an RF signal exceeds the Maximum Permissible Exposure (MPE):**

- **Frequency** of the signal
- **Power density** of the signal
- **Duty Cycle** of transmissions

Frequency: Radiation exposure limits vary with frequency because the human body absorbs more RF energy at some frequencies than at others. The greatest absorption, and thus the lowest Maximum Permissible Exposure limit, is found for the VHF band of 30 to 300 MHz. Note that this includes the popular 2m band (near 144 MHz) and 6m band (near 50 MHz). The HF frequencies are less readily absorbed by the human body than VHF or UHF.

	Wavelength Band	Evaluation Required if Power* (watts) Exceeds
MF	160 meters	500
HF	80 meters	500
	75 meters	500
	40 meters	500
	30 meters	425
	20 meters	225
	17 meters	125
	15 meters	100
	12 meters	75
	10 meters	50
VHF	All bands	50
UHF	70 cm	70
	33 cm	150
	23 cm	200
	13 cm	250
SHF	All bands	250
EHF	All bands	250

* Power = PEP input to antenna

Figure 7.9: You must evaluate your station for RF exposure compliance if the transmitter power exceeds established power limits.

Power Density: *Power Density* is the measure of RF power over area. Typi-

RF Exposure

cally, this is expressed as milliwatts per square centimeter (mW/cm^2). The MPE values are expressed in these units for each frequency band, as summarized in Figure 7.13, an FCC bulletin extract at the end of this section. Power density is determined primarily by the *output power* and *antenna distance* from the exposure location, and antenna gain must also be factored into the evaluation.

Power Output: Greater power output from your antenna increases the power density of the RF field. **A routine RF exposure evaluation must be performed to ensure compliance with RF safety regulations when transmitter power exceeds levels specified in FCC Part 97.13.** These transmitter power levels, expressed in watts, are summarized by frequency band in Figure 7.9. Regardless of power transmitted, **make sure MPE limits are not exceeded in occupied areas if you install an indoor transmitting antenna.**

Distance from Antenna: Radio frequency energy spreads out as distance from the antenna increases, reducing the power density. Specifically, power levels fall off as the square of the distance, so doubling the distance from the antenna reduces your exposure by a factor of four (1/4). Thus, relocating or elevating antennas is one of the most common actions an amateur might take to prevent exposure to RF radiation in excess of FCC-supplied limits.

Antenna Radiation Pattern & Gain: Directional antennas will concentrate power in one direction, increasing the power density in that direction as compared to isotropic or dipole antennas. Assessments of RF exposure should take into account the power gain of all antennas used by the station. The output power must be determined with the antenna gain as a multiplying factor.

Duty Cycle: The ratio of on-air transmission time to total operating time of a transmitted signal is duty cycle. Duty cycle affects the **time-averaged RF radiation exposure (the total RF radiation exposure averaged over a certain time).** So, duty cycle is a factor used to determine safe RF radiation exposure levels. **A lower transmitter duty cycle permits greater short-term exposure levels,** while a greater duty cycle allows less exposure over time.

Duty cycle varies with the mode of transmission used. FM signals transmit at 100% power for the entire transmission time. SSB signals vary in power with your audio, dropping to near zero between words and sentences, and causing the duty cycle to be reduced. The ratio of transmission time to receive time also impacts the exposure calculation.

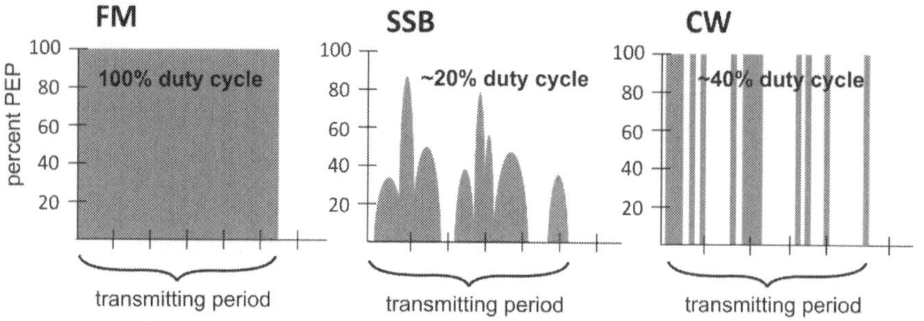

> The duty cycle of transmission modes is determined by transmitter "on air" time and percent PEP within any single transmission. For 100% PEP modes (FM, CW) duty cycle is simply the ratio of "on air" time to total operating time. Multiple transmitter operating periods and receiver "listening periods" may comprise a standard averaging period of 6 or 30 minutes for estimating RF exposure levels.

Figure 7.10: Duty cycle of a transmitter varies with mode.

Complying with Limits: If your station requires an exposure evaluation, **you can determine that your station complies with FCC RF exposure regulations by any of the following methods of determining compliance:**

- **By calculation based on FCC OET Bulletin 65** (see upcoming Practical Advice topic)
- **By calculation based on computer modeling** (see upcoming Practical Advice topic)
- **By measurement of field strength using calibrated equipment** (Accurate measurement of an RF field requires a calibrated field-strength meter instrument with a calibrated antenna.)

If an evaluation of your station shows RF energy radiated from your station exceeds permissible limits you must take action to prevent human exposure to the excessive RF fields. Figure 7.11 characterizes common actions to prevent excessive exposure. For example, **if evaluation shows that a neighbor might receive more than the allowable limit of RF exposure from the main lobe of a directional antenna, you can take precautions to ensure that the antenna cannot be pointed in their direction.** A mechanical stop or limiters on an antenna rotator system may help to accomplish this mitigating action. Elevating the antenna or narrowing its elevation pattern with stacked elements may also alleviate this type of exposure problem.

Practical Advice on RF Exposure Compliance:

Most ham stations are not going to require an evaluation if antenna placement has been well planned, if space constraints are not too imposing, and if high output power levels are not used. But if you plan to use higher power levels, if you plan to use a directional antenna with substantial gain figures, or if your antenna must be in close proximity to people, it is your responsibility to ensure your station is not exposing humans to RF levels in excess of the Maximum Permissible Exposure limits defined in FCC OET Bulletin 65.

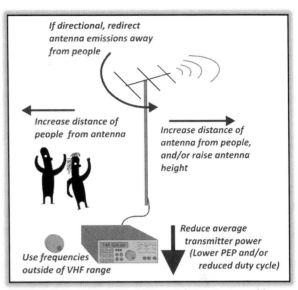

Figure 7.11: RF exposure can be mitigated by several methods or combinations of methods.

The FCC Office of Engineering and Technology (OET) Bulletin 65 from August 1997 contains more information than most new hams are likely to absorb in a short time. However, the tables and graph of MPE from the bulletin's appendix A is quite useful. Armed with a computed estimate of exposure in mW/cm^2 (milliwatts per square centimeter), you can use these tables to make a good estimate of whether or not your station is complying with MPE limits.

How can you easily make such a computation, you ask? The internet comes to the rescue! In addition to commercial and freeware computer software programs, several good internet sites are now available to estimate exposure levels using basic information that is easily known to you about your station and the exposure environment. Most of these sites utilize the formulas given in FCC OET Bulletin 65, but research sufficiently to be sure these equations are indeed used. An internet search of "RF Exposure Calculator" will turn up multiple options. You will also find links to online exposure calculators in the learning media at HamRadioSchool.com.

In most software or online MPE calculators using the FCC formulas, you will need to enter the following types of information:

- **Average PEP** power at the antenna. This should be close to your

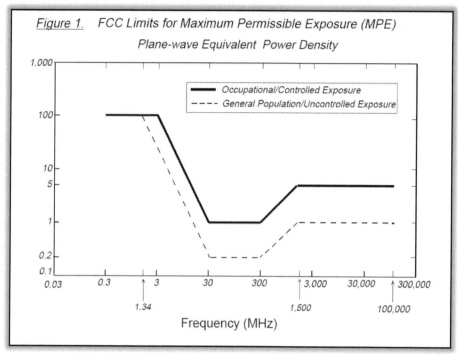

Figure 7.12 OET Bulletin 65 Chart of MPE (mW/cm2) by Frequency.

transmitter PEP, taking into account feedline losses for the length and type of feedline used, and you may also measure closer to your antenna with a power meter on the feedline. You may also need to adjust the power value for the duty cycle that is typical of your operational mode.

- **Gain** of your antenna in the direction of interest, or the isotropic gain.

- **Distance** to the area of interest for your measurement. That is, how far from your antenna to the living room or to your neighbor's house.

- **Frequency** of transmission, usually in MHz.

To use the FCC tables:

1. Make your estimates of exposure power density in mW/cm^2, perhaps using an online calculator as described above.

2. Reference the frequency range in megahertz in the left column of the

RF Exposure

OET Bulletin 65 table (included at the end of this section)

> Note that MPE is specified for controlled exposure (you, the operator) and for uncontrolled exposure (other people), and note that some frequency ranges require a simple MPE calculation based upon the specific frequency of exposure.

3. Compare your computed exposure level for your station with the MPE values in the table to determine if your station is exceeding the MPE.

4. If you find your station is exceeding the MPE, take steps to reduce the exposure.

Congratulations! You have completed all of the testable material for your FCC General Class VE exam! Review the last set of question pool items for this section, take plenty of practice exams, and go upgrade your license!

HamRadioSchool.com/general_media

Good luck, and we'll catch you on the HF bands soon! 73. WØSTU, clear.

Table 1. LIMITS FOR MAXIMUM PERMISSIBLE EXPOSURE (MPE)

(A) Limits for Occupational/Controlled Exposure

Frequency Range (MHz)	Electric Field Strength (E) (V/m)	Magnetic Field Strength (H) (A/m)	Power Density (S) (mW/cm^2)	Averaging Time $\|E\|^2$, $\|H\|^2$ or S (minutes)
0.3-3.0	614	1.63	(100)*	6
3.0-30	1842/f	4.89/f	(900/f^2)*	6
30-300	61.4	0.163	1.0	6
300-1500	--	--	f/300	6
1500-100,000	--	--	5	6

(B) Limits for General Population/Uncontrolled Exposure

Frequency Range (MHz)	Electric Field Strength (E) (V/m)	Magnetic Field Strength (H) (A/m)	Power Density (S) (mW/cm^2)	Averaging Time $\|E\|^2$, $\|H\|^2$ or S (minutes)
0.3-1.34	614	1.63	(100)*	30
1.34-30	824/f	2.19/f	(180/f^2)*	30
30-300	27.5	0.073	0.2	30
300-1500	--	--	f/1500	30
1500-100,000	--	--	1.0	30

f = frequency in MHz   *Plane-wave equivalent power density

NOTE 1: *Occupational/controlled* limits apply in situations in which persons are exposed as a consequence of their employment provided those persons are fully aware of the potential for exposure and can exercise control over their exposure. Limits for occupational/controlled exposure also apply in situations when an individual is transient through a location where occupational/controlled limits apply provided he or she is made aware of the potential for exposure.

NOTE 2: *General population/uncontrolled* exposures apply in situations in which the general public may be exposed, or in which persons that are exposed as a consequence of their employment may not be fully aware of the potential for exposure or can not exercise control over their exposure.

Figure 7.13: FCC OET Bulletin 65 Table of MPE Limits.

Appendices

Index of Terms

A-Index 309
Amplitude Modulation (AM) 269, 318
Amplifier Adjustment 466
Amplifier Classes 462
Analog IC 469
Analog-to-Digital Conversion (ADC) 350
Antenna Analyzer 361, 395
Antenna Clearance (power lines) 498
Antenna Gain 361
Antenna Radiation Pattern 360
Antenna Tuner 361, 398
Arcing 486
AREDN 295
ARES 250
ASCII 284
Auroral Propagation 309
Auto Controlled Digital Stations 289
Automatic Level Control (ALC) 329, 467
Automatic Repeat Query (ARQ) 285
Azimuthal Projection Map 274
Balanced Modulator 326
Batteries 456
Baudot Code 286
Beacon 251, 316
Beverage Antenna 378
Bipolar Junction Transistor 428
Bleeder Resistor 454
Blocking Diode 458
Break-in Telegraphy 279
Capacitance Hat 380, 441
Capacitive Reactance 386
Capacitor 420
Capacitor, polarized 422
Carson?s Rule 338
CERT 20 250
Chassis Grounding 487, 489
Choke Input 455
Climbing Gear 499
Clipping 328
Codes and Ciphers 258
Common-mode Currents 485
Connectors (feedline) 400
Connectors (other) 474
Coronal Ball 381
Coronal Holes 300
Coronal Mass Ejection 301
Critical Angle 306

CSCE 239
CW 277
CW Time Ratio 279
CW Transmitter 322
dBi vs. dBd 361
D Layer Absorption 305
Decibels 236, 406
Delta Loop Antenna 389
Digital Counter 472
Digital Filtering 351
Digital IC 470
Digital Logic Gates 471
Digital Memory 474
Digital Shift Register 473
Digital Signal Processing (DSP) 350
Digital Sub-bands 284
Digital-to-Analog Conversion (DAC) 350
Diode 415, 426
Direct Digital Synthesis (DDS) 356
Director (Yagi) 385
Drive Power 461, 465
Duty Cycle 505
DX 232, 253
E Skip 312
Electrical Generators 496
Emergency Communications 249
Equivalent Component 434
Exam Credit (VE) 240
F2 Skip 311
Fan Dipole 376
FCC Monitoring Stations 256
FCC OET Bulletin-65, 506, 510
Feed Point 360
Feedlines 396
Ferrite Chokes 485
Ferrite Core (Inductor) 425
Field Effect Transistor 430
Field Strength Meter 482
FM Deviation 317, 335
FM Receiver 342
FM Transmitter 339
Foreign Contacts 254
Forward Error Correction 285
Frequency Domain View 235
Frequency Modulation (FM) 335
Frequency Separation 265
Frequency Shift Keying (FSK) 287

Topic Index

Front-to-Back Ratio 385
FT8 Mode 294
Full-wave Bridge Rectifier 453
Full-wave Rectifier 453
Fundamental Overload 484
Fuse 493
Gamma Match 386
General Class Privileges 241
Geomagnetic Storms 309
Ground Fault Circuit Interrupter 494
Ground Loop 487
Ground Plane 370
Grounding 487
Half-wave Dipole 363
Half-wave Rectifier 452
Halo Antenna 377
Harmonic Multiplier 339
Harmonics 485
Heterodyning 324
HF operations 232
Household Circuits 492
I and Q Signals 355
IF Shift 334
Image Response 334
Impedance 359
Impedance Matching 393
Inductive Reactance 442
Inductor 423
Integrated Circuit (IC) 469
Intermediate Frequency (IF) 330
Intermodulation 357
Inter-turn Capacitance (inductor) 425
Ionization 302
Ionosphere Layers 304
Isotropic Antenna 361
ITU 254
JT65 / JT9 294
Junction Diode 426
Key / Keyer 278
K-Index 309
Kirchoff?s Law 433
LC Circuit 444
Light Emitting Diode 427, 474
Lightning Feedline Protectors 489, 500
Lightning Grounding 499
Linear Amplifier 463
Liquid Crystal Display (LCD) 474
Loading Coil 379

Loading Techniques 379
Local Oscillator 326, 330
Log Book 262
Log Periodic Antenna 390
Long Path 274
Lower Sideband 271, 319
Lowest Usable Frequency (LUF) 307
Magnetosphere 308
Maximum Permissible Exposure 504
Maximum Power Transfer Theorem 446
Maximum Usable Frequency (MUF) 307
Microcontroller 473
Microprocessor 473
Mixer 324, 330
Mobile HF Antenna 380
Modes 233
Monolithic Microwave IC (MMIC) 473
Morse Code 277
MOSFET (transistor) 430
Multiband Antennas 373
Multiband Transmitter 325
Multimeter 479
Mutual Inductance 425
NAK (Not Acknowledged) 291
National Electric Code (NEC) 492
Neutralization (amplifier) 467
Noise Reduction 354
Notch Filter 353
NVIS 313, 369
Ohm?s Law 404
Omnidirectional Antenna 267, 361
Oscillator Circuits 237, 444
Overmodulation (AM, SSB) 328
Packet 284
PACTOR 291
Parallel Circuits 434
Parasitic Elements 360, 384
Peak Envelope Power 410
Peak-to-Peak Voltage 410
Phase Modulation (PM) 342
Phase Relationship 342
Pile Up 269
PN Junction 426
Polarization 360
Potentiometer 420
Power Law 405
Power Limits 245
Prosigns 258, 281

513

PSK31 292	SSB Transmitter 326
Q Factor 398	SSB vs. AM 269, 318
Q Signals 281	Standing Wave 393
QRP 273, 282	S-Unit 346
Quad Antenna 388	Sunspot Cycle 299
Quarter-wave Vertical Antenna 370	Sunspots 298, 315
RACES 250	Superheterodyne 329
Random Wire 374	Switch-Mode Power Supply 456
Reactance 237, 441	SWR 237, 393
Reactance Modulator 339	SWR Curve 399
Reciprocal Agreements 255	SWR Meter 361, 394
Rectifier 452	Tapped Coil 380, 424
Reflector (Yagi) 384	Thermistor 419
Resistor 417	Third Party International Contact 255
Resistor Values 419	Time Domain View 234, 408, 480
Resonance 443	Transformer 450
Reverse Sideband 281	Transistor 415, 427
RF Burns 374, 489	Transmission Line Loss & SWR 397
RF Exposure Calculations 506	Trap Antenna 374
RF Exposure Factors 504	Trimmer 420
RF Exposure Limits 503	Trimming (antenna) 398
RF Hot Spots 489	Two Tone Test 481
RF in the Shack 488	Unintentional Receivers 484
RMS Voltage 409	Universal Serial Bus (USB) 475
RTTY 287	Upper Sideband (USB) 271, 319
Running Barefoot 273	Vacuum Tube 464
Safety Interlock 494	Variable Frequency Oscillator 271
Sampling 350	Variable Frequency Transmitter 323
Scatter 314	Volunteer Examiner (VE) 247
Schottky Diode 427	Volunteer Monitor 248
Secondary Privileges 257	VOX 273
Selectivity 353	Winlink 292
Semiconductor 426	Wire Current Ratings 493
Series Circuits 434	Yagi Antenna 383
Signal-to-Noise Ratio 347	Zener Diode 427
Single Point Ground 487	Zero Beat (CW) 280
Single Sideband 319	
S-Meter 345	
Software Defined Radio (SDR) 354	
Solar Flare 300, 315	
Solar Flux Index (SFI) 299	
Solar Power 458	
Soldering 497	
Solid State Amplifier 461	
Speech Processor 347	
Splatter 486	
Split Mode 269, 272	

Element 3 General Class Exam Pool Question Page Index

G1		G1D01	240	G2C01	279	G3	
G1A01	241	G1D02	247	G2C02	282	G3A01	299
G1A02	242	G1D03	239	G2C03	282	G3A02	315
G1A03	242	G1D04	248	G2C04	282	G3A03	300
G1A04	244	G1D05	247	G2C05	280	G3A04	315
G1A05	244	G1D06	240	G2C06	280	G3A05	299
G1A06	244	G1D07	247	G2C07	263	G3A06	309
G1A07	242, 246	G1D08	248	G2C08	282	G3A07	315
G1A08	244, 245	G1D09	239	G2C09	282	G3A08	309
G1A09	242	G1D10	247	G2C10	282	G3A09	309
G1A10	241	G1D11	240	G2C11	282	G3A10	299
G1A11	241					G3A11	301
G1A12	242	G1E01	255	G2D01	248	G3A12	309
G1A13	242, 244	G1E02	242	G2D02	248	G3A13	309
G1A14	244	G1E03	289	G2D03	249	G3A14	300
G1A15	242	G1E04	256	G2D04	274		
		G1E05	255	G2D05	266	G3B01	313
G1B01	257	G1E06	254	G2D06	274	G3B02	307
G1B02	251	G1E07	295	G2D07	268	G3B03	315
G1B03	251	G1E08	257	G2D08	262	G3B04	316
G1B04	259	G1E09	290	G2D09	268	G3B05	308
G1B05	259	G1E10	252	G2D10	273	G3B06	307
G1B06	258	G1E11	289	G2D11	316	G3B07	307
G1B07	258					G3B08	307
G1B08	264	G2		G2E01	287	G3B09	311
G1B09	251	G2A01	271	G2E02	292	G3B10	312
G1B10	251	G2A02	271	G2E03	292	G3B11	307
G1B11	262	G2A03	271	G2E04	284		
G1B12	254	G2A04	271	G2E05	294	G3C01	305
		G2A05	271	G2E06	287	G3C02	305
G1C01	242	G2A06	318	G2E07	284	G3C03	305
G1C02	245	G2A07	320	G2E08	293	G3C04	306
G1C03	244	G2A08	268	G2E09	291	G3C05	315
G1C04	245	G2A09	271	G2E10	292	G3C06	314
G1C05	245	G2A10	273	G2E11	294	G3C07	314
G1C06	245	G2A11	265	G2E12	476	G3C08	314
G1C07	288	G2A12	329	G2E13	292	G3C09	314
G1C08	288			G2E14	288	G3C10	313
G1C09	288	G2B01	264	G2E15	294	G3C11	305
G1C10	288	G2B02	268				
G1C11	288	G2B03	267				
G1C12	244	G2B04	265				
G1C13	289	G2B05	265				
G1C14	244	G2B06	264				
G1C15	242	G2B07	264				
		G2B08	265				
		G2B09	251				
		G2B10	250				
		G2B11	251				

Element 3 General Class Exam Pool Question Page Index

G4							
G4A01	353	G4D01	347	G5C01	450	**G7**	
G4A02	281	G4D02	349	G5C02	452	G7A01	455
G4A03	272	G4D03	349	G5C03	436	G7A02	455
G4A04	467	G4D04	345	G5C04	436	G7A03	453
G4A05	467	G4D05	346	G5C05	439	G7A04	452
G4A06	399	G4D06	345	G5C06	451	G7A05	452
G4A07	461	G4D07	346	G5C07	460	G7A06	453
G4A08	467	G4D08	321	G5C08	439	G7A07	453
G4A09	280	G4D09	321	G5C09	438	G7A08	456
G4A10	278	G4D10	321	G5C10	438	G7A09	431
G4A11	334	G4D11	322	G5C11	436	G7A10	428, 431
G4A12	272			G5C12	439	G7A11	431
G4A13	347	G4E01	380	G5C13	436	G7A12	431
G4A14	329	G4E02	381	G5C14	436	G7A13	424, 431
G4A15	485	G4E03	495	G5C15	437		
G4A16	353	G4E04	495	G5C16	451	G7B01	467
G4A17	354	G4E05	379	G5C17	422	G7B02	464
		G4E06	379	G5C18	422	G7B03	471
		G4E07	487			G7B04	471
G4B01	481	G4E08	458	**G6**		G7B05	473
G4B02	481	G4E09	458	G6A01	456	G7B06	473
G4B03	481	G4E10	458	G6A02	457	G7B07	470
G4B04	481	G4E11	459	G6A03	427	G7B08	462
G4B05	480			G6A04	422	G7B09	445
G4B06	479	**G5**		G6A05	426	G7B10	463
G4B07	482	G5A01	441	G6A06	418	G7B11	464
G4B08	482	G5A02	441	G6A07	429		
G4B09	482	G5A03	442	G6A08	425	G7C01	328
G4B10	395	G5A04	441	G6A09	430	G7C02	328
G4B11	395	G5A05	442	G6A10	465	G7C03	330
G4B12	395	G5A06	441	G6A11	426	G7C04	330
G4B13	395	G5A07	446	G6A12	465	G7C05	356
G4B14	479	G5A08	446	G6A13	422	G7C06	401
G4B15	481	G5A09	441	G6A14	421	G7C07	331
		G5A10	446			G7C08	342
G4C01	485	G5A11	446	G6B01	424	G7C09	355
G4C02	486			G6B02	473	G7C10	355
G4C03	484	G5B01	406	G6B03	470	G7C11	354
G4C04	485	G5B02	434	G6B04	474	G7C12	353
G4C05	489	G5B03	406	G6B05	474	G7C13	353
G4C06	489	G5B04	405	G6B06	469	G7C14	352
G4C07	500	G5B05	405	G6B07	401	G7C15	353
G4C08	485	G5B06	411	G6B08	427	G7C16	356
G4C09	487	G5B07	409	G6B09	474		
G4C10	487	G5B08	408	G6B10	485		
G4C11	489	G5B09	408	G6B11	401		
G4C12	354	G5B10	407	G6B12	476		
G4C13	495	G5B11	412	G6B13	401		
		G5B12	409				
		G5B13	412				
		G5B14	412				

Element 3 General Class Exam Pool Question Page Index

G8		G9			
G8A01	287	G9A01	398	G9D01	369
G8A02	342	G9A02	396	G9D02	400
G8A03	335	G9A03	398	G9D03	377
G8A04	342	G9A04	393	G9D04	374
G8A05	319	G9A05	397	G9D05	385
G8A06	294	G9A06	397	G9D06	390
G8A07	320	G9A07	396	G9D07	390
G8A08	339	G9A08	399	G9D08	380
G8A09	294	G9A09	396	G9D09	378
G8A10	329	G9A10	396	G9D10	390
G8A11	319	G9A11	395	G9D11	376
G8A12	294	G9A12	397	G9D12	369
		G9A13	397	G9D13	378
G8B01	330			G0	
G8B02	334	G9B01	374	G0A01	503
G8B03	324	G9B02	372	G0A02	504
G8B04	339	G9B03	373	G0A03	506
G8B05	291	G9B04	363	G0A04	505
G8B06	338	G9B05	368	G0A05	506
G8B07	340	G9B06	371	G0A06	499
G8B08	289	G9B07	367	G0A07	505
G8B09	353	G9B08	366	G0A08	505
G8B10	288	G9B09	373	G0A09	506
G8B11	330	G9B10	364	G0A10	506
G8B12	357	G9B11	364	G0A11	505
		G9B12	372		
G8C01	295			G0B01	493
G8C02	294	G9C01	385	G0B02	493
G8C03	285	G9C02	384	G0B03	494
G8C04	286	G9C03	384	G0B04	496
G8C05	291	G9C04	361	G0B05	494
G8C06	292	G9C05	385	G0B06	492
G8C07	285	G9C06	388	G0B07	499
G8C08	292	G9C07	384	G0B08	499
G8C09	292	G9C08	384	G0B09	496
G8C10	286	G9C09	386	G0B10	498
G8C11	287	G9C10	385	G0B11	500
G8C12	292	G9C11	267	G0B12	494
G8C13	293	G9C12	387	G0B13	496
G8C14	293	G9C13	388	G0B14	498
		G9C14	388		
		G9C15	361		
		G9C16	387		

Made in the USA
Columbia, SC
23 July 2021